MAPPING THE ROCKUMENTARY

Traditions in World Cinema

General Editors
Linda Badley (Middle Tennessee State University)
R. Barton Palmer (Clemson University)

Founding Editor
Steven Jay Schneider (New York University)

Titles in the series include:

Traditions in World Cinema
by Linda Badley, R. Barton Palmer and Steven Jay Schneider (eds)

Japanese Horror Cinema
by Jay McRoy (ed.)

New Punk Cinema
by Nicholas Rombes (ed.)

African Filmmaking
by Roy Armes

Palestinian Cinema
by Nurith Gertz and George Khleifi

Czech and Slovak Cinema
by Peter Hames

The New Neapolitan Cinema
by Alex Marlow-Mann

American Smart Cinema
by Claire Perkins

The International Film Musical
by Corey Creekmur and Linda Mokdad (eds)

Italian Neorealist Cinema
by Torunn Haaland

Magic Realist Cinema in East Central Europe
by Aga Skrodzka

Italian Post-Neorealist Cinema
by Luca Barattoni

Spanish Horror Film
by Antonio Lázaro-Reboll

Post-beur Cinema
by Will Higbee

New Taiwanese Cinema in Focus
by Flannery Wilson

International Noir
by Homer B. Pettey and R. Barton Palmer (eds)

Films on Ice
by Scott MacKenzie and Anna Westerståhl Stenport (eds)

Nordic Genre Film
by Tommy Gustafsson and Pietari Kääpä (eds)

Contemporary Japanese Cinema Since Hana-Bi
by Adam Bingham

Chinese Martial Arts Cinema (2nd edition)
by Stephen Teo

Slow Cinema
by Tiago de Luca and Nuno Barradas Jorge

Expressionism in Cinema
by Olaf Brill and Gary D. Rhodes (eds)

French Language Road Cinema: Borders, Diasporas, Migration and 'New Europe'
by Michael Gott

Transnational Film Remakes
by Iain Robert Smith and Constantine Verevis

Coming of Age in New Zealand
by Alistair Fox

New Transnationalisms in Contemporary Latin American Cinemas
by Dolores Tierney

Celluloid Singapore: Cinema, Performance and the National
by Edna Lim

Short Films from a Small Nation: Danish Informational Cinema 1935-1965
by C. Claire Thomson

B-Movie Gothic: International Perspectives
by Justin D. Edwards and Johan Höglund (eds)

Francophone Belgian Cinema: Filmmaking in Wallonia since 2001
by Jamie Steele

The New Romanian Cinema
by Christina Stojanova (ed) with the participation of Dana Duma

French Blockbusters: Cultural Politics of a Transnational Cinema
by Charlie Michael

Nordic Film Cultures and Cinemas of Elsewhere
by Anna Westerståhl Stenport and Arne Lunde (eds)

New Realism: Contemporary British Cinema
by David Forrest

Contemporary Balkan Cinema: Transnational Exchanges and Global Circuits
by Lydia Papadimitriou and Ana Grgić (eds)

www.edinburghuniversitypress.com/series/TIWC

MAPPING THE ROCKUMENTARY
Images of Sound and Fury

Edited by Gunnar Iversen and Scott MacKenzie

EDINBURGH
University Press

Edinburgh University Press is one of the leading university presses in the UK. We publish academic books and journals in our selected subject areas across the humanities and social sciences, combining cutting-edge scholarship with high editorial and production values to produce academic works of lasting importance. For more information visit our website: edinburghuniversitypress.com

© editorial matter and organisation Gunnar Iversen and Scott MacKenzie, 2021, 2023
© the chapters their several authors, 2021, 2023

First edition published 2021
Revised edition published 2022

Edinburgh University Press Ltd
The Tun – Holyrood Road
12(2f) Jackson's Entry
Edinburgh EH8 8PJ

First published in hardback by Edinburgh University Press 2021

Typeset in 10/12.5 pt Sabon by
Servis Filmsetting Ltd, Stockport, Cheshire

A CIP record for this book is available from the British Library

ISBN 978-1-4744-7802-1 (hardback)
ISBN 978-1-4744-7803-8 (paperback)
ISBN 978-1-4744-7804-5 (webready PDF)
ISBN 978-1-4744-7805-2 (epub)

The right of Gunnar Iversen and Scott MacKenzie to be identified as the editors of this work has been asserted in accordance with the Copyright, Designs and Patents Act 1988, and the Copyright and Related Rights Regulations 2003 (SI No. 2498).

CONTENTS

List of Figures viii
List of Contributors x
Traditions in World Cinema xviii

    Introduction: Images of Sound and Fury 1
    Gunnar Iversen and Scott MacKenzie

PART I. HISTORIES

1. *Music Makers of the Blue Ridge* (aka 'Bluegrass Roots,' David Hoffman, USA, 1966) 21
   Greil Marcus

2. "I Don't Make Culture, I Sell It!": The Early History of Music Documentation, 1920s-1970s 24
   Laura Niebling

3. *Monterey Pop* and the Maturation of the Concert Film 37
   Laurel Westrup

4. The Sound of Rockumentary: A Consideration of the Documentary Soundtrack 50
   Michael Brendan Baker

CONTENTS

5. False Endings 64
   Scott MacKenzie

PART II. GENDER

6. "Start Me Up": The Place and Displacement of Women in the Cinema of The Rolling Stones 85
   Catherine Strong and Stephen Gaunson

7. Madonna on Film: Geopolitics, Globalization, and Gender Politics 97
   Anna Westerstahl Stenport

8. The Freedom to Speak: The Dixie Chicks, Observational Documentary, and *Shut Up & Sing* 113
   Heather McIntosh

9. Rock 'n' Roll Family Romances: The Rockumentary as Male Melodrama 125
   Gunnar Iversen

10. Performing Dylan: The Many Lives of Bob Dylan in *I'm Not There* 140
    Magdalena Fürnkranz

PART III. AESTHETICS AND POLITICS

11. U2's *Rattle and Hum*: God, Sex, Rock 'n' Roll and God Again 157
    Karine Bertrand

12. Punk City Symphony: The Clash and *Rude Boy* 173
    Celine Bell

13. Listening from the Empty Booth: Performing the Grateful Dead Community in *Long Strange Trip* 185
    Randolph Jordan

14. Minimum and Maximum Rock 'n' Roll: Nick Cave and the Bad Seeds and Rockumentary Form 198
    Anthony Kinik

15. "Everything Was Stories": The Aesthetic Imaginaries of *Searching for the Wrong-Eyed Jesus* 212
    Asbjørn Grønstad and Øyvind Vågnes

PART IV. COUNTER-CULTURES

16. Chile: The Rock of Political Culture and the Hard Place of Cultural Policy — 225
    Jorge Saavedra Utman and Toby Miller

17. Psychedelia and Rebelliousness in Times of Dictatorship: Argentinian Rockumentaries (1973–1983) — 239
    Javier Campo and Tomás Crowder-Taraborrelli

18. *Harmonium in California*: Musically Imagined Communities and the Rockumentary Form — 250
    Eric Fillion

19. Stations of the Crass: Counter-Culture and the Anarcho-Punk Movement — 263
    Asbjørn Tiller

20. Cars and Guitars, or, Detroit and the MC5: On Representations of Music and Place in *MC5: A True Testimonial* — 276
    Lindsey Eckenroth

PART V. FUTURES

21. Unknowable Dogs — 291
    Gary Kibbins

22. "*This is a F**king Business*": The Concert Show and Tour in 1970s Hollywood Fiction Films — 303
    Julie Lobalzo Wright

23. Live from the Multiplex: The Concert Film as Event Cinema since the 2000s — 314
    Ian Robinson

24. Documenting Deities: Touch and K-pop Fandom on YouTube — 330
    Eric Chalfant and Ali Na

25. Ritual in Transfigured Time — 344
    Greil Marcus

Index — 349

FIGURES

3.1	Trumpeter Jimmy McPartland joins a line of dancers coming towards the camera, beckoning the viewer into *Jazz Dance* (1954).	40
3.2	Close-ups of Janis Joplin performing "Ball and Chain" ring true emotionally, even if the performance we see in *Monterey Pop* (1968) is actually a composite.	45
4.1	The Nagra III portable reel-to-reel tape recorder by Kudelski SA, c. 1958.	54
4.2	Three stagehands work to identify a faulty microphone cable in *Dont Look Back*.	55
4.3	Promotional image for the Ampex AG-440-8, the first mass-produced eight-track recorder available in North America.	59
5.1	Alex directly addressing the camera and audience in *The Cry of Jazz* (1959).	67
5.2	John Lennon: "I'd like to say thank you on behalf of the group and ourselves and I hope we passed the audition," *Let It Be* (1970).	72
6.1	Hysterical fan from *Charlie is My Darling* (1966).	87
6.2	Groupie in *Cocksucker Blues* (1972).	92
7.1	Madonna and staged *cinéma vérité* in *Truth or Dare* (1991).	102
7.2	Performing bodies: Carlton Wilborn and Luis Xtravaganza Camacho with Madonna in *Strike a Pose* (2016).	109

FIGURES

9.1	Metallica working out their issues in *Metallica: Some Kind of Monster* (2004). Therapist Towle in the background.	130
9.2	Tom and Matt Berninger discussing the editing of *Mistaken for Strangers* (2013).	135
10.1	Civil Rights March on Washington, D.C. Close-up view of vocalists Joan Baez and Bob Dylan, 28 August 1963 by Rowland Scherman.	147
10.2	Allen Ginsberg and Bob Dylan by Elsa Dorfman in 1975.	149
11.1	U2, *The Joshua Tree* press photo, 2007.	162
11.2	Bono and B. B. King performing on stage during Love Town Tour.	168
12.1	Police officers prepare to face off against British youth in *Rude Boy* (1980).	175
12.2	Joe Strummer (left) and Ray Gange debate contemporary political issues in *Rude Boy* (1980).	181
14.1	Uli M. Schüppel's *The Road to God Knows Where* (1989) as it appears in the opening montage of Iain Forsyth and Jane Pollard's *20,000 Days on Earth* (2014), roughly 12,152 days into the life of Nick Cave.	202
14.2	Nick Cave reads his last will and testament from 1987 to two archivists (and to the camera) in Forsyth and Pollard's *20,000 Days on Earth* (2014).	209
18.1	Harmonium on stage at the Starwood in Los Angeles, California. Source: National Film Board of Canada.	257
18.2	Limited theatrical release of *Harmonium in California* on October 19–24, 1979. Source: *La Presse*.	259
19.1	Crass art.	270
21.1	An Affront to Humanism. Laurie Anderson's *Heart of a Dog* (2015).	292
21.2	The Anthropological Machine is switched off. Laurie Anderson's *Heart of a Dog* (2015).	295
23.1	*8th Annual Grateful Dead Meet-Up at the Movies* poster.	321
23.2	Coldplay's *A Head Full of Dreams* poster.	322
24.1	Still image from Fancam, Blackpink world tour in LA.	334
24.2	Screenshot from viral YouTube Fancam.	337

CONTRIBUTORS

Michael Brendan Baker is a Professor of Film Studies at Sheridan College in the Faculty of Humanities & Social Sciences. He specializes in documentary film and video, music and the moving image, and media history. He is author of numerous book chapters and journal articles on a range of subjects including documentary, popular music and film, and new media. Baker is co-editor, with Tom Waugh and Ezra Winton, of *Challenge for Change: Activist Documentary at the National Film Board of Canada* (McGill-Queen's University Press, 2010) and is Chair of the editorial board of the *Canadian Journal of Film Studies*.

Celine Bell is a Ph.D. candidate in the Cinema Studies Program at the University of Toronto. Her Ph.D. research focuses on female friendship in classical Hollywood cinema. Her other research interests include the development of film canons, genre studies, and feminist film theory. Her previous research in the MA program at York University focused on the female narrator in film noir. She has taught courses on the woman's film and on *film noir*.

Karine Bertrand is an Assistant Professor of French Canadian and Indigenous ancestry (Québec, Algonquin) in the Department of Film and Media, Queen's University. Her research interests are centered around Indigenous film and poetry, Quebec cinema, road movies, transnational cinemas and oral practices of cinema. She is a member of the Vulnerable Media Lab at Queen's and lead researcher for the Archive Counter Archive research project (financed by SSHRC) working with the Arnait Video Productions collective of Inuit women. Her latest publications include an article on Indigenous women and testimonies (Canadian Journal of Film Studies, 2020) on Québécois cinema and Americanité (*American Review of Canadian Studies*, 2019) and a book chapter on Canadian and Québécois Indigenous cinemas (*Oxford Handbook to Canadian Cinema*, 2019). She is presently working on a project involving the creation of an international network for Indigenous women filmmakers, with her partners from the Wapikoni Mobile and the INAAC (the International Network for Aboriginal Audio-Visual Creation).

Javier Campo holds a Ph.D. in Social Sciences (University of Buenos Aires). He is a researcher at CONICET; co-director of *Cine Documental* magazine; Associate Editor of *Latin American Perspectives*; Professor of Film Aesthetics (UNICEN); Author of *Revolución y Democracia. El cine documental argentino del exilio* (2017); *Cine documental argentino. Entre el arte, la cultura y la política* (2012); co-editor of *A Trail of Fire for Political Cinema. The Hour of the Furnaces Fifty Years Later* (2018); *Cine documental, memoria y derechos humanos* (2007); co-author of *Directory of World Cinema. Argentina* (2014 and 2016, two volumes) and *World Film Locations: Buenos Aires* (2014), among other publications; and Director of the Department of History and Art Theory (Faculty of Art, UNICEN).

Eric Chalfant is an independent scholar and has a Ph.D. in Religion and Modernity from Duke University. His research lies at the intersection of Media Studies and Religious Studies. Theoretically, his work draws heavily on Critical Media Studies and several shades of material media analysis, including Affect Studies, Sound Culture Studies, Interface Studies, and Algorithmic and Network Culture.

Tomás Crowder-Taraborrelli received his doctorate in Spanish and Portuguese at the University of Irvine, California. He is an Associate Producer for ITVS and POV, from the Public Broadcasting Service in the United States. He is on the editorial board of the journal *Latin American Perspectives*, of which he is co-editor of the film section. He is co-editor of *Film and Genocide* (University of Wisconsin Press, 2012) and *El documental político en Argentina, Chile y Uruguay* (LOM Ediciones, 2015). Currently, he is a visiting professor of Latin American Studies at Soka University of America, California.

Lindsey Eckenroth is a musicologist and flutist currently based in Brooklyn. She is a doctoral candidate in Musicology at the CUNY Graduate Center, where her dissertation research focuses on Rockumentaries. Her writing has been published in *Rock Music Studies*, *American Music Review*, and *Women* *and Music: A Journal of Gender and Culture*. She has taught in the music department of Brooklyn College since 2010. Eckenroth is also employed at *Répertoire International de Littérature Musicale* (RILM), where she works with both the technology team and the editorial staff as Data Coordinator. As a flutist, Lindsey performs regularly with The Curiosity Cabinet, an interdisciplinary new music ensemble.

Eric Fillion is a fellow in the Department of History at the University of Toronto. He holds a Ph.D. in History from Concordia University. His research explores the social and symbolic importance of music, within countercultures and in Canadian international relations. His ongoing work on cultural diplomacy builds on the experience he has acquired as a musician. It also informs his current project, which examines international music festivals as transnational, contested sites of cultural performance during the long sixties. An affiliate of the North American Cultural Diplomacy Initiative, he is the founder of the Tenzier archival record label and the author of *JAZZ LIBRE et la révolution québécoise*.

Magdalena Fürnkranz studied Theatre, Film and Media Studies and Gender Studies at the University of Vienna. She is a postdoctoral fellow at the Department of Popular Music at the University of Music and Performing Arts Vienna. As co-leader of the project 'Performing Diversity' and leader of the project 'Female Jazz Musicians in Austria', her recent research has focused on performativity, gender and intersectionality in popular music, Austrian music scenes, and European jazz cultures. She is co-editor of *Performing Sexual Identities. Nationalities on the Eurovision Stage* (2017), co-author of *Performing Diversity* (2018), and author of *Elizabeth I in Film und Fernsehen. De-/Konstruktion von weiblicher Herrschaft* (2019).

Stephen Gaunson is a Senior Lecturer in the Media program at RMIT University. He is the author of *The Ned Kelly Films* (2013) and co-editor (with Adrian Danks and Peter Kunze) of the book *American-Australian Cinema: Transnational Connections* (2018). In 2017 Dr Alexia Kannas and he were the recipients of the 'Citation for Outstanding Contributions to Student Learning', Australian Awards for University Teaching.

Asbjørn Grønstad is Professor of Visual Culture in the Department of Information Science and Media Studies, University of Bergen. He is founding director of the Nomadikon Center for Visual Culture and the author/editor of nine books, the most recent of which are *Gestures of Seeing in Film, Video and Drawing* (co-edited with Henrik Gustafsson & Øyvind Vågnes, Routledge, 2016) and *Film and the Ethical Imagination* (Palgrave, 2016).

Gunnar Iversen is Professor of Film Studies in the School of Art and Culture at Carleton University. He was Professor of Film and Media Studies at the Norwegian University of Science and Technology between 1992 and 2017. He has published widely on Norwegian and Scandinavian film history, documentary films, early and silent cinema and Sound Studies. He has published more than twenty books in Norwegian. His many essays have been published in nine different languages, and English language essays have appeared in journals such as *Film History*, *Early Popular Visual Culture*, *Journal of Scandinavian Cinema*, *Scandinavian Studies*, and *European Journal of Scandinavian Studies* as well as in many anthologies. In English he has co-edited the books *Unwatchable* (Rutgers University Press, 2019), *Historical Dictionary of Scandinavian Cinema* (Scarecrow Press, 2012), *Beyond the Visual: Sound and Image in Ethnographic and Documentary Film* (Intervention Press, 2010), and he also co-wrote *Nordic National Cinemas* (Routledge, 1998).

Randolph Jordan is a media scholar/practitioner and is currently Assistant Professor of Film Studies in the School of Image Arts at Ryerson University in Toronto, Canada. His work lives at the intersection of film sound, acoustic ecology, and critical geography, investigating the ways in which we can rethink the boundaries of documentary media through attention to the role of sound in facilitating engagement with place. He has three major projects on the go: a monograph for Oxford University Press entitled *An Acoustic Ecology of the Cinema*; a collection of new essays for Palgrave entitled *Sound, Media, Ecology*, co-edited with Dr Milena Droumeva at SFU; and a multimedia project entitled *Bell Tower of False Creek*, currently on the festival circuit. Whenever he gets the chance, he also writes about his other two obsessions: *Twin Peaks* and the Grateful Dead.

Gary Kibbins is Associate Professor and Head of the Department of Film and Media, Queen's University. He is a media artist and writer, who previously taught at the California Institute of the Arts. Books of his essays and scripts include *Grammar Horses* (Agnes Etherington Art Centre, 2003), and *Grammar & Not-Grammar: Selected Scripts and Essays* (YYZ Books, 2005). His recent media works include *Or So We Say* (2017), *God Hates Himself* (2017), *Mama Minde* (2016), *The Child's Concept of Chance* (2016), *Grading Greek Philosophers* (2016), *The Wide Wide World* (2016), *We Move Only Ourselves* (2015), *Ocean View* (2015), and *Only Believe Things That Are Easy To Understand* (2014).

Anthony Kinik is Associate Professor of Film Studies, Brock University. His areas of specialization include documentary film, experimental film, Canadian and Québécois cinema, and cinematic representations of the urban environment. Together with his colleagues Steven Jacobs and Eva Hielscher, he recently co-edited a collection entitled *The City Symphony Phenomenon: Cinema, Art, and Urban Modernity Between the Wars* (Routledge, 2018). His essay 'Celluloid City: Montreal and Multi-screen at Expo 67' appeared in the *Reimagining Cinema: Film at Expo 67* anthology (McGill-Queen's University Press, 2014), and he is currently working on a book on sixties Montréal as a cinematic city.

Scott MacKenzie is Professor of Film and Media, Queen's University. His many books include: *Cinema and Nation* (w/ Mette Hjort, Routledge, 2000); *Purity and Provocation: Dogma 95* (w/ Mette Hjort, BFI, 2003); *Screening Québec: Québécois Moving Images, National Identity and the Public Sphere* (Manchester University Press, 2004); *The Perils of Pedagogy: The Works of John Greyson* (w/ Brenda Longfellow and Thomas Waugh, McGill-Queen's University Press, 2013); *Film Manifestos and Global Cinema Cultures* (University of California Press, 2014); *Films on Ice: Cinemas of the Arctic* (w/ Anna Westerstahl Stenport, Edinburgh University Press, 2015); *Arctic Environmental Modernities* (w/ Lill-Ann Körber and Anna Westerstahl Stenport, Palgrave, 2017); *Arctic Cinemas and the Documentary Ethos* (w/ Lilya Kaganovsky and Anna Westerstahl Stenport, Indiana University Press, 2019); and *Process Cinema: Handmade Film in the Digital Age* (w/ Janine Marchessault, McGill-Queen's University Press, 2019).

Greil Marcus writes on popular music and cultural history. His many books include *Mystery Train: Images of America in Rock 'n' Roll Music* (E. P. Dutton, 1975), *Lipstick Traces: A Secret History of the 20th Century* (Harvard University Press, 1989), *Dead Elvis: A Chronicle of a Cultural Obsession* (Harvard University Press, 1991), *Ranters & Crowd Pleasers: Punk in Pop Music, 1977–1992* (Doubleday, 1993), *The Dustbin of History* (Harvard University Press, 1995), *Invisible Republic: Bob Dylan's Basement Tapes* (Henry Holt, 1997), *The Manchurian Candidate* (BFI Film Classics, 2002), *The Shape of Things to Come: Prophecy in the American Voice* (Picador, 2006), *Bob Dylan by Greil Marcus: Writings 1968–2010* (Public Affairs, 2011), *The Doors: A Lifetime of Listening to Five Mean Years* (Public Affairs, 2011), *The History of Rock 'n' Roll in Ten Songs* (Yale University Press, 2014), *Three Songs, Three Singers, Three Nations* (Harvard University Press, 2015), and *Real Life Rock: The Complete Top Ten Columns, 1986-2014* (Yale University Press, 2015). His edited volumes include *Psychotic Reactions and Carburetor Dung: The Work of a Legendary Critic: Rock 'n' Roll as Literature and Literature as Rock 'n' Roll* (Vintage Books, 1988), and *A New Literary History of America* (w/ Werner Sollors, Harvard/Belknap Press, 2009).

Heather McIntosh is an Assistant Professor of Mass Media at Minnesota State University, Mankato, USA. Her research focuses on documentary representations, technologies, and institutions. Her work has appeared or is forthcoming in *Journal of Film and Video*, *Quarterly Review of Film and Video*, and *Journal of Popular Film and Television*. She is co-editor of *Documenting Gendered Violence: Representations, Collaborations, and Movements*. She also has written about documentary as a blogger for PBS's POV series.

Toby Miller is Stuart Hall Professor of Cultural Studies, Universidad Autónoma Metropolitana–Cuajimalpa and Sir Walter Murdoch Distinguished Collaborator, Murdoch University. He was a Professor at the University of California Riverside for a decade and New York University for eleven years. The author and editor of over fifty books, his work has been translated into Spanish, Chinese, Portuguese, Japanese, Turkish, German, Italian, Farsi, French, Urdu, and Swedish. His most recent volumes are *Violence* (2021), *The Persistence of Violence: Colombian Popular Culture* (2020), *How Green is Your Smartphone?* (co-authored, 2020), *El trabajo cultural* (2018), *Greenwashing Culture* (2018), *Greenwashing Sport* (2018), *The Routledge Companion to Global Cultural Policy* (co-edited, 2018), *Global Media Studies* (co-authored, 2015), *The Routledge Companion to Global Popular Culture* (edited, 2015), *Greening the Media* (co-authored, 2012) and *Blow Up the Humanities* (2012). *The Covid Charter* is in press.

Ali Na is an Assistant Professor in Film and Media at Queen's University and holds a doctorate in Communication from the University of North Carolina at Chapel Hill. As a media scholar working at the intersections of race, queer, and feminist studies, her research focuses on how media performances define and defy conceptions of Asian/Asian diasporic bodies. Drawing on transnational cultural histories, she theorizes resistance, complicity, and ambivalence in new border crossings facilitated by digital media.

Laura Niebling is a Lecturer and Postdoctoral Research Fellow in Media Studies at Regensburg University. She has worked extensively on popular music and film, particularly the history, theory and industry of rockumentaries and is the author of *Rockumentary. Theorie, Geschichte, und Industrie* (Schüren, 2018) as well as the editor of *Populäre Musikkulturen im Film* (/w Carsten Heinze, Springer VS, 2016). In recent years her work focus has shifted to the history of material and digital culture with an upcoming anthology on music objects in German pop music history and a current research project on the digitization of German (tele)medicine since the 1960s.

CONTRIBUTORS

Ian Robinson, prior to joining the Department of Film and Media Studies at Queen's, was a Visiting Assistant Professor in the North American Studies MA Program at the University of Bonn. His current research is focused on Canadian film and media industries, urban film cultures, the role of film festivals as sites of exhibition, the emergence of event cinema and new modes of distribution, and the intermediality of cinema. He completed his Ph.D. at York University and did postdoctoral work at McGill. He has previously taught at the University of Waterloo and OCAD University. His research has been published in several journals and anthologies on film and media culture.

Anna Westerstahl Stenport is Professor of Global Studies and Chair of the School of Modern Languages at the Georgia Institute of Technology. Her many books include: *Locating August Strindberg's Prose: Modernism, Transnationalism, and Setting* (University of Toronto Press, 2010), *The International Strindberg: New Critical Essays* (Northwestern University Press, 2012), *Nordic Film Classics: Lukas Moodysson's 'Show Me Love'* (University of Washington Press, 2012), *Films on Ice: Cinemas of the Arctic* (w/ Scott MacKenzie, Edinburgh University Press, 2015), *Arctic Environmental Modernities: From the Age of Polar Exploration to the Era of the Anthropocene* (w/ Lill-Ann Körber and Scott MacKenzie, Palgrave, 2017), *August Strindberg and Visual Culture: The Emergence of Optical Modernity in Image, Text, and Theatre* (w/ Eszter Szalczer and Jonathan Schroeder, Bloomsbury Academic 2018), *Nordic Film Cultures and Cinemas of Elsewhere* (w/ Arne Lunde, Edinburgh University Press, 2019), and *Arctic Cinemas and the Documentary Ethos* (w/ Lilya Kaganovsky and Scott MacKenzie, Indiana University Press, 2019).

Catherine Strong is a Senior Lecturer in the Music Industry program at RMIT in Melbourne, Australia. Among her publications are *Grunge: Music and Memory* (2011), and *Death and the Rock Star* (2015, edited with Barbara Lebrun). Her research deals with various aspects of memory, nostalgia and gender in rock music, popular culture, and the media. She is currently Chair of IASPM-ANZ and co-editor of *Popular Music History* journal.

Asbjørn Tiller, Ph.D., is an Associate Professor at the Department of Art and Media Studies at the Norwegian University of Science and Technology in Trondheim, Norway. Tillers Ph.D. thesis focused on spatial experience in experimental sound installations and audiovisual expressions. He teaches practical film and video production. Tillers main research area lies within the use and experience of sound in a broad range of audiovisual expressions. He also has a background in practical sound production for music and film.

Jorge Saavedra Utman is an Affiliated Lecturer at the Department of Sociology, University of Cambridge. He has written on the media and communicative practices of non-mainstream politics, media systems and cultures of participation, and Latin American cultural politics, and has taught at Goldsmiths, University of London, Brunel University London, and Pontificia Universidad Católica de Valparaíso, Chile. He is the author of *The Media Commons and Social Movements: Grassroots Mediations Against Neoliberal Politics* (Routledge, 2018); and *Historia Social de los Teatros en Chile: Melipilla en el Siglo XX* (Chancacazo, 2012).

Øyvind Vågnes is Professor of Visual Culture in the Department of Information Science and Media Studies, University of Bergen. His *Zaprudered: The Kennedy Assassination Film in Visual Culture* (University of Texas Press, 2011) received honorable mention from the American Publishers Awards for Professional and Scholarly Excellence. He has published widely in scholarly journals and anthologies, and is the author of five novels in Norwegian.

Laurel Westrup received her Ph.D. in Cinema and Media Studies from UCLA, where she is now a continuing lecturer with Writing Programs and the Honors Program. She is co-editor, with David Laderman, of *Sampling Media* (Oxford University Press, 2014), and her work has also appeared in the journals *Spectator* and *Projector*, and several collections. Laurel is currently working on an edited collection, with Paul Reinsch, on soundtrack albums.

Julie Lobalzo Wright is a Teaching Fellow in Film and Television Studies at the University of Warwick. Her monograph, *Crossover Stardom: Popular Male Music Stars in American Cinema*, was released in December 2017 and she is the co-editor of *Lasting Screen Stars: Images that Fade and Personas that Endure* (Palgrave, 2015). Her work has focused on the overlap between popular music and film and she has published on David Bowie's film stardom and Bowie's music video oeuvre.

TRADITIONS IN WORLD CINEMA

General editors: **Linda Badley and R. Barton Palmer**
Founding editor: **Steven Jay Schneider**

Traditions in World Cinema is a series of textbooks and monographs devoted to the analysis of currently popular and previously underexamined or undervalued film movements from around the globe. Also intended for general interest readers, the textbooks in this series offer undergraduate- and graduate-level film students accessible and comprehensive introductions to diverse traditions in world cinema. The monographs open up for advanced academic study more specialized groups of films, including those that require theoretically-oriented approaches. Both textbooks and monographs provide thorough examinations of the industrial, cultural, and socio-historical conditions of production and reception.

The flagship textbook for the series includes chapters by noted scholars on traditions of acknowledged importance (the French New Wave, German Expressionism), recent and emergent traditions (New Iranian, post-Cinema Novo), and those whose rightful claim to recognition has yet to be established (the Israeli persecution film, global found footage cinema). Other volumes concentrate on individual national, regional or global cinema traditions. As the introductory chapter to each volume makes clear, the films under discussion form a coherent group on the basis of substantive and relatively transparent, if not always obvious, commonalities. These commonalities may be formal, stylistic or thematic, and the groupings may, although they need not, be popularly identified as genres, cycles or movements (Japanese horror, Chinese martial arts cinema, Italian Neorealism). Indeed, in cases in which a group of films is not already commonly identified as a tradition, one purpose of the volume is to establish its claim to importance and make it visible (East Central European Magical Realist cinema, Palestinian cinema).

Textbooks and monographs include:

- An introduction that clarifies the rationale for the grouping of films under examination
- A concise history of the regional, national, or transnational cinema in question
- A summary of previous published work on the tradition
- Contextual analysis of industrial, cultural and socio-historical conditions of production and reception
- Textual analysis of specific and notable films, with clear and judicious application of relevant film theoretical approaches
- Bibliograph(ies)/filmograph(ies)

Monographs may additionally include:

- Discussion of the dynamics of cross-cultural exchange in light of current research and thinking about cultural imperialism and globalisation, as well as issues of regional/national cinema or political/aesthetic movements (such as new waves, postmodernism, or identity politics)
- Interview(s) with key filmmakers working within the tradition.

INTRODUCTION: IMAGES OF SOUND AND FURY

Gunnar Iversen and Scott MacKenzie

"Where is my camera?" shouts Becky in the girl-punk group Something She, in an emblematic scene in the feature film *Her Smell* (Alex Ross Perry, USA/Greece, 2018). Elisabeth Moss plays the self-destructive rock star on the verge of total mental breakdown in this fictional rockumentary. In the scene, Becky is backstage, two hours late for her concert and surrounded by an entourage of voodoo priests, hangers-on and a film team. Becky may be falling apart but she knows the importance of audio-visual representation and documentation, and she wants even her most painful moment of failure to be recorded, so she screams that the cinematographer should continue filming and record her mental collapse and artistic downfall. Backstage is the real space of display and performance, and Becky is performing just as much backstage as on-stage. The fact that recording both the public and private life of a rock star takes central stage in a fiction film demonstrates the rockumentary's importance to the contemporary scene. Today, *to be* is *to be filmed*, and any rock star or band needs to have their own rockumentary.

Throughout its history, the rockumentary has been not only an important vehicle for image control by artists and the music industry, but also a revealing mirror showcasing rock 'n' roll excesses. It is also a popular documentary form that fans can enjoy, seeing and hearing their favorite artists both on- and off-stage. Michael Brendan Baker notes: 'The genre as a whole is a vast archive of rock's many styles and myriad tropes of live performance. In a very practical sense, rockumentary fims exist as a reservoir of popular music history, documentary history, and film technology' (2011: 67), becoming the meeting between documentary history and practice on the one hand, and popular music history and performance on the other.

Rockumentaries in cinemas and on television have been, since the early 2000s, supplemented by numerous Internet websites where fans lovingly post videos of their idols. YouTube is a treasure trove for music enthusiasts, and audio-visual representations of popular music bring together new virtual transnational audiences experiencing music and performance. Today, fans access performances of their favorite popular music artists on their computers and cell phones, creating sonorous communities in transnational contexts, but they can also access the rockumentary archive of music and performance and feelings by looking and listening to older films and videos online. Old rockumentaries, or documentaries about popular music before the industrialization of rock 'n' roll in the 1960s, exist side by side on YouTube with the latest fancam videos of yesterday's concerts uploaded by eager fans. During the COVID pandemic, bands recognized the central importance of the Internet for their fans and turned their web platforms on YouTube into Event Cinema sites, streaming time-limited material from their archives, such as Pink Floyd's Free Film Fridays, which featured works such as *Pink Floyd: Live at Pompeii* (Adrian Maben, UK/Belgium/West Germany, 1972) for twenty-four hours. Spike Lee's adaptation of David Byrne's Broadway musical *American Utopia* (USA, 2020) demonstrates a new form of rockumentary concert film emerging in the COVID era.

The term "rockumentary" was probably first coined in the late 1960s. It can be traced back to its use in a radio context in the United States. Radio host Bill Drake used the term in the radio show *History of Rock 'n' Roll* in 1969 (Landau 1973). Even if the exact origin of the term is unclear, by the beginning of the 1970s it was used as a portmanteau for a number of popular documentaries about successful new rock music. Films like *Dont Look Back* (D. A. Pennebaker, USA, 1967), *Monterey Pop* (D. A. Pennebaker, USA, 1968), *Woodstock* (Michael Wadleigh, USA, 1970), and *Gimme Shelter* (Albert Maysles, David Maysles and Charlotte Zwerin, USA, 1970) represented the breakthrough of a new genre of popular music documentary.

These rockumentaries were imitated in similar films about rock music or concert events around the world and helped shape both documentary form and popular music performances. *Woodstock* especially had many imitators, from the Argentinean *Rock Until the Sun Sets* (Aníbal Uset, Argentina, 1973) to the Norwegian *Ragnarock* (Arne Philip Fraas, Norway, 1973). These feature-length rockumentaries celebrate a new youth culture and identity politics through the concert and the festival, signaling a global change in attitudes towards music, film, and youth.

Beginning in the 1960s, the role of recorded musical performances, and, indeed, the act of witnessing pop and rock artists perform, especially at music festivals or big arenas, became more and more important for youth cultures globally. Young people created new identities all over the world, as they aligned themselves with rock music, rock artists, and rock identities. Since then, as Baker has argued in detail in his PhD dissertation, the first comprehensive study of the genre, the rockumentary has played a huge role in shaping youth culture, audio-visual representations of artists, and live musical performances (Baker 2011: 6). Furthermore, as Baker notes, the rockumentary establishes and then reworks most of the conventions of audio-visual representation of popular music (see Baker 2011: 6).

A few rockumentaries, like the pioneering *Lonely Boy* (Wolf Koenig and Roman Kroitor, Canada, 1962) and *Dont Look Back*, are considered important for the development of *cinéma vérité* in the 1960s, but rockumentary as a documentary genre, Baker aside, has received scant attention in the growing field of documentary studies. Relatively little is written about the central importance played by the rockumentary in the development of documentary forms like *cinéma direct*, self-reflexive documentary, and expanded cinema and IMAX, or the rockumentary's intersections with underground and *avant garde* film, or punk/post-punk DIY-documentaries. In popular music studies, the same situation is obvious. Even though visual representation has been so central to popular music since the 1960s, the rockumentary has not received the full attention it deserves. Part of the disparagement of the rockumentary in documentary studies come from the portmanteau nature of the term. The strong claim we are making in this volume is that "rock" (and its pop cultural status) overdetermines one's understanding of the genre, and that the rockumentary has as much – and, at times, more – to say about gender, politics, cultural appropriation, race, class, postmodernism, intersectionality, colonialism, cultural history, geopolitics, the epistemology of the image and the representation of the real as the documentary writ large does.

Today – as the fiction film *Her Smell* illustrates in an interesting and compelling way, as well as numerous rockumentaries from *Dont Look Back* about Bob Dylan's tour of England in 1965, to *Truth and Dare* (Alek Keshishian, USA, 1991) about Madonna's Blond Ambition tour in 1990, to the band Coldplay on tour around the world in *Coldplay: A Head Full of Dreams* (Mat Whitecross, UK, 2018) – to be a rock artist is to be filmed and recorded.

A Documentary Genre

Even though the term rockumentary itself seems to indicate that it is only used in a rock context, the term usually encompasses a number of different popular musical genres, including pop, blues, jazz, country, and hip hop. Mediated music has a long history that starts with Warner Bros. and the many Vitaphone short sound films made in the United States between 1926 and 1932, and the television show *American Bandstand* (1952–89) with its numerous musical performances. As Laura Niebling notes in this volume, in these early depictions of popular music before the late 1950s and early 1960s, two key factors are relevant for the later rockumentary form: how the popularization and canonization of urban musical styles are linked to their depiction in moving images, and the way in which the films already at this early point in history were associated with the early music industry. This is an important aspect with many of the most canonical rockumentaries and music documentaries, from *Jazz on a Summer's Day* (Bert Stern, USA, 1959) to *The Last Waltz* (Martin Scorsese, USA, 1978).

Even though film and music always have been tightly knitted together, something new happened in the post-war period of documentary. A catalyst for a new documentary style was the English cinematographer and director Richard Leacock (1921–2011). Right after the end of World War II Leacock got a job as cinematographer on a short film directed by Irving Lerner and Willard Van Dyke. *To Hear Your Banjo Play* (USA, 1946) was inspired by the folk revival in the United States and depicts how folk music shapes the modern America. In the film, the history of the banjo is presented and it offers short portraits of Pete Seeger and Woody Guthrie, but the film most importantly conveys the raw social power in the music when Seeger is playing at a dance or Guthrie is playing with Black musicians, a raw social power that soon changed the musical landscape of America. The blend of folk and blues conveys a glimpse of a social and aesthetic utopia where race is unimportant and where music represents the aesthetics of hope.

Leacock was not happy about his work on *To Hear Your Banjo Play* or the later short *Jazz Dance* (Roger Tilton, USA, 1954). The use of heavy 35mm unsynchronized cameras created technical limitations that affected the aesthetic form. The use of new lightweight and hand-held synchronized 16mm cameras in what became known as direct cinema or *cinéma vérité*, which Leacock was instrumental in creating in the early 1960s, paved the way for a more improvised, intimate, raw, energetic and free depiction of musical performance as well as life backstage. Leacock had first used the new camera and sound technology in 1957 on *Bernstein in Israel*, filming the American conductor on a trip to Tel Aviv for the inaugural concert of the new home of the Israel Philharmonic, but the gear was still cumbersome and created a number of problems and artistic limitations (Chanan 2013, 339). When D. A. Pennebaker released *Dont Look Back* ten years later, a new language for conveying both musical performance and artists' backstage life had been invented.

While Leacock in the United States was making music documentaries and slowly trying out new technologies for depicting artists and musical forms, Karel Reisz and Tony Richardson made *Momma Don't Allow* (UK, 1956) in

England. Included in the very first Free Cinema programme at the National Film Theatre in London in February 1956, but filmed during the winter of 1954–55, Reisz and Richardson's film is a portrait of a jazz club in a pub in North London. Filmed on 16mm, without sync sound, but conveying the excited energy of jazz and skiffle music, *Momma Don't Allow* was a deliberate attempt to challenge the dominant Griersonian school of British documentary. Its attitude towards documentary form as well as the people depicted is quite distinct from contemporaneous documentaries.

Without any voice-over interpreting the images or the events, the filmmakers follow a young dental assistant, an assistant to a butcher, and a young cleaner when they spend their Saturday night out at the jazz pub. While *To Hear Your Banjo Play* mixes Black and White musicians, *Momma Don't Allow* mixes working-class youth and an upper-class couple who just want to hear the new exciting rhythmic music. Initially, the appearance of these "toffs" creates some unruliness in the crowd, but the couple throw themselves into the energetic dance and become part of the dancers. Important themes in later rockumentaries, and especially the festival films, are the new mixed audiences and the social utopic space that music and events create. In *To Hear Your Banjo Play* and *Momma Don't Allow*, musical subcultures are depicted, but within this depiction, there is also a social utopia where Black and White or different classes can dance and listen to artists performing together as one big musical family.

This theme is also important in the film that is most often singled out as the first rockumentary, even though it is not much about rock at all: Bert Stern's *Jazz on a Summer's Day*. Like many later rockumentaries, Stern's film depicts a kind of social and musical melting pot, where people from different classes and races interact, all performing or listening to the same musical mix. Documentary scholar Michael Chanan has written that: "*Jazz on a Summer's Day* is already more than a transcription of concert performances, but an almost ethnographic portrait of the audience in its natural habitat" (Chanan 2013, 339).

Even if the artists on stage at the Newport Jazz Festival at Rhode Island in 1958 are the most important in Stern's film, the depiction of the audience is central to its presentation of the event itself and of the new youth culture and mixed audience bought together by the music. *Jazz on a Summer's Day* mixes different musical genres, from Dixieland and bebop to gospel, but also includes Chuck Berry performing "Sweet Little Sixteen." By including "The Father of Rock 'n' Roll," as Berry is often called, playing his hit song from earlier in 1958, Stern's film also shows the popular musical idiom that soon will replace jazz as the music of the young. Berry's hip gyrations and extravagant guitar playing not only bring out big smiles on the faces of his fellow musicians in frequent cuts from Berry to his band and the audience, but also get a young couple dancing. Instead of the audience sitting still and listening to the jazz, rock creates a different kind of interactivity with its audience, and the many short depictions of the audience are another example of how *Jazz on a Summer's Day* is pointing towards the concert rockumentaries from the late 1960s and the early 1970s to today.

Jazz on a Summer's Day is the first feature-length music rockumentary and introduces the subgenre of the concert film, which became so important in the late 1960s. The film also exemplifies some important technological and industrial issues of the rockumentary. While other filmmakers experimented with new technology, especially the 16mm format, and used black-and-white film, Stern turned to 35mm color film and magnetic audio recordings. The need for high-quality audio recordings of filmed live events, in order to sonically represent the original performance and capture music in a quality so that it met the requirements of theatrical reproduction – and later the release of live albums – is important to the genre. In the case of *Jazz on a Summer's Day*, the sound recording equipment was provided by Columbia Records, and this meant that Stern had to give away the editorial control to the record company. The selection of artists and songs included in the film was to a large degree given to executives at Columbia Records to ensure the profitability of the recorded live music. *Jazz on a Summer's Day* also then illustrates what documentary scholar Michael Brendan Baker has called "the synergistic relationship between filmmaker, artist, studio, and record company so central to subsequent rockumentaries" (Baker 2011, 102).

Another important precursor that signals the new genre in documentary filmmaking is the National Film Board of Canada/Office national du film's rockumentary *Lonely Boy*. If *Jazz on a Summer's Day* is innovative in the depiction of the audience and how audience members react to the music and in the process establishes many of the conventions of the concert film, Kroitor and Koenig explore the behind-the-scenes aspects of an artist's life. *Lonely Boy* is an early backstage documentary, but the film also depicts Paul Anka's performances and the ecstatic female fans at his concerts in the United States.

An early example of direct cinema or *cinéma vérité*, *Lonely Boy* follows Anka into the private spaces of backstage and the dressing room, promising the audience something new and more real than the older, more expository documentaries. The famous scene in Anka's dressing room, where he strips down to his underwear in front of the camera crew, is an emblematic moment in documentary history and points to the new self-reflexivity in the documentary. "Just forget that they are there," he says to a photographer who reacts to the presence of the camera crew. In another scene, where Anka gives Copacabana owner Jules Podell a kiss on the cheek, the directors ask Anka to repeat the kiss. Self-consciousness is also apparent in some of the concert scenes. Some of his many female fans are crying and screaming, but others look around and to the camera, searching for an appropriate way of acting – and performing – as a fan at a concert.

The depiction of the audience changes dramatically between *Jazz on a Summer's Day* and *Lonely Boy*. In Stern's film the audience members are usually listening coolly to the different jazz musicians, and only rarely dance or interact in other ways. In *Lonely Boy* the teen idol and his relationship to the female fans are foregrounded, even including a short interview with Anka where he says that 60 per cent of his attraction is due to emotions and sex. The ecstatic fans at Anka's concerts are seen as a curious new sociological and psychological phenomenon by the two Canadian filmmakers. Soon this behavior would get a new name: Beatlemania. Indeed, the aesthetics of *Lonely Boy* foreshadow one of the templates for future rockumentaries and the representation of rock more generally in works such as *What's Happening! The Beatles in the U.S.A.* (Albert and David Maysles, USA, 1964) and The Beatles' own early mockumentary *A Hard Day's Night* (Richard Lester, UK/USA, 1964).

In the later, now classic, rockumentaries of the late 1960s and early 1970s, different views of the audience show the changes in the genre as well as changes in celebrity culture and conceptions of stardom. Film scholar Julie Lobalzo Wright has written convincingly about the differences in audience representation in *Woodstock* and *Gimme Shelter*. The former emphasizes the natural environment and community, creating what Wright calls a "communal gaze," while the latter emphasizes the artificial, man-made environment and individualism, creating a "disconnected gaze" (Wright 2013, 73). *Woodstock* is often seen as the epitome of the new young generation's hope for the future and peaceful co-existence. As its dystopian double, *Gimme Shelter*, with its violence and anger, illustrates that the Summer of Love definitively is over.

The breakthrough films of the late 1960s and early 1970s, like *Monterey Pop*, *Woodstock*, and *Gimme Shelter* are very different, even though they all represent concerts and festival events. These films not only explore the new social spaces of the concert events, and the new experience of being in a big crowd of fans, but also create new images of performers. Especially through close-ups, fans and other cinema spectators come closer to performers than ever before, and the films often single out small intimate moments on-stage where the performer is presented in a way unique to the rockumentary form.

These films also chart the changes in the portrait of the artist. In *Lonely Boy*, Anka is depicted as "just a lonely boy from Ottawa," but his youthful 19-year-old innocence is combined with a candid portrait of the making of a star. Anka himself and his manager openly discuss how he needed to lose weight, change his hair style, and even undergo plastic surgery in order to become an attractive star. The film points out that stardom, feelings, and charisma are carefully constructed. Of course, these constructions can also be seen as ephemeral. At one point, Anka's manager states that "God has given [Anka] something that I don't think he has given to anyone in the last 500 years . . . I truthfully believe that Paul will be the biggest star, with an overall career, that this world has ever known." This, perhaps to the surprise of no one, did not turn out to be the case.

Five years later, when *Dont Look Back* premiered, Bob Dylan remained mystical. He seldom lost his cool. His entourage also presented a very different image of stardom. "I can't pose," folk singer Joan Baez says in a central scene, but Dylan poses all the time. His pose, however, is a very different one than Anka's. Only in some short moments does Dylan lose his controlled and reserved poise, or his scepticism about his own fame, especially when he scolds a journalist when he is being interviewed. Suddenly, in a brief moment, the mask slips and Dylan becomes just as dogmatic and ordinary as the journalists, even using the same "dirty" rhetoric in order to punish the journalist.

These films illustrate that the rockumentary is also about fandom, stardom, and celebrity culture. Since these canonical documentaries from 1959 to the early 1970s, numerous rockumentaries have explored both the new social spaces of rock and pop culture, the new identities created by fans and concertgoers, and performance styles. And, often, the performance continues, like in *Lonely Boy* and *Dont Look Back*, even backstage and in more intimate settings. These moments in many rockumentaries have been used for image building and image control by numerous artists. Indeed, this image control has led to the banning of some rockumentaries as the producers are also the subjects. Michael Lindsay-Hogg had to deal with four different band member producers while editing *Let It Be* (UK, 1970). Robert Frank's *Cocksucker Blues* (USA, 1972), a backstage account of The Rolling Stones' 1972 American concert tour, and Lindsay Anderson's *If You Were There* (UK, 1985), about Wham!'s tour of The People's Republic of China just as the country was beginning to open up to the West, were both placed under highly restrictive viewing parameters to "protect" the interest and image of the artists.

The Rockumentary and its Subgenres

Throughout its history, the rockumentary has encompassed a number of subgenres. Documentary scholar Michael Brendan Baker distinguishes between five rockumentary trends, broad currents, or subgenres (Baker 2014). These different subgenres point to the variety of forms grouped together under the term rockumentary and show the centrality of this documentary form to documentary film history as well as the development of popular music.

The first subgenre is the rockumentary biography or artist portrait. In this type of documentary, the filmmakers present either a living or a dead artist. Sometimes the films are celebrations of important stars and artists, summing up their careers, like *George Harrison: Living in the Material World* (Martin

Scorsese, USA, 2011) or Jim Jarmusch's portrait of Iggy Pop in *Gimme Danger* (USA, 2016). Sometimes the biographies or portraits focus on more tragic and problematic aspects of a star's life, like Asif Kapadia's portrait of singer Amy Winehouse in *Amy* (UK, 2015). These portraits or biographies use archival material in order to create a depiction of an artist's life and career.

The second subgenre is the concert film or other performance-based rockumentaries. Even though these films focus on the performances themselves, in a variety of ways, they can have a very different attitude and aesthetic form, and range from rigorously choreographed and composed spectacles, like *Stop Making Sense* (USA, 1984), Jonathan Demme's concert film about Talking Heads, to raw and rough low-budget, even fan-made films, like the Beastie Boys' concert film *Awesome; I Fuckin' Shot That!* (Adam Yauch, USA, 2006). Concert films, despite their documentary status, at times also contain fantasy and fictional elements to contrast with, illustrate, or highlight aspects of the documentary work, such as Peter Clifton and Joe Massot's *The Song Remains the Same* (UK, 1976) filmed during Led Zeppelin's three night stand at Madison Square Garden in 1973 interspersed with quasi-runic fantasies, and Lasse Hallström's *ABBA: The Movie* (Sweden, 1977), which interweaves the band's 1977 tour of Australia with a fictional account of a DJ seeking an interview.

The third subgenre is the tour film or making-of documentary. This type of rockumentary is different from the artist portrait or the concert film in the way it focuses on a single event, either a tour or the act of making an album or planning a special event. An example of the tour film is *Coldplay: A Head Full of Dreams*. On television there have been numerous rockumentaries focusing on important or classic rock albums, tracing the production of albums such as Pink Floyd's *Atom Heart Mother* (1970), Black Sabbath's *Paranoid* (1970), Lou Reed's *Transformer* (1972), The Sex Pistols' *Never Mind the Bollocks, Here's the Sex Pistols* (1977), and Jay-Z's *Reasonable Doubt* (1996).

The fourth subgenre is what Michael Brendan Baker has called "ethnographic studies of rock music, its subgenres, and subcultures" (Baker 2014). This type of rockumentary does not necessarily focus on artists at all, but more on subcultures or fan cultures. Sometimes a band or a musical style is at the center of the film, but the aim of the rockumentary is broader than just giving a portrait of an artist or a band. Dutch filmmaker Alexander Oey's *There is No Authority but Yourself* (The Netherlands, 2006) falls into this category, being more an exploration of the anarcho-punk movement in the UK in the 1970s and 1980s than about the central band Crass. Penelope Spheeris' *The Decline of Western Civilization* (USA, 1981), Ice-T's *Something from Nothing: The Art of Rap* (USA, 2012), and the Canadian web series *Hip-Hop Evolution* (HBO Canada/Netflix, 2016-) are also exemplars of this category.

The fifth and last subgenre, according to Baker, is the compilation or archive project. This is a type of rockumentary that often is found on television and the Internet, and it relies more than other rockumentaries "on the structure and expository mode of address of classical documentaries with the subordination of the images to a singular rhetorical position and a reliance on didactic commentary" (Baker 2014: 6). The borders between this type of rockumentary and the others are, however, sometimes hard to draw. Baker's examples of this type of rockumentary could easily be subsumed under other categories. The Who's *The Kids Are Alright* (Jeff Stein, UK, 1979), the Sex Pistols' *The Filth and the Fury* (Julien Temple, UK, 2000), Jay-Z's *Fade to Black* (Patrick Paulson and Michael John Warren, USA, 2004) and The Rolling Stones' *Crossfire Hurricane* (Brett Morgen, USA, 2012) might be seen as band portraits, and the television mini-series *The History of Rock 'n' Roll* (1995) might be seen as a "making of" documentary.

A sixth subgenre could be added to Baker's typology: the music industry rockumentary. This could be seen as a separate subgenre with its focus on aspects of the music business or music industry, which only parenthetically involve artists or bands. In James D. Cooper's *Lambert and Stamp* (USA, 2014), a portrait of Chris Stamp and Kit Lambert – the first two managers of The Who – the band and their career certainly are at the centre, but the focus is on the managers not the artists. In a more experimental vein, there is Craig Baldwin's *Sonic Outlaws* (USA, 1995), on the copyright infringement case surrounding Negativland's sampling of U2. An even better example may be *All Things Must Pass: The Rise and Fall of Tower Records* (Colin Hanks, USA, 2015), which tells the fascinating story of Tower Records, a chain of record stores in Sacramento and San Francisco. If this is seen as an "ethnographic study" of rock culture, it is a different one than the most common studies. Instead of either focusing on musical genres, fan cultures, or subcultures, Hanks' film discusses the industrial and technological aspects of popular music culture through the rise and fall of a series of record stores due to the decline of the vinyl and CD formats.

Many classic as well as modern rockumentaries are hybrid forms, combining two or several of these suggested subgenres. Certainly, Pennebaker's *Dont Look Back* is both a tour film and a portrait of Bob Dylan, and *Lonely Boy* is both a portrait of Paul Anka and an ethnographic study of the new phenomenon of fan and celebrity culture. Other subgenres might be added; for instance the political rockumentary, such as Yoko Ono and John Lennon's *Bed Peace* (UK, 1969), about their "Bed In" in Amsterdam during their honeymoon to bring awareness to their peace imitative, and Rubika Shah's *White Riot* (UK, 2019), about the 1970s "Rock Against Racism" movement in the UK, or the rockxploitation movie, such as Stanley A. Long's *Bread* (UK, 1971), which uses the Isle of Wight festival in 1970 as a setting and refers to *Woodstock* and *Gimme Shelter*. One could expand the area further with the inclusion of the rockudrama biopic, with works such as Anton Corbijn's *Control* (UK/USA, 2007), about Joy Division lead singer Ian Curtis, Bill Pohlad's *Love & Mercy* (USA, 2014), about Beach Boy Brian Wilson, and F. Gary Gray's *Straight Outta Compton* (USA, 2015), about the seminal gangsta rap group N.W.A. Some rock operas that draw on bands' biographies can also, if one takes a catholic approach to the rockumentary, be considered another kind of docudrama; for example Franc Roddam's *Quadrophenia* (UK, 1979), and Alan Parker's *Pink Floyd: The Wall* (UK, 1982). The main point here is not to close down the discussion of a documentary genre through taxonomy, but rather to open the discussion up by pointing out the variety of forms and types of documentaries that are grouped together under the term rockumentary. In this book, all of the types of rockumentaries above will be discussed.

THE ROCKUMENTARY TODAY

Genre theorists often say that a genre is fully formed when one can make fun of it. The combination of audience and industry recognition is met when one can make a parody or a satire of a genre. If this is the case, the release of the mockumentary *This is Spinal Tap* (Rob Reiner, USA, 1984) marks the beginning of another phase of the genre. Musical parodies that could be called mockumentaries, making fun of pop culture and rock bands, were certainly made before Reiner's phony road movie and celebration of the wonderful ridiculousness of heavy metal. The inventive *The Rutles: All You Need is Cash* (Eric Idle and Gary Weis, UK/USA, 1978), with its parody of The Beatles and Beatlemania, is one example. However, *This is Spinal Tap* is important in the way it uses and exposes the many conventions of the rockumentary genre. The film lovingly makes fun of heavy metal culture, with its masculine excess, but also of fan and celebrity culture or the trope of being 'on the road' between gigs, as well as parodying *cinéma vérité* (de Seife 2007, 43–7). In a vertiginous manner, the mockumentary *This is Spinal Tap* becomes the intertextual influence on the heavy metal rockumentary *Anvil!: The Story of Anvil* (Sacha Gervasi, USA, 2008), about a hapless Canadian metal band whose glory days are long behind them. Intertextual mockery can also be present as an aspect of a rockumentary. *1991: The Year Punk Broke* (Dave Markey, USA, 1992), while in many ways a straight performance rockumentary about Sonic Youth touring the UK with some support bands, also features backstage scenes where Kim Gordon and Kurt Cobain restage and parody aspects of *Truth or Dare*.

The rockumentary seems to be everywhere these days; every country has its rock heroes and rockumentaries about them, and rockumentaries are shown in cinemas, on television, and flourish on YouTube and other Internet platforms. Some films are "official," in the sense that they are authorized by the artist or band, and work as a form of image building and image control. Other films may be more critical or fancam-based and present a different picture of the artist or the music.

Since the rockumentary emerged at a turning point in the history of popular music and rock 'n' roll, when the musical form changed from the dominance of the three-minute pop song to a higher degree of complexity or even seriousness and longer songs, the media forms and the industry and publicity apparatuses around popular music have changed drastically. All the subgenres of the rockumentary could be used for different documentary purposes, and there are numerous examples of popular music and rockumentaries being used for important social and political purposes.

An example that shows how rockumentary can be used for a more political purpose, and at the same time illustrates how the genre is no longer restricted to the USA and the UK, is *Sumé: The Sound of a Revolution* (Inuk Silis Høegh, Greenland/Denmark/Norway, 2014). This rockumentary from Greenland gives a striking portrait of the band Sumé. Between 1972 and 1976, this band, which consisted of only Indigenous members, was not only popular in Greenland, but also in Denmark, and other parts of Scandinavia and northern Europe.

As the title suggests, *Sumé: The Sound of a Revolution* is much more than a mere portrait of a band; it is a socially critical documentary showing how music and rock can be tools in the mobilization of Greenlanders to fight against colonization and for self-governance and independence. In the film, Greenland's trajectory from Danish colony to country with more and more independence is mixed with the role the band Sumé and its music had in the fight for independence. *Sumé: The Sound of a Revolution* is one of many recent Indigenous rockumentaries that combine the protest of pop, rock, and hip hop with Indigenous stories of decolonization, including Derek Aqqiaruq's *Northern Haze: Living the Dream* (Canada, 2011), *Arctic Superstar* (Simen Braathen, Norway, 2016), about Sámi hip hop artist SlinCraze, *Rumble: The Indians Who Rocked The World* (Catherine Bainbridge and Alfonso Maiorana, Canada, 2017), which traces the history of rock artists with Indigenous backgrounds, from Link Wray and Mildred Bailey, to Jesse Ed Davis and Jimi Hendrix, to Buffy Sainte-Marie and Robbie Robertson, and *WE UP: Indigenous Hip Hop in the Circumpolar North* (Priscilla Naunġaġiaq Hensley and David Holthouse, USA, 2018).

We tend to think of popular culture as first and foremost a tool of globalization and even "Americanization." In countries all over the world, from Argentina to Greenland, from South Korea to Norway, popular music and rockumentaries have not only signaled personal freedom and a new identity politics, but have also presented filmmakers and audiences with tools for social and political liberation. This is another aspect of the social utopia of popular music as the aesthetics of hope. Today, the variety of the rockumentary form is larger than ever, and many documentaries of rock or other types of popular music are fascinating hybrids, mixing two or several of the rockumentary subgenres or types mentioned earlier. Some even use rock music and exciting images in order to try to change the world for the better.

Contributions

The contributors in this book explore the history of rockumentary and the genre's malleability through a variety of perspectives and examples. We have organized the twenty-five chapters into five sections. In the first section, "Histories," different aspects of the history of the genre are discussed. Greil Marcus opens the book with his evocative, poetic piece on David Hoffman's documentary *Music Makers of the Blue Ridge* (USA, 1966), a film about bluegrass roots, thus starting the journey towards modern pop and rock by pointing to the American folk and blues roots. The pre-history of the rockumentary is explored by Laura Niebling, who points out how the history of the rockumentary genre must be seen as a continuation of mediated music on film, television, and in radio from the 1920s to the late 1960s. The radio connection is especially important here, via the canonization of music through experts, hits, and stars. Laurel Westrup focuses primarily on *Monterey Pop* as the pivotal pop festival and concert film. Pennebaker's film wove together aesthetic ideas from previous concert documentaries and ultimately produced a concert film style that continues to influence concert film production today. Michael Brendan Baker's chapter discusses the different strategies for sonic representation of musical performances in rockumentaries. By pointing out how rockumentaries are intensely mediated audio-visual representations of already mediated events, through examples like *Dont Look Back* and *The Last Waltz*, Baker shows how the concepts of liveness and authenticity are problematic. In the last chapter in section one, Scott MacKenzie examines how rockumentaries function as false endings to different cultural, political and historical moments in the history of rock music, youth cultures, and political moments, from Edward O. Bland's *The Cry of Jazz* (USA, 1959) to Michael Lindsay-Hogg's *Let It Be* (UK, 1970), to more recent works on death and trauma, such as The Tragically Hip rockumentary *Long Time Running* (Jennifer Baichwal and Nicholas de Pencier, Canada, 2017) about the band's last tour after lead singer Gord Downie was diagnosed with glioblastoma, and a rockumentary about the lingering trauma of The Who's concert in Cincinnati in December 1979, *The Who: The Night That Changed Rock* (Emily Maxwell, USA, 2019).

In the second section of the book, "Gender," different conceptions of gender in rock culture and rockumentaries are explored. Catherine Strong and Stephen Gaunson use rockumentaries with and by The Rolling Stones as a case study for a discussion of how women have been portrayed in rockumentaries about the band. Which roles women have been given access to and have been expected to perform are discussed through especially designated roles as groupies, wives and girlfriends, to out-of-control fans. How The Rolling Stones, through gender roles, have created themselves as rock outlaws is also important in the chapter, and it is followed by Anna Westerstahl Stenport's discussion of Madonna and the depiction of her Blond Ambition Tour in 1990 in *Truth or Dare*. In Stenport's chapter, gender politics are supplemented with larger issues of geopolitics and globalization, showing how Madonna, in the midst of MTV fever, became a complex and contradictory geopolitical agent, pop culture icon, and international media brand. Heather McIntosh uses the controversy over a comment by one of the Dixie Chicks as a way to discuss the freedom to speak and how women are portrayed in country music. Focusing on Barbara Kopple and Cecilia Peck's *Shut Up & Sing* (2006), McIntosh discusses how the group responded to the media backlash. In his essay, Gunnar Iversen focuses on masculinity and how the rockumentary genre also contains melodramatic depictions of family relations. By comparing *Metallica: Some Kind of Monster* (Joe Berlinger and Bruce Sinofsky, USA, 2004) and *Mistaken for Strangers* (Tom Berninger, USA, 2013), Iversen points out how many rockumentaries are family melodramas. In the last chapter in this section, Magdalena Fürnkranz looks closely at Todd Haynes's *I'm Not There* (USA/Germany, 2007) and how this "rockudrama" creates different identity representations, and how sexual identities are performed.

In the third section of the book, "Aesthetics and Politics," different connections between politics and aesthetics are explored. Karine Bertrand examines what could be seen as the turning point from earnestness to postmodern irony by the Irish band U2 through an analysis of *Rattle and Hum* (Phil Joanou, USA, 1988). Celine Bell uses *Rude Boy* (Jack Hazan and David Mingay, UK, 1980) and the punk group The Clash to examine representations of British youth and punk music and their relationship to London as an urban metropolis in the 1970s. The connections between The Clash and their fans are important, and this is also the core of Randolph Jordan's chapter. By analyzing *Long Strange Trip* (Amir Bar-Lev, USA, 2017) about the Grateful Dead, Jordan discusses not only the relationship between the band and the audience, but also how technological solutions were used by the band to create community and how fan taping was accepted as part of family building. Anthony Kinik explores Nick Cave's shifting engagement with the rockumentary through two very different rockumentaries about the artist. By comparing *The Road to God Knows Where* (Uli M. Schüppel, Germany, 1990) with the much later *20,000 Days on Earth* (Iain Forsyth and Jane Pollard, UK, 2014), Kinik discusses opposing trends or forces within the genre, anti-rockumentaries, and meta-rockumentaries. Issues of performativity and authenticity, and mystifications in the rockumentary are also important in Asbjørn Grønstad and Øyvind

Vågnes' chapter on *Searching for the Wrong-Eyed Jesus* (Andrew Douglas, UK, 2003). Grønstad and Vågnes invoke Greil Marcus's aesthetic imaginary of "the old weird America" and the literary trope "the Southern Gothic" in order to explore the elusive identity of Southern music and culture, and the multiple ways the performative rockumentary engages with the South.

In the fourth section of the book, "Counter-cultures," the main theme is how rockumentaries can work as and within counter-cultures. As a direct continuation of the different thematizations of aesthetics and politics, the first two chapters look at rock and rockumentaries in Latin America. In their chapter, Jorge Saavedra Utman and Toby Miller discuss documentaries about popular music in Chile and how Chilean popular music becomes a political gesture. They also show how rockumentaries in Chile have contributed to an ongoing reflection about social and political identity. In Argentina, the situation is similar, as Javier Campo and Tomás Crowder-Taraborrelli point out in their chapter. Discussing two Argentinean rockumentaries, *Rock Until the Sun Sets* (Aníbal Uset, Argentina, 1973) and *Buenos Aires Rock* (Héctor Olvera, Argentina, 1983), the authors not only trace important historical lines in Latin American rock and rockumentary history, but also the audio-visual genre as an important part of a social and political counter-culture. How rock and rockumentary can be used for purposes of nation building is the topic of Eric Fillion's chapter. In September 1978, the progressive rock band Harmonium accompanied Québec Premier René Lévesque on a cultural mission to the USA, and Robert Fortier's rockumentary *Harmonium in California* (Canada, 1979) is a striking example of cultural diplomacy and nation building through rock music. If the Québécois documentary looks at national self-representation, Asbjørn Tiller discusses in his chapter the British anarcho-punk movement, where the dissolving of nations and national jingoism is central. By using Alexander Oey's *There is No Authority but Yourself* (The Netherlands, 2006) focusing on Crass as the main example, Tiller shows how both popular music and audio-visual representation worked as integral parts of the anarcho-punk movement. The rockumentary seen as a form of psychogeography is a topic that is further explored by Lindsey Eckenroth in her chapter on the American band MC5. David C. Thomas's rockumentary *MC5: A True Testimonial* (USA, 2002) becomes the entry into a discussion about the relationship of rock and urbanity, and especially the many striking connections between Detroit and MC5.

In the fifth and final section of the book, "Futures," the theme is more experimental and exploratory, extrapolating futures of the genre and its audience. Gary Kibbins uses Laurie Anderson's experimental rockumentary *Heart of a Dog* (USA, 2015) as a way to explore non-identity filmmaking and Anderson's essayistic and highly ironic film. How live music, star culture, and concert tours were reflected in fiction films in the 1970s is the topic of Julie Lobalzo

Wright's chapter. By focusing on two Hollywood films, and especially *The Rose* (Mark Rydell, USA, 1979), Wright sees how fiction films in the 1970s document the expansion of the popular music business and establish many of the clichés that have come to be associated with the contemporary rock concert tour. The recent feature *Her Smell* is a modern example of this. Ian Robinson points to the future in his chapter dealing with the phenomenon of alternative content in cinemas since the early 2000s. Event Cinema has become more and more common and important for cinemas as well as for artists, and Robinson discusses how this new hypermediated livecasting creates a new conception of liveness and authenticity. If event cinema is one future where rock and visuality meet, another is Fancam recordings uploaded on YouTube or other platforms. In their chapter, Eric Chalfant and Ali Na use K-pop to explore this phenomenon, but they also discuss new fan cultures and fan formations. Questions of touch and stanning are especially important, and Chalfant and Na show how questions of touch become important among transnational K-pop fans who are physically dispersed but affectively connected. We end the book as it begins, with a short piece by Greil Marcus, one of the social historians of rock who have inspired this collection. If bluegrass, blues, and jazz are the main roots of rock and pop music, Marcus points out alternative pasts and futures by using Bruce Conner's experimental film *The White Rose* (USA, 1967) in the final chapter, discussing a film where art, touch, jazz, and ritual create a new aesthetic space.

The many contributions in this book show us how important the rockumentary has been and still is for the documentary and for the popular music industry. But they also point out how the wide range of films that fall into the rockumentary genre work as a space for image making and image control for artists, how they constitute an alternative archive of history through rock and popular music, how they are a space for identity politics and a variety of performance styles, and how the rockumentary is an archive of feelings in the form of music and images.

References

Baker, Michael Brendan. 2011. *Rockumentary: Style, Performance and Sound in a Documentary Genre*. Ph.D. thesis. Montréal: McGill University, Montréal.

Baker, Michael Brendan. 2014. "Notes on the Rockumentary Renaissance." *Cinephile* 10(1): 5–10.

Chanan, Michael. 2013. "Music, Documentary, Music Documentary." In *The Documentary Film Book*, ed. Brian Winston. London: Palgrave Macmillan/BFI. 337–44.

de Seife, Ethan. 2007. *This is Spinal Tap*. London: Wallflower Press.

Landau, Jon. 1973. "Let the Good Times Roll 'indeed'." *Rolling Stone*, July 19, 1973. 62–3.

Wright, Julie Lobalzo. 2013. "The Good, The Bad, and the Ugly '60s: The Opposing

Gazes of Woodstock and Gimme Shelter." In *The Music Documentary: From Acid Rock to Electropop*, eds Robert Edgar, Kirsty Fairclough-Isaacs, and Ben Halligan. London: Routledge 71–86.

PART I

HISTORIES

1. *MUSIC MAKERS OF THE BLUE RIDGE* (AKA 'BLUEGRASS ROOTS,' DAVID HOFFMAN, USA, 1966)

Greil Marcus

In May and June of 1965 David Hoffman, working for what was still called National Educational Television, took a crew to South Turkey Creek, North Carolina, to make a film with Bascom Lamar Lunsford.

At eighty-three in 1965, Lunsford, who died in 1973, was the unchallenged grandee of old-time music. Very much the country squire in his speech and bearing – a lawyer, salesman, and politician but most of all a song collector, he'd founded the Mountain Dance and Folk Festival in Asheville in 1928, and in 1939 he'd performed at the White House for President and Mrs Roosevelt and King George VI of England.

Lunsford was Hoffman's tour guide. They got in a car with Lunsford's wife, Freida Lunsford, and unseen crew members, and Hoffman started shooting out the window.

Right from the start, the moving-car shots of the North Carolina mountains – in not the highest resolution black-and-white footage – are otherworldly, receding from your eyes as you watch. The mountains are evanescent; you want to reach through the screen and touch them, to prove to yourself that they're real. Hoffman keeps sticking his camera out the window, and the mountains never become any more factual. As Lunsford talks about the disappearance of the old ways and how the young people don't know how to play the music anymore, the mountains seem less like landscape than a visible memory. It's as if you're looking at the mountains as they were 100 or 200 years before. Throughout the short film, they will appear again and again, counterpoint to the music Lunsford is looking for – its handmaiden and its rebuke.

Lunsford takes Hoffman to meet banjo players, fiddlers, buck dancers, and dulcimer players. On his front porch, in front of his rocks-and-mortar house (an enormously impressive handmade structure), Bill MacElreath kicks his feet out from under himself, "knocking out the tune with the feet," as Lunsford and his wife accompany him on banjo and guitar. MacElreath – a long, lean, older man – hits the ground and knee-walks. As Lunsford stands up and sings in a high, keening voice, MacElreath takes the banjo, finds a beat, and then begins to chant.

It's ordinary, but it's also an event – as repeatable as a high school science experiment, as unique as a face. Lunsford asks his wife for "East Virginia Blues." She has clearly sung the song hundreds of times; you get the feeling everyone else in the area has, too. But Lunsford wants to hear her sing it. She sings it very slowly, as if everything that happens – "*I was born/In East Virginia*" – happened to her, and left her scarred. She stretches the lines out further than Clarence Ashley did, further than Bob Dylan would, as far as she can see them.

From house to house they go. There are interludes at a hall in town where people sing from a stage, at a house parry where a string band – four old men, one young – rocks the floorboards as children square dance. Even if you were forced to square dance as a child in school, even if you hated not only square dancing but also the very concept, even if nothing on earth could have seemed more square, even to your ten-year-old sense of cool, another world can open up out of the moments Hoffman captures. The people moving on the floor are happy. They know that what they are doing is their birthright and that it might never feel like this again.

This is the internal rhythm of the film: between the ordinary and the extraordinary. You can't begin to tell one from the other, but the tension is never lessened. Can Lunsford really summon up these miracles at will, just by waving his magic hand? In one sequence he visits a farmer. The man is old and exhausted. He is so tired he can barely complain. He is covered in dirt. He seems ready to quit – to quit life. Why has Lunsford stopped the car and brought the crew out to film this man? What does he play? He's the best something in the area, everyone Lunsford stops for is, but what that is we're not going to find out, because Lunsford knows that to do anything but leave this man alone would take away all he has left: his right to be left alone. The sequence leaves a hole right in the middle of the film. Obviously it could have been omitted. It says that there are some songs you're never going to hear. It's another of Lunsford's miracles, and it's a miracle that Hoffman understood what Lunsford was showing him.

At the end of the film, Lunsford takes Hoffman into Wilkes County, where in

1886 Tom Dula ("Tom Dooley") and Annie Melton killed Laura Foster. "Lost John" lives here – real name Jesse Ray, Lunsford explains, a tenant farmer and the best fiddler around – and something in Lunsford's tone, a certain deepening, suggests that a word like *best* isn't exactly going to cover the story. Soon, surrounded by friends playing banjo, guitar, dulcimer, and autoharp, Ray is slick, then dissonant. He plays with his eyes closed, a beatific smile all across his face, and his technique is flatly amazing: he leaves out pieces of the melody, of the rhythm, forcing his listeners to jump across the old songs as if they were rushing creeks. He takes "Little Maggie" fast, faster – he's so good it's almost unbearable. And then there is a cut: it's later, Lost John has changed into a checked shirt, and with a hat on his head he is standing, running the bow on his fiddle, blowing down everything around himself: the other musicians, the mountains, the past, the future. The idea of folk music breaks up. You don't believe that 200 years of music-making in these hills can account for what this man with a moon face and a few teeth is doing now. You don't believe that time and this place could have made Lost John's sound. You don't believe that 200 years could take that sound away from him, and give it back to a folk, any more than Faulkner's place and time could claim his books as theirs, not his. You listen, and you know that the human species has never made anything better. Outside of the memories of those who knew him, and the courthouse records of Wilkes County, *Music Makers of the Blue Ridge* is probably the only proof that Jesse Ray ever lived.

2. "I DON'T MAKE CULTURE, I SELL IT!": THE EARLY HISTORY OF MUSIC DOCUMENTATION, 1920S–1970S

Laura Niebling

The emergence of the festival film between the end of the 1950s and its heyday in 1970 is often understood as the beginning of rockumentary history. While films such as *Jazz on a Summer's Day* (Bert Stern and Aram Avakian, USA, 1959), *Dont Look Back* (D. A. Pennebaker, USA, 1967) and the legendary *Woodstock* (Michael Wadleigh, USA, 1970) are in retrospect connoted as the first rockumentaries (cf. Winston 2000, 53 or Cohen 2012, 23), the practices of music documentation in written form predate them by several centuries. Particularly the transformation of live performance into mediatized recordings, however, shaped contemporary music culture: "Little more than a century ago all music was necessarily heard live while today vastly more music around the globe is heard in mediatized form" (Clarke 2015, 26). And even though "mediatized events were modelled on live ones" (Auslander 2008, 11) at first, when music on stage became music on film, music on the radio and eventually music on television in the first half of the twentieth century, it was shaped by the forms of its mediatization. Particularly music documentation also brought back a visual plane to the "primarily audio one, sound without vision" (Ibid., 73) established through the recording of music on sound carriers. Music recording technology changed the way music could be perceived, particularly with regards to its repeatability and its detachment from traditional places of reception. This made music more affordable as well as widespread and therefore often popular – a dynamic that industrial agents drew on almost immediately and that would become central for rockumentaries.

To better understand these origins of music documentation, the following chapter looks at ways this mediatization took shape in cinema, on radio, and on television in the United States between the 1920s and 1970s. It relies on the mediation levels as proposed by Keith Negus (cf. Negus 1996, 66–71), particularly "the use of various media technologies in the transmission of popular music, and in the discourse around popular music" (Percival 2011, 104). Through the popular examples of jazz on *Vitaphone Varieties*, music shows such as *American Bandstand* (1952–89) on television, and the first ever rockumentary *The History of Rock & Roll* (Bill Drake, USA, 1969) on the radio, the emergence of music as a topic on screen and radio pre-1960 is discussed. From these premises, the chapter concludes with a transfer of these early forms of music documentation into a definition of what today could be a "rockumentary."

Music in Cinema: Jazz on *Vitaphone Varieties* (1929)

While early cinema had its history of scores before the advent of the sound film (Marks 1997, 29), it was the marrying of sound with pictures in the mid-1920s that created new opportunities for the presentation of music on screen. Among them was the Vitaphone sound film system, which was licensed by Warner Bros. (WB) and became standard practice for over a thousand films (cf. Deaville 2015, 44) between 1926 and 1932. Vitaphone was the last technology to feature sound-on-disc instead of sound-on-film, to which even WB changed in 1930 when the phonograph discs ended up being too cost-intensive and the synchronization "frequently unreliable" (Alleyne 2009, 23).

In its golden age, however, Vitaphone was applied to many of the early popular talkies such as *The Jazz Singer* (Alan Crosland, USA, 1927), but as John Mundy notes in *Popular Music on Screen*, it was less a focus on voices than on music, which played a central role in WB's decision for the technology. They aimed to record "a range of music, from popular vaudeville music acts to popular classics" (Mundy 1999, 40), therefore reducing the cost of live performances during movies. The shorts aired during this period were organized in series such as *Broadway Brevities*, *Melody Masters*, or *Vitaphone Varieties*. The last one was a particularly influential series in the late 1920s, which gained its title in 1929 as a result of WB's shifting program. Diverging from an initial focus on opera performances, these news shorts now presented "forms of entertainment in line with the rhythms of big city life" (King 2017, 61). Warner renovated their stage in Brooklyn in 1928 to create a newly equipped space for the recording of these artists and "to better tap the Broadway talent pool" (Ibid., 61). Two key factors later relevant for rockumentaries are already at play in these early depictions of music: a popularization and canonization of (urban) musical styles through their depiction and the way the films were already associated with the early music industry.

The new performers of the *Vitaphone Varieties* were popular musicians, who represented up-and-coming musical genres such as jazz in its manifold shapes like New Orleans, Swing, or Dixieland. Particularly notable with regards to the following history of music on screen is the way these genres were visualized. In the attempt to bring popular musicians from the city to any place with a cinema, the technology allowed for full performances (Deaville 2015, 44) producing "a faithful record of the performance as it would be seen and heard from a seat in the theatre" (Cohen 2012, 13). Such a "faithful" reproduction required synchronous voices, which at best turned the "motion picture experience" of the shorts into the experience of an actual "stage show" (O'Brien 2019, 65). The shorts were at times even advertized as a "better" (Allen and Gomery 1985, 196) alternative to the live performance. Not only were they cheaper (Ibid., 196), but reports noted the new sound technology even aided the immersive features of the musical shorts, leading to audiences applauding an absent musician after a Vitaphone short "as if the featured artist were there in person" and even, as one critic notes, establishing in them "the mentality that one brings to the music-hall or a concert" (O'Brien 2019, 65).[1] Overall synchronous sound marked a significant step in the "attribution of realism to sound cinema" (Ibid., 65), which became a critical factor in the immersive strategies of rockumentary filmmaking.

With the new sound came a change in visuals. When the Vitaphone premier *Don Juan* featured close shots of opera singer Marion Talley, it elicited "blatantly sexist" (Crafton 1995, 77) demands, with one magazine even claiming the camera had come too close to her face: "long shots – and good, long ones – were just invented for that girl" (Ibid., 77). Most of the films in the Vitaphone series, such as the jazz short *Hazel Green and Company* (Bryan Foy, USA, 1927), were indeed rather static at first, featuring long and medium-long shots, which allowed for a presentation of music groups. In the following decade, the pace and variety of perspectives increased, however, predating the dynamic editing of music pieces and a focus on frontmen and band leaders (cf. Strank et al. 2014, 16), which can also be found in many rockumentaries after 1960.[2]

The productions offered working conditions for a limited section of musicians. With the connection to Broadway, the performers represented "the showier firmament of musical revues" (King 2017, 61), which focused on a representable selection of club and Vaudeville performers. One result of this was the preferential booking of already established African American jazz musicians, who would provide some guarantee for success and best "conformed to white models and easily took direction" (Cripps 1993, 225). In those shorts WB's approach became a balancing act between the recognition of the new popular music genres associated with African American culture and a servicing of White middle-class spectators through often racist and sexist stereotypes (cf. Fleeger 2014, 106). Even with changing socio-cultural parameters, this aim for the broadest compatibleness of music images, however problematic with regards to marginalized artists, continued throughout the decades.

The production of the films using sound carriers opened a market beyond the Vitaphone shorts and enabled a lucrative cooperation with the music industry, which would become central to rockumentaries. Starting from the early *Vitaphone Varieties* shorts, major label groups of the era like HMV or Columbia were in charge of pressing the accompanying discs (cf. Shaman, Collins and Goodwin 1999, xxii). Songs became popular nationally, utilizing an increasingly connected mediatization and reproduction, which included the films, radio broadcasts, sheet music, and phonograph records. With the success of the films abroad, they are also an example of the early limitations of licensing as a "recurring problem was the music, for which Warner could sometimes not get copyright clearance" (Liebman 2003, 398) in certain countries. The problem of music rights remains relevant until today, as does WB's solution to resort to public domain music (Ibid., 398) or to even incorporate publishers into the company (cf. Crafton 1997, 195).

Overall, early Vitaphone shorts can be read as formative predecessors of the rockumentary with regards to their general impact on sound film history, their cost-reductive broad distribution of documented performances, their contribution to and perpetuation of viewing patterns of musical genres, their implicit regulation of musicians' careers through screen time and their association with the early music industry. As exemplarily discussed with regards to African American jazz musicians, this happens in an often two-sided dynamic, which features selected artists while also often subjugating them to stereotypical perceptions of their (music) culture.

Music on Television: *American Bandstand*

Already highly anticipated in the 1920s, television in the United States "made its long awaited public debut" (Anderson 1999, 422) in 1939 with a report from the New York World's Fair, from which it soon grew to offer a broader program. Cheaper television sets and an increasing variety of channels helped with its popularity during the 1940s and turned it into a mass medium. Television broadcasters understood early on that television's role in music presentation could become comparable to that of radio. It became especially significant to the emerging economy surrounding pop music, as "the popular music industry realised at once that television was a potentially fundamental component of the star-making machinery whatever the music involved" (Frith 2016, 185). Aside from films, which gave musicians a career in both music and Hollywood, television shows presenting new music grew in popularity.

Among them, the game and dance shows of the "golden age of television" (Huff 2013, 240) – the 1950s – stand out as they are often centered on popular music topics. They followed popular hit shows such as *Your Hit Parade*, which aired on radio from 1935 to 1955 and on television from 1950 to 1959. Particularly the shows of the 1950s focused on a recording of a song, either live or on tape, which was increasingly paired with additional information given by a host. Running from 1952 to 1989, *American Bandstand* is probably the most popular example of a show centered around musical performances. The show was originally designed for a local channel in Philadelphia – WFIL-TV – and was hosted by radio and television broadcaster Bob Horn, first airing under the name *Bob Horn's Bandstand*. The young radio host Dick Clark took over in 1956; a year later the show moved to ABC, when it was officially renamed and broadcasted nationwide. The concept was based on performances of Top 40 songs, to which teenage couples danced and gave their opinion in a rate-the-record segment, which actively "impacted record sales" (cf. Lehman 2008, 71). Over the decades, the show increasingly shifted to a stationary studio audience and featured Clark sitting among the young spectators or talking to the bands about new records and trivia. Fundamental for this development was the improvement of sound and image recording in the studio. Early on the show featured zooms, pans, and cuts between field sizes comparable to the *Vitaphone Varieties* shorts, however with increasing pace in editing and more close-ups. The artists lip-synching, and Clark using a hand-held microphone with a long cable run, made the show especially mobile in its spatial impact without great loss of sound quality. This especially allowed for "an opportunity to perform in ways that the mechanics of live music would make difficult or impossible" (Austen 2005, 46).

Relevant to the discussion of the early television series with regards to rockumentaries is the serial nature of performance, and its consequential impact on the perception of hits. Not only was there a great number of shows with popular songs, but some like *American Bandstand* also ran every day in a family-friendly spot at 3:30pm. Throughout the shows, music was visualized and connoted as entertainment and youthful leisure with a history of "bland, pleasant performances" (Austen 2005, 229) once again suited for the traditional American middle-class family – a tradition which continued all the way to *American Idol*. This depiction of popular music both relied on sponsors – mostly tobacco companies at the time – and was a factor of an industrial co-dependency of television and music entertainment. The show gave exposure to a variety of artists and music genres, with Clark's winning manner easing parental generations into critically-perceived new genres such as rock 'n' roll (cf. Ashby 2006, 346). In his interviews, Clark also increasingly communicated a sympathetic knowledge of music and musicians, which he allegedly did not possess from the start, but adapted as part of his involvement with musicians and his stance "I don't make culture, I sell it" (Clark quoted in Ibid., 346). In this regard, he was also involved in a payola scandal in 1960. He "successfully deflected" (Delmont 2012, 146) the charges, discontinued financial relations with the music business, and ABC helped to rebuild the image of their prolific host. His growing "entertainment enterprise" (Diefenbach 1998, 74), however, soon included interests in the industry again. Most shows of the era relied on hosts who were already famous on radio. Their role as knowledgeable and seemingly neutral commenters and advertizers put them in a complicated position between the recording industry, the show industry and the audience they affirmatively addressed. This notion gained in relevance the more diverse and commercial music culture became, and it became an essential aspect in the perception of rockumentary filmmakers as objective documentarists of music culture.

Overall, the role of popular music on television was highly anticipated and soon implemented through hit, game and dance shows in the 1950s, creating a family-friendly yet also youthful and entertaining surrounding for the presentation of new music. While the game shows of the time, which are not discussed in this chapter, provided a playful and subtle inclusion of new songs, series such as *American Bandstand* directly promoted new music on screen. Both approaches are fundamental in the evolving history of music documentation with their focus on hits, their broad appeal, their adapting visual dynamics in the presentation of music, their representation of music through popular figures, and their seemingly impartial nature with a simultaneous concealed entanglement with the music industry. It might even be argued that in taking the edge out of youth genres these shows are direct predecessors of contemporary pop music films for teenagers, such as *One Direction: This Is Us* (Morgan Spurlock, USA, 2013).

Music on the Radio: *The History of Rock & Roll* (1969)

While radio existed mostly contemporaneously to any development of music on screen, the context under which the term rockumentary was first developed and used is essential for today's understanding of it and shall, therefore, be discussed further in the following. As the number of radios drastically increased from 12,000,000 to 30,000,000, radio became "the major source of family entertainment" (Chorba 2013, 239) in the 1930s and 1940s. Next to comedy shows and soap operas, "[m]usical programming . . . attracted a broad audience" (Lenthall 2007, 61) and was even the "most-played genre on air" (Ibid., 61) in the 1930s. A professor of music education, Peter Dykema, even stated in a brochure on music on the radio in 1935 that radio had the effect of making people musically literate, with music, in turn, holding great emotional power: "Music keeps our hearts responsive and extends our sympathies" (Dykema 1935, 363). This emotional connection became particularly relevant after World War II "as radio became a *mediator* between the worlds of the listener and the activity of the musicians, publishers, and recording companies, so radio broadcasting began to have an important impact on the distribution of music knowledge, style and preferences" (Negus 1996, 77).

The key players of the targeted circulation of popular music were the established RKO programming consultant Bill Drake, and sales manager Gene Chenault. In the form of their syndication service, Drake Chenault Enterprises (DCE), they consulted radio stations such as Los Angeles-based KHJ in the late 1960s, helping it become number one in California within a year (cf. Shane 2011, 46). Aesthetically and technically, the shows of KHJ followed the "Boss Radio" strategy of DCE, which consisted of less talking by the disc jockeys, limited commercial time and more music (cf. Denisoff 1995, 238). They hired broadcaster Ron Jacobs, who as program director for KHJ had a significant impact on this strategy and also helped create a new chart series called *The History of Rock & Roll*, which was produced by DCE. The program "was met with phenomenal success" (Ibid., 47), syndicated and broadcasted nationwide in various constellations.

The History of Rock & Roll, which ran in 1969 and in revised and updated versions in 1978 and 1981, is of particular interest for the history of the rockumentary because of its label "KHJ Rockumentary." It was even billed in a front advertisement in *Variety* as "Modern music's first rockumentary" (Baker 2015, 240). The term was one of the many neologisms attributed to Jacobs according to journalist Jerry Hopkins (cf. Niebling 2016, 114), who back in 1969 wrote the show's review for *Rolling Stone* magazine (cf. Hopkins 1969, 9). The interesting phrasing suggested not only an understanding of the history of music documentation, but also signaled a new beginning. It promised an in-depth look at the phenomenon of rock music, which the show mainly served through its sheer range. Pete Johnson, a former pop music critic for the *Los Angeles Times*, wrote the script. It took four months to assemble (cf. Hall 1969, 35) and Johnson stated that it included "nearly every record" (Johnson, quoted in Hopkins 1969, 9) he had ever heard, framing "Rock 'n' Roll" rather as pop(ular) music "from the pre-'Sh-Boom' era to the present" (Ibid., 9). With a total length of forty-eight hours in the first edition, the show featured the history of particular music genres and "then a pop 'chartsweep' (the hits)" (Ibid., 9), with some hours dedicated to popular musicians such as The Beatles or The Stones, while again mostly excluding the social dimension of rock music history. It relied on archived and new exclusive interviews with over 100 prominent "artists, producers and music biz executives" (Ibid., 9), framed by an exchangeable local host (cf. Hall 1969, 35).

The History of Rock & Roll did not so much follow non-fiction reporting techniques, which were established on the radio in the 1940s, but in tone and pace rather resembled the early stylized festival films on television like *Jazz on a Summer's Day* (1959), which presented music as an event within a context.

Part of the Drake Chenault formula for successful radio stations was their engineering team, who used new technology for changing tapes while on air, enabling "a variety of contemporary-sounding formats" (Shane 2011, 47). With the smooth and fast music arrangements and a star-studded cast retelling the history of music, *The History of Rock & Roll* established the archetypical form of rockumentaries. The success of the initial series also "caused Drake and Chenault to create a new division within DCE" (Ibid., 47), which should produce further radio music documentaries in the same form.

Overall, radio's role in the history of popular music on screen is often one of direct influence, with radio shows and hosts changing between radio and television. Over the decades radio grew to be an important platform for the recording industry to present songs, but the individual stations also competed amongst themselves through the presentation of music – a situation which also increasingly affected the audio-visual rockumentary corpus. *The History of Rock & Roll* is an example of a particularly successful attempt at a radio music format. The affirmative and often rather superficial canonization and historicization of music through hits, stars and experts, the attempt at a technologically-enabled fast and smooth flow, and a broad musical and personal appeal to both national and local audiences are aspects of the first self-proclaimed radio "rockumentary," but they also become the modus operandi for rockumentaries in cinema and on television.

From Mediatized Performances to Rockumentaries

Individually, the forms of mediatized performance discussed in this chapter are set pieces of music media history. But as Robert Niemi finds in *History in the Media*, "music history films constitute something of an informal chronicle of American popular culture, from vaudeville to hip-hop" (Niemi 2006, 237). The socio-musical research of countries or regions, cultures or groups regularly uses films as an audio-visual document, in which cultural questions manifest and through which history can be told. Adhering to a trend in the narrative of music films after 1960, that "the events . . . presented had a wider cultural significance" (Strachan and Leonard 2003, 27), their understanding is often not only a discussion of music fans but especially of Northern American youth or even post-war culture in general. The era of rock music is particularly epitomized in the success of the rockumentary, with the films being "celluloid bookmarks," as they "mark the beginning, middle and epilogue of the rock culture" (Plasketes 1989, 56). Looking at the predecessors of rockumentary history before 1960, however, it becomes apparent why this historical understanding of rockumentaries, as well as any terminological restriction implicit in the term, is problematic. So, what can be said about the nature of the rockumentary against the backdrop of early mediatized music culture?

Firstly, it is noticeable that even the precursors of the festival films discussed at the beginning of the chapter all share an already commercial nature. The jazz shorts, radio and television shows already seek to directly promote the songs and artists on display, contributing to a fundamental understanding of music documentation as a promotional instrument. This makes them distinguishable from forms of music documentation in the newsreel or ethnographic films, which, too, emerge in the earliest stages of film history and put into focus the social circumstances of music production.

I have suggested differentiating between the "rockumentary" and these forms of "music documentary" (Niebling 2018, 77f.), which are not designed as an aesthetic, affirmative (re)presentation but rather as a report or document of "people making music" (Titon 2015, 175–185). The main distinctive feature of these early traditions of the rockumentary compared to the music documentary are the industrial agents behind-the-scenes such as record labels, publishers or major music festivals. When the new popular music was turned into an increasingly concentrated system after World War II, filming music became instrumental for this growing music industry. To this end, the complicated role of both hosts and early shows as disguised advocates of this industry between bribes, sponsorship, and a documentary claim is particularly interesting.

The rise of rockumentary films as cinematic entertainment during the era of direct cinema in the 1960s saw a new generation of filmmakers hired to depict musicians and music events, who at times seemed to directly follow Dick Clark's sentiment of just being a sympathetic *merchant* of music culture. A schism arose between the established production contexts of mediatized music and the mythical idea that the topics and forms of music documentation enabled a somehow "authentic" presentation of music culture and artists (cf. for the often debated authenticity of (rock) music and media: Goodwin 1993, 8, Auslander 2008, 74). As shown with regards to the Vitaphone shorts an attribution of "realism" to sound films, however, can already be traced back to the use of synchronous sound and recorded music. The notion of an immersive, "real" music experience is a vital part of the history of music documentation before the advent of direct cinema rockumentaries and their success in promoting an allegedly unaltered, "fly-on-the-wall" perspective on music culture.[3]

Secondly, it can be found that even in these early forms of performance display, the popularity of a variety of musical styles has played a role. This notion of popular music predates the industrialization of rock music culture after World War II, with which rockumentary films of the 1960s are usually associated. The early performance films in cinema and on television provided a platform for commercially viable artists and genres of the time. Film documentation therefore always reflects upon the changing public taste in music, as it is mediatized for a mainstream audience. This often implies an appropriation of marginalized music cultures and artists, who face demands for their depiction or whose access to audio-visual (re)presentation is restricted or virtually non-existent.

The term "rockumentary" in its first use encompassed a broad selection of popular music. At the core of *The History of Rock & Roll*'s formula lay a "pop 'chartsweep' (the hits)" (Johnson, quoted in Hopkins 1969, 9). The program combined music, interviews, and a narrative framework with its concept of a historical overview adhering to an early pop music nostalgia.[4] The simple pattern of presenting popular musicians and their hits in a historically unique context (often of a specific event) using the latest (film) techniques and technologies was already present in early festival films of the time and became the trademark of many rockumentary films of the 1960s, and particularly the festival films such as *Woodstock* and *Gimme Shelter*. It remains a central approach to rockumentary filmmaking to the present day.

Lastly, the documentation of performance soon exceeded the mere copying of live situations and rather included an increasingly complex context to better understand and assess music culture in its ever-changing form. From the complex documentary nature of performances on cinema and television to the canonization of pop music history on radio, I have argued that the term rockumentary transcends the notion of a specific genre (cf. Niebling 2016, 115), such as the "rock performance film" (Winston 1995, 255) proposed by Brian Winston, or the concert film used by Keith Beattie (cf. Beattie 2004, 97). It should rather be understood as a *mode* of film production, which exceeds not only platforms of screen media, but also specific genres, as Roy Shuker has noted (cf. Shuker 2017, 108). This way, rockumentaries can be read and compared with regards to the changing production contexts – from the financing over the role of individual agents to the evolution and implications of sound technology and visual aesthetics in particular. They are affirmative and rely on an emotional framework provided by the music to both sell the underlying hits and the form in which they are presented.

A commercial framework, a latitude of musical styles, and a particular, affirmative way in which music was depicted created a peculiar form, which took ultimate cinematic shape in the incredibly successful tour and festival films of the 1960s. These films, today commonly referred to as rockumentaries, broke first ground for what became – and until today remains – one of the most popular and widespread fields of documentary filmmaking. Rockumentaries have become a staple in musicians' catalogs, on all media platforms and in the writing of pop music history. Their phenomenal success, however, did not simply happen by chance.

Notes

1. Slightly displaced synchronization was occasionally a topic of early film criticism, as reactions to the premiere of *Don Juan* (Alan Crosland, USA, 1926) show (cf. Crafton 1997, 77).
2. There are also more experimental narrative contributions like *Yamekraw* (Roth 1930), which rather resembles a music video (cf. Friedman 2011, 83).
3. It is noteworthy that the Maysles brothers, responsible for *What's Happening! The Beatles in the USA* (Albert & David Maysles, USA, 1964) and the infamous Stones concert film *Gimme Shelter* (Albert & David Maysles, Charlotte Zwerin, USA, 1970), considered direct cinema to be a technique rather than a philosophy. They claimed their films had made them "known in the advertising business as the leading practitioners of 'real people' commercials" (Maysles 1981, 31), calling their works 'Convincing Corporate Films'. Given the commercial history of music documentation before and during the first wave of rockumentary filmmaking, I have argued to discuss rockumentaries in the context of documentary strategies established in industrial filmmaking (cf. Niebling 2018, 158).
4. Ian Inglis argues that both popular music and film can evoke "attractions of an idealised past," with a fusion of "these two symbolic mediums" creating an "extraordinarily potent device through which the practice of nostalgia is activated" (Inglis 2003, 83–4). This is the case for documentary forms such as the rockumentary, and fictional genres such as the musician's biopic.

References

Allen, Robert C. and Douglas Gomery. 1985. *Film History: Theory and Practice*. New York: McGraw-Hill.
Alleyne, Mike. 2009. "Sound Reel: Tracking the Cultural History of Film Sound Technology." in *Sound and Music in Film and Visual Media*, ed. Graeme Harper. New York: Bloomsbury. 15–42.
Anderson, Christopher. 1999. "Television and Hollywood in the 1940s." in *Boom and Bust: American Cinema in the 1940s*, ed. Thomas Schatz. Berkeley, CA: University of California Press. 422–45.
Ashby, LeRoy. 2006. *With Amusement For All: A History of American Popular Culture Since 1830*. Lexington, KY: The University Press of Kentucky.
Auslander, Philip. 2008. *Liveness: Performance in a Mediatized Culture*. 2nd edn. Abingdon: Routledge.
Austen, Jake. 2005. *TV a-Go-Go: Rock on TV from American Bandstand to American Idol*. Chicago: Chicago Review Press.
Baker, Michael Brendan. 2015. "Martin Scorsese and the Music Documentary." In *A Companion to Martin Scorsese*, ed. Aaron Baker. Malden: Wiley Blackwell. 239–59.
Beattie, Keith. 2004. *Documentary Screens: Non-Fiction Film and Television*. Basingstoke: Palgrave MacMillan.
Chorba, Frank J. 2013. "Golden Age of Radio." in *History of the Mass Media in the United States*, ed. Margaret A. Blanchard. London: Routledge. 239–40.
Clarke, Eric. 2015. "Ideological, Social and Perceptual Factors in Live and Recorded Music." In *Musical Listening in the Age of Technological Reproduction*, ed. Gianmario Borio. London: Routledge. 23–41.
Cohen, Thomas F. 2012. *Playing to The Camera. Musicians and Musical Performance in Documentary Cinema*. London: Wallflower.

Crafton, Donald. 1997. *The Talkies: American Cinema's Transition to Sound 1926–1931*. Berkeley, CA: University of California Press.
Cripps, Thomas. 1993. *Slow Fade to Black: The Negro in American Film, 1900–1942*. Oxford: Oxford University Press.
Deaville, James. 2015. "Sound the World: The Role of Music and Sound in Early 'Talking' Newsreels," In *Music and Sound in Documentary Film*, ed. Holly Rogers. New York: Routledge. 41–56.
Delmont, Matthew F. 2012. *The Nicest Kids in Town: American Bandstand, Rock'n'Roll and the Struggle for Civil Rights in 1950s Philadelphia*. Berkeley, CA: University of California Press.
Denisoff, R. Serge. 1995. *Solid Gold: The Popular Record Industry*. New Brunswick: Transaction.
Diefenbach, Donald. 1998. "Clark, Dick." In *Historical Dictionary of American Radio*, eds Donald G. Godfrey and Frederic A. Leigh. Westport, CT: Greenwood. 74–5.
Dykema, Peter W. 1935. *Music as Presented by the Radio*. New York: Radio of the Audible Arts.
Fleeger, Jennifer. 2014. *Sounding American: Hollywood, Opera, and Jazz*. Oxford: Oxford University Press.
Friedman, Ryan Jay. 2011., *Hollywood's African American Films: The Transition to Sound*. New Brunswick: Rutgers University Press.
Frith, Simon. 2016. *Taking Popular Music Seriously: Selected Essays*. London: Routledge.
Grossberg, Lawrence. 1993. "The Media Economy of Rock Culture – Cinema, Postmodernity, and Authenticity." In *Sound and Vision: The Music Video Reader*, eds Simon Frith, Andrew Goodwin, and Lawrence Grossberg. London: Routledge. 185–209.
Hall, Claude. 1969. "Jacobs' Brainchild a Swinger." *Billboard Magazine*, 15 March 1969. 35.
Hopkins, Jerry. 1969. "Rockumentary Radio Milestone." *Rolling Stone* 30. 9.
Huff, Kelly W. A. 2013. "Golden Age of Television." In *History of the Mass Media in the United States*, ed. Margaret A. Blanchard. London: Routledge. 240–3.
Inglis, Ian. 2003. "The Act You've Known for All These Years: Telling the Tale of The Beatles." In *Popular Music and Film*, ed. Ian Inglis. London: Wallflower. 77–91.
King, Rob. 2017. *Hokum! The Early Sound Slapstick Short and Depression-Era Mass Culture*. Oakland, CA: University of California Press.
Lehman, Christopher P. 2008. *A Critical History of Soul Train on Television*. Jefferson, TX: McFarland.
Lenthall, Bruce. 2007. *Radio's America: The Great Depression and the Rise of Modern Mass Culture*. Chicago: Chicago University Press.
Liebman, Roy. 2003. *Vitaphone Films: A Catalogue of the Features and Shorts*. Jefferson, TX: McFarland.
Marks, Martin Miller. 1997. *Music and the Silent Film: Context and Case Studies, 1895-1924*. Oxford: Oxford University Press.
Mundy, John. 1999. *Popular Music on Screen: From Hollywood Musical To Music Video*, Manchester: Manchester University Press.
Negus, Keith. 1996. *Popular Music in Theory*. Cambridge: Polity.
Niebling, Laura. 2016. "Defining Rockumentary. A Mode and its History." In *Populäre Musikkulturen Im Film. Inter- und transdisziplinäre Perspektiven*, eds Carsten Heinze and Laura Niebling. Wiesbaden: VS Verlag. 113–31.
Niebling, Laura. 2018. *Rockumentary: Theorie, Geschichte und Industrie*. Marburg: Schüren.

Niemi, Robert. 2006. *History in The Media. Film and Television*. Santa Barbara, CA: ABC-Clio.
O'Brien, Charles. 2019. *Movies, Songs, and Electric Sound: Transatlantic Trends*. Bloomington, IN: Indiana University Press.
Percival, J. Mark. 2011. "Meditation of Popular Music in The UK." In *Stereo: Comparative Perspectives On The Sociological Study Of Popular Music In France And Britain*, eds Hugh Dauncey and Philippe Le Guern. London: Routledge. 105–19.
Plasketes, George M. 1989. "Rock on Reel: The Rise and Fall of the Rock Culture in America Reflected in a Decade of 'Rockumentaries'." *Qualitative Sociology* 12(1): 55–71.
Richards, Larry. 1998. *African American Films Through 1959: A Comprehensive Illustrated Filmography*. Jefferson, TX: McFarland.
Shaman, William, William J. Collins, and Calvin M. Goodwin. 1994. *More EJS: Discography of the Edward J. Smith Recordings*. Westport, CT: Greenwood Press.
Shane, Ed. 2011. "Chenault, Gene 1919-2010." In *The Biographical Encyclopedia of American Radio*, ed. Christopher H. Sterling New York: Routledge. 45–8.
Shuker, Roy. 2017. *Popular Music: The Key Concepts*. 4th edn. London: Routledge.
Strachan, Robert and Marion Leonard. 2003. "Film and Television Documentaries." In *Continuum Encyclopedia of Popular Music of the World: Volume I – Media, Industry and Society*, ed. John Shepherd. London: Continuum. 26–9.
Strank, Willem and Claus Tieber. 2014. "Einleitung. Jazz im Film: Ein weites Feld." In *Jazz im Film: Beiträge zur Geschichte und Theorie eines intermedialen Phänomens*, eds Willem Strank and Claus Tieber. Wien: Lit. 11–27.
Titon, Jeff Todd. 2015. "Ethnomusicology as the Study of People Making Music." *Musicological Annual*, 51(2): 175–85.
Winston, Brian. 1995. *Claiming the Real: The Griersonian Documentary and its Legitimations*. London: BFI.
Winston, Brian. 2000. *Lies, Damn Lies and Documentaries*. London: BFI.

3. *MONTEREY POP* AND THE MATURATION OF THE CONCERT FILM

Laurel Westrup

The Monterey International Pop Festival, which took place in June 1967, is often remembered as the first of the big 1960s rock festivals. But the significance of the festival lies as much in its concert film *Monterey Pop* (D. A. Pennebaker, USA, 1968) as in the festival event itself. The film spread counter-cultural ideals, spawning other rock festivals, happenings, and be-ins. The organizers of Woodstock, for instance, were famously inspired by the film (Bell 1999, 53). *Monterey Pop* knits together performances from the festival's "international" line-up – soul singer Otis Redding, sitar legend Ravi Shankar, rock acts from LA, San Francisco, and the UK (The Mamas and the Papas, Janis Joplin, Jimi Hendrix) – as well as footage of the roughly 50,000 concertgoers communing with each other and with the performers. *Monterey Pop* was certainly not the first rock concert film, but in this chapter I argue that it is one of the most pivotal because it wove together aesthetic ideas from previous concert documentaries, ultimately producing a mature concert film style that continues to influence concert film production, and rockumentaries more broadly, to this day. The film's box office success also suggested the economic viability of the concert film at a crucial moment in the genre's development.

While *Monterey Pop* is a pivotal text in the history of the concert film, it has not always been treated as such. Overshadowed by two other counter-cultural concert films that came out a couple of years later – *Woodstock* (Michael Wadleigh, USA, 1970) and *Gimme Shelter* (Albert and David Maysles and Charlotte Zwerin, USA, 1970) – *Monterey Pop* has functioned largely as a footnote rather than a main attraction. *Woodstock* has dwarfed *Monterey Pop* in discussions of the concert film in part because it was hugely successful, both critically and commercially, and in part because it has figured as one half of a powerful (if overdetermined) opposition with *Gimme Shelter*, with the former representing the apotheosis of flower power and the latter representing the demise of the counter-culture.[1] Despite the more prominent role that these films have played in the rockumentary conversation, *Monterey Pop* has not gone totally unremarked. It did not make *IndieWire*'s 2014 list of the Top Ten concert films, but its influence is mentioned not only in the entries for *Woodstock* and *Ziggy Stardust and the Spiders from Mars* (D. A. Pennebaker, UK/USA, 1973), but also in the wrap-up for the piece, where the author is almost apologetic about leaving it off the list (Brock 2014). *Monterey Pop* was also deemed significant enough to warrant Criterion's release of deluxe DVD/Blu-ray editions packaged with photographs, extra performance footage, and other bonus features, upon the festival's thirty-fifth anniversary in 2002 and its fiftieth anniversary in 2017.

Scholar David James devotes a great deal of attention to the film in his *Rock 'N' Film: Cinema's Dance with Popular Music* (James 2016). There, he argues that in *Monterey Pop*, Pennebaker adapted Direct Cinema norms to develop "new cinematic languages for the representation of musical performance and its social context" (Ibid., 200). Key to these new languages is the articulation of a cultural space in which performers and fans are equally involved. In this regard, James argues, *Monterey Pop* borrows much from other live performance documentaries, particularly *The T.A.M.I. Show* (Steve Binder, USA, 1964), where "The uninterrupted chorus of screams from the audience and the cutaways to them ... the numerous shots that include both performers and audience, and the minimal breaks between acts all together sustain a delirious interactive communality among fans and performers and dancers" (James 2016, 193). *Monterey Pop* similarly, through its shot composition and editing, weaves together footage of audience and performers.

But while *The T.A.M.I. Show* records an event staged for the screen, James argues that *Monterey Pop* adheres more closely to the structure of *Jazz on a Summer's Day* (Bruce Stern and Aram Avakian, USA, 1959) insofar as the mediation of the event was not the occasion for its production. Both the Newport Jazz Festival recorded in *Jazz on a Summer's Day*, and the Monterey International Pop Festival recorded in *Monterey Pop*, would ostensibly have gone on even if the cameras had not rolled. And, as James points out, this lack of reliance on the ancillary film renders these events less commercial in nature, and the recordings more organic and free from commercial interest (James 2016, 215). In the case of *Monterey Pop*, this idea of an organic, authentic representation of "music, love, and flowers" (as the festival's publicity had it) was further bolstered by the non-profit nature of the festival. While there was some discussion of producing the festival for profit, Los Angeles concert promoter Alan Pariser initially conceived it as a non-profit event, and festival organizers Lou Adler and John Phillips ultimately presented it as a charity event to appease a skeptical Monterey City Council (Santelli 1980, 22–5). The film was also a non-profit venture. However, the narrative of Monterey Pop and *Monterey Pop* as non-commercial entities does deserve further scrutiny, and I will return to this aspect of the concert film at the end of the chapter.

While James's articulation of *Monterey Pop*'s contributions to a concert film language provide a strong foundation for reevaluating the film's significance, he ultimately places *Woodstock* as the "apogee" of the concert film, in part because of its commercial success and in part because of its further articulation of the fan-performer relationship via the introduction of additional innovations like the split screen (James 2016, 242). The assertion of a community formed by performers and fans alike is certainly one of the most important things about both of these films, but *Monterey Pop* develops another aspect of concert film language that I would argue is equally important, and to which James does not attend as fully: the experiential quality of the event. *Monterey Pop*'s focus on "being there" is developed through a filmic vocabulary that is partly inherited from Direct Cinema but that also seems to respond to the unique requirements of documenting the concert experience.

The Direct Cinema movement, which emerged alongside the rock festival in the 1960s and 70s, influenced the concert film in a couple of key regards. First, by eschewing voice-over narration and by approaching material in an observational rather than didactic manner, Direct Cinema placed more emphasis on the experience of events – both by those present at those events and by those in the film's audience. If the traditional documentary told viewers *about* an event, Direct Cinema sought to place them *inside* it. Inspired by the immediacy of televisual reportage, Direct Cinema leader Robert Drew and his "Associates," Pennebaker among them, tried to capture what filmmaker Richard Leacock described as "the sense of what happened, what it was like to be there when it happened" (Macdonald and Cousins 1996, 257). This emphasis on the feeling of "being there" is arguably the most important legacy of Direct Cinema for the concert film. It has persisted even when some other Direct Cinema conventions, such as the eschewal of interviews and quick cutting, shifted with the Associates' interest in musical subjects. As James argues, in Pennebaker's first foray into documenting the musical counter-culture, *Dont Look Back* (USA/UK, 1967), the director both retained features of Direct Cinema's film language, such as long takes shaped by in-camera editing (zooms, pans, etc.) while introducing staged elements like Bob Dylan's lyrical "Subterranean Homesick Blues" sequence (James 2016, 204, 210). In *Dont Look Back*, Pennebaker gives the audience access to Dylan, both behind and, to a lesser extent, on stage. But the language of presence he developed in *Monterey Pop* actually looks back, however unwittingly, to some earlier experiments with recording the concertgoing experience.

Monterey Pop's Predecessors

An important and oft-overlooked predecessor to *Monterey Pop* is *Jazz Dance* (Roger Tilton, USA, 1954), a twenty-minute short that was shot in part by Pennebaker's eventual producing partner, Richard Leacock. The film was shot in black-and-white and was possibly intended for distribution on television.[2] It begins with a scrolling title card that rather grandiosely claims "Jazz music and jazz dancing are America's greatest folk expressions," followed by some history of jazz's American evolution. It then proceeds to focus much more on the present, continuing, "[Jazz's] pulse is the pulse of America ... This film records the living spirit of jazz as it actually was one night in 1954 at the Central Plaza Dance Hall in New York City." The title card announces not just a record of a jazz performance, but also the experience of that performance. The film notably opens (underneath the scrolling titles) with an image of a subway car that somewhat recalls Pennebaker's first film, *Daybreak Express*

3.1 Trumpeter Jimmy McPartland joins a line of dancers coming towards the camera, beckoning the viewer into *Jazz Dance* (1954).

(USA, 1953), which sets the experience of subway riding to Duke Ellington's song of the same name. In *Jazz Dance* this footage works to ferry us to the venue where we will join the musicians and audience/dancers in experiencing "the living spirit of jazz."

Jazz Dance develops several key features of the concert documentary that Pennebaker would further refine in *Monterey Pop*. First, it places emphasis on musical virtuosity through close-ups of the performers. James discusses this kind of shot in *Woodstock*, where the whole screen becomes filled with "[Richie] Havens's mouth, Joe Cocker's boot, or Hendrix's hands chording the neck of his guitar," consequently rendering each of these moments both "intimate and monumental" (James 2016, 236). While it is true that Wadleigh achieved a more exaggerated effect by shooting close-up with a wide-angle lens, the intimate monumentality James discusses can also be glimpsed on several occasions in *Jazz Dance*. About twelve minutes in, we get exactly this kind of shot of trombone player Jimmy Archey as he solos. Shortly thereafter is a similar shot of George Foster working the strings of his bass as he takes over the solo. What is particularly interesting about this sequence is not only its emphasis on the mastery of the musicians, but also its interweaving of that mastery with its effects on the audience. A brief close-up at the beginning of Archey's solo is followed by a jazz dancer kicking his leg rhythmically to the music, and the sequence includes other shots of the crowd listening, clapping, and dancing (while standing on a chair, in one case), sometimes in close-up and sometimes in medium or long shot. This stitching together of the musicians and the audience through editing supports James's argument about the concert film's articulation of a community that includes both groups, but *Jazz Dance* also portrays this relationship in a more continuous/contiguous manner that does not rely on editing. In a shot about eighteen minutes into the film, we are positioned on stage behind Archey, watching a man dancing ecstatically to this final number of the film, a raucous rendition of "When the Saints Go Marching In." This shot, even more than the reaction shots edited into the performance, works to represent a common, and celebratory, musical space.

The film's presentation of this common musical space is significant, especially so many years before the big 60s rock festival documentaries. But the film also seems concerned with allowing the audience to experience the performance in a more dynamic way that replicates the experience of "being there." Tilton and his team experiment with several techniques to place us inside the action. One of the most important is the placing of the camera within the crowd, so that we are not only watching the dancers from afar, but interacting with them close-up. A particularly resonant shot places us in the middle of the dancefloor as a train forms and approaches the camera directly. Watching this shot, we feel as though the line of dancers brushes past us, inciting us to join them as they snake around the club. Several shots of tapping shoes also prompt us to tap our own feet. In addition to these experiential shots, Tilton and his team also attempted to capture the vibrations of the club aurally and visually. In several instances we can hear hands clapping rhythmically on the soundtrack, and these sounds are often paired with footage of people sitting at their tables, or gathered around the dancefloor, clapping. The clapping sounds as it would at an actual club: fairly faint under the music and general commotion. In an impressionistic shot towards the end of the film, part of a montage that captures the full fervor of the "Saints" number, we see glasses and a pitcher of beer sloshing on a table that is swaying rhythmically to the music. Remarkably for a film made with only the most rudimentary equipment for sound-image synchronization, we really feel the pulse of the club and the music and revelry within it. Leacock recalls of shooting the film, "I was all over the place having the time of my life, jumping, dancing, shooting right in the midst of everything," an experience which opened his eyes to a form of documentary that would put the viewer into the action (Saunders 2007, 10). While *Jazz Dance* predates Drew's convening of the Direct Cinema Associates, the film's emphasis on dynamic space over a static representation of the stage points the way to *Monterey Pop* and later concert films.

In comparison to *Jazz Dance*, *Jazz on a Summer's Day*, which is often cited as a predecessor to the rock concert film, feels rather static. The film, which documents the 1958 Newport Jazz Festival, occasionally places us within a dancing audience, particularly in the parts of the film that take place at night, but otherwise the shots of the audience tend to be more conventionally shot from the stage looking out at the sea of people, or else are close-ups of individuals that do not necessarily seem tied to particular moments in the music we hear. Nonetheless, the beautiful shots of water rippling rhythmically in the harbor featured at the beginning of the film, and occasionally throughout, help to capture something of the experience of "jazz on a summer's day." Stern and Avakian seem more interested in representing the experience of musicians, and *Jazz on a Summer's Day* attends to this experience more fully than *Jazz Dance* does. Much of the footage in *Jazz on a Summer's Day* is shot from on stage or sufficiently close-up so that we get a strong sense of the performers' physicality. In the sequence featuring the Chico Hamilton Quintet, we first get an alternation between musicians and audience that focuses on musical mastery and concentration, in keeping with the emcee's introduction of the band's blend of "emotion, technique, precision, and imagination." As the set continues, though, and particularly during a long take of Hamilton playing a drum solo, we see beads of sweat emerge on his face, indicating not only the work of performing the music, but also the experience of being on stage under hot lights. Conversely, toward the end of Mahalia Jackson's set, performed in the cool of late night, we can see her breath, not to mention the breath's movement of her body, as she performs "The Lord's Prayer." Elsewhere in her set, we can hear her unamplified hand claps. These sequences seem to build upon the vocabulary of performance that Tilton began to develop in *Jazz Dance*.

These innovations begin to come together in Murray Lerner's *Festival!* (USA, 1967), which weaves together performance footage and interviews from four years of the Newport Folk Festival (1963–66). Like the previous two films, *Festival!* articulates a common space where performers and audience interact. This is especially important to the film's underlying (and not-so-subtle) thesis: folk music is music made by the people rather than sold to them. Consequently, the film spends almost as much time capturing festivalgoers making music as watching their more famous counterparts on stage. While *Jazz on a Summer's Day* gives us a few brief scenes of life in Newport outside of the festival, *Festival!* is arguably the first film to really capture the festival experience away from the stage. At one point, over the sounds of Joan Baez and Donavan performing "Colours," we see festivalgoers waking in their sleeping bags on the fairgrounds or the nearby beach. Toward the beginning of the film, we also hear the ruckus of hundreds of attendees arriving on the grounds.

Like *Jazz Dance*, *Festival!* frequently puts us inside the festival's crowds, and it also puts emphasis on musicality. For instance, in a sequence focusing on the Paul Butterfield Blues Band, many of the shots are from behind the musicians, looking out at the audience. Sometimes, when the camera is close to the musicians, the audience is blurred, but we get some long shots that unite the stage space with the audience beyond. We are also given entrée into the musicians' experience of the music. Guitarist Mike Bloomfield is frequently featured in profile, his face contorting as he plays. Directly following the performance, he tells an interviewer that his experience of the blues is about his body and the music becoming united. He says that you play the blues not with your hands but with "every part of you." This lived musicality is represented in the film through alternations between impressionistic close-ups and longer shots of people interacting with each other and with the music. However, the frequent recourse to interviews and voice-over narration sometimes takes us out of the concertgoing experience, and places *Festival!* more in the mold of a traditional documentary with a point to make.

Monterey Pop and Concert Film Style

With the exception of a few very brief interview segments, *Monterey Pop* eschews this kind of didacticism or message-setting, instead weaving together the three earlier films' innovations for portraying the concert experience. In his commentary track for the 2002 Criterion DVD release of the film, Pennebaker says that before working on *Monterey Pop* "I'd never done a concert film – I don't think I'd even seen one before." Whether or not this is true (*Dont Look Back* contains at least some concert footage, and as a jazz fan who was friends with Leacock he likely would have seen *Jazz Dance* and *Jazz on a Summer's Day*), Pennebaker's self-reported amateurism as a rockumentarian might actually have been a virtue. As his DVD co-commentator Lou Adler points out, Pennebaker approached the film as just another member of the audience, one who was hearing and seeing many of the acts for the first time. Consequently, the sense of wonder that sometimes comes across in the film is, at least in the footage he shot, genuine. Adler sees Pennebaker as almost a proxy for the film's audience, allowing them access to the experience of being at the show. He says to Pennebaker, "But I think . . . the fact that you were filming it as a person that was watching a concert and not someone that had blocked out all the shots is why the film is much more emotional . . . What you go to is something that excited you at that moment and not something preconceived . . . so that we're seeing it with the same excitement." Pennebaker notes in the commentary that when he saw cameraman Jim Desmond's footage of Jimi Hendrix performing "Wild Thing," he thought "there was no reason to cut." The long take here simulates the audience's rapt attention to the performance. Like the filmmakers previously discussed, Pennebaker not only emphasizes performers' musical virtuosity through framing and lighting, but also gives weight to the experiential quality of the event. The Direct Cinema approach underlying Pennebaker's film is evident here, since he and his crew follow events as they happen around the grounds rather than shooting only what is happening on stage. This allows for a much more dynamic representation of the festival.

We see (and hear) this dynamism in Janis Joplin's riveting performance of "Ball and Chain." Pennebaker opens the sequence with a blurry pan of some flowers as we hear the first, somewhat abrasive, chords of the song. The image signifies the altered state of much of the audience, the "drug mood" that Pennebaker says he tried to capture throughout the film. After some shots of Joplin's band, Big Brother and the Holding Company, playing, we come to a close-up of Joplin as she begins to sing, softly and pensively, "Standing by the window, just looking out at the rain." In this first shot, we see her in profile, long hair covering most of her face. As a bright guitar note sounds, we get an in-camera edit: a zoom out to a medium shot of Joplin, who we can now see is grasping the microphone with one hand as she gestures with the other. This kind of reframing, which we see often throughout the film, signals a kind of shift of attention.

As Adler indicates, this tendency of Pennebaker's (and the other camera operators who worked on the film) to "go to what excited you at the moment" mimics the shifting attention of the audience. When we watch a performance, we do not necessarily experience it in long shot. Rather, we attend closely to what the drummer's doing during a solo, and then maybe to the way a singer brushes the hair from her face. Sometimes, we try to take in the whole

MONTEREY POP AND THE MATURATION OF THE CONCERT FILM

3.2 Close-ups of Janis Joplin performing "Ball and Chain" ring true emotionally, even if the performance we see in *Monterey Pop* (1968) is actually a composite.

spectacle of the band's interaction with one another. Pennebaker captures the significance of this experience especially well during the close-ups of Joplin's feet stomping, which recall Bloomfield's comment about Blues involving "every part of you." Throughout this sequence, the music animates Joplin fully, and like the camera operators, we can scarcely take our eyes off her. We identify fully with Mama Cass Elliot who, in one of the few cutaways from the stage, mouths "Wow" as she watches her fellow performer.

There is a fiction at the heart of this sequence, though, and it is an important one to consider with regards to the concert film's evolution. Joplin and Big Brother initially refused to sign the release that would allow Pennebaker and his crew to film them.[3] The crew did manage to sneak some shots of Joplin and Big Brother's Saturday afternoon performance of "Ball and Chain" and the response to it, including Mama Cass's reaction shot. However, they would not have had sufficient footage for the film had they not struck a deal with the band before a special encore appearance the next evening, during which they only performed two songs, one of them "Ball and Chain." Consequently, the performance we see in *Monterey Pop* is actually a composite of the two performances at the festival. In the commentary track, Pennebaker points out that the sequence is quite obviously a composite, given the significant changes in natural light (and thus time of day) visible in the long shots. This clear violation of chronology would seem to negate the concert film's emphasis on "being there." After all, the Joplin performance we see in *Monterey Pop* is one that would have been impossible for us to experience live. Nonetheless, there is an emotional quality to the performance that feels genuine. It is true to the overarching experience of Joplin at the Monterey Pop festival even if it is not absolutely true to reality as it unfolded.

The same can be said of the film as a whole, and as Pennebaker notes in his commentary track, the film ends with Ravi Shankar's performance not because

45

this was the final performance of the event, but because it felt like the culmination of the festival. The catharsis we witness over the course of the nearly twenty-minute sequence is not entirely manufactured, either. As Pennebaker tells us, all of the audience footage was recorded with synchronized sound, and it was edited, in most cases, so that we see the audience respond to particular points in the music. Perhaps better than any concert film sequence before or since, the Shankar sequence portrays the intermingling of audience, performers, and instruments that comprises the concert experience. Early shots take us around the grounds, listening to the music from afar, and recall the shots of festival life in *Festival!*. About 3:30 minutes in, we are drawn closer to the stage, entering the festival seating area, where some in the crowd are silently contemplating the music and some are starting to groove with it. Then, as the raga begins to build, about seven minutes in, we are introduced to the performers. We first meet Alla Rakha: we see his head moving to the music and then pan down to a close-up of his hands playing the tabla drums. Then we see, seated next to him, Ravi Shankar on sitar. Shots begin to alternate between the two musicians, with close-up emphasis on their musicianship, and the audience, who we hear clap at one point. Eventually, the third member of the trio, taboura player Kamala, enters the mix. In a particularly memorable shot that recalls *Jazz Dance*'s emphasis on rhythm, we see, in the foreground, Shankar's foot tapping to the beat while, a bit blurry in the background, Rakha's hands continue to work the tabla. The performance culminates with a standing ovation, which we are shown from many angles, thus allowing us to feel part of this filmic finale.

In the Shankar sequence, and throughout *Monterey Pop* as a whole, Pennebaker pushes beyond merely recording the event to put the viewer in the middle of the action, whether that action was on-stage or in the audience. He was not the first to develop the building blocks of a successful concert film. Nonetheless, his naïve amazement at the event as it unfolded, when paired with his considerable experience by 1967 as a documentary filmmaker with experimental tendencies (see, for instance, the end of *Daybreak Express*), produces a film that feels, somehow, both unplanned and meticulous, a description that might also describe the best moments of live musical events. The minimally-planned shoot gives us the feeling that we are experiencing the festival organically, while Pennebaker and Nina Schulman's thoughtful editing keeps it from feeling totally haphazard. While *Woodstock* would certainly build on this model of the concert film, it did not significantly alter it: the language of performance and of the experience of performance remains largely unchanged from *Monterey Pop*. More recent concert films are often hybridized with other rockumentary forms, which focus more heavily on biography and behind-the-scenes footage. Yet when it comes to the concert itself, directors continue to rely on the repertoire of shots that come together in *Monterey*

Pop: close-ups of performers' musical mastery, long shots from the stage that articulate communication between performer and audience, and a variety of shots that convey the audience and their responses to the music.

MONTEREY POP AND THE CONCERT FILM BUSINESS

Monterey Pop helped to solidify the language of the concert film, but its industrial contributions to the concert/festival film genre are also worth some brief discussion. The tension between the San Francisco and Los Angeles contingents at the festival – between a genuine counter-culture and the "slick" music industry – have been well-documented. Chet Helms of San Francisco's Avalon Ballroom (a key hippie venue) remembers, "Basically, we all resisted Monterey Pop because we felt it was kind of slicko L.A. hype. We felt that they were coat-tailing a bunch of L.A. acts on the success of what was happening in San Francisco" (Mayes 2002, 57). Adler minimizes the stereotype of "slick LA" and the SF–LA rift as a whole in his commentary for the *Monterey Pop* DVD. But the tension between counter-cultural and commercial interests is significant in part because of the way it would also come to inflect *Woodstock* and, eventually, other counter-cultural music scenes and the films made about them. This tension is captured, for instance, in *1991: The Year Punk Broke* (Dave Markey, USA, 1992), which documents Sonic Youth's 1991 European Tour, complete with significant concert footage.

Monterey Pop also proved that concert films could be lucrative. Before the festival took place, there was significant media interest in the event. According to *Variety*, television network ABC put up the initial funding for the film – $300,000 – with the expectation that it would screen on the network ("ABC-TV Reject" 1969). However, as the apocryphal story goes, when Pennebaker screened footage of Jimi Hendrix alternately humping and setting fire to his guitar, the network passed on further involvement. *Hollywood Reporter* suggested, decades after the fact, that Pennebaker had intentionally screened the risqué footage with the hope that the network would cut him loose to make the film on his own terms (Abel 2002, 12). The ABC debacle delayed the film's release and also likely indebted Pennebaker to ABC for the initial outlay of capital ("ABC-TV Reject" 1969). The film was finished in 1968, and Pennebaker and Leacock ultimately released it under the auspices of "The Foundation," short for the Monterey International Pop Foundation, a joint non-profit venture with Lou Adler and John Phillips. To this day, all of the proceeds from the film and its ancillaries go to charity.

But while the film did not technically make any profits given the arrangement with The Foundation, it was nonetheless successful at the box office. In May of 1969, *Hollywood Reporter* announced in a headline, "'Monterey Pop' Looms As Champ Doc Grosser," and reported that the film had grossed over

$300,000 in just four dates. The author predicted that when the film entered wider release in summer 1969, it would "gross more than $2,000,000 in this country and from $500,000 to $1,000,000 overseas" ("'Monterey Pop' Looms" 1969). While the actual box office for the film is difficult to determine with any accuracy, it was certainly successful enough to give the impression that concert films could succeed in the market. The trade press reported on the film's success, and word traveled. Director Michael Wadleigh reportedly told Lewis Teague, one of *Woodstock*'s production managers, "you know... Monterey Pop made a lot of money" (Bell 1999, 28–9). Warner Bros., who released *Woodstock*, undoubtedly took note. *Monterey Pop* has continued to make money for The Foundation via a plethora of ancillary releases, including soundtrack albums, VHS, DVD, and Blu-ray releases, anniversary screenings, and recycled works like Pennebaker's *Jimi Plays Monterey* (USA, 1987).[4] The success of these ventures reveals the vast market for concert film intertexts and paratexts.

While it might never be as financially successful or widely celebrated as *Woodstock*, *Monterey Pop* nonetheless established a model for the successful concert film, both in terms of its cinematic language and its ability to drive viewers to the box office (and to ancillary products). While most of the film's successful techniques for representing the experience of the concert can be glimpsed in earlier, less widely-released films, *Monterey Pop* was perhaps the first film to put these techniques together in a film that reached a large audience. Consequently, despite its oft-remarked innocence, we might see it as marking the maturation of the concert film. In its emphasis on "being there" above all else, it set a standard that concert films continue to emulate today.

Notes

1. For a more nuanced reading of the Altamont concert and its portrayal in *Gimme Shelter*, see Coates 2006.
2. The credits for the film indicate that Tilton used the facilities of Visual Transcriptions, Inc., and while this company's history has proven obscure, it seems to have produced musical shorts for television.
3. There is some disagreement about why the band wouldn't sign the release. Santelli presents the decision as one of creative control: the band worried they would not have a say over how their performance was edited and presented in the film (1980, 40–1). However, in the 2002 commentary track, Pennebaker and Adler imply that Albert Grossman (Bob Dylan's then-manager), who was in the process of negotiating a contract with the band on behalf of Columbia, forbade them from signing the release.
4. For more on the cyclical commodification of Monterey Pop and the film *Monterey Pop* see Westrup (Forthcoming).

REFERENCES

"ABC-TV Reject Making It Now as a Theatrical." 1969. *Variety* (weekly), 1 January 1969.

Abel, Glenn. 2002. "Monterey Pop." *Hollywood Reporter*, 25 November 2002. 12.

Adler, Lou and D. A. Pennebaker. 2002. "Commentary Track." *The Complete Monterey Pop* (DVD). Criterion.

Bell, Dale. 1999. *Woodstock: An Inside Look at the Movie That Shook up the World and Defined a Generation.* Studio City, CA: M. Wiese Productions.

Brock, Ben. 2014. "The 10 Best Concert Movies Ever." *IndieWire*, 17 July 2014, <https://www.indiewire.com/2014/07/the-10-best-concert-movies-ever-274407/> (last accessed 12 August, 2019).

Coates, Norma. 2006. "If Anything, Blame Woodstock. The Rolling Stones: Altamont, December 6, 1969." In *Performance and Popular Music: History, Place and Time*, ed. Ian Inglis. England: Ashgate. 58–69.

James, David E. 2016. *Rock 'N' Film: Cinema's Dance with Popular Music.* New York: Oxford University Press.

Macdonald, Kevin and Mark Cousins. 1996. *Imagining Reality*, London: Faber and Faber.

Mayes, Elaine. 2002. *It Happened in Monterey: Modern Rock's Defining Moment, The Monterey International Pop Festival, Monterey, California, June 16, 17, 18, 1967.* Culver City, CA: Britannia Press.

Santelli, Robert. 1980. *Aquarius Rising: The Rock Festival Years.* New York: Dell.

Saunders, Dave. 2007. *Direct Cinema: Observational Documentary and the Politics of the Sixties.* London: Wallflower.

Westrup, Laurel. Forthcoming. "Monterey Pop and the Memorial Machine." In *Wounded Galaxies: 1968*, eds Charles Cannon and Joan Hawkins.

4. THE SOUND OF ROCKUMENTARY: A CONSIDERATION OF THE DOCUMENTARY SOUNDTRACK

Michael Brendan Baker

The rockumentary genre emerged in the 1960s as part of a larger shift in the character and content of Western youth culture and popular music. Its swift ascent to the status of the preeminent theatrical documentary during this period occurred directly in proportion to the growth of rock music as a cultural and economic force, as well as the innovation of the live rock spectacle. As I've written elsewhere, rockumentary contributes to and draws upon the reorientation and commodification of live rock performance through the 1970s and beyond, and the concert film is a major current within the genre (Baker 2011).

As an audio-visual genre, rockumentary participates in and comments upon broader cultural discourses which emerged through the mid-twentieth century concerning the relationship between recorded musical objects and audiences, as the separation between live musical performance and recorded music grew exponentially upon several waves of technological innovation. The emergence of discourses on sound fidelity, and debates concerning the relative status of recordings better understood as realist versus spectacle – the latter describing audio objects which "through a union of science and the arts, would provide listeners with sensational renditions of the real" (Anderson 2006, 114) – were rooted in anxieties concerning the "liveness" of popular music as stereo and other sound reproduction technologies emerged. These same anxieties persist in contemporary popular culture. The specific rockumentary category of the concert film illustrates a transformational period whereafter *the recording* supplants *live performance* in the cultural, industrial, and aesthetic landscape.

The genre highlights a continuing cultural fascination with the *live* in a socio-industrial context dominated by the *recorded* (Gracyk 1996, 42–3). As these music documentaries adopt and popularize particular sound technologies and practices, they challenge conceptions of the documentary soundtrack as both realist and evidentiary. The soundtracks of these films should be understood not as historical evidence but rather as historical documents of sound reproduction technology and practice, along with cultural expectations for recorded sound at a given moment in time. This chapter uses the concert rockumentary in its earliest years to interrogate sound-image relationships in non-fiction film within a particular historical moment to chart a shift in the sound design of concert films and, more generally, audio-visual representations of music within non-fiction. It expands upon established theoretical models pertaining to sound in cinema in order to better incorporate documentary cinema into existing scholarly discussion of the subject.

The Documentary Soundtrack

While the documentary image receives its share of attention in film scholarship, the documentary soundtrack is a relatively neglected object. The development of theoretical and historical models for evaluating and critiquing the ethical position of the documentary filmmaker and the impact of specific image-making technologies in non-fiction film has not been matched by similar developments addressing the shifting uses and impact of sound technologies and music in documentary cinema. The rockumentary genre, and the concert film subgenre in particular, provide a focused body of work facilitating an examination of the documentary soundtrack.

The limited selection of theories of sound in documentary cinema mirror the theorization of sound in cinema generally, with its focus on a constructed binary of realism and illusion distinguishing between the central sonic representational strategies evinced in non-fiction film. Major figures including Eisenstein (1928), Vertov (1930), and Bazin (1945) offer founding contributions to the theoretical discourse on image and sound in cinema in the form of debates on the merits of illusory approaches to cinematic representation versus realist projects, and how sound factors in both. Of the three, Vertov's position is crucial to an understanding of sound in non-fiction film not least because of his status as one of cinema's earliest theorists and practitioners of a documentary cinema. Vertov develops his theory and practice of sound in documentary from an experimental position, challenging synchronicity and naturalistic sound-image relationships by employing "the abstract and disassociative techniques of audiovisual collage" (Fischer 1985, 250). Advocating for an illusory representational practice within non-fiction filmmaking, Vertov provides an early precedent for evaluating the complex sound-image relationships epitomized by those featured within concert films and offers a link to contemporary debates concerning the mediatization of musical performance.

In practice, the rockumentary concert film is the consumption of a recording often perceived as an encounter with an authentic or unmediated performance. In the context of the present discussion, I use the term *authentic* in keeping with Benjamin's description of an art object or performance's unique existence in time and space (Benjamin 1936, 214). Jonathan Sterne, in his cultural history of sound reproduction technology, argues "recording [does] not simply capture reality as it [is]; it [aims] to capture reality suitable for reproduction" (Sterne 2003, 236). It is about "realism," he explains, "not reality itself" (Ibid., 245). I would suggest this distinction between *reality* and that which is suitably *realistic* establishes a framework for the rockumentary audience's expectations of sound-image relationships outside of any knotty conception of authenticity. Concert films are intensely mediated audio-visual representations of already mediated events. The evidentiary link between the original audio-visual event or performance and its subsequent mediation is profoundly compromised, and thus the evidentiary status of these works is immensely complicated.

Concert film sound strives to re-imagine the original performance legibly for absent audience members. As constructions, the sound designs of these films need only be comprehensible as "concert sound" and invoke the *liveness* of the original event by presenting an audio-visual object perceived as "live" within the cultural context of its production and exhibition. There is no evidence, per se. Theorist and composer Michel Chion suggests such intelligibility hinges on the grasp of the differing qualities of *definition* and *fidelity* as characteristics of any recorded sound:

> A sound recording's *definition*, in technical terms, is its acuity and precision in rendering of detail ... [*Fidelity*] is a tricky term; strictly speaking it would require making a continuous close comparison between the original and its reproduction ... However, it happens that today *definition* is (mistakenly) *taken as proof of fidelity*, when it's not to be confused with fidelity itself. (Chion 1994, 98)

Contemporary sound technologies like Surround Sound or lossless soundtracks on HD media, for example, do not offer fidelity – since that would require something approaching a quantitative real-time comparative analysis of the film presentation and its source material – but instead present an acute and precisely rendered representation of the already mediated performance. Viewers mistakenly perceive a well-*defined* representation of an acoustic event as a sign of audio fidelity and too quickly progress to an evaluation of the original event rather than its representation. As a result, a misconception resides at the centre of discourses concerning concert films generally, and rock concert films

A CONSIDERATION OF THE DOCUMENTARY SOUNDTRACK

especially. The confusion stems on the one hand from the problematic nature of visual representations of music, which often emphasize the image component at the expense of the auditory, and on the other, from evaluations of the auditory element of these texts as representative of an *original* event, somehow authentic and faithful to a set of *original* sounds. If we want to evaluate concert films more effectively and address the true complexity of sound-image relationships in this corpus and other non-fiction films, we must confront the fallacy that is central to the experience: the sonic event *as it happened* does not exist in its representation, no matter the faithfulness of the motion picture to the pro-filmic event. Accepting this provides us with the opportunity to shift our inquiries into fields such as rock music production – and what scholars including Theodore Gracyk (1996) and Lee B. Brown (2000) describe as *works of phonography* with their *aesthetic intentions* and *artistic representations* – in order to better grasp the representational possibilities of the documentary soundtrack.

Two Strategies for the Sonic Representation of Musical Performance

Concert films shape reception via a complex visual interface and layers of sound reproduction technologies in an effort to convince viewers of being privy to a well-defined reproduction of the original sonic event. To reiterate a point made above, concert film sound strives to re-imagine the original acoustic event legibly for absent audience members. In an effort to more accurately describe and analyze the evolving relationship between the audio dimensions of these non-fiction films and the intricate, often contradictory, claims cooperatively established by the sound-image relationship, I propose we approach the issue of sound in concert films with an understanding of two differentiated sonic strategies adopted by the filmmakers: *the journalistic* and *the illusionistic*. In the context of the concert film current of the rockumentary, these two sonic representational strategies occupy two points along a quick evolution of sound practices within rockumentary beginning with the most basic documentation of a musical event to the technologically-intensive sound design of an audio-visual text (e.g. stereophonic or spatialized sound). Both encourage the 'being there' discourse surrounding live popular music performance that pre-dates the rockumentary genre, extending back to early-to-mid-1950s developments and marketing of "high-fidelity" sound recording and reproduction systems (see Anderson 2006), but differ in terms of their respective emphasis upon the image and sound elements.

The first strategy, appearing at the inception of the genre, is premised upon basic access to the emerging images and sounds of rock and rock culture which these documentaries offered viewers. A soundtrack indicative of the journalistic strategy is best understood as a straightforward representation of the original performance that does not necessarily seek to conceal the limits of its definition imposed by the performance environment and available sound recording technologies. The approach is proximate to the field recording aesthetic exemplified within ethnomusicology. The truth claims invoked by this sonic strategy are generally supported by photojournalistic portraiture of events rather than self-conscious formal techniques which might otherwise serve to conceal more advanced sound design. D. A. Pennebaker's *Dont Look Back* (USA, 1967) – and the concert sequences featured therein – is perhaps the most widely screened example of this approach, its run-and-gun shooting style and use of a Nagra III reel-to-reel tape recorder befitting Bob Dylan's folk aesthetic and anti-celebrity posturing.

Dylan revels in both the acoustics of the Royal Albert Hall and the richness of the piano sound in the backstage dressing room while the soundtrack recording crackles and pops with traces of its age and materiality. In one telling sequence, the crowd sits patiently as Dylan begins his set with a faulty microphone; stagehands scurry to correct the problem and when Dylan's voice is finally heard over the PA, the crowd erupts in applause.

An often-overlooked detail of presentations such as *Dont Look Back* is the audibility of the audience during the performance of each song – most

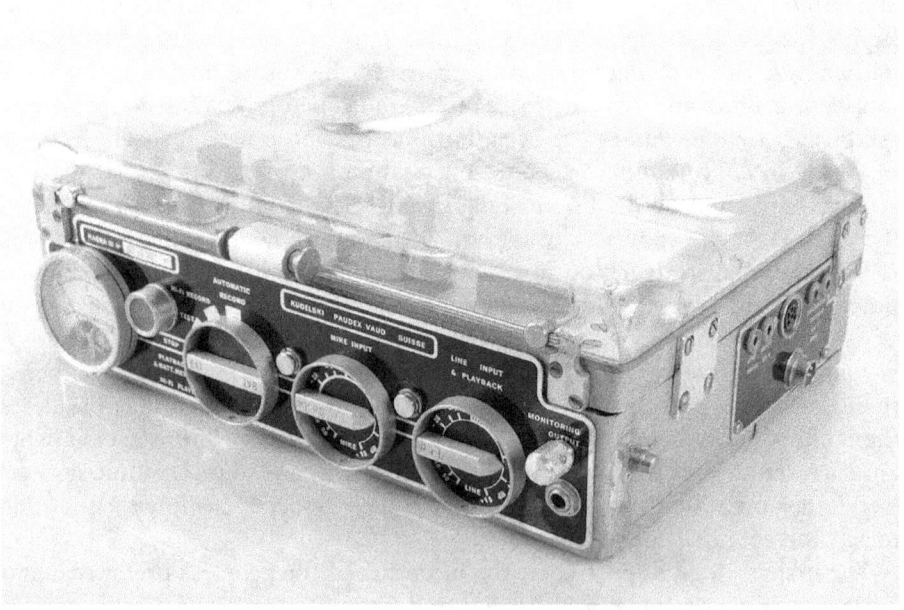

4.1 The Nagra III portable reel-to-reel tape recorder by Kudelski SA, c. 1958.

A CONSIDERATION OF THE DOCUMENTARY SOUNDTRACK

4.2 Three stagehands work to identify a faulty microphone cable in *Dont Look Back*.

contemporary concert films completely remove any trace of audience noise for the duration of each song (a noteworthy subversion of this trend is Morrissey's *Who Put the M in Manchester?* (Bucky Fukumoto, UK, 2005) which opens and closes with an extended overture comprised entirely of chanting audience members). In many ways, the ascribed authenticity of films such as *Dont Look Back* is as dependent upon the technological limits of the original soundtrack recordings as it is its visual style.

The second sonic strategy appearing within the early evolution of the rockumentary concert film is the initiation of a project wherein concert filmmakers strive not to merely document the event but to play an active part in shaping the production to ensure its sonic reproducibility in theaters and at home. In practice, it is not dissimilar from live sound engineering or studio recording technique. With the aid of ever-evolving sound reproduction technologies, particularly spatialized sound systems like Dolby Stereo and Surround Sound, the soundtracks of these concert films re-imagine the experience of hearing the music within the space of the original event. Curiously, this approach often excludes any trace of sound that is not generated by the on-stage performers; the audience is silenced during the performance of each song. The viewer is thus offered a sonic representation that exceeds the original in terms of its phonographic clarity and reveals a commitment to designing and capturing sonic material most suitable for its subsequent reproduction, not its evidentiary link to an original performance.

For a clear illustration of both approaches I turn to a single film, *The Last Waltz* (Martin Scorsese, USA, 1978). It is a significant film because of its historical place within the genre and the way in which it foreshadows how subsequent concert film soundtracks blur the line between the simple documentation of the event and the staging of the event itself. Scorsese's meticulous approach to pre-production, the complex staging and lighting, and a dedication to capturing a "high-fidelity" audio recording of the on-stage performances are all of a piece with the slick presentation expressly demanded by the noted filmmaker. The production team was afforded a full complement of sound reinforcement technology, and the result of this coordinated effort is a live performance not solely intended for mechanical reproduction, but one ultimately tailored to ensure its successful reproducibility. Yet to have people perform for machines fundamentally changes the process of representation and the event's subsequent reproduction. For example, *The Last Waltz* presents us with on-stage and choreographed soundstage performances that are post-dubbed to enrich and correct the original, and overdubs to live guitar tracks in an effort to expand the arrangements and conceal mistakes (particularly those made during solos) (Helm and Davis 2000, 257). Additionally, the decision is made (by both The Band and the filmmaker) to mute Robertson's microphone for large portions of the evening to obscure his notoriously flat vocal delivery (Ibid., 257). His "silent" performance is only rendered audible on-screen.

Only ten years after the guerrilla aesthetics of *Dont Look Back*, *The Last Waltz* begins with a title card proclaiming "This Film Should Be Played Loud!" Interestingly enough, Jay Cocks (a frequent Scorsese collaborator) explains this command had the opposite of its intended effect: projectionists across the United States turned the volume *down* for fear that the soundtrack would damage theater equipment (Jay Cocks, *The Last Waltz: Special Edition* DVD commentary, 2002). And yet this had no impact on the film's success, ironically because its high-production values assured a stunning photographic presentation even in instances that found its audio presentation lacking. The film did not need to be played loud – perhaps few, if any, concert films do. They need only introduce us to the original acoustic event before convincing us of its faithful reproduction within a merely *legible* representation of concert sound that otherwise requires that we *look* at the sophistication of the sound-image relationship to confirm its authenticity. Such audacious sleight of hand becomes ever more possible as sound reproduction technology re-shapes both studio recording and live concert sound in the late-1960s and early 1970s.

Technological Innovation and the Rockumentary Soundtrack

A crucial aspect of the rockumentary during both its emergence and evolution is the deployment of sound reproduction technology: sound reinforcement systems for live music events, recording devices for film sound and in studio, and sound reproduction systems for theatrical exhibition. The technical apparatus of rock is reproduced in rockumentary. In the first wave of direct cinema-styled rockumentary biographies, single-microphone synchronized sound recording reinforced notions of immediacy, intimacy, and spontaneity that were deemed foundational to this type of portraiture. Early concert films, however, only rarely exhibited similar tendencies, relying as they did on a more sophisticated audio recording of the on-stage performance that would facilitate successful post-synchronization with the images. Such requirements ultimately establish multitrack recording and the phonographic practices of professional recording studio and post-production audio within the context of large-scale concert showcases and their cinematic rendering.

Gracyk, in response to Camille Paglia's claims that the audience-artist bond was destroyed by the increasing size of rock concert loudspeakers and a preference for special effects, argues "these were the very things that first made rock concerts into something more than party music" (Gracyk 1996, 193). He offers a historical sketch that takes the reader from the early days of rock and the "package" show featuring an assortment of musical acts performing only a handful of songs each – as seen in *T.A.M.I. Show* (Steve Binder, USA, 1964) – to the feature-length rock spectacle pioneered by major acts including Led Zeppelin and The Rolling Stones. Gracyk cites Stones drummer Charlie Watts, who explains set lengths rarely exceeded twenty minutes before the late 1960s, when improved technology made amplification systems cheaper and louder, and stage monitors ensured musicians could hear themselves and each other, thus ensuring the quality of the concert event for performers and audiences alike. Here we find fertile ground for the discussion of the technological nature of the representation of concert sound in the rockumentary genre: the rock concert is a mediated construct and any consideration of its cinematic representation must negotiate this technological reality.

Sound exhibition technology through the 1960s and a good portion of the 1970s remained essentially unchanged until the introduction and widespread adoption of Dolby Stereo's multitrack system toward the end of the decade (Kerins 2011, 29). During this same period, however, sound recording practices in cinema underwent a series of revolutionary changes, not least of which was the arrival of truly mobile, multitrack recording and high-fidelity wireless microphone systems. Robert Altman is often credited with introducing multitrack recording to American feature-film production, specifically his use of mobile eight-track recorders (and wireless lapel microphones) in his work on

California Split (USA, 1974) and *Nashville* (USA, 1975). In actual fact, these technologies were first introduced within the context of documentary production several years earlier, specifically concert film production in the late 1960s. Barry Salt's preliminary research into this field supports such a claim although more contemporary accounts of film sound technology largely overlook these contributions (Salt 1992: 263). Moreover, these technologies were directly related to, if not one and the same as, those employed by recording studios of the era. In two key instances, documentary filmmakers literally wheeled the recording studio into the field and forever changed location sound practice and the conception of the documentary soundtrack.

Monterey Pop (D. A. Pennebaker, USA, 1968) is often celebrated for its visual style yet it boasts a soundtrack recording of startling clarity and dynamic range relative to other documentaries of the era. It was tailored to a cinema experience and sought to capture and convey the energy of live rock performance; in doing so, Pennebaker and his associates established a sonic template for subsequent rockumentaries. Recalling a relationship between filmmaker and record label first established during the production of *Jazz on a Summer's Day* (Bert Stern, USA, 1959) – wherein a commitment from Columbia Records to release audio recordings of the concert guaranteed funds for the production of the film – later concert rockumentaries would benefit greatly from record label investment in attaining a high-quality soundtrack recording without necessarily asserting control over the material featured in the finished film. The involvement of Lou Adler and John Phillips with *Monterey Pop* guaranteed Pennebaker had the necessary resources for his soundtrack as well as the support of the musicians with regard to the filmmaker's music selections. The performances were recorded in eight-channel audio by Wally Heider using an Ampex multitrack recorder borrowed from no less a pop music titan than Beach Boys pioneer Brian Wilson (Lovece 1986). Though the project began as a television feature which would have required a mono mix, this approach provided Pennebaker with the necessary raw material to produce a 4-track stereo mix for the film's original theatrical release (Rosenthal 1971, 195) and it remains the source for multichannel remixes of the soundtrack for *Monterey Pop*'s various contemporary home video iterations. The improvised mobile multitrack recording technology – distinct from mobile mixing units used by Hollywood productions – was likely an Ampex AG-440-8, the first mass-produced commercially available 8-track recorder available in North America (see Figure 4.3), and provided the filmmakers with the ability to preserve individual channel strips for mixing and mastering later in the production process (Miller 2009).

In *Monterey Pop*, multichannel and multitrack sound technology delivers to film audiences a record of musical performances that is distinct from the experience of those in attendance at the event and sets the genre on a path towards

A CONSIDERATION OF THE DOCUMENTARY SOUNDTRACK

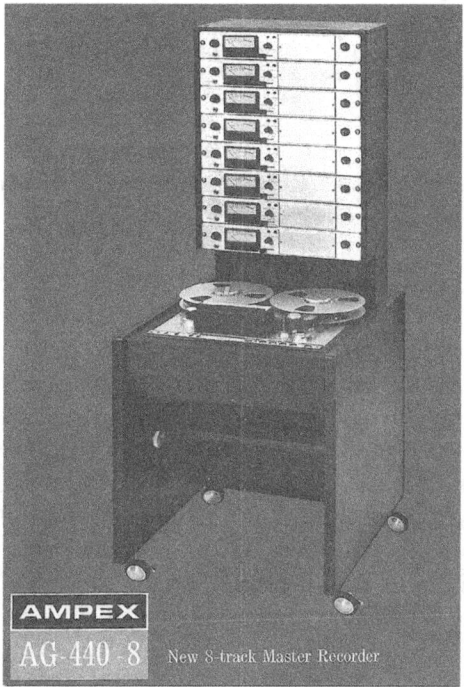

4.3 Promotional image for the Ampex AG-440-8, the first mass-produced eight-track recorder available in North America.

the exploration of new horizons in audio recording and sound design with an emphasis on the preparation of soundtrack albums using the phonographic conventions of rock music production.

Released on 26 March 1970, *Woodstock* (Michael Wadleigh, USA, 1970) played in theaters throughout 1970 and ranks among the most successful rockumentaries of all time (IMDB Pro). The soundtrack of *Woodstock* represents one of the most ambitious and commercially successful sound enterprises in the history of documentary. It is with *Woodstock* that filmmakers and musicians permanently make the jump from monoaural and two-channel stereo soundtrack recordings to the multitrack mobile recording units and multichannel theatrical soundtracks originally foreshadowed by *Monterey Pop*. Chion argues the decision to adopt multichannel sound in *Woodstock* and other musical films of the early 1970s had a profound impact upon the theatrical experience:

> These rock movies were made with the intent to revitalize filmgoing by instituting a sort of participation, a communication between the audience shown in the film and the audience in the movie theatre. The space of

the film, no longer confined to the screen, in a way became the entire auditorium, via the loudspeakers that broadcast crowd noises as well as everything else. (Chion 1994, 151)

Multichannel sound design works in harmony with the image-track in the service of communicating a sensorial experience of the original event to the film audience. Moreover, *Woodstock* conventionalizes the practice of coordinating the production of a concert film with the recording and release of a live album, an exercise that firmly embeds the synergistic relationship between film studios and record labels (foreshadowed by *Jazz On A Summer's Day*) within the fabric of the rockumentary genre.

Eddie Kramer, whose career as an engineer began in the UK working with artists including The Beatles, The Rolling Stones, and Small Faces, was selected to record the Woodstock performances because of his relationship as producer for Jimi Hendrix. Concert audio was engineered and recorded with a soundtrack release in mind and Kramer found the production equipment supplied to him by Warner Bros., as primitive as it was, exceeded that of both live sound engineer Bill Hanley and Wadleigh's crew (who arrived at the site with the knowledge there was not enough film stock to capture each performance in whole or in part). Meanwhile, Kramer and his technical assistant Lee Osborne had enough tape at their disposal to record each performance in its entirety (Hobson 2005). The audio recording equipment consisted of two mobile 1" 8-track recorders (of a similar vintage to those used for *Monterey Pop*), two 12-channel mixing boards, and a large selection of Shure microphones customized by Hanley, the concert's director of sound. The 8-track recorders, housed in a trailer nearby the front-of-house production stage, used ten 1/2"-reels which necessitated a change-over every twenty-five minutes – the machines were each paired with one of the 12-channel mixing boards and operated serially in order to capture the performances and stage announcements without interruption. Concert audio was mastered in 6-track stereo for theatrical exhibition in 70mm prints and 4-track stereo for 35mm release prints (which could not accommodate the six magnetic soundtracks of the 70mm format); these technologies predict the film industry's turn toward multichannel stereo sound presentations through the 1970s and the central influence of Dolby sound technologies in particular (Sergi 2004, 11–34). The details of *Woodstock*'s soundtrack recording, in combination with the efforts involved in the recording of *Monterey Pop* and other rockumentary concert films from the genre's first decade, represent a major shift in the documentary soundtrack whereafter any predisposition for maintaining an evidentiary or journalistic representational strategy falls away in favour of an increasingly mediated, illusionistic sonic text which adopts the technologies and principles of record production and reflects the changing nature of live concert sound.

Conclusion

Concert films are both sonic artefacts and fully artefactual sonic events which highlight the disjunction between cursory summaries of individual films ("It's just like being there!") and the true complexities involved in the audio-visual representation of a live musical event. The history of sound reproduction technology within the rockumentary informs the evolution of the genre and prompts a reconsideration of the evidentiary status of the documentary soundtrack as a whole. It is a chapter in a much larger narrative concerning changing conceptions of music and recorded sound in post-war Western society, in large part because of the dynamic influence of emerging technologies, but it is a significant one.

With the continuing evolution of high-definition theatrical and home theater exhibition spaces as the principal sites for viewing concert films, a misapprehension regarding the evidentiary status of mediated sound now seems firmly embedded within the language used to discuss these films and the means by which they find validation as exceptional media experiences. Robbie Robertson of The Band, commenting on the rerelease of Martin Scorsese's seminal concert film *The Last Waltz*, explains:

> We went to the original master tapes and mixed all the music and sound again in stereo and 5.1 Surround Sound. It is amazing what we can do with today's technology to *improve* and *enhance* the whole experience of this movie. (Robbie Robertson, *The Last Waltz: Special Edition* DVD commentary, 2002; emphasis added)

Moving further away from the qualities and character of the original acoustic event – and in many cases diminishing or destroying the film's value as an artefact of the event – is now considered to improve the concert film experience, perhaps proving enhancement and supplementation is the objective of these representational practices, rather than fidelity or mimesis. There is nothing new about this propensity for improvement, enhancement, or outright replacement; among rockumentary's earliest entries resides a concert film – *The Beatles at Shea Stadium* (Bob Precht, USA, 1966) – with a soundtrack that all but abandoned the original location recordings in favor of studio-recorded takes which assured the film's sonic legibility in light of the original material's unintelligibility. And yet, in the contemporary moment, one of the largest areas of growth and innovation within the genre involves performance films re-embracing a journalistic strategy for the sonic representation of musical performance. Filmmakers for non-fiction web series such as *The Take Away Show* (France, 2006–) and *Southern Souls* (Canada, 2009–) adopt field recording techniques to capture well-defined performances which summon the immediacy and authenticity so closely associated with the earliest rock concert films and assert the evidentiary status of these soundtracks.

In conclusion, the rockumentary concert film soundtrack is a sophisticated construct that challenges our understanding of the status of non-fiction film sound as realist and evidentiary and collapses distinctions between cinema sound and music production. In critical instances, it may very well be better approached from the perspective of record production than established methodologies of contemplating the film soundtrack. The technical apparatus of rock music is reproduced in rock concert films, and in our analysis and critique of the rockumentary soundtrack we discover what is perhaps the genre's most significant contribution to documentary studies as a whole.

References

Anderson, Brian. 2015. "The Wall of Sound." *Motherboard*, 5 July 2015, <https://motherboard.vice.com/en_us/article/wnnayb/the-wall-of-sound> (last accessed 27 July, 2018).

Anderson, Tim. 2006. *Making Easy Listening: Material Culture and Postwar American Recording*. Minneapolis: University of Minnesota Press.

Baker, Michael Brendan. 2011. "Rockumentary: Style, Performance, and Sound in a Documentary Genre." Ph.D. diss. Montréal, Quebec: McGill University.

Bazin, André. 1967. "The Ontology of the Photographic Image [1945]." In *What is Cinema?*. Berkeley, CA: University of California Press. 9–16.

Benjamin, Walter. 1992. "The Work of Art in the Age of Mechanical Reproduction [1936]." In *Illuminations*. London: Fontana. 217–52.

Brown, Lee B. 2000. "Phonography, Rock Records, and the Ontology of Recorded Music." In *The Journal of Aesthetics and Art Criticism* 58: 361–72.

Chion, Michel. 1994. *Audio-vision: Sound on Screen*. New York: Columbia University Press.

Durant, Alan. 1984. *Conditions of Music*. London: Macmillan.

Eisenstein, Sergei, V. I. Pudovkin, and G. V. Alexandrov. 1949. "A Statement on the Sound-Film [1928]." In *Film Form: Essays in Film Theory*. New York: Harcourt and Brace. 257–60.

Fischer, Lucy. 1985. "Enthusiasm: From Kino-Eye to Radio-Eye." In *Film Sound: Theory and Practice*, eds Elizabeth Weis and John Belton, New York: Columbia University Press. 247–64.

Gracyk, Theodore. 1996. *Rhythm and Noise: An Aesthetics of Rock*. Durham. NC: Duke University Press.

Helm, Levon and Stephen Davis. 2000. *This Wheel's on Fire: Levon Helm and the Story of the Band*. Chicago: Chicago Review Press.

Hobson, Mike. 2005. "Interview with Eddie Kramer." In *Jimi Hendrix: Live at Woodstock*. Classic Records.

IMDB Pro. n.d. "Woodstock." <http://pro.imdb.com/title/tt0066580/> (last accessed 16 August, 2009).

Kerins, Mark. 2011. *Beyond Dolby (Stereo): Cinema in the Digital Sound Age*. Bloomington: Indiana University Press.

Lovece, Frank. 1986. "Monterey Pop Vid Transfer No Easy Job: After Post-Production Snafus, '68 Film Out on Tape." *Billboard*, 22 March 1986: 48.

Miller, Larry. n.d. "Ampex History Project." *Audio Engineering Society*. <http://www.

aes.org/aeshc/docs/company.histories/ampex/ampex_history_project.html> (last accessed 5 October, 2009).

Rosenthal, Alan. 1971. *The New Documentary in Action: A Casebook in Film Making.* Berkeley, CA: University of California Press.

Salt, Barry. 1992. *Film Style and Technology: History and Analysis.* London: Starword.

Sergi, Gianluca. 2004. *The Dolby Era: Film Sound in Contemporary Hollywood.* Manchester: Manchester University Press.

Sterne, Jonathan. 2003. *The Audible Past: Cultural Origins of Sound Reproduction.* Durham: Duke University Press.

Vertov, Dziga. 1972. "The Vertov Papers [1930]." *Film Comment* 8(1): 46–51.

5. FALSE ENDINGS

Scott MacKenzie

When I began teaching at university, I half-jokingly told myself that as long as the students were born before The Beatles broke up in 1970, I could identify with them.[1] Time passed, and I told myself that as long as they were born before John Lennon was assassinated in 1980, I could identify with them.[2] Time passed, and I gave up on this practice. The notion of thinking that as long as students were born before George Harrison released *Cloud Nine* in 1987, or before he died in 2002, seemed pointless. This points to two things: one, that my lines of demarcation were arbitrary and two, that they were nevertheless quite real. These lines of demarcation as to when things change – or of moments of *zeitgeist* that are shared by all – as meaningful markers, are a central and unexplored aspect of the rockumentary, as well as rock and pop culture writ large. Despite all the claims to revolution, popular music and rock music itself are equally infused with nostalgia, with supposedly profound moments of loss as to an imagined Platonic ideal of the past. This chapter addresses some of these "ends" as recurrent moments in the history of the rockumentary and the cultural and political shifts that various films seem to demarcate. A number of films take center stage in this argument: Edward O. Bland's *The Cry of Jazz* (USA, 1959), Michael Lindsay-Hogg's *Let It Be* (UK, 1970), Mandy Stein's *Burning Down the House: The Story of CBGB* (USA, 2009), Jennifer Baichwal and Nicholas de Pencier's *Long Time Running* (Canada, 2017), Emily Maxwell's two versions of *The Who: The Night That Changed Rock* (USA, 2019), and Peter Jackson's as-yet unreleased *The Beatles: Get Back* (UK/New Zealand, 2021).

I argue that these nostalgic, melancholic – or perhaps, more properly, what is called *vemod* in Scandinavian languages, a not easily translated concept to which I shall return at the chapter's conclusion, but which could be defined as a positive form of reflective melancholy about something lost – "false ending" rockumentaries are a recurrent and distinct category. As such, they need to be understood as different from a number of other kinds of endings that exist in the rockumentary, such as:

1) retrospective rockumentaries, such as *The Kids Are Alright* (Jeff Stein, USA/UK, 1979) about The Who; the television series *The Beatles Anthology* (Geoff Wonfor and Bob Smeaton, UK, 1995); Jay-Z's *Fade to Black* (Pat Paulsen, USA, 2004); or the recent streaming series *Laurel Canyon* (Alison Ellwood, USA, 2020);
2) "final concert" or "final tour" rockumentaries, such as *Cream: Farewell Concert* (Tony Palmer, UK, 1969); *Ziggy Stardust and the Spiders from Mars* (D. A. Pennebaker, UK, 1979); or *Rush: Time Stand Still* (Dale Heslip, Canada, 2016);
3) the recent spate of "Lion in Winter" rockumentaries – which engage in a different form of nostalgia without postulating end-points (other than encroaching death) – such as *David Crosby: Remember My Name* (A. J. Eaton, USA, 2019); and *Once Were Brothers: Robbie Robertson and the Band* (Daniel Roher, Canada, 2019); or
4) what Monika Kin Gagnon (2014) has called "posthumous cinema," with rockumentaries such as *Tupac: Resurrection* (Lauren Lazin, USA, 2003); or *Michael Jackson's This Is It* (Kenny Ortega, USA, 2009).

"False ending" rockumentaries also need to be distinguished from new beginnings that retrospectively become a kind of ending, such as Elvis Presley's "comeback" and return to his roots in *Elvis* (Steve Binder, USA, 1968), often referred to as the *'68 Comeback Special*. What makes the "false ending" category of rockumentary I discuss herein distinct is that either the film itself, or the cultural and sociological discourses that surround it (and, at times, both) present the work as demarcating an "end" that goes beyond a performance proper, whether these ends are real or not. More often, they are the endings of things other than the supposed subject of the rockumentary in question. "False endings," in this context, should not be construed as untruths or lies; instead, "false endings" highlight how endings that seem decisive at one moment become something decidedly less so over time. The "false endings" in songs – from Glenn Miller's "In the Mood" (1939), The Contours' "Do You Love Me" (1962), The Beatles' "Rain" (1966) and "Strawberry Fields Forever" (1967), to Hüsker Dü's "Ice Cold Ice" (1987), and Metallica's "Sad But True" (1991) – are never the end; indeed, the songs are only understood by the ends that come after the false end. This, I claim, is equally true as to the meaning of "false ending" rockumentaries.

Ends that are Beginnings

In 1959, Edward O. Bland made a short independent documentary in Chicago called *The Cry of Jazz*.³ Interspersing documentary images of Sun Ra and his group Solar Arkestra playing different forms of jazz, with images of Chicago ghettos and White bourgeois suburbs intercut with a staged docudrama of the "Parkwood Jazz Club," a biracial jazz club debating the form's meaning, the film was quite distinct from the much better known *Jazz on a Summer's Day* (Aram Avakian and Bert Stern, USA, 1959), which seems more of a transition film than an ending proper. *The Cry of Jazz* can also be seen as the antithesis to the Hipster classic *Pull My Daisy* (Robert Frank and Alfred Leslie, USA, 1959), also released the same year, and Norman Mailer's 'The White Negro: Superficial Reflections on the Hipster,' first published in *Dissent* in 1957.

The Cry of Jazz begins with Alex (George Waller), a Black man, completing the minutes for a meeting with his jazz club. The membership of the club is both Black and White, and the group obviously socializes together. Bruce (Gavin McFadyen), a White member of the group, states that "rock 'n' roll is jazz." Alex counters that rock 'n' roll is merely an offspring of R&B. The group debates this, and when Alex is asked if jazz is not rock 'n' roll then what is it, he states that the "Negro alone could create jazz." He talks about how jazz is a response to the "Negro condition" and that White jazz musicians play "follow the leader." The film cuts from this debate to a close-up of an African statute on the mantle, and then to a montage of scenes from Chicago ghettos and Black jazz players. Over these images, Alex discusses jazz's formal elements as a dialectic between restraint and freedom, between pain and joy. Restraint is a chain and the denial of the "Negro" to the American way of life, while freedom is the utopian desire. Jazz, then, is an expression of the recreation of the eternal present in the face of the "Negro's" annihilation by White America. As the soundtrack changes to White-infused cool jazz, the city images shift to White suburbia, train stations, and poodle grooming. Over these images, Alex describes the "futureless future" (eighteen years before the Sex Pistols' "no future" in 1977's "God Save the Queen" foreshadowing the same sense of history at an end) which American life has bestowed on the "Negro" and that jazz reflects both the ideal of freedom and the actuality of restraint. As John Szwed notes: "This is the 'worship of the present' in the face of having no future, life as it should be versus what it is" (Szwed 2020, 162).

The film then returns to the living room. A White woman states that she doesn't see why "Negroes" see things differently than anyone else, as everyone in the world suffers. Alex replies by stating that because of the outrageous savagery of "you white Americans" that "The Negro is the only human American" as "you wiped out our past with slavery, wiped out today and with present day savagery you wipe out tomorrow." Compounding this critique, there is a biracial gender dynamic taking place, with Faye (Melinda Dillon), who is White, holding Alex's hand, as Bruce and John look on with White male jealousy, and implicitly, the fear of miscegenation. The film then cuts back to jazz performances, with Alex recounting the history of jazz from New Orleans jazz, to the White derivative Dixieland, to swing, to bebop, and cool jazz. According to Alex, all jazz culminates with Sun Ra (whose band plays all the various styles in the film). Back at the party, Faye asks what will happen next with jazz. Alex replies that jazz is dead. Loud arguments ensue as Alex says that the "Negro needs more room to tell history." Faye talks about how jazz can be used to fight the Cold War, as there is a great deal of mistrust about White Americans globally. John (Andrew Duncan), another White man, gets very agitated by this, claiming "slavery was over in 1863 so why do Negroes cry the blues?" At this point, the veneer of integration that film begins with has been stripped away. Alex argues that the jazz body is dead, but its sprit is still alive. His soliloquy unfolds over the image of Sun Ra playing jazz on a piano. The film then cuts back to burning ghettos, while Alex argues that the "Negro controls America's destiny" and that White Americans must accept them or

5.1 Alex directly addressing the camera and audience in *The Cry of Jazz* (1959).

disappear like a handful of smoke. Bruce calls this Black chauvinism, but Alex counters that it is Black Americanism, and engages in a critique of capitalism, decrying White America's focus on possessions. The film offers no resolution, as Alex turns his attention away from the group and addresses the camera directly, finishing his analysis.

In response to a query from Jonas Mekas, Bland, drawing on the thesis he advanced in the film, stated that: "Jazz is a musical expression of the Negro's eternal re-creation in the eternal present" (1960, 29). He claims that jazz is dead as it has exhausted its form and has become an empty aesthetic text, as evidenced by the White jazz aficionados in the film: "Since the Jazz body cannot grow, it can only repeat itself" (1960, 30). He states that one of the main critiques of the film – which is sadly prescient in terms of current responses in some parts of White America to the "Black Lives Matter" movement that "All Lives Matter" – is that "not only Negroes suffer economic woes" (1960, 32). He responds, echoing the film itself, that ". . . the nature of being a Negro in the United States opens the Negro to every potentiality of suffering that which the non-Negro can expect plus the suffering visited upon him for being born Negro" (1960, 32).

The end of jazz postulated in the film is a false ending in a number of ways. First, the ending addressed in the film is not that of jazz as much as it is a call for the end of the dehumanized conditions Black people in the United States live under, which are constructed by White hegemony and racism. Second, the end of jazz in *The Cry of Jazz* is in part a product of White acceptance and appropriation of the form, continuing it in a debased manner. Yet despite the film's claims, jazz was not dead, as the film was released the same year as Miles Davis's *Kind of Blue*, which took the form into new territory, modal jazz, and Ornette Coleman's free jazz album *The Shape of Jazz to Come*, two other examples of the revivification of the form. And in many ways, more so than an ending, *The Cry of Jazz* actually consists of a number of firsts. In one of the few positive reviews of the film upon its release, Ernest Callenbach and Dominic Salvatore argue: "This is the first anti-white film made by American Negroes, and it is fitting that it deals ostensibly with jazz, both in principle and because this will help it find an audience among whites. The film is badly made; but in its intentions it is exceedingly interesting" (1959, 58). They go on to note: "Thus the film's thesis is the film, very largely. Bland's view is that jazz is the cry of the Negro confronting the hazards and suffering of being a Negro in America; that jazz is now aesthetically dead; and that in a moral sense the Negro controls the destiny of America – for he poses to the whites their worst problem of conscience, which keeps them less than human" (1959, 58). With this rhetoric and form, *The Cry of Jazz* is both the first punk rockumentary and the first hip hop rockumentary. It also inaugurates the radical political protest rockumentary, foreshadowing works such as Santiago Álvarez's

Now! (Cuba, 1965), which juxtaposes found footage of racial unrest and discrimination in the US with Lena Horne's incendiary "Now" (1963), Jean-Luc Godard's *1+1/Sympathy for the Devil* (UK, 1968), which intercuts The Rolling Stones recording "Sympathy for the Devil" with figures of Black Panthers quoting texts from Amiri Baraka and Eldridge Cleaver, Ismail Shammout's *The Urgent Call of Palestine* (Palestine, 1973), featuring Palestinian Egyptian singer Zeinab Shaath singing the eponymous title song, the style of which she says was greatly influenced by Joan Baez, intercut with a statement by PLO spokesperson Kamal Nasser, who was assassinated shortly after filming by Israeli Special Forces in Lebanon (see Sela 2018), and Julien Temple's *Jubilee! Day 1977 On the River: Sex Pistols* (UK, 1977), an account of the Sex Pistols' cruise down the River Thames playing a three song set, and then being arrested during the celebration of Queen Elizabeth II's jubilee. In these ways, the film offers a series of new possible beginnings disguised as false endings.

The End of the 1960s

Let It Be was released on 13 May 1970 in New York City, and 20 May 1970 in London. Paul McCartney had announced the break-up of The Beatles via a press release that accompanied his first solo album *McCartney* on 10 April 1970, a little over a month earlier.[4] Yet, at this point, as Peter Doggett notes: "It was too soon for any claims that this event marked the death of the 1960s; such theorising, applied to any number of apparently epoch-defining moments, would come later" (2009, 130). Yet, for the first time, none of The Beatles attended the premiere of their film (Neaverson 1996, 110). Originally, the material shot for *Let It Be* was for a behind-the-scenes television special documenting The Beatles preparing for their first live performance in two-and-a-half years at The Roundhouse in London: "The footage of the rehearsals that would become part of the film *Let it Be* was not initially shot with the intention of becoming a feature film. Only a small part of the filmed rehearsals were to become part of the television concert show 'Get Back'" (Matteo 2004, 27). These initial plans rapidly changed many times over the course of the month of intermittent filming and the live concert went through many transformations before becoming the rooftop concert at the Apple headquarters at 3 Savile Row. Director Michael Lindsay-Hogg claims that playing on the roof was his idea, and that the band prevaricated a great deal up until the last minute, when John Lennon stated, just before taking the roof-stage: "Oh fuck it. Let's do it" (Lindsay-Hogg 2011, 142).

Alongside *Gimme Shelter* (Albert and David Maysles and Charlotte Zwerin, USA, 1970), released six months later, *Let It Be* is understood as the demarcation of the demise of the 1960s. It is also understood as a rockumentary "about" the break-up of The Beatles. Part of this reading is based on two key scenes in the film; indeed, *Let It Be* is overdetermined by its two most famous moments of dialog. The first is from Harrison as he rows with McCartney in the first third of the film as the band tries to learn "Two of Us": "I'll play whatever you want me to play. Or I won't play at all if you don't want me to play. Whatever it is that will *please you*, I will do it." The second is Lennon's closing line in the film, at the end of the rooftop concert: "I'd like to say thank you on behalf of the group and ourselves and I hope we passed the audition," which has a perhaps unintended tone of ironic finality to it.

Let It Be is understood to be a rockumentary about the break-up of the band, and hence the end of the 1960s; for instance, Bob Neaverson notes that: "[*Let It Be*] makes no secret of the fact that the Beatles are in the process of splitting up . . ." (1996, 111). Yet, this reading of the film is not really supported by the content of the film itself, besides the brief row between Harrison and McCartney. And in the end, *Let It Be* has carried this weight for a long time because The Beatles themselves have rewritten their memories of the filming over the decades (and have spoken of these recollections while leaving the film unreleased since the early 1980s). Harrison had the most negative memories of the time, noting in *The Beatles Anthology* TV series (Geoff Wonfor and Bob Smeaton, UK, 1995) that "Hanging out with Bob Dylan and The Band and having a great time and for me to come back to the winter of discontent with The Beatles in Twickenham was very unhealthy." The TV series then cuts to the aforementioned iconic row from *Let It Be* and Harrison states: "And they were filming and recording us having a row, it was terrible really." Lennon's account was more reflective: "The whole pressure of it finally got to us . . . it became petty, but the manifestations were all on each other as we were the only ones we had." McCartney downplays the problems and there are no comments from Starr. McCartney concludes that: "in fact what happened was we showed how the break-up of a group works because we didn't realise that we were breaking up as it was happening." There were certainly negative things going on with the band at this point, including the out-of-control spending of the band's company Apple (see Doggett 2009, 53–86; see also The Beatles 2000 for the band's account of this period). As Johnathan Cott and David Dalton note: "Apple's attempts to integrate the Beatles' own personal aspirations with the mechanics of a business was proving a fruitless task" (Cott 1973, 266; see also Doggett 2009). Yet these issues do not make it into the film proper.

Given this narrative on the part of the band members as to what the film actually documents, perhaps it's worthwhile to examine what *does* actually happen in the film. *Let It Be* is built on a tripartite structure. The first part begins with roadies setting up The Beatles' gear at Twickenham Film Studios with the various band members then arriving. The group starts running through and learning their new songs, while taking numerous breaks (McCartney reminisces, not for the last time, about the group's past with the film crew). It is in the "Twickenham" section where the only direct account of the stress within the band flares up, with the confrontation between Harrison and McCartney. Later in this section Harrison does mention he does not want to do a concert, but this doesn't lead to fights, though it does lead to some apathy on Lennon's and Starr's parts.

The second section takes place when the band move to their own studios in the basement of their Apple headquarters. Pianist Billy Preston joins them, and the mood is more buoyant; rehearsals are interspersed with group discussions often led by McCartney in a manner that might seem paternalistic and condescending, but again, without any major or minor blow-ups. The band had endless debates about where to hold the concert, be it in London, on a cruise ship, or in Tunisia (Sulphy and Schweighardt 1998, 105–6), some of which make it into the film. The "Apple" section ends with three complete songs as performances (actually recorded the day after the rooftop concert): the acoustic "Two of Us," and the piano-driven "Let It Be" and "The Long and Winding Road."

The final section of the film is the infamous "rooftop concert" (while this was seen as yet another innovative move on The Beatles' part, Jefferson Airplane performed "House at Pooneil Corners" on 19 November 1968 on the roof of the Schuyler Hotel in New York City – whether The Beatles knew about this performance is speculation; see Gleason 1969) which took place on 30 January 1969.[5] The mood among The Beatles, and between Lennon and McCartney in particular, is again buoyant (as the concert proceeds, the performance is intercut with *vox pops* on the street below, commenting on the concert: a few find it off-putting but most are pleased). Later in the concert, performances are intercut with the arriving police. Amps are turned off, and then back on, and McCartney adlibs at the end of "Get Back" about "You've been playing on the roofs again" and "She's gonna have you arrested" (they had hoped to have been arrested, McCartney and Starr claimed retrospectively, but were not). The song ends, and Lennon closes the gig with his famous quip.

So, *Let It Be* contains conflict but ends in harmony, literally and figuratively. The Beatles did not set off to make a rockumentary about their demise, and nor did they, despite all the later claims. As The Beatles themselves produced the film and individually oversaw Lindsay-Hogg's editing, any notion that this rockumentary is *cinéma vérité* and was a warts-and-all account is dubious at best. As David James notes: "... the absence of structure, information, or any discursive element appear to allow an unmediated personal intimacy with the four; ... This ostensive *vérité* is, of course, constructed" (2016, 172). The constructed, if not fictive, nature of the film – and the rooftop concert in particular – is described by James as a "... *cinéma vérité* reproduction of Lester's technique in *A Hard Day's Night*" (2016, 174). Jonathan Cott notes that: "But because this is not cinema vérité, but a documentary made by the

5.2 John Lennon: "I'd like to say thank you on behalf of the group and ourselves and I hope we passed the audition," *Let It Be* (1970).

Beatles themselves, the emphasis quite naturally is not on the tensions" (Cott 1973, 274). Both of these accounts, forty years apart, note both the constructed nature of the film and the avoidance of conflict. Yet, somehow both the band and its audience see *Let It Be* as a documentary of the end of the band, filled with arguments and anger.

Over the decades the band has intermittently tried to rewrite this end that they themselves created, this supposedly negative end which *Let It Be* represents, yet is not actually on-screen, in a work they have now kept out of official circulation for forty years. The release of the album *Let It Be . . . Naked* in 2003 (McCartney's attempt to rewrite the false ending of the Phil Spector production on the original album) brought back the question again of what the film was about. John Kimsey argued that: ". . . *Let It Be . . . Naked* has a case to make; namely, that the popular reading of the 1970 album and film as documenting the group's hateful and hurtful collapse – is wrong. In his liner notes, Kevin Howlett attributes this impression to . . . Lindsay-Hogg's having cut the film to emphasize moments of conflict" (2009, 242). Yet, the film itself makes no such claim. Indeed, if The Beatles had not broken up just before the film's release, *Let It Be* could easily be read in the following manner: *Let It Be* is a *cinéma vérité* classic, which offers an unvarnished account of the behind-the-scenes debates that go on in the world's most famous band as they produce their art. The film ends with a joyous concert, offsetting any of the quite natural disagreements that go into working together and through consensus. This, of course, is as spurious a reading as the one constructed by The Beatles.

Let It Be . . . Naked was not the end of this ongoing attempt to rewrite a false ending. On 30 January 2019, an Apple press release reported that director Peter Jackson would be culling through the fifty-five hours of footage shot and 144 hours of audio recorded during the making of *Let It Be* to make a new work, *The Beatles: Get Back*, using the techniques he deployed for *They Shall Not Grow Old* (Peter Jackson, New Zealand/UK, 2018), his remediation of World War I footage. Jackson stated that "I was relieved to discover the reality is very different to the myth. . . . After reviewing all the footage and audio . . . 18 months before they broke up, it's simply an amazing historical treasure-trove. Sure, there's moments of drama – but none of the discord this project has long been associated with. Watching John, Paul, George, and Ringo work together, creating now-classic songs from scratch, is not only fascinating – it's funny, uplifting and surprisingly intimate" (The Beatles 2019).[6] With *The Beatles: Get Back*, the recording sessions for *Let It Be* are no longer an ending infused with acrimony and discord. The narrative that surrounds the new film is about the joy the band had making the music (see, for instance, accounts of the filmmaking process and what it has "discovered," such as Robinson 2000 and Sheffield 2000).

The false endings that surround this film are copious. The band has spent fifty years trying to rewrite the ending they claim *Let It Be* embodies, though it is clear that this ending is not in the film itself, but instead in all the cultural and historical context that surrounds the work. The 1960s did not end on 30 January 1969; while dates can be debated, more likely contenders are Richard Nixon's resignation in August 1974 or the American withdrawal from Vietnam in April 1975. And The Beatles, at least as a corporation, are still going strong with no end in sight, generating more revenue now than they ever did in the 1960s. The desire to rewrite their end is a means to try and make their break-up disappear, or at the very least, disappear from the realm of representation, creating anew a false ending. They, as much as their audience, were caught in the utopian *zeitgeist* of the 1960s and its demise, supposedly brought on by the end of their band.

The End of Life

Founded in Kingston, Ontario in 1984, The Tragically Hip only skirted with American success. Fellow Kingstonian Dan Aykroyd got them a gig on *Saturday Night Live* in 1995; despite later opening for The Stones and

The Who, this was the peak of their American exposure. Their relative lack of success in the USA – they were popular in border towns like Detroit and Buffalo – paradoxically made them all the more popular in Canada. Lead singer Gord Downie's lyrics were infused with historical and contemporary references to Canadiana, weirdly paralleling the (four fifths Canadian) group The Band's nostalgic Americana.

Long Time Running offers an account of The Tragically Hip's last Canadian tour in 2016 and was directed by Jennifer Baichwal and Nicholas de Pencier, best known for working together on environmental documentaries such as *Manufactured Landscapes* (Canada, 2006) and *Anthropocene: The Human Epoch* (Canada, 2018). In 2015, a year before the tour, Downie was diagnosed with terminal glioblastoma. Downie states in the opening minutes of the film that: "I don't know what we were planning, a tour? Uh, the record was made. I guess we probably wondered what we would do next. And then [laughs], uh, y'know, yeah brain cancer, hmm, yeah." Guitarist Rob Baker stated that Downie, while going through chemotherapy, kept talking about going on tour, but felt: "I did not think there was any chance in hell that we would make it to the tour." There were good reasons for this. Downie states over rehearsal footage, "First rehearsal; I actually couldn't remember a damn thing. I think I started to cry." *Long Time Running* came about at the last minute: "Five days before the tour started . . . , the filmmakers got a call asking them to come and film the whole experience. 'Make the film I've never seen,' Downie told them. The movie was Downie's idea. The band was reluctant. There was enough pressure on the tour already" (Barclay 2018, 419). The tour was a success and the film was shot over the fifteen days on the road, with follow-up interviews afterwards.

Perhaps ironically, the band finally got coverage in the USA and the UK when Downie and the band went on this final Canadian tour while facing death. In *The New Yorker*, Stephen Marche wrote: ". . . dying hasn't stopped the tour. Downie is coming out on stage every night to burn out publicly. It has been glorious." Marche goes on to offer context for the band in Canada, arguing that the band ". . . has always sung about uniquely Canadian themes, often to the point of absurdity. Bill Barilko, who scored the winning goal for the Maple Leafs in the 1951 Stanley Cup Finals, disappeared on a fishing trip that summer, and his body was not found until 1962, the next time the Leafs won the Cup. That story may not sound like a natural subject for a rock song, but Downie got 'Fifty-Mission Cap' out of it . . ." He concludes with: "Gord Downie has entered the iconography of the Northern survivor. He has proved his endurance by crossing an impossible country while dying" (Marche 2016).

Long Time Running is infused with Canadiana nature shots, as was the tour, with a five-minute lightning break moving across Georgian Bay, to give Downie a rest. These images nevertheless echo the Northern survivor trope mentioned above. These images, backstage footage and interviews dominate. As Michael Barclay notes: "There are only four full songs in the film – it's not a concert movie" (2018, 420). The final gig takes place in Kingston, the band's hometown. After the band talks about the difficulties of playing there, we see the crowds gathering at the 6,000-seat arena, and outside in Springer Market Square, where the concert was simulcast to an audience of 25,000 people (and broadcast live on the CBC [Canadian Broadcasting Corporation] to an audience of 11.7 million people or just under a third of the country's population).[7] Here, what passes for Canadian nationalism kicks in, with copious Canadian flags and Prime Minister Justin Trudeau walking through the crowd and posing for selfies. Yet this supposedly benevolent Canadian national narrative is challenged in the film, with a move towards bringing it to an end. With the band riffing on their 1993 song "Courage (for Hugh MacLennan)" and playing to what is most likely the band's largest audience ever, and what was the second largest broadcast audience in Canada, Downie, who could have spent his time talking about anything, in one of the few comments he made, and the only one not about the concert/tour/the band's origins, went into a long monologue and stated that in terms of Indigenous peoples in Canada, as a society, "that we [White settler Canadians] were trained our entire lives to ignore, trained our entire lives to hear not a word of what's going on up there." Which is, of course, true – sadly and undeniably true – but a White settler Canadian could certainly have a double take at this point, thinking, "did he really say that?" This was not the anodyne "we're Canadians, we can fix this" sentiment that plays a central role in all the White settler (Anglo) Canadian flag waving in the film; it was an indictment of these very activities and their blind spots, the country's national rhetoric of inclusion, and the ideological structures that turn the Canadian North into a blank, white, uninhabited space, utterly and willfully ignoring its Indigenous populace. And while this was rhetorically framed as a statement of support in Trudeau and what he would accomplish, it also put the Prime Minister and the Canadian government on notice by a guy that has been transformed into a dying Canadian national icon, in a broadcast that a third of the population was watching, that things must change. Trudeau has done little to solve these structural problems, but Downie's statement functioned as a way of challenging the knee-jerk Canadian nationalism that surrounded the band's tour – and the band itself – that was otherwise infused throughout the film with all the metaphorical and literal flag waving. Which raises the question: what exactly is the subject of the rockumentary here? Certainly, the tour, and the stamina it must take to perform after brain surgery for glioblastoma. And certainly, there is an end here: The Tragically Hip are coming to an end as Downie's cancer is terminal. Yet, the other death at the heart of the film – and the end that one ought not to mourn – is that of a certain kind of unreflective, Anglo-Canadian "we're peaceful and generous" nationalism, withering in the face of Canada's TRC report of 2015, and Downie's public statement for Indigenous reconciliation, when a whole country who adored him were watching and listening.

The End of Trauma

Two rockumentaries, both called *The Who: The Night That Changed Rock* (Emily Maxwell, USA, 2019), commemorate the events that took place at Riverfront Stadium, outside a Who concert in Cincinnati, Ohio on 3 December 1979, where eleven fans were asphyxiated trying to get into a concert with festival seating (for a comprehensive, contemporaneous account of the event, see Flippo 1980). The Who left the city the day after the tragedy to play their next gig in Buffalo, New York. For the next forty years, they toured the USA many times, but never played Cincinnati again. This event became another form of false ending in rock lore: the end of rock idealism. In his career-spanning biography of the band, Dave Marsh wrote in 1983 that: "The real difference between the old Who and the new one was in what happened after the incident." The event was "... soon forgotten, dredged up only in passing in press accounts of the band's career" (1983, 513). Indeed, the event was only covered in cursory ways in Daltrey and Townshend's respective autobiographies (Daltrey 2018; Townshend 2012) and Entwistle's official posthumous biography (Rees 2020). Marsh goes on to note: "That didn't mean that Townshend didn't feel badly about those who died. He did. But Pete's comments indicate that his time as a rock idealist was past" (1983, 514). Townshend's own position as a so-called rock idealist was made more complicated by a fairly sarcastic and incendiary interview he gave to Greil Marcus about the event in 1980. At first, Townshend expressed how he thought the event would change the band in a positive way: "It's changed the way we feel about our audience. In terms of affection, and also remembering constantly that they are human beings – and not just people in rows. And I hope the reverse: that people who come to see the band will know that we're human beings too, and not this *myth* you were talking about earlier." But then he suddenly switched gears: "I mean, I watched Roger Daltrey cry his eyes out after that show. I didn't, but he did. But now, whenever a fucking journalist – sorry – asks you about [it] they expect you to come up with a fucking theatrical tear in your eye! You know: 'Have you got anything to say ... ?' 'Oh, we were *deeply* moved, terrible tragedy, the horror, loss of life, *arrrrghh* –' What do you do? We did all the things we thought were right to do at the time: sent flowers to the fucking funerals. All ... *wasted*. I think when people are dead they're dead" (Marcus 1981, 411). While speaking sarcastically, his words in print seemed callous, and shortly thereafter the whole band stopped speaking of the event, which only served to reaffirm the end of idealism and the triumph of capital in rock.

Broadcast and streamed on 3 December 2019 on the fortieth anniversary of the event, WCPO, an ABC affiliate in Cincinnati, released two versions of the rockumentary: *The Who: The Night That Changed Rock, A WCPO 9 On Your Side Special* (43 min.), a live broadcast, and while a rockumentary, structured much like many news documentaries; and *The Who: The Night That Changed Rock: A Documentary About The Who's Last Concert in Cincinnati* (48 min.), a standalone web-stream rockumentary, focusing far more on the community of Finneytown – a suburb of Cincinnati, where three of the dead went to Finneytown High School – than on the band itself.[8] Like *Long Time Running*, neither work focuses very much at all on music or performance. The two versions provide different kinds of endings to the events that took place at Riverfront Stadium. The news special concentrates as much on the experiences of The Who (Daltrey, Townshend, and manager Bill Curbishley all talk separately about how they have not talked about the incident in detail before, Townshend's interview with Marcus notwithstanding), intercut with interviews with the families of those who died, and survivors of the concert. The intercutting foregrounds the trauma experienced by both the band and the community over the incident, and the parallel editing implies a need to find a point of reconciliation to bring the event to an ending of sorts. The standalone rockumentary takes a different approach. The first two thirds of the broadcast concentrates on the families and the survivors, the experiences of police and paramedics that night, using archival news footage shot by the same station in 1979, and the community outcome of the event in Finneytown, which led to the establishment of PEM grants (an acronym for the three students who died from Finneytown High School) in the arts. Daltrey, Townshend and Curbishley only appear for any length of time in the last third of the rockumentary. Each appears separately, and their interviews are not intercut with the voices from the community; their accounts focus on their own difficulty processing the incident. The band's trauma is addressed in these works in quite a different manner to that of Mick Jagger and Charlie Watts in *Gimme Shelter*, another rockumentary that deals with death and questions of culpability. In both cases the band fled the scene – Townshend states in his interview that the band "ran away"' and ought to have stayed – but in *Gimme Shelter*, Jagger and Watts watching the murder of Meredith Hunter on a Steenbeck while being filmed leaves their own feelings and experiences opaque (see Austerlitz 2018). Indeed, they became avatars for the viewers, with Jagger becoming, as Austerlitz notes ". . . aligned . . . with the investigators, and not the culprits" (2018, 229). The Who, on the other hand, while not making any claims to culpability, demonstrated the lingering effects of trauma and guilt. No doubt part of this is the fact forty years have passed, whereas Jagger and Watts were shot in London watching the footage a few months after Altamont.

This version of the rockumentary concludes with the announcement that

The Who will return, for the first time since the tragedy, to play the Cincinnati area, in April 2020 (this concert was then postponed and will be rescheduled to a later date due to the COVID-19 pandemic, again delaying closure and a new end). The endings of these works could be seen in the first instance as being about the end of life and the death of eleven fans at a concert, and more metaphorically, the end of rock idealism. But on closer inspection, another ending is apparent: the end of trauma for the survivors, the families of those lost, and the band. The end of trauma is brought about in part by the same event that caused the trauma itself: a rock concert. Which is an example of rock idealism. Which had supposedly ended. What these two rockumentaries attempt to provide then, are new endings to this tragedy, both for the band and for Cincinnati. And, for that to happen, these new forms of closure and healing that break down the barrier between performer and audience – the same barrier that was lamented as a consequence as an end of rock idealism – have to happen in tandem.

Not an Ending: Same As It Ever Was

Despite all these rockumentaries being about metaphorical or literal death, they all offer viewers a form of pleasure. While not actually works of *Schadenfreude* they are perhaps more akin to the Swedish, Danish and Norwegian word *vemod*, which does not have a direct English translation, but can be best understood, as noted above, as a positive form of reflective melancholy about something lost. And while the term itself denotes something that will not return, it does allow for a certain form of repetition. One can experience *vemod* about the end of summer, for instance, yet there will be yet another summer next year, which one can feel *vemod* about all over again as it ends. This potentially endless experience of ends, loss, melancholy and repetition is well illustrated at the conclusion of *Burning Down the House: The Story of CBGB* (Mandy Stein, USA, 2009). The rockumentary tells the story of the closing, and the last years in the life of the formative Bowery club CBGB. Directed by Mandy Stein – the daughter of Seymour Stein, the founder of Sire Records, who signed The Ramones and Talking Heads based on their performances at the club – the film offers a variety of accounts of the importance of the venue. Director Jim Jarmusch returns to the club after it has closed down to explore the graffiti on the wall and engage in nostalgia. Stein interviews Steve Van Zandt, who is part of a group trying to keep CBGB open, along with customers and neighbourhood denizens. *Burning Down the House* also provides a history of the space and spends a good deal of time focusing on the club's halcyon days in the late 1970s. The last part of the film concentrates on Hilly Kristal's attempt to keep the club open, and its final night. While the rockumentary's signifier is the end of CBGB and its demise at the hands of Bowery Residents' Committee's

Executive Director Muzzy Rosenblatt (who would not be interviewed for the film, but had a long-term animosity towards the club and its owner Kristal), *Burning Down the House*'s signifier is not ultimately the club, the bands that played there, or the plight of Kristal, who died soon after, but the process of gentrification rampant in Manhattan in the early twenty-first century that brought inexpensive living in the borough to an end. It is the existence of affordable urban spaces that is coming to an end through the process of gentrification, not necessarily any great musical movement or moment. As Patti Smith said from the stage on the closing night of CBGB: "This place is not a fuckin' *temple*; it's just what it is. And the greatest thing about it . . . is just show an example of what ya can do. Ya just get a place, some crappy place that nobody wants, where ya got one guy who believes in ya, and ya just do your thing. And anyone can do that, anywhere in the world. Any time" (Hermes 2011, 285). And this is where Smith destroys the mythos of the "false ending" – the closing of a club far past its prime – through a statement infused with *vemod*. We can mourn the past, and mistake the past, and what ended when, and what an ending meant, and if it was an ending at all, but the hope for the future is, of course, that there will be more times and places and events that we will miss when they are over. New "false endings" to enjoy and lament in equal measure.

Notes

1. I was born in 1967, so my connection to The Beatles' break-up, and its significance, was an imaginary one. It no doubt had all the more significance because it was imaginary.
2. I was thirteen when Lennon was shot. My Aunt awoke me, knowing I would want the news, as I was by then a Beatles fan. She announced, with concern, that "Jack Lemmon" had been killed. Not a film scholar yet, I responded with "Oh, OK. Who's Jack Lemmon?"
3. *The Cry of Jazz* was added to the Library of Congress's National Film Registry in 2010 and can be streamed from its YouTube Channel: https://www.youtube.com/watch?v=fE00fzXpI04
4. After its initial release the film was unseen for many years. *Let It Be* was released by United Artists on VHS and Laserdisc in 1981 but has been unavailable since – except as a bootleg – despite many announcements that it would be rereleased from the 1990s onwards. There was contention between the surviving members (and spouses who stood in for Lennon and Harrison at Apple after their deaths) because the film was seen as painting various members in a bad light. The copy consulted for this chapter is a bootleg of a broadcast on Thames Television, the ITV television network serving London. Fairly detailed rehearsals and group discussions recorded during the *Let It Be* sessions can be found in the 8-CD bootleg *The Beatles: Rockin' Movie Stars* (Orange/Yellow Dog Records, 2000). See also Cott and Dalton 1969, Sulphy and Schweighardt 1998, and Mansfield 2018. For a detailed analysis of the recording process, see MacDonald 2005.
5. This performance, two-and-a-half months earlier, was shot as part of a never

completed film *One A.M.*, by Jean-Luc Godard, and later released as *One P.M.* by the film's cinematographer D. A. Pennebaker, in 1972.
6. After this release, *Let It Be* will finally be released on Blu-ray, according to Apple. Don't hold your breath.
7. The broadcast was subsequently released on DVD/Blu-ray as *The Tragically Hip: A National Celebration* (Dave Russell, Canada, 2017), recycling the title given to the live broadcast.
8. Both versions can be streamed at https://www.wcpo.com/news/the-who-the-night-that-changed-rock. Most coverage of the event on broadcast media largely blamed the band. One of the few mass media platforms to offer a sympathetic account of the event was the sitcom *WKRP in Cincinnati* with its episode "In Concert" (Season 2, Episode 19), broadcast on 11 February 1980.

References

Austerlitz, Saul. 2018. *Just a Shot Away: Peace, Love, and Tragedy with The Rolling Stones at Altamont*. New York: Thomas Dunne/St. Martin's.
Barclay, Michael. 2018. *The Never-Ending Present: The Story of Gord Downie and The Tragically Hip*. Toronto: ECW Press.
Beatles, The. 2000. *The Beatles Anthology*. San Francisco, CA: Chronicle Books.
Beatles, The. 2019. Press Release. "New Film Project: Announcing an Exciting New Collaboration Between The Beatles And the Acclaimed Academy Award Winning Director Sir Peter Jackson." <https://www.thebeatles.com/news/new-film-project-announcing-exciting-new-collaboration-between-beatles-and-acclaimed-academy> (last accessed 23 July, 2020).
Bland, Edward O. 1960. "On *The Cry of Jazz*." *Film Culture* 21: 28–32.
Callenbach, Ernest and Dominic Salvatore. 1959. "Review: *The Cry of Jazz*." *Film Quarterly* 13(2): 58–60.
Cott, Jonathan and David Dalton. 1969. *The Beatles: Get Back*. London: Apple Corps.
Cott, Jonathan and David Dalton. 1973. "Daddy Has Gone Away Now: *Let It Be*." In *He Dreams What is Going on Inside His Head: Ten Years of Writing*, ed. Jonathan Cott. San Francisco, CA: Straight Arrow Books. 266–79.
Daltrey, Roger. 2018. *Thanks A Lot, Mr. Kibblewhite*. New York: Henry Holt.
Doggett, Peter. 2009. *You Never Give Me Your Money: The Beatles After the Breakup*. New York: Harper.
Flippo, Chet. 1980. "Rock & Roll Tragedy: Why Eleven Died in Cincinnati." *Rolling Stone*, 24 January: 10–12, 22–4.
Gagnon, Monika Kin. 2014. "Unfinished Films and Posthumous Cinema: Charles Gagnon's *R69* and Joyce Wieland's *Wendy and Joyce*." In *Cinephemera*, eds Zoë Druick and Gerda Cammaer. Montréal: McGill-Queen's University Press. 137–58.
Gleason, Ralph. 1969. *The Jefferson Airplane and the San Francisco Sound*. New York: Ballentine.
Hermes, Will. 2011. *Love Goes to Buildings on Fire: Five Years in New York That Changed Music Forever*. New York: Farrar, Straus and Giroux.
James, David E. 2016. *Rock 'n' Film: Cinema's Dance with Popular Music*. Oxford: Oxford University Press.
Kimsey, John. 2009. "'An Abstraction, Like Christmas': The Beatles for Sale and for Keeps," in *The Cambridge Companion to The Beatles*, ed. Kenneth Womack. Cambridge: Cambridge University Press. 230–54.
Lindsay-Hogg, Michael. 2011. *Luck and Circumstance: A Coming of Age in Hollywood, New York, and Points Beyond*. New York: Knopf.

MacDonald, Ian. 2005. *Revolution in the Head: The Beatles Records and the Sixties*, 2nd edn. London: Pimlico.
Mansfield, Ken. 2018. *The Roof: The Beatles' Final Concert*. New York: Post Hill Press.
Marche, Stephen. 2016. "Watching Canada's Biggest Rock Band Say a Dramatic Goodbye." *The New Yorker*, 20 August. <https://www.newyorker.com/culture/culture-desk/watching-canadas-biggest-rock-band-say-a-dramatic-goodbye> (last accessed 23 July, 2020).
Marcus, Greil. 1981. "The Rolling Stone Interview: Pete Townshend." In *The Rolling Stone Interviews: 1967-1980*, ed. Peter Herbst. New York: St. Martin's/Rolling Stone Press. 404–13.
Marsh, Dave. 1983. *Before I Get Old: The Story of the Who*. New York: St. Martin's.
Matteo, Steve. 2004. *Let It Be*. 33⅓ Series. London: Bloomsbury.
Neaverson, Bob. 1996. *The Beatles Movies*. London: Cassell.
Rees, Paul. 2020. *The Ox: The Authorized Biography of The Who's John Entwistle*. New York: Hachette.
Robinson, John. 2020. "Long and Winding Road." *Uncut* 279: 64–75.
Sela, Rona. 2018, "The Urgent Call of Palestine: An Interview with Zeinab Shaath." <http://www.ronasela.com/en/details.asp?listid=85> (last accessed, 23 July 2020).
Sheffield, Rob. 2020. "And in the End." *Rolling Stone* 1343: 32–7, 74–5.
Sulphy, Doug and Ray Schweighardt. 1998. *Get Back: The Beatles' Let It Be Disaster*. London: Helter Skelter.
Szwed, John. 2000. *Space is the Place: The Life and Times of Sun Ra*. rev. edn. Durham, NC: Duke University Press.
Townshend, Pete. 2012. *Who I Am: A Memoir*. New York: HarperCollins.

PART II
GENDER

6. "START ME UP": THE PLACE AND DISPLACEMENT OF WOMEN IN THE CINEMA OF THE ROLLING STONES

Catherine Strong and Stephen Gaunson

Introduction

Since its establishment in the early 1960s, the rockumentary has been a staple of rock culture. In considering its connections with observational direct cinema, rockumentary, as Keith Beattie (2005, 21) argues, "emphasises showing over telling; that is, rockumentary privileges the visual capacities of documentary over patterns of exposition." As Beattie notes, the focus of the rockumentary has remained on performance, yet as this chapter will argue, in the past there has been too much emphasis on the performance of the musicians without enough serious discussion of other crucial social actors and how the way they are depicted has helped to create and maintain the myth of the "rock star." By looking at the way women have been portrayed in the rockumentary, using The Rolling Stones as a case study, we will illuminate the very specific roles that women have been given access to, and have been expected to perform, including the designated roles of groupies, screaming out-of-control fans, wives and girlfriends to band members. The way women are shown performing these roles helps to shore up the myth of the masculine "rock god," and the ideal of the authentic artistic genius that underpins the narrative that has been created around the rock canon.

This chapter will examine how classic rock documentaries help to reinforce these gendered roles and how their treatment of women mirrors and reinforces that found in the music industry more generally. Specifically, we will focus on how the footage from three early Stones documentaries, *Charlie is My Darling* (Peter Whitehead, UK, 1966), *Gimme Shelter* (Albert Maysles, David Maysles and Charlotte Zwerin, USA, 1970) and *Cocksucker Blues* (Robert Frank, USA, 1972), has been reused in the more recent anthology documentary *Crossfire Hurricane* (Brett Morgen, USA, 2012). We argue that the earlier documentaries present women in problematic ways that reinforce their marginal status in the rock world, but in other ways also show women as agentic and as personalities who help shape the culture around the band. *Crossfire Hurricane*, by contrast, features women far less, and when they are present, they are reduced to simple "groupie, fan or girlfriend" roles in a way that portrays them as mindless accessories to the band's hedonism. Given that The Rolling Stones have retained increasingly tight control over their cinematic representation, the way they choose to include or omit women becomes part of a decades-long arc of how the band performs its own identity.

Understanding this portrayal also helps to construct an image of where women fit into the rock landscape, and how it is acceptable to treat them, which will contribute to a better understanding of women's historical exclusion from this genre. There is currently a substantial body of literature that examines gender inequalities in popular music. Women have been consistently marginalized within this field: studies have shown that the number of performers who are women is significantly lower than the number of men (figures from performing rights associations from various countries put women's participation at 15–25 per cent of those making money from music (see Strong and Cannizzo 2017)). The roles that have been made available to women as performers have been very carefully circumscribed; certain types of music (folk, "singer-songwriter," pop) have been coded as more "feminine" than others (such as rock, metal and electronic music), leading to gendered differences across musical genres (Leonard 2007). Where women have been involved their contribution has often been downplayed or completely left out in historical accounts (Strong 2015; Reddington 2010). The collective memory of rock in particular, and the construction of the canon in this field, has been very much about white men (von Appen and Doehring 2006). In terms of documentaries, in recent years film has been one of the places where somewhat of a corrective to women's omission from music history has been taking place. Acclaimed films such as *Amy* (Asif Kapadia, 2015) (on Amy Winehouse) and *Whitney* (Kevin Macdonald, 2018) (on Whitney Houston) incorporate these artists into the "tragic rock star" pantheon using similar tropes to those used for male stars. Performance-focused documentaries on artists in the once-denigrated pop genre, such as Madonna, Katy Perry and Lady Gaga, have also received very positive receptions. However, the portrayal of women in rockumentaries focused on male stars has been less closely interrogated (although see Hassan 2010). Focusing on how women are portrayed helps explain the legacy of The

Rolling Stones, a band who are not only recognized as progenitors of the "sex, drugs and rock 'n' roll" lifestyle (Hassan 2010) but who also have increasingly maintained strict control over the cinematic output relating to them. This will also provide insight into how gender roles have been defined and maintained in rock, and how this has changed over time as rock becomes an aging and nostalgic art form.

Documentary Depictions of The Rolling Stones: An Overview

Over the course of their career, The Rolling Stones have been the subject of many documentaries, ranging from those based almost purely on concert footage, to tour films that focus more on off-stage events (which are the focus here). What has always been the case with The Rolling Stones is their involvement and copyrighted control of the documentaries that have been produced depicting their public image. We argue that this creative control has increased over time. It should be noted that everything seen in all of the Rolling Stones documentaries discussed in this chapter has been in agreement with, and approved by, the Stones themselves, and Mick Jagger more directly, who remains the copyright holder and producer of their cinema. This section will give an overview of the history of the four movies being considered here,

6.1 Hysterical fan from *Charlie is My Darling* (1966).

with a view to tracing the input of the band into how they are being portrayed.

Charlie is My Darling is a 1966 Peter Whitehead documentary covering two days in the life of The Rolling Stones during their second tour of Ireland in September 1965. This documentary was produced by Rolling Stones manager Andrew Loog Oldham. The film claims to show the band "in a way the world had never seen them before; as a band just coming into their own – raw, visceral, innocent and with purpose" (Gochanour 2013). Even in this film, which following its premiere was not seen for the next fifty years following a theft of the film reels, women (mostly in the form of screaming fans) are presented as important and crucial to the image of The Rolling Stones as significant rock icons.

Gimme Shelter, largely considered to be one of the most important rockumentaries ever made, is a very different type of film despite being made only a few years later. It famously documents the disastrous 1969 Altamont festival, where there were four deaths among the 300,000 attendees, including the eighteen-year-old Black man, Meredith Hunter, who was stabbed and bludgeoned by the Hells Angels hired by the Stones as security (for the modest fee of $500 and a case of beer). This terrible incident overshadowed one of the greatest rock line-ups ever staged, including Santana, Jefferson Airplane, The Flying Burrito Brothers, and Crosby, Stills, Nash & Young. The Grateful Dead were scheduled to play but refused as the perilous environment of the event became evident. Shooting Hunter's attack from the stage, the film's camera crew captured the chaotic moment that saw a number of Angels jump into the crowd as the Stones played their hit song, "Under My Thumb." In the aftermath, the band were criticized for not walking off-stage during the commotion, and for hiring the Angels in the first place. Premiering on 6 December 1970, exactly one year after the horrific incident, *Gimme Shelter* gave the Stones a right of reply. In the film, Jagger sits with co-director David Maysles at the editing table, seemingly disturbed by the live footage that plays in flashback. "It looks like a scuffle . . . it's just awful," he harmlessly says. As Amy Taubin (2009) writes, "compared to the Angels and the kids crowding the stage, stoned on bad acid and speed, they seem like the good guys."

In 1971, Jagger hired Robert Frank, Swiss photographer and filmmaker who had worked with beat poets Jack Kerouac and Allen Ginsberg in the 1950s, to create a documentary on their next American tour. The film's title, *Cocksucker Blues*, is taken from a deliberately "unreleasable" Stones song which Jagger wrote to fulfill the group's contractual obligations with Decca Records. Having formed their own private label, Rolling Stones Records, and dumped Allen Klein as their manager, by the early 70s the band was becoming a more professional unit. Frank's film documents the last real wild tour of the Stones; however, besides one brilliant performance of "Midnight Rambler," *Cocksucker Blues* is not the brilliant tour film that many want to believe it is.

Although film director Jim Jarmusch may be right that it is "one of the best movies *about* rock and roll" (cited in Gaunson 2010), it is monotonous and dull. Indeed, scenes which depict the Stones as living an ugly, vacant and decadent existence, fuelled by their notorious cohort of drug dealers, groupies and celebrities, are hardly enthralling. In addition to the band themselves, Frank is equally interested in the sleazy world of these hangers-on, who spend most of their time strung out in hotel rooms, often waiting for the band to turn up. Frank paints a vivid, unattractive and monotonous portrait of the debauched rock world.

Running at ninety-three minutes, *Cocksucker Blues* was scheduled for an 18 November 1972 release; however, after watching Frank's rough cut, Jagger demanded that it not be shown, on account of its "heavy scenes." At the time, Jagger was reported to have said,

> Why can't [Robert Frank] go and do something else? It was my idea of making that stupid movie. He was just paid to film what I told him to do ... it's our movie. And if I want to go shred it in the shredder, or if I want to show it to my friends, or if I want to put it in general release, it's up to me. (quoted in Gaunson 2010)

Frank claimed that as director of the material, he was its true author, and therefore the copyright belonged to him. Taking the matter to court, the judge peculiarly ruled that the film could screen just once a year and only if Robert Frank was in attendance. As well, Frank was instructed to insert an absurd disclaimer at the start of his film that implied the lewd antics were merely staged for the camera (Gaunson 2010). However, as evident from the footage, this is not the Stones playing it up for the camera, but the camera exposing their seedy and decadent lifestyle. Surely this disclaimer does not fool anyone.

Released much later than the other three documentaries, *Crossfire Hurricane* (2012) is a film about nostalgia for an earlier – or mythical – version of a band that has continued to exist in a fragmented and reduced form over five decades. For many, their connection to the band comes from excerpts from the previous documentaries posted on YouTube or compilation albums or, of course, their numerous stadium concert tours, which in themselves are a performance of and about nostalgia. What director Brett Morgen offers in this archival film is a selection of fragmented clips unscrambled from the documentaries discussed above and other unseen archival material, focusing almost completely on the first fifteen years of the band's career. As the clips play, new audio interviews with the Stones act as a running commentary from the inner sanctum of the band's perspective. The purpose is to offer an eye into the world of being a Rolling Stone, which the chosen footage represents as a haze of sex and drugs, with women given a mostly reductive and sexualized role.

From Screaming Fans to Groupies and Beyond: Stones Documentaries and Women

Norma Coates (2003, 65) has noted that:

> ...the use of "teenyboppers" or "groupies" to identify female fans of popular music belies a disturbing reality of rock culture for women: for decades, those were essentially the two ways to imagine the relation of women to rock. The normative power of these prescribed identities remains potent, even though women are increasingly visible in rock culture as musicians and critics.

As we will demonstrate here, these are the main modes of presentation of women in the Rolling Stones documentaries, despite the occasional inclusion of more complicated depictions of women around the band. The teenybopper and the groupie are both identities connected to desire for men in bands, but with a different emphasis. Teenyboppers are associated with a more innocent desire for romantic interactions, whereas groupies are "a more extreme type of female fan who seeks intimate emotional and/or sexual relations with musicians" (Larsen 2016, 398). The image of the "screaming teen girl" is almost a signifier for unthinking, overly-emotional consumption, and the types of music associated with women, particularly "pop," have historically not been taken very seriously by critics. The teenybopper, then, has been a key figure in the general dismissal of feminine culture and tastes (Kearney 2017). The groupie, on the other hand, is a complicated figure in rock history, framed as poised almost perfectly between the ideal of the liberated woman who has complete agency in how she uses her body, and who unapologetically pursues her desires, and a much more debased figure who is exploited and used by men for sex. Forthright accounts of women like Pamela des Barres and Cynthia Plastercaster, who foreground their own pleasure, and their value to the bands, in the stories they tell sit uncomfortably alongside stories in rock biographies – and scenes such as that in *Cocksucker Blues* discussed below – of women being degraded and exploited by tour crews and musicians alike. Larsen (2016, 398) has highlighted the ways that "the labelling of certain people as 'groupies' works as an othering practice that serves to support and maintain the gendered norms of rock and thus exclude women from creative production." One of the ways in which this occurs is through the use of the figure of the groupie to delegitimize women who attempt to make their way into music spaces. Numerous studies have documented women artists' accounts of being reduced to a sexual object by gatekeepers such as bouncers, sound engineers and venue owners, through questions such as "are you with the band?" (see also Leonard 2007). This could imply "girlfriend" or "wife" status as well as implying that the woman in question is a groupie, and this serves another role that is available for women in popular music; the supportive partner. Either way, the implication is that women do not belong in music spaces unless they are there with, or for, a man.

In *Charlie is My Darling* the teenybopper/screaming fan depiction of female fans is foregrounded as a central motif of the film. We see teenage girls invading stages in 1965. Bill Wyman, discussing this scene decades later in *Crossfire Hurricane*, explains how "I could see the water flowing between the seats . . . it was a flood of urine . . . girls always urinate when excited." In this footage, the band barely complete live performances before fans storm the stage.

The hysteria that the Stones create sparks boys with long hair and girls in beehives to literally force the band to hightail across the train tracks for a safe exit at a Belfast station. The song that seems to create the most hysteria across the film is "Satisfaction," the song that would remain one of their most popular and a staple of live performances for decades to come. "*I can't get no satisfaction/I can't get no satisfaction/'Cause I try and I try and I try and I try/I can't get no/I can't get no*": the lyrics are sung like a dare to their female fans to give the band members some of that satisfaction they desire. At the time of the film, "Satisfaction" was an international hit, taking the Stones to stardom. While the film promises to depict the band before they became a legend, it more accurately establishes cinematic representations of hedonism that would come to define their collective identity as rock outlaws. *Charlie is My Darling* is relatively innocent compared with later films, but hysterical women unable to control themselves are on display in practically every scene. Where fans are not seen, they are discussed by interviewers or the band themselves: Jagger explains, "On stage there is a sexual thing between the audience and the group."

In *Gimme Shelter*, we see a different type of female fan emerging. The Stones' members in this documentary are more mature and self-confident, and more overtly sexualized. Screaming fans are relied on less to validate the band's standing in popular culture, and women are given more range across the film. Certainly, the identity of women as something closer to groupies becomes apparent with young women shown waiting outside the band's trailer hoping to glimpse or speak to their beloved rock stars. The most prevalent images of women in the film are either here, or as part of the massive crowds; not screaming or hysterical, as the qualities of fandom shifted in the free-love and hippie era, but still subsumed into an uncritical (and in this instance dangerous) mass. Women, though, have other roles, particularly as performers. Andrew August (2009, 79) has argued that despite criticism of the band's lyrics for being sexist, a close examination of their songs shows a more complex picture, revealing the band as "conflicted and ambivalent, rather than uniformly hostile, to changing gender roles." Of the documentaries being considered here, *Gimme Shelter* and *Cocksucker Blues* can most clearly be regarded in a similar manner. A standout moment in the former film is the mesmerizing performance of Tina Turner's "I've Been Loving You Too Long" at Madison Square Garden. Then, in the latter part of the film, at Altamont, Grace Slick of Jefferson Airplane is shown not only performing but taking control of a violent situation and attempting to calm both the Angels and the crowd. "Both sides are fucking up temporarily. Let's not keep fucking up," she implores. The moments when the film breaks from the Stones to show Turner or Slick identifies the importance that women played in this rock scene during the 1960s, offering agency and significance beyond the typical depictions of women in the music and behavior of the Stones' members. These are, however, few and far between, and are at times undercut by the band. For example, while Jagger appears awestruck by Turner's performance, he is ultimately dismissive, stating "It's nice to have a chick occasionally." This speaks volumes about how Jagger depicts himself in these films.

Cocksucker Blues goes further in showing a complicated version of the women around the Stones. While on the one hand we again see the typical roles for women emerging – groupies, screaming fans and wives and girlfriends – they are very visible and less one-dimensional, often depicted as agentic participants in the culture surrounding the band, helping create its character.

Women are shown enthusiastically partaking in the drug taking that is docu-

6.2 Groupie in *Cocksucker Blues* (1972).

mented in unflinching detail throughout the film, with one woman notably enthusing about her first encounter with heroin that is captured on tape, and another talking to the camera while high and naked in a hotel room in a scene that is in equal parts titillating and ugly, but which avoids seeming entirely exploitative due to the apparent enthusiasm of the woman for the situation. Elsewhere, women are shown as constantly present in the everyday life of the band, from Bianca Jagger's apparent boredom with life on the road, to women back-up singers and support acts. Even female fans are given a certain amount of substance: the fan who talks about having had her baby taken away because of her drug taking is sad and strange, but she has a personality and is given a chance to tell her story.

In other places, however, the film portrays some of the worst aspects of the milieu being documented. The most problematic scene in the movie, and the one where the tensions between readings of women in these documentaries as agentic or exploited become most obvious, is where members of the groups and entourage engage in explicit (and explicitly shown) sexual activities with young women on their private plane. While some of this activity appears consensual, it crosses uncomfortable lines at times. Most notably, one of the women has her clothes removed while laughing but protesting and trying to pull away at the same time. Keith and Mick grin away at the scene as it unfolds for their entertainment. This has been read as obscene on more than one occasion: as Brody (2016) notes: "At one point, a young woman is undressed and lifted and spun around, and, though her shrieks at times sound like laughter, her protests and demands to be put down are unambiguous. Even if it's a playful moment, it's an ugly one and a painful one to watch." Similarly, Mulholland (2010, 123) writes, "we realise that the Stones are leading a crowd of men who are encouraging the girl to go further by verbal cajoling and the beating of drums. Another girl is roughly manhandled into toplessness by the meathead ... she's laughing, but it still feels uncomfortable." Elsewhere, the encounter has been described as "dubiously consensual" (Hamilton 2013) and the woman as "reluctant looking" (Doyle 2009). At a moment in time when the #MeToo movement has drawn unusually strong attention to the nature of women's strategies for avoiding harm at the hands of men, this woman's laughter and smiles are easy to read as ways of not being too "difficult" while trying to say no in a situation – surrounded by horny men on a plane – that is potentially very dangerous for her. The men push on through her protests – perhaps they would have done so no matter what. The fact that more has not been made of this (at best) ambiguity by the (male) writers who have noticed it when discussing the movie is also noteworthy, but beyond the scope of discussion here. Frank would later deflect the consensual issues of the sequence by claiming the entire thing was staged (Mulholland 2010, 122). But was it? And if so, why stage this? Why would this be an image the Stones would want depicted?

Footage from all the above films is used in *Crossfire Hurricane*, which draws on and helps to solidify a mythology of The Rolling Stones that emphasizes the "dangerous" aspects of their youthful personas at a time when the actual Stones are safely ensconced in old age. In doing so, it to a large extent elides the role of women, who, despite the extensive footage of them available to draw from, hardly feature in the film at all. Unlike the more complex depiction of women from the earlier films, Morgen seems solely interested in the representation of women-as-hysterical-fans. Again Jagger plays the role of Producer, hiring the director as he has continued to do across all of his and the band's documentaries. Why Morgen was chosen becomes clear after watching his previous movies: notably *Montage of Heck*, where he was hired by Courtney Love to unscramble the home movie footage of Nirvana frontman Kurt Cobain. As with that film, in his Stones documentary he delivers a visually stimulating film that never challenges the mythology behind the footage that is being shown or wants to consider what exactly it says of the band. Through the footage, roughly chronicling the band up to 1981, the band remain young men (save a clip to end the film pulled from Martin Scorsese's concert film *Shine a Light*). Though we hear the older Stones reflecting back, they are never seen, with the film remaining entrenched in this earlier mythology of the band as the dangerous renegades of rock 'n' roll. *Crossfire Hurricane* encourages us to read the band for its hedonistic desire of getting satisfaction through drugs and sex. Clips of the band snorting cocaine (such as Mick from *Cocksucker Blues*) are front and center, framed by songs that could be read as auto-critiques of their own exploits (Patterson 2012). For example, the song "Brown Sugar" is matched by the African American groupie seen across one sequence with various band members. The film never critiques such moments, never wanting to probe beyond the banner of bad band of rock brothers.

In addition to this, *Crossfire Hurricane* uses some of the footage from the group sex scene in *Cocksucker Blues*. Small segments of it, so short that it is only just understandable what they are, are inserted in a section of the film where sex is being discussed. These disjointed, out-of-context images speak to the parts of the rock 'n' roll mythology where women's bodies become endlessly available to stars while removing the discomforting aspects of the scene as originally presented. This is almost a new type of violence being perpetrated on the woman in question; not only were her original protests over-ridden, but here they are omitted altogether as she is presented as a sexualized, willing participant in a way that works only to shore up the Stones' self-presentation as sex gods.

CONCLUSION

What this chapter keeps returning to is the idea of performance, both the performance of The Rolling Stones as dangerous rock outlaws, and the women in designated roles as subordinates. The Rolling Stones are both symptomatic, yet an extreme case, of the nostalgic male rock culture, in how women are reduced to classical cliché and stereotypes, there to fulfill the depiction of the hedonistic lifestyle. Across the history of the rockumentary it is hard to find a band that so heavily relies on and reduces the depiction of women to those designated roles of groupies, screaming out-of-control fans, or wives and girlfriends to band members. Although at times women are shown to be dominant and in control of their sexual identity, they are invariably cut down to size. Women can be shown, but only occasionally and within limits, and always they are expendable and replaceable. This seems to be the attitude of Jagger (as Producer) in all of the Stones documentaries, which is all the more apparent in a film like *Crossfire Hurricane*, intended and marketed as the definitive Stones documentary, capturing the true essence of the band that was and continues today.

Across its duration, under the watch of the band themselves, the women that seemed so present and important to the earlier films of *Gimme Shelter* and *Cocksucker Blues* are reduced to the clichés of screaming fans or background props for the band members. In many respects, what makes women so crucial to *Crossfire Hurricane* is not their presence, but absence, in the ongoing marginalization of women as a significant omission of rock culture, rock history, and rock nostalgia. What such histories now require is more discussion on how the objects of the (male) rock stars' hedonism are never given a chance to be the subject, but are almost always reduced and marginalized to subordinates in the male milieu. Rather than accepting this as an unfortunate part of the culture, we require more scrutiny on how these depictions are supported and scaffolded throughout broader media, including rock journalism and of course the documentaries themselves.

REFERENCES

August, Andrew. 2009. "Gender and 1960s Youth Culture: The Rolling Stones and the New Woman." *Contemporary British History* 23(1: 79–100.
Beattie, Keith. 2005. "It's Not Only Rock and Roll: 'Rockumentary', Direct Cinema, and Performative Display." *Australasian Journal of American Studies* 24(4): 21–41.
Brody, Richard. 2016. "'Cocksucker Blues': Robert Frank's Suppressed Rolling Stones Documentary Comes to Film Forum." *The New Yorker*, July 20. <https://www.newyorker.com/culture/richard-brody/cocksucker-blues-robert-franks-suppressed-rolling-stones-documentary-comes-to-film-forum> (last accessed 19 October, 2018).
Coates, Norma. 2003. "Teenyboppers, Groupies, and Other Grotesques: Girls and Women and Rock Culture in the 1960s and early 1970s." *Journal of Popular Music Studies* 15(1): 65–94.

Doyle, Patrick. 2009. "Rolling Stones' Controversial Tour Documentary 'Cocksucker Blues' Screens in New York." *Rolling Stone*, October 26. <https://www.rollingstone.com/movies/movie-news/rolling-stones-controversial-tour-documentary-cocksucker-blues-screens-in-new-york-79448/> (last accessed 19 October, 2018).

Gaunson, Stephen. 2010. "*Cocksucker Blues*: The Rolling Stones and Some Notes on Robert Frank." *Senses of Cinema* 56. <http://sensesofcinema.com/2010/feature-articles/cocksucker-blues-the-rolling-stones-and-some-notes-on-robert-frank/> (last accessed 19 October, 2018).

Gochanour, Michael. 2013. "Director's Statement – The Rolling Stones – Ireland 1965 (a/k/a Charlie is my Darling)." <http://www.mickgochanour.com/directors-statement-2.html> (last accessed 19 October, 2018).

Hamilton, Jack. 2013. "Why did you want to film that?" *Slate*, July 9. <http://www.slate.com/articles/arts/culturebox/2013/07/cocksucker_blues_robert_frank_s_rolling_stones_documentary_revisited.html> (last accessed 19 October, 2018).

Hassan, Nedim. 2010. "'Girls, Girls, Girls'? The Los Angeles Metal Scene and the Politics of Gender in *Decline of Western Civilization Part II: The Metal Years*," *Popular Music History* 5(3): 243–63.

Kearney, Mary Celeste. 2017. *Gender and Rock*. Oxford: Oxford University Press.

Leonard, Marion. 2007. *Gender in the Music Industry: Rock, Discourse and Girl Power*. Aldershot: Ashgate.

Larsen, Gretchen. 2017. "'It's a Man's Man's Man's World': Music Groupies and the Othering of Women in the World of Rock." *Organization* 24(3): 97–417.

Mulholland, Garry. 2010. *Popcorn: Fifty Years of Rock and Roll Movies*. London: Orion.

Patterson, Troy. 2012. "Sympathy for the Devils." *Slate*. <http://www.slate.com/articles/arts/television/2012/11/rolling_stones_hbo_documentary_crossfire_hurricane_reviewed.html> (last accessed 18 October, 2018).

Reddington, Helen. 2012. *The Lost Women of Rock Music*. Sheffield: Equinox.

Strong, Catherine. 2015. "Shaping the Past of Popular Music: Memory, Forgetting and Documenting." In *The Sage Handbook of Popular Music*, eds A. Bennett and S. Waksman. London: Sage Publications. 418–33.

Strong, Catherine and Fabion Cannizzo. 2017. *Australian Women Screen Composers: Career Barriers and Pathways: Research Report*. Melbourne, Australia: RMIT University. <http://apraamcos.com.au/about-us/industry-research/australian-women-screen-composers/> (last accessed 22 January, 2018).

Taubin, Amy. 2009. "*Gimme Shelter*: Rock-and-Roll Zapruder." Criterion Collection, DVD, Production Notes. <https://www.criterion.com/current/posts/103-gimme-shelter-rock-and-roll-zapruder> (Last accessed 19 October, 2018).

von Appen, Ralf and Andre Doehring. 2006. "Nevermind the Beatles, Here's Exile 61 and Nico: 'The Top 100 Records of all Time': A Canon of Pop and Rock Albums from a Sociological and an Aesthetic Perspective." *Popular Music* 25(1): 21–39.

7. MADONNA ON FILM: GEOPOLITICS, GLOBALIZATION, AND GENDER POLITICS

Anna Westerstahl Stenport

With seismic changes in the geopolitical order underway at the end of the 1980s and in the early 1990s, popular culture became one of the arenas in which these shifts were most conspicuously addressed, even though scholarship in the field of geopolitics has explored the ramifications of popular culture in the "New World Order" only sporadically. This was also at the height of American musician, lyricist, vocalist, and performer Madonna's fame, influence, popularity, and global reach. Madonna's pop culture power is demonstrated by the success of the albums *Like A Prayer* (1989) and the greatest hits compilation *The Immaculate Collection* (1990); the three-continent Blond Ambition Tour in 1990; and the internationally released rockumentary made about it: *Madonna: Truth or Dare* (a.k.a. *In Bed with Madonna*, Alek Keshishian, USA, 1991). This chapter situates visual documentation about the Blond Ambition tour and the rockumentary *Truth or Dare* in their geopolitical contexts and as artefacts of a particular moment in time.

At the fall of the Berlin Wall in 1989, political theorist Francis Fukuyama famously proclaimed "the end of history" (1989; see also 1992), prompting the field of geopolitics, international relations, and political theory to address the end of the Cold War. At the same time, globalization theory and discourse came into prominence, signifying "an apparently 'borderless' world in which trade, commerce, and money can enjoy unimpeded movement over space and through time" (Dodds 2014, 5). This globalization ideology aligns with Madonna's statements and production at the time, including what could be called her international mandate. As J. Ann Tickner affirms: "Globalization involves more than economic forces; it has also led to the spread of Western-centered definitions of human rights and democracy" (2001, 7). These are the tensions and registers examined in this chapter.

Scholars of geopolitics and globalization responded to these changing times in three significant ways. First, the study of "critical geopolitics" emerged; a response at least in part to globalization theory (Ó Tuathail 1996). Influenced by post-structuralism, critical geopolitics is informed by discourse and media analysis, integrating both a "linguistic turn" as well as a "visual turn" (Dodds 2008). Second, popular culture – movies, magazines, music – began to be recognized as important to the study of both geopolitics and globalization, which cannot be understood outside of their own mediatization (e.g., Sharpe 2000, Dodds 2007). Third, feminist perspectives emerged, with J. Ann Tickner's work particularly noteworthy, as it articulated how geopolitics had been "gendered masculine" for decades; for instance in its emphasis on "nuclear strategy and Cold War rivalry between the United States and the Soviet Union" (2014, xv) or Western-centric nation state politics. Indeed, in 1990, feminist scholar Cynthia Enloe "suggested that international relations were so thoroughly gendered that no one had noticed that women were missing" (see Tickner 2014, xvii). This was the dominant societal and scholarly framework at the time. Critiques of globalization as assuming a male, Western, (upper) middle-class, White prerogative of mobility, autonomy, and freedom ensued.

These changes in geopolitical thinking cannot be separated from the changes in the global media landscape in the late 1980s and early 1990s. Deregulation of public radio and television in Europe, for instance, led the way for new "borderless" English-language satellite and cable networks such as Sky TV. These provided international linkages beyond what national television and radio had done before. Transmitting over satellite, MTV not only became a symbol of this new era; it arguably also had geopolitical ambitions, announced by its influential slogan: "One World, One Image, One Channel MTV." Carla Freccero, for instance, argues that MTV became a loudspeaker for a particular form of Western popular culture, propagated "under the veil of democracy" (1992, 165; see also Kaplan 1987 and Mitić 2015). The music industry soon became one of the key conveyors of globalization, with "borderless" peer-to-peer (P2P) music popularized by Napster in 1999. By the time Madonna embarked on the Blond Ambition tour and *Truth or Dare* was made, critical theory engaged full-on with gendered and ethnic assumptions of stardom, mediated mega-fame, and the challenge to "natural" boundaries between sex and gender in relation to discursively, culturally, or socially constituted gender (e.g., Negra 2001; Butler 1990, 1993).

Madonna's *Truth or Dare* as a Document of Its Time

A number of political, scholarly, and pop culture movements thus conjoined at the pivotal moment at the end of the 1980s and early 1990s. There are several explanatory paradigms that I seek to integrate in this chapter. The overarching one is the discourse of globalization, including the institutionalizing of global media outlets (transnational corporations as well as smaller DIY venues) and discourses of free, open, and digital democratic information sharing. The mainstreaming of a "world" popular youth culture aesthetics and set of practices, exemplified among other venues by MTV – and Madonna's presence in MTV's rotation – is key in this instance. Indeed, the "free movement" of popular culture was facilitated through the deregulated public sector media and new private sector cable and satellite television phenomena, such as Sky, which needed a constant supply of audio-visual moving image material, pop videos and filmed stage concerts among them. A related paradigm, with particular relevance to how *Truth or Dare* has been received by a generation of scholars and critics, is the radical and transformative gender and identity politics movement of the early 1990s, when burgeoning alliances and simmering conflicts between LGBTQ rights, third wave feminism, and racial and ethnic tensions came into focus, of which Madonna's ongoing HIV/AIDS advocacy work was a significant aspect. The HIV/AIDS epidemic, moreover, was also the first disease of globalization, a viral epidemic with geopolitical implications (Treichler 1999; Colvin 2011).

The Madonna Megastar Phenomenon, *Truth or Dare*, and the Global Concert Tour

At this transformative moment of the late 1980s and early 1990s, there was one megastar whose productions and performances linked all of these movements: globalization and the new geopolitics; a transforming media landscape; and gender and queer identity politics including HIV/AIDS advocacy. That person, or, perhaps better, persona, was Madonna. These three paradigms and discourses – the end of the Cold War and the start of globalization; global media networks and the digital information society; and gender and racial politics – run through *Truth or Dare* in numerous ways that allow one to make the argument for this rockumentary as both an artefact of geopolitical trends at the time and as a document imbued with political agency in service of a globalization ideology.

Blond Ambition is part of the stadium concert tour phenomenon, which emerged in the early 1980s and held prominence well into the 1990s. The stadium concert tour phenomenon exemplifies globalization and a new post-Cold War geopolitical world order. Heralding the seemingly free movement of rock stars around the world, concert tours were staged in ways that looked and sounded strikingly similar – indeed were designed precisely to do that – regardless of location. These concerts were also frequently recorded and filmed for a loyal fan base who could subsequently enjoy the concert phenomenon at home on vinyl, CD, Laserdisc and VHS platforms. These stadium concerts drew massive live audiences for the first time in the history of pop and rock, including loyal fans traveling from location to location.

Pop and rock performances are not always linked to geopolitics, but at this moment in time several certainly were. The example of the collective Band Aid's 1984 charity recording *Do They Know It's Christmas?* is illustrative. Collecting funds for famine relief in Ethiopia, while discursively maintaining a neo-colonial power hierarchy with the lyrics dismissively othering the intended recipients: "Do they know it's Christmas time at all?" Band Aid promoted a uniform world order of Western Christianity for sub-Saharan Africa. As a collective of recognized pop stars, the impact of Band Aid subsequently spawned the two-continent massive Live Aid concert in the summer of 1985, held at Wembley Stadium in London and the John F. Kennedy Stadium in Philadelphia. The Live Aid concerts – essentially a live, televized rockumentary – linked two continents through satellite technology with a globalization ethos; namely, to mitigate world hunger, caused not insignificantly by the impact of an old colonial world order. These concerts raised massive awareness of the lingering effects of an old geopolitical world order, while the new world order was nevertheless propagated through global dissemination of popular culture.

Madonna was on the bill for Live Aid, performing in Philadelphia in 1985, placing her in front of her largest audience to date. Post-Live Aid, no other woman performer consistently filled stadiums around the world during the 1980s and 1990s to the extent of Madonna. A conservative estimate puts the total number of tickets sold worldwide for the Blond Ambition Tour at 1,000,000.[1] Similarly, no other solo woman performer spearheaded anything quite like the rockumentary *Truth or Dare*. While *Truth or Dare* is aesthetically distinctive from the male-dominated rockumentaries that came before, it is complemented by at least five other films directly related to the Blond Ambition World Tour: four concert films were officially released, as well as the rockumentary *Strike a Pose* (Ester Gould and Reijer Zwaan, The Netherlands/Belgium, 2016), which focuses on the Blond Ambition dancers.[2]

Part concert film, part behind-the-scenes rockumentary, *Truth or Dare* covers the singer's Blond Ambition World Tour, which brought Madonna, her musicians, performers, and entourage to Japan, Canada, the United States, and eight European countries between April and August 1990. *Truth or Dare* was a success with critics and audiences, grossing nearly $30 million upon its worldwide release, with about half of that sum coming from international sales (Box Office Mojo). In the USA, the film remains in the top twenty grosses of all documentaries. Upon the twenty-fifth anniversary of its release, the Museum of Modern Art in New York City staged a commemorative screening, demonstrating its significance for critics and audiences; it remains a gay, lesbian, and queer cult film, as demonstrated by the Los Angeles LGBT Outfest screening the film in 2015.

The impact of the Blond Ambition tour on global popular culture still resonates. For instance, Drew Mackie wrote in a celebratory article in *People* magazine in 2015, on the occasion of the tour's twenty-fifth anniversary, that Madonna's "Blond Ambition changed the pop-culture landscape" and "reinvented the concert tour" by making it a performance and theatrical event, through five distinct acts, which paid attention and homage to current and past trends in fashion, art, cinema, and choreography (Mackie 2015). Similarly, the BBC credited the tour with "invent[ing] the modern, multimedia pop spectacle" (Savage 2015). Madonna herself directed and choreographed most aspects of the concert performance, which included a range of intermedial and intertextual references, imbued with nods to pornographic imagery, film history (from German Expressionism – Fritz Lang's *Metropolis* (Germany, 1927), to Broadway backstage films such as Mervyn LeRoy's *Gold Diggers of 1933* (USA, 1933), to films about showbusiness – especially as a man's world – including Bob Fosse's 1972 *Cabaret* (USA, 1972) and Richard Attenborough's *A Chorus Line* (USA, 1985)); to burlesque and vaudeville, to fashion photography, contemporary dance (Vogueing and breakdancing) and religious performances (e.g., the Catholic Mass) with both Christian and mystical iconography. Its postmodern intertextuality also demonstrates a stark break from rockumentaries past, with the exception perhaps of Talking Heads' *Stop Making Sense* (Jonathan Demme, USA, 1984).

Blond Ambition's rich set of aesthetic intertexts were not 'global' in the sense of representing multiple regions of the world, but they certainly presented Madonna as a figure whose registers engaged numerous international influences, produced to appeal to a range of audiences in multiple countries, yet adhering to fundamentals of globalization as the references and intertexts were primarily Western. Madonna's attention to a global media language is thus not trivial. Indeed, Madonna's mediated persona and the ways in which she as an artist, creative director, and businesswoman manages media relations is well-known (O'Brien 2007, 162–69). This careful attention to the power of mediated spectacle on an international scale has produced both a global brand – "Madonna" – as well as a deep commitment to inter-media references executed on the diegetic level in a range of her productions. Blond Ambition and *Truth or Dare* are early examples of impactful global media aesthetics at this pivotal historical moment. These attributes also have geopolitical contexts.

The New Globalization Intimacy and Personified Geopolitics

Directed by twenty-six-year-old Alek Keshishian, *Madonna: Truth or Dare* was the director's first major production. It intermixes black-and-white "behind-the-scenes" faux-*cinéma vérité* footage with color shots of the concert performances. The choice of monochrome color scheme signals originality and authenticity, through the intertext of low-budget hand-held 16mm, newsreel, and *cinéma vérité* footage, shot with one microphone and one camera. The aesthetics of *cinéma vérité* – a central rockumentary trope as well as one of unadorned reportage – would have been recognized by the early 1990s as a mediated and constructed way to signal accuracy, impartiality, and authenticity. Madonna, "the person," is captured in black-and-white, often speaking directly to the camera, in voice-over, or directing the camera movement or the scenes.

The monochromatic, one camera and one microphone approach is offset against the complex camerawork in color with multiple audio uptakes used to capture the choreographed and rehearsed on-stage spectacle. As E. Deirdre Pribram notes, the film addresses "cultural dichotomies between ... onstage and offstage, public and private, reality and appearance, or truth and arti-

7.1 Madonna and staged *cinéma vérité* in *Truth or Dare* (1991).

fice" (1993, 189). *Truth or Dare*, however, gives the impression that the artist is almost as much in full control backstage as "the persona" featured in the concert scenes. As important as the choreography and spectacle are, the lyrical content of Madonna's songs, addressing female experience, female sexuality, and feminist empowerment, are also central to the performance and the rockumentary. While these lyrics no doubt come from the position of a straight, White subjectivity – performed against a backdrop of queer dancers who are People of Color – songs such as "Like a Prayer," "Express Yourself," and "Papa Don't Preach" express female subjectivity in a manner not seen in rockumentaries, or in much of popular music, before. Much like geopolitics, popular music was also largely gendered masculine.

The dual rockumentary aesthetic – one construed as "authentic" in black-and-white; the other "performance" in color – speaks on two levels to Madonna's control of the means of production and the spectacle: on one level the film implies she has "authorized" unlimited access to her life on tour as if through a journalistic reportage; on the other, she controls the stage itself. With twenty-five years' hindsight, Keshishian describes the process as, for him, on the one hand, having "technically complete independence" yet always knowing that Madonna was funding the film, thereby exercising control (Coscarelli 2016). Keshishian thereby acknowledges that the supposedly private and intimate behind-the-scenes moments are authorized to appear as if they were directed and planned by Madonna nearly to the same level as the stage show it captured. For instance, her then-partner Warren Beatty remarks directly on the staged aspects of the documentary: "she doesn't want to live off-camera." Indeed, Madonna loved the rough-cut, says Keshishian: "She was laughing at the right moments . . . , thrilled with it the first time she saw it. . . . she didn't ask me to lose anything. She only wanted to keep more. I think it captured the roller coaster that she had been on; that had been her goal" (Coscarelli 2016).

The roller coaster portrayed in the film is certainly one of intense and physically demanding on-stage and off-stage labor, as Madonna, her singers, dancers, and musicians perform their sets in varied venues in multiple countries and on a tight schedule. Another aspect of the "roller coaster" Keshishian references is the fact that the both the on-stage performance and the backstage interactions elicited intense emotions among all those involved. For Madonna, that involved breaking up with one romantic partner and identifying a new one, while relating nearly 24-7 to a diverse group of individuals in her entourage. As the dancers articulate in *Strike a Pose* two decades later, the setup and the near-constant camera attention was grueling (three dancers sued for violation of privacy). This roller coaster was also a global tour, spanning Asia, Europe, and North America. For many involved in the production, this would have been their first international experience.

In its emphasis on international travel and global audiences, *Truth or Dare* can be productively positioned in relation to feminist international relations and popular geopolitics, fields of academic study that emerged in the 1990s at the same time as discourses of globalization. A range of scholars have charted the field of popular geopolitics, mobilizing especially Hollywood blockbusters or European art cinema for the inquiry (see for example Dodds 2007; 2008; 2014). But if we move beyond this framework to also include gender components, the paradigm of popular geopolitics must extend beyond what Dodds calls "national security cinema" (2008, 481), such as Ridley Scott's *Black Hawk Down* (USA, 2001) or *Collateral Damage* (Andrew Davis, USA, 2002).

Instead, scholars such as Joanne Sharpe and J. Ann Tickner use post-1989 paradigms to query the field of International Relations' indebtedness to military-security studies and political "neorealism and neoliberalism, approaches that share rationalistic methodologies and assumptions about the state of the international system" (Tickner 2001, 3). In the traditional "big politics" International Relations frameworks, there would be no room to situate the performer Madonna, the Blond Ambition tour, or *Truth or Dare*, as a set of geopolitical agents or documents. Similarly, when the fields of communications and film and media studies have addressed the intersections between geopolitics and popular culture, the focus has tended to remain on "war and terrorism" (e.g. Downing 2013). But when geopolitics, especially in relation to theories of globalization, is expanded beyond a narrow set of approaches to include critical inquiries into mediated and gendered components, a range of new interpretive paradigms open up.

Madonna: The Center Stage Stateswoman

Blond Ambition and *Truth or Dare* are products of an era when, for the first time, the portrayal of a woman being in control of the modes and mechanisms of production could be seen across the world. *Truth or Dare*, among other things, can thereby be seen as an extension of the tour, bringing it to an even wider global audience where the performers did not or could not travel. This extended Madonna's geopolitical reach. These media products stand in sharp contrast to most depictions of women in Cold War popular and cinematic geopolitics, where women are in the minority and marginalized as eye candy, captive innocents, tantalizing virgins, maternal and sage goddesses, or eroticized anti-heroines, leading the military-industrial complex astray. James Bond films, action films such as *Top Gun* (Tony Scott, USA, 1986), or classic Cold War science fiction films from *Forbidden Planet* (Fred M. Wilcox, USA, 1956) to *Star Wars* (George Lucas, USA, 1977) adhere to this depiction of women. As intertexts, Blond Ambition and *Truth or Dare* together provide one of the first times that a certain image of women's power can be, literally, center stage.

Blond Ambition and *Truth or Dare* mobilize, moreover, a complex and gendered negotiation of the articulation of power, including S & M aesthetics and practices, or relationships wherein the woman in charge does not appear as benevolent or altruistic. This kind of powerful woman of wealth, prestige, influence, and pop-cultural megawattage, and captivating persona – the one on stage – had not been seen on this scale or in a global context before. Madonna in this articulation becomes a states(wo)man.

Madonna's concert performance conformed in many ways to Western patriarchal expectations of what a woman in power would stereotypically look like, meaning that the only way to demonstrate power would be to "perform" it. The portrayal of the performer on stage in *Truth or Dare* and in her behind-the-scenes statements enacts a moment in time when US world domination was in full force through globalization. The USSR was dismantled as the film was being shot. The Eastern Bloc and the Berlin Wall were disappearing into memory as geopolitical constructs, no longer there to uphold the power balance. It was in this vacuum that Madonna swept in to proclaim – for a moment – a new world order where a (albeit straight, White) woman literally took center stage.

In the geopolitical vacuum of the immediate post-Cold War era, Madonna at the time can be construed as a states(wo)man advocating for freedom of expression, secular liberalism, and political autonomy, all of which were well-known aspects of US foreign policy at the time. She was a woman in full control of her show – directing and leading a large group of people – being "the boss" – while also simulating the performance of sexual acts, such as masturbating on stage, or praying and performing the sacrament of reconciliation, an encounter between confessant and priest. The concert choreography thus rests on a continuous set of juxtapositions of realms that span private and public and personal and political, which are also central to *Truth or Dare*. This set of complexities, as Jennifer L. Fluri argues, relate to the work of feminist scholars who "effectively identify the interrelationship between the personal and the geopolitical" as well as the concept of "intimate geopolitics [which] seeks to disrupt the customary divisions between global/local, familial/state, and personal/political by showing how they are mutually constituted, affected, and integrated" (2017: 132; 143). The depiction of a woman calling the shots on-stage and off-stage should be recognized for its radical representation at the time, also because it integrates the performance of intimacy, on-stage and off.

Madonna's privilege should not be disassociated from being White and Western. Bleached blonde and light-skinned, Madonna performs on-stage and in the rockumentary against a cast of BIPOC dancers and singers, whose races, ethnicities, and nationalities offset the image of her Western Whiteness. At the same time, Madonna self-identifies as a proud Italian-American, for whom Italy is an imaginary homeland. For most of this crew, traveling to Japan,

Europe, and multiple locations in North America is presented as their first opportunity to represent not only American culture abroad, but also to project an alternative to contemporary mainstream US ideology, namely one of gay male bodies and queer identities. Their excitement is palpable, as this period also coincides with the acceleration of mass-tourism by Westerners. In addition, for audiences outside of the US, including in Japan, the cast's multiracial and multiethnic composition signaled Madonna's global ambassadorship of bringing the US notion of the multicultural melting pot of teamwork, camaraderie, and showbusiness to the wider world.

This performance of multicultural unity is part of the geopolitical register of globalization, especially in its promotion of "Western-centered definitions of human rights and democracy" (Tickner 2001, 7) against its histories of suppression, repression, violence, and persecution. A number of scholars have discussed the racial and ethnic stereotypes of *Truth or Dare*, including identifying the dynamic of "mistress/slave" that informs it (Jack Waters 1992: 73). bell hooks' incisive criticism of *Truth or Dare* in the stringently titled essay "Madonna: Plantation Mistress or Soul Sister?" is to the point: "I was angered by her visual representation of her domination over not white men (certainly not Warren Beatty or Alek Keshishian), but people of color and white working-class women," demonstrating that Madonna "can only think of exerting power along very traditional, white supremacist, capitalistic, patriarchal lines" (1992,162). hooks' analysis is accurate; it also demonstrates that theories of globalization and proclamations about "the end of history" at the end of the Cold War do not necessarily address the kind of intertwined power dynamics of sexuality, race, identity, and power that also inform the representation and exertion of geopolitical power.

The Blond Ambition tour was politically controversial, with the expression of female and queer sexuality a geopolitical point of contention. For instance, the tour set itself up against a powerful foe: the global Catholic Church and the Pope. The official Vatican paper *L'Osservatore Romano* condemned the show as sinful and requested it to be banned (see Mackie 2015). Madonna indeed cancelled two of the three Rome shows. These controversies are mobilized in *Truth or Dare*, becoming part of the geopolitical plot that undergirds it. Madonna's well-known on-camera speech in response to the Vatican's proclamation is a political statement worthy of American ideology about democracy and art: "My show is not a conventional rock show but a theatrical presentation of my music. And, like theater it asks questions, provokes thought and takes you on an emotional journey. Portraying good and bad, light and dark, joy and sorrow, redemption and salvation. I do not endorse a way of life but describe one, and the audience is left to make its own decisions and judgments. This is what I consider freedom of speech, freedom of expression and freedom of thought." In these instances, it becomes clear that the tour and the rockumentary not only reflect but also shape discourses of globalization.

Madonna the stateswoman – the person and the persona – enacts a US version of a globalized world order following the end of the Cold War, as one of freedom of movement across countries with the privilege of artistic expression. At other points, Madonna states that she is interested in being both political and provocative. For instance, an extended sequence shot in Canada explicitly challenges the local authorities' demand that Madonna modify a masturbation scene to avoid charges of public indecency. Refusing to back down, Madonna makes a geopolitical comment in *Truth or Dare* about "the fascist state of Toronto" and performs the set unchanged.

Global Showbusiness and Geopolitics of the HIV/AIDS Epidemic

Part of Madonna's political legacy lies in her involvement with HIV/AIDS activism. For example, an insert into the album *Like A Prayer* (1989) presents a call to action to practice safe sex and recognize the dangers of HIV/AIDS. In *Truth or Dare*, she is presented as a global public health ambassador for HIV/AIDS advocacy, dedicating the last Blond Ambition show in New York City to HIV/AIDS support, in memory of artist Keith Haring, who had died earlier that year. Just a few years later, through the publication of her lavishly illustrated photo book *Sex* (1992), Madonna continued to explore mediated, performed, and globally-disseminated modes of sexuality.

The geopolitical implications of the HIV/AIDS epidemic are a mostly unstated backdrop in *Truth or Dare*. Global public recognition of the disease as an epidemic was being enacted along numerous fronts at the time with the medical, biological, and public health aspects only some of the factors, while official US governmental discourse under George H. W. Bush still largely ignored it. As Paula A. Treichler argues in *How to Have Theory in an Epidemic: Cultural Chronicles of AIDS*, the discursive constitution of the phenomenon and the questions – often stereotyped according to sexuality, class, and race – raised by Western media portrayal made it impossible not to recognize that by "the end of the 1980s, the AIDS epidemic had been invested with an abundance of meanings and metaphors" (1999, 1). *Truth or Dare* intervenes in this context of widely varying understandings of the origin, spread, effects, and long-term ramifications of the disease for individuals and communities. In the discipline of global health, the geographical and geopolitical aspects of the disease are significant. Christopher J. Colvin argues, for instance, that "HIV/AIDS has always been one of the most thoroughly global of diseases. From its still hazily understood emergence as a zoonotic infection in colonial and post-colonial West and Central Africa and the early moral panics over a globe-trotting 'Patient Zero' to the current situation of global pandemic, it has always been intimately bound up in globalized structures and processes" (2011, 1). Yet, these globalized frameworks are rarely explicitly addressed in *Truth or Dare*, which foregrounds one specific locale in its direct address of HIV: New York City.

Truth or Dare foregrounds an emphasis on the choreography of vogueing, with the film referencing that several of the dancers are members of the queer community of the late 1980s in New York City, a community that was ravaged by HIV/AIDS. In addition, *Truth or Dare* includes footage from a rally and march in support of gay rights, filmed in New York City. A range of connections also exist between *Truth or Dare* and Jennie Livingston's queer classic *Paris is Burning* (USA, 1990) about the New York City queer scene of cross-dressing, balls, and vogueing.

While a burlesque of varied gender roles and sexual practices are performed on stage, attention to queer presence is also enacted in *cinéma vérité* style backstage in *Truth or Dare*. These sequences engage in the film's problematic and contradictory production of "authenticity": the film celebrates gay and queer identities and that performing a range of gendered and sexual behaviors on-stage and off-stage is entirely acceptable. These cinematic, sexual, gendered, and political power relations between how black and brown bodies are portrayed in *Truth or Dare* relate closely to a recent revisionist documentary that seeks to address the means of production of that film, especially in relation to its HIV/AIDS advocacy: Gould and Zwaan's *Strike a Pose*.

Repurposing scenes and cinematic strategies from *Truth or Dare*, the rockumentary *Strike a Pose* tells the little-known story of the Blond Ambition Tour dancers. One of the most interesting strategies is the inversion of its color scheme, with the scenes from the Blond Ambition tour conveyed in black-and-white and the contemporary interviews and scenes in color. *Strike a Pose* crosscuts several narratives, which are accentuated by the color strategies. First, it shows that *Truth or Dare*, despite its claims to embrace a range of sexual identities and praise of gendered empowerment, nevertheless elided the actual narratives of the dancers; especially that three of them were HIV positive and that none revealed this to Madonna, foregrounding the profound stigma associated with the disease at the time, despite Madonna's HIV/AIDS advocacy.

Second, *Strike a Pose* argues that the dancers themselves had little control over their own backstage portrayal – and express that they perceived they were not empowered to tell their own stories. Three of them ended up suing Madonna for breach of privacy. *Strike a Pose*, then, delineates the difference between having power and empowering others, though even this is complex: while documentary ethics may be challenged by some of the film's narrative strategies and choices, *Truth or Dare*, as delineated in the letters read by queer fans in *Strike a Pose*, nevertheless empowered a generation of female, queer, and male audiences and served a political purpose, especially for HIV/AIDS advocacy.

7.2 Performing bodies: Carlton Wilborn and Luis Xtravaganza Camacho with Madonna in *Strike a Pose* (2016).

It is important to note that in addition to its queer politics, *Truth or Dare* also posits two versions of White femininity against one another, and that these assumptions relate in inverse ways to the film's professed support for HIV/AIDS advocacy. Anal rape is part of this complexity. In a compelling sequence of *Truth or Dare*, the stylist Sharon Gault, calling herself "mama makeup" in the rockumentary, describes, casually, how she wakes up one morning bleeding out of her anus, assuming that she has been drugged and anally raped by a man or group of men she met in a bar. She retells this event on camera as if it were nothing. Madonna laughs off the report, attributing it to Gault's attention-seeking. Chuckling, as if a stylist has overstepped her boundaries – and as if her White womanhood has been compromised – Madonna appears to blame the victim. Nearly thirty years after its release and in the wake of the #MeToo movement, the scene is even more fraught. Sequences such as these foreground the complexity of feminist spectacle(s), by which the "feminist in charge" – backstage in supposedly black-and-white "authenticity" – can also be a patriarch, or, rather, oblivious to the multiplicity of gendered and sexualized power positions. Madonna backstage (filmed in black-and-white), appears to be only partially aware of the power she herself holds, and that "Blond Ambition" is possible only if you are powerful and control the means of production.

Yet *Truth or Dare* is also a global HIV/AIDS epidemic advocacy film and a queer and gay rights film. It is one of the first rockumentaries to show camaraderie, friendship, and a community of gay men who are dedicated professionals and skilled experts in what they do. Similarly, *Truth or Dare* emphasizes that the notion of "family" is a construct, revisited in the final act of the concert that also concludes the film. As Lucas Hilderbrand argues in his book about *Paris is Burning*: "Seeming to appropriate the language of the [queer NYC] ball scene, the Blond Ambition tour's finale, 'Keep It Together'/'Family Affair' staged the concept of an alternative queer and interracial family to a broad audience, and Madonna refers to herself as a 'mother' to her dancers" (2013, 97).

The global HIV/AIDS epidemic is a background to this depiction. New York City, the queer scene of vogueing and balls, and the 1990 Pride Parade captured on screen is one set of locales in which acceptance of queer identities and homosexuality would be possible as part of the globalization rhetoric of Western democracy and freedom of expression, while at the same time, mainstream US ideology exercised rampant homophobia and suppression of queer politics, at home and abroad. This complexity lies at the heart of *Truth or Dare*. Indeed, as Jeremy Kinser writes in *Queerty* at the time of the twenty-fifth anniversary of *Truth or Dare*: "in the many decades since gay stories have been honestly depicted on the big screen, there are still just a handful of films that can be thought of as transformative viewing experiences" (2015). Through Madonna's Blond Ambition global tour and the rockumentary about it, HIV/AIDS activism through popular and mediated cultures became a geopolitical reality.

Madonna, then, as a complex and contradictory geopolitical agent, a pop culture persona, and international media brand, raises salient issues about the importance of analyzing cultures of globalization and soft power as a means of achieving the "New World Order" so often imagined at the time of the fall of the Iron Curtain. Moreover, her body of work, and the global reach of *Truth or Dare*, speaks to the way in which questions of gender, so often marginalized in the study of geopolitics, take a central role in terms of popular culture, media representation, and the contested roles that the sexualities of women and queer men play in discourses of "freedom" propagated by the new American imperialism that followed the end of the Cold War. The dichotomies and contradictions that lie at the heart of the rockumentaries *Truth or Dare* and *Strike a Pose* demonstrate – because of their echoes in the contemporary political landscape – that globalization theory's discourses of "freedom," whether about gender or geopolitics, are still sites of contestation today.

Notes

1. Wikipedia's entry for Blond Ambition Tour only lists 781,000 tickets, omitting sales for all Japanese venues as well as for several in Europe.
2. Wikipedia's entry for *Blond Ambition World Tour Live* includes information about the release. *Blond Ambition World Tour Live* (1990) features footage from Nice, France, on the last day of the tour. It was released by Pioneer Artists on LaserDisc and earned Madonna her first Grammy in 1992; the same footage was used by HBO for the television program *Madonna: Live! Blond Ambition World Tour 90*. Then there is the *Blond Ambition Japan Tour 90* by Sire Records and Warner Pioneer; and *Blond Ambition Tour 1990* (unauthorized), released in Germany by Falcon Neue Medien.

References

Box Office Mojo. n.d. "Madonna: Truth or Dare." (last accessed December 1 2019.)
Butler, Judith. 1990. *Gender Trouble: Feminism and the Subversion of Identity*. London: Routledge.
Butler, Judith. 1993. *Bodies That Matter. On the Discursive Limits of 'Sex'*. London: Routledge.
Colvin, Christopher J. 2011. "HIV/AIDS, Chronic Diseases and Globalisation." *Globalization and Health* 7(31): 1–6.
Coscarelli, Joe. 2016. "After 25 Years, How Well Has Madonna's 'Truth or Dare' Aged?" *The New York Times*. < https://www.nytimes.com/2016/08/26/arts/music/madonna-truth-or-dare-alek-keshishian.html> (last accessed 1 December, 2020).
Dodds, Klaus. 2007. *Geopolitics: A Very Short Introduction*. Oxford: Oxford University Press.
Dodds, Klaus. 2008. "'Have You Seen Any Good Films Lately?' Geopolitics, International Relations, and Film." *Geography Compass* 2(2): 476–93.
Dodds, Klaus. 2014. *Global Geopolitics: A Critical Introduction*. London: Routledge.
Downing, John D. H. 2013. "'Geopolitics' and 'the Popular': An Exploration." *Popular Communication: The International Journal of Media and Culture* 11(1): 7–16.
Dyer, Richard. 1997. *White: Essays on Race and Culture*. London: Routledge.
Fluri, Jennifer L. 2017. "Feminist Political and Geography and Geopolitics." In *Feminist Spaces: Gender and Geography in a Global Context*, eds Ann M. Oberhauser, Jennifer L. Fluri, Sharlene Mollett, and Risa Whitson. London: Routledge. 131–52.
Freccero, Carla. 1992. "Our Lady of MTV: Madonna's 'Like a Prayer'." *boundary 2 – Feminism and Postmodernism* 19(2): 163–83.
Fukuyama, Francis. 1989. "The End of History." *National Interest* supplement, Summer.
Fukuyama, Francis. 1992. *The End of History and the Last Man*. New York: Free Press.
Hilderbrand, Lucas. 2013. *"'Paris is Burning': A Queer Film Classic*. Montréal: Pulp Arsenal Press.
hooks, bell. 1992. *Black Looks: Race and Representation*. Boston: South End Press.
Kaplan, E. Ann. 1987. *Rocking Around the Clock: Music Television, Postmodernism, and Consumer Culture*. New York: Methuen.
Kinser, Jeremy. 2015. "Madonna's 'Truth or Dare' Changed a Generation of Gay People; the Director takes us Behind uhe Scenes." In *Queerty*, July 11. < https://www.queerty.com/madonnas-truth-or-dare-changed-a-generation-of-gay-people-the-director-take-us-behind-the-scenes-20150711> (last accessed 1 December, 2020).

Mackie, Drew. 2015. "25 Reasons Madonna's Blond Ambition Tour Still Rules, 25 Years Later." *People Magazine*, April 13. <https://people.com/celebrity/madonnas-blond-ambition-tour-25-years-later/> (last accessed 1 December, 2020).

Madonna. 1992. *Sex*. New York: Ediciones.

Mitić, Katarina. 2015. "Madonna: Feminist or Antifeminist? Domination of Sex in her Music Videos and Live Performances from the 20th Century to the Present Day" *AM Journal of Art and Media Studies* 8: 68–72.

Negra, Diane. 2001. *Off-White Hollywood: American Culture and Ethnic Female Stardom*. London: Routledge.

O'Brien, Lucy. 2007. *Madonna: Like an Icon – The Definitive Biography*. London: Bantham.

Ó Tuathail, Gearóid. 1996. *Critical Geopolitics: The Politics of Writing Global Space*. London: Routledge.

Pribram, E. Deirdre. 1993. "Seduction, Control, & the Search for Authenticity: Madonna's *Truth or Dare*." In *The Madonna Connection: Representational Politics, Subcultural Identities, and Cultural Theory*, ed. Cathy Schwichtenberg. Boulder: Westview Press: 189–212.

Savage, Mark. 2015. "Madonna Returns to Scene of Brits Fall." BBC News. <https://www.bbc.co.uk/news/entertainment-arts-34979759#:~:text=Madonna%20has%20put%20the%20painful,by%20a%20malfunctioning%20matador%20cape> (last accessed 1 December, 2020).

Sharpe, Joanne. 2000. "Reconfiguring Geopolitics. The *Reader's Digest* and Popular Geographies of Danger at the End of the Cold War." In *Geopolitical Traditions: Critical Histories of a Century of Geopolitical Thought*, eds David Atkinson and Klaus Dodds. London: Routledge. 332–52.

Tickner, J. Ann. 2001. *Gendering World Politics. Issues and Approaches in the Post-Cold War Era*. New York: Columbia University Press.

Tickner, J. Ann. 2014. *A Feminist Voyage Through International Relations*. Oxford: Oxford University Press.

Treichler, Paula A. 1991. *How to Have Theory in an Epidemic: Cultural Chronicles of AIDS*. Durham, NC: Duke University Press.

Wikipedia. n.d. *Blond Ambition World Tour*. < https://en.wikipedia.org/wiki/Blond_Ambition_World_Tour> (last accessed 1 December, 2020).

Wikipedia n.d. *Blond Ambition World Tour Live*. < https://en.wikipedia.org/wiki/Blond_Ambition_World_Tour_Live> (last accessed 1 December, 2020).

Wikipedia. n.d. *List of Highest-grossing Concert Tours*. < https://en.wikipedia.org/wiki/List_of_highest-grossing_concert_tours> (last accessed 1 December, 2020).

8. THE FREEDOM TO SPEAK: THE DIXIE CHICKS, OBSERVATIONAL DOCUMENTARY, AND *SHUT UP & SING*

Heather McIntosh

The Dixie Chicks achieved new career heights with their album *Home*. Propelled by hit songs such as "Travelin' Soldier" and "Landslide," the album topped the Billboard 200 and the Top Country music charts (RIAA n.p.). The female country trio's album earned three-times multiplatinum status within three months of its August 2002 release. Building on this success, the group's "Top of the World" tour opened in Europe, just as global tensions arose around the United States' possible invasion of Iraq in March 2003.

The Dixie Chicks started their tour at the London venue Shepherd's Bush Empire. After singing "Travelin' Soldier," a song about a girl who waited for a Vietnam War soldier who never returned, lead singer Natalie Maines bantered with the audience. According to a concert review in British newspaper *The Guardian*, Maines said, "Just so you know, we're ashamed the president of the United States is from Texas" (Clarke 2003, n.p.). Reviewer Betty Clarke followed the quote with, "It [the comment] gets the audience cheering –at a time when country stars are rushing to release pro-war anthems, this is practically punk rock" (Clarke 2003, n.p.).

Several days later The Associated Press put the review on its wire service, distributing the quote globally and inciting a wave of backlash against The Dixie Chicks. Media pundits and bloggers criticized Maines' remarks. Former fans protested the group's concerts. Radio stations' publicity stunts encouraged former fans to trash the trio's CDs; one radio station even steamrolled them. Fans threatened radio station boycotts if DJs played the group's music.

Cumulus Media even instituted a ban of the group's music on its country stations' playlists. In all, country music fans felt betrayed by The Dixie Chicks.

But The Dixie Chicks also felt betrayed by country music. The trio faced both personal and professional repercussions from the disproportionate reactions to Maines' statements. Critics questioned the trio's patriotism, their right to free speech, their support of soldiers, their places as artists, their roles in country music, and even their statuses as "proper" women. Maines apologized for her remarks, attempting further clarification, but those comments only seemed to incite further backlash. Instead of backing down, however, The Dixie Chicks confronted the situation and reinvented themselves as both free speech advocates and music artists.

Barbara Kopple and Cecilia Peck's *Shut Up & Sing* (USA, 2006) picks up the group's story during these phoenix-rising-from-the-ashes moments. The film appears an unlikely concert documentary. Classic rockumentaries such as *Gimme Shelter* (Albert Maysles, David Maysles, and Charlotte Zwerin, USA, 1970) feature male artists occupying masculine spaces and showcasing masculinity through their on-stage performances and their hypersexual off-stage antics (Plantinga 2014, 339–55). Women in these worlds serve as adornments and sex objects, not active subjects, and they are represented as disrupting the male bonding as so thoroughly spoofed in the mockumentary *This Is Spinal Tap* (Rob Reiner, USA, 1984; Plantinga 2014, 339–55). Classic concert documentaries also avoid politics in favor of performers' lifestyles and their authenticity as artists, as shown through impromptu performances or rehearsal/recording sessions. *Woodstock* (Michael Wadleigh, USA, 1970), for example, incorporates anti-war talking heads, but those voices drown among the cacophony of concert performances and more talking heads in double and triple split screens across the film's three-hour runtime.

Shut Up & Sing also focuses on the questions of artists, their lifestyles, and their authenticity, but it does so in the wake of a publicity crisis during the highly charged political era following the September 11 2001 attacks on the Twin Towers and the subsequent US military actions against Iraq and Afghanistan. During a three-year period from 2003-2006, *Shut Up & Sing* stays in the moment with Maines, Martie Maguire, Emily Robison, and others as they balance career challenges with domestic ones, facing the waves of backlash and even death threats while navigating the musical scene outside the country music genre that had been their home for many years. Similar to other observational documentaries, the film allows intimate access to the singers and their lives, creating the potential for fans to connect with these celebrities in these off-stage moments and struggles.

This chapter analyzes *Shut Up & Sing* as an observational concert documentary within the contexts of Maines' comments and their aftermath through two related themes. The first theme connects celebrity and politics via the way the group's public status forces them to engage the critics and fight to continue their careers. The second theme connects gender stereotyping and country music, which expects more traditional gender roles for women. Overall, this chapter demonstrates how in *Shut Up & Sing* Kopple and Peck use the observational approach to create a space that allows The Dixie Chicks both to challenge and affirm the norms of country music, to mitigate the critics' voices, and to speak freely for themselves during their image crisis and image repair.

Observational Documentary, Concert Films and Celebrity

Concert films, or films that focus on popular music artists, their on-stage performances, and their off-stage lives, often follow the conventions of the observational documentary mode, wherein the director appears to cede control over the filmed events and allow them to unfold without intervention (Nichols 1991, 38). Filmmakers adopting this approach become metaphorical "flies on the wall," and in theory life plays out as it would without the camera present. This approach creates a sense of intimacy with the participants, as it allows the cameras to capture people's experiences and emotions spontaneously, unprompted by the filmmaker but perhaps prompted by extenuating circumstances. The imperfections of these production-driven realities seem to affirm this sense of intimacy: shaky cameras as cinematographers follow participants, muffled sound and voices as multiple people speak near and far from microphones, and longer takes as scenes unfold before the seemingly ignored camera.

Despite assumptions, observational documentary filmmakers still exert control over their productions. Choosing scenarios with built-in climaxes offers a way to ensure a timely end to the production such as the election win (*The War Room*, D. A. Pennebaker and Chris Hegedus, USA, 1993) or the big race (*On the Pole*, Robert Drew, USA, 1960). This format also provides a narrative arc and dramatic tension, which suggests a potential resolution. Filmmakers further exert control in the editing process, where much of these documentaries' stories emerge.

Observational documentary makers frequently turn their cameras to celebrity subjects. Barbara Kopple in particular has made a long career of this practice with films such as *Fallen Champ: The Untold Story of Mike Tyson* (USA, 1993), *Wild Man Blues* (about Woody Allen; USA, 1997), *Running from Crazy* (about Mariel Hemingway; USA, 2013), and *Miss Sharon Jones!* (USA, 2015). While the term "celebrity" might evoke reverence or awe at the perceived popularity, unimagined achievements, and elevated distance from everyday audiences, contemporary celebrities are quite diverse and, thanks to social networking sites such as Twitter and Instagram, seemingly more accessible. This duality of public distance and personal access points to a key idea informing definitions of celebrity: "The contemporary celebrity will usually have emerged from the sports or entertainment industries, they will be highly visible through the media, and their private life will attract greater public interest than their professional life" (Turner 2014, 4–5).

Celebrities struggle to balance their public and private lives. Their public lives are highly managed through multiple vested groups, including the media industry, the publicity industry, and social media, not to mention the celebrities themselves. These public lives require public presentation, or a staged activity designed to garner further publicity and maintain or elevate the celebrity's status. This public presentation allows celebrities to reserve their private self for themselves. This separation of the public and private selves splits the "I" from the "Me." "I," or the veridical self, refers to the private self, while the "Me" refers to the self presented for others to see (Rojek 2001, 39).

Though criticized for being idealistic or naïve about its claims to greater levels of truth (Hall 1991, 237–54; Taylor 2011, 45–60), observational documentary provides a unique venue for balancing the celebrity "I" and "Me." In these documentaries celebrities still manage their presences, but they can do so in more nuanced ways than the mainstream media and other publicity appearances allow. Instead of focusing only on the public self, they can incorporate aspects of their veridical selves – carefully managed aspects, but still aspects that offer glimpses into their "real" selves (Tolson 2001, 444).

Celebrities' publicity stories often feature a rise-and-fall narrative arc; these lend themselves well to the crisis structure guiding some observational documentaries (Redmond 2014, 218–20). These arcs are a common structure in music documentaries, however the fall is not necessarily the end but a new beginning. According to Redmond, "Of course, the rise-and-fall trajectory for the celebrity can also have a further 'act,' one where a resurrection or rebirth takes place, and the celebrity is seen to rise again, having cleaned up their act and learned from past mistakes" (Redmond 2014, 218–20). Music documentaries such as *Searching for Sugar Man* (Malik Bendjelloul, Sweden/UK/Finland, 2012), whose bootleg boosted Rodriguez's career in the unlikely location of South Africa, and *A Band Called Death* (Mark Covino and Jeff Howlett, USA, 2012), whose discovered 1974 demo tape introduced the group to another generation of audiences, show this narrative arc. This loss and reclamation of public image remains a key theme within documentaries about celebrities more generally, and in concert films in particular (Edgar et al. 2013, 18).

This combination of revealing elements of the veridical self, obtaining access behind-the-scenes in celebrities' lives, and riding this narrative arc creates a coded opportunity for revelations of an "authentic" celebrity. While multiple ways exist to classify celebrities, P. David Marshall organizes them according to their origins, such as politics, sports, television, or music. Among these, he develops a category for the "popular music celebrity." Authenticity is central to that category: "At the center of these debates concerning the authentic nature of the music is the popular music performer, how he or she expresses the emotionality of the music and his or her own inner emotions, feelings, and personality and how faithful the performer is to the intentions of the music score are all part of how the individual performer is determined to be authentic" (Marshall 2014, 9–12).

The observational documentary shapes *Shut Up & Sing* and its representation of celebrity through its structure and editing, and its access and authenticity. The crisis structure of a celebrity story and the dramatic climax of that structure inform the film's overall structure. Kopple and Peck join the trio after Maines' on-stage comments ignite a crisis that calls into question the group's reputation, earning potential, and even physical safety. Kopple and Peck's documentary observes their struggles to handle the rejection from country music and to redefine themselves within an industry that expects a certain earning potential and a certain female image. Kopple and Peck manipulate the tensions in *Shut Up & Sing* through editing. Instead of following a linear arc to the climax –a sold-out show in Texas, of course –they intercut across the timeline, mixing events during the three-year filming period. This approach slowly unwinds multiple themes and creates a balance among the facets of these celebrities' lives.

Kopple and Peck also had access to multiple aspects of The Dixie Chicks' lives, both professional and personal, which contributes to the film's building of their authenticity as artists and as country women. The professional aspects include moments such as studio recording sessions, producer meetings, and record label conference calls. These scenes show the group's attempts to maintain their place in the music industry. Supporters step away and venues become challenges to fill in certain geographical areas. Kopple and Peck also show the group's struggles to reinvent themselves musically. Studio sessions showcase their "true" performance abilities, while other sessions showcase how they work through conceptualizing themselves in a new light. An intense conversation with producer Rick Rubin shows part of that struggle. The casual inclusion of Rubin and Chad Smith, Red Hot Chili Peppers drummer, further validates their connections to the music scene and by extension their authenticity as artists. Interestingly enough, male musicians and producers provide this affirmation, not female ones.

Celebrity and Politics

Celebrities such as actors and musicians represent fantasies for audiences. As Rojek explains, "The audience's connection with celebrities, celetoids and celeactors is dominated by imaginary relationships. The physical and cultural remoteness of the object from the spectator means that audience relationships carry a high propensity of fantasy and desire" (2001, 25). These fantasies and desires propel audiences to develop parasocial relationships. Contemporary social networking sites such as Twitter and Instagram allow these audiences to connect with their faves seemingly directly, thus bringing access to the celebrities' supposedly intimate everyday lives and shifting the perceived fantasy toward a more possible documented reality. According to Marwick and Boyd, "Twitter conversations between fans and famous people are public and visible, and involve direct engagement between the famous person and their follower" (2011, 148).

The intrusion of politics and political issues into entertainment, then, serve as rude reminders of the vagaries of the real world within these fantasies. Their intrusion into the relationships between celebrities and their fans evokes an even stronger reaction. Fans frequently get upset when celebrities become "political" in their social media feeds, such as through comments on governmental policies, military movements, or global issues. Celebrities also receive an immense amount of vitriol online. Some attacks address their career choices (and failures), their appearance, and other aspects of their personal lives. Other attacks threaten sexual assault, further physical violence, and even death. This "e-bile," as Emma Jane defines it, forces some celebrities to fear for their mental health and for their safety, and even to close their accounts altogether (2017, 7).

Shut Up & Sing addresses less about the political issues surrounding the war itself and focuses more on the political fallout from The Dixie Chicks speaking up, speaking their minds, and handling the consequences for doing so. The backlash is multisided, swift, and virulent. Kopple and Peck's observational approach in *Shut Up & Sing* creates an immersive world that controls what criticisms reach the trio, how those criticisms reach the trio, and how the trio responds to them. For the most part, criticisms of the group are relegated to areas outside the band's intimate spaces such as their homes, studio rehearsals, and backstage. In particular the criticism appears in archival footage from news sources and former fan interviews. If the criticism reaches the group, they control how they respond.

The film's opening scene illustrates this idea of a managed, safe space within the observational world of *Shut Up & Sing*. The film begins with the group jamming in a studio session. During a break, musician David Grissom reads some scathing comments found online. The comments he reads dismiss the trio, calling them "talented lamebrains" or observing, "I thought their 15 minutes were up a long time ago." Martie Maguire also reads some comments: "I mean, they're not like an important band where you know all their names, like the Beatles" and "The Dixie Chicks suck. They don't know what they're talking about and should shut the fuck up." Raucous laughter accompanies them as they read. This scene allows the group to introduce the comments they want to share, and it allows them to respond in the ways that they see fit. In this case the laughter takes the power out of the comments and reinforces the group's solidarity.

The concert stage becomes another venue for allowing the trio to speak in a way that addresses and controls the criticism. The first footage comes from the Shepherd's Bush Empire concert where Maines utters those infamous words. *The Guardian* review quotes only a portion of what she says, eliminating some key context that ultimately shows how Maines banters with the audience. But *Shut Up & Sing* allows Maines' full comments to be spoken and heard: "Just so you know, we are on the good side with y'all. We do not want this war, this violence, and we are ashamed that the President of the United States is from Texas." While this extended quote might not have prevented the overall backlash as the original quote elicited much speculation as to its meaning (Katz 2008, 142), it may have toned down the virulence of it. A later concert sequence shows the group inviting the negative audience response. Maines encourages people who want to "boo" them for fifteen seconds to get it out of their systems, but the roaring cheers from the crowd drown out any boos.

Shut Up & Sing also focuses extensively on how the group responds to the backlash. In doing so, it gives The Dixie Chicks a safe space to raise their voice and say what they want to say and how they want to say it. One sequence shows a particularly important moment for Maines. First, archival footage reveals an interview of then-President George W. Bush responding to the comments and the fallout. Walking along with the reporter, Bush states, "I mean, the Dixie Chicks are free to speak their mind. They can say what they want to say. And just because – they shouldn't have their feelings hurt just because some people don't wanna buy their records when they speak out. You know, freedom is a two-way street." Situating the comments within archival footage removes them from the safe space created by the observational film. In the film's present moment Maines reads the comments from a sheet: "'They shouldn't have their feelings hurt'? What a dumb fuck." She looks right at the camera with the next line – "You're a dumb fuck" – as if addressing the former President directly. She can express her honest reaction openly within the observational space and without response from her critic. This moment also reveals more of her veridical self, giving a controlled yet intimate look at her inner feelings.

Interestingly, the film skims the more political side of The Dixie Chicks and their responses to the situation and its fallout. Adolphson (2014, 53) argues that the trio engaged in dissent through their *Entertainment Weekly* cover story, for which they posed nude with scathing words written on their bodies, including "Traitors" and "Dixie Sluts." *Shut Up & Sing* represents the *Entertainment Weekly* cover shoot as a publicity event, one that publicist

Cindi Berger strongly questions: "My concern is that the average person isn't gonna get it. They're going to be horrified when they see that." Watson and Burns (2010, 328) note that the group also joined the Vote for Change tour with artists such as Bruce Springsteen and Bonnie Raitt. Advocacy group Moveon.org organized the tour to bring the acts to swing states to encourage higher voter turnouts. Though within the film's timeline, this tour remains unmentioned.

Politics and Gender in Country Music

The film's skimming of The Dixie Chicks' more political engagements might come back to the intersections of country music, politics, and gender identity. As a genre, American country music "has always been associated with pastoral white America and its values, such as independence, patriotism, and religion" (Rossman 2004, 68), but the genre generally avoids commenting on politics and political issues. In a study of country music song lyrics, Van Sickel found that the genre remains largely apolitical, with few songs commenting directly on political issues (2005, 314). Instead, artists' political engagement "comes through the activities and statements of country artists, rather than through the lyrics of their songs" (Van Sickel 2005, 314). In the wake of the events of September 11 2001, however, country music supported then-President George W. Bush and, by extension, his wars on Iraq and later Afghanistan through writing and performing pro-war and pro-troops songs. Patriotism in these instances evoked unquestioned pride (Van Sickel 2005, 318).

Women in country music face gender expectations following more "traditional values." These expectations frequently shape their public images, their fans' responses, and their music and lyrics. According to Pruitt, "In American country music, certain gendered discourses dominate, wherein men are expected to exhibit traits considered masculine, such as aggressiveness, reason, rationality, and protection; women should demonstrate the corresponding feminine attributes: peacefulness, caring, emotion, and vulnerability" (2007, 86). Gender expectations in country music echo gender expectations of other music and media genres. In general, women belong to the domestic sphere. Women stay home, while men ramble, or wander (Poey 2010, 3–4). Women remain dependent on men for their livelihoods and their identities, and their lives gain value and meaning from that dependence. In addition to their domestic obligations and dependencies, women are constructed as sex objects, focusing on revealing clothing, appealing physical attributes, sexual availability, and general sex appeal. Contemporary country music lyrics appear to reinforce both the domestic expectations and the sexual objectifications (Rasmussen and Densley 2017, 199).

If female country artists take stands about political issues in their music, they must do so in ways that avoid offending "the industry's male gatekeepers at record labels, publishing companies, and radio stations, where the sexist double standard is alive and well" (Keel 2004, 131). They also must soft pedal their messages so as to avoid offending fans (Keel 2004, 131). These restrictions, however, fail to prevent female artists from asserting their views and their values. Keel (2004, 131–2) describes a seventeen-year period within country music of women taking feminist stances, promoting values such as independence and strength. Keel includes The Dixie Chicks among these forerunners, as well as Shania Twain, Gretchen Wilson, and Faith Hill (2004, 132).

These constraints fail to stop female country music artists from speaking out about particular issues and injustices. They often speak from specific subject positions, such as through their domestic roles and dependence on men. For example, many songs address cheating and abusive men who mistreat their wives and girlfriends. In Martina McBride's "Independence Day" the female narrator burns down the house with the drunk, abusive husband inside (Poey 2010, 5). Carrie Underwood's "Before He Cheats" offers a less violent version, as she instead destroys his truck with a Louisville slugger before handing him the keys to the annihilated vehicle. The Dixie Chicks themselves also offer a take on the deficient-man genre with "Goodbye Earl" from their earlier album *Fly*. In this song, Earl abuses his wife, putting her in the emergency room, and his wife and her best friend poison and kill him in revenge.

In *Shut Up & Sing*, The Dixie Chicks assert their views from both beyond the domestic sphere and from within the domestic sphere. The backlash against The Dixie Chicks addressed their speaking out against the war, for engaging in a political subject outside their expected gendered place of home. The trio has used music to speak against war before. "Travelin' Soldier," which the group played before Maines' infamous remarks, is an anti-war song. Griffiths (2015, 237) notes, "Some critical studies recognise this song as the only prominent anti-war statement the group made at the level of their artistic repertoire in this period." The song tells the story of a young woman who falls in love with a soldier who is eventually killed in the Vietnam War. The polysemic lyrics framed by the story structure common in country music allow multiple interpretations, and with those some political ambiguity (Griffiths 2015, 237).

Shut Up & Sing shows how The Dixie Chicks use these gendered expectations in ways that both align with country music and subvert it within domestic spaces. Concert films traditionally serve as masculine spaces and platforms for affirming the group's image and lifestyle; Kopple and Peck's film creates a feminine space that affirms this group's image and lifestyle. One brief example is The Dixie Chicks' children. They appear throughout the film, including backstage after shows and in the recording studio. The babies regularly tour with the trio as well.

An extended sequence demonstrates the importance of family and home life for The Dixie Chicks. All three women have husbands and young children, and the film visits each of their homes and introduces each of their husbands. In San Antonio, Texas, Emily talks about the importance of her horses and her family as a grounding point. In her home in Austin, Texas, Martie talks about her husband, Gareth Maguire, serving as the househusband who cares for the children while the band is on tour. These home visits allow insights into these celebrities' domestic and private lives, and these moments are warm, familiar, and almost inviting. Gareth Maguire himself even jokes about not always putting dinner on the table on time.

Another female issue that arises is fertility, arguably an unusual topic for a concert film, but an issue still important for the trio. Both Emily Robison and Martie Maguire experience fertility issues, and each sister undergoes treatment to help them conceive. *Shut Up & Sing* offers an extended sequence wherein Emily struggles with getting pregnant, goes through in vitro fertilization, finally gets pregnant, and eventually goes into labor. Kopple and Peck's camera even joins them in the delivery room as Emily breathes through contractions. Martie talks on camera openly about her struggles, too, even though both she and Emily have twins, which is one-third more likely with in vitro treatments.

The film gives the trio space to joke about their roles as mothers and wives, and to joke in what some might consider an inappropriate way. While sharing their stories about being too tired to wake up and tend to the children, the trio laugh about offering their respective spouses $1,000 or blow jobs to get up with the child asking for a parent. Funnily enough, none of their spouses take them up on the offers.

These sequences both affirm and poke fun at the traditional gender expectations for women in country music. The affirmations come through their representations as mothers and wives, their domestic obligations, and the importance of their homes. The subversions are more subtle. The trio's spouses gain some screen time, but ultimately the men are relegated to the background. The trio assert their sexuality and subject status through joking about blow jobs. They further focus on a contemporary issue plaguing many women, in this case the struggle to become mothers through IVF.

These domestic sequences in *Shut Up & Sing* create a more feminine space within the concert film genre. This space allows The Dixie Chicks to speak from their expected gender roles as country music artists, mothers, and wives. But it also allows them to subvert the expectations as almost demanded by their celebrity in that the spouses tend the home and hearth in their absences for performances and recording sessions. This subversion allows them to push beyond the expectations of country music, part of their mission with the reinvention of their images as artists and their new album.

The observational style, then, adjusts to accommodate artists outside the traditional rock 'n' roll concert film. Instead of locking The Dixie Chicks into those rigid gender roles, it allows them to define their gender roles and assert their sexuality within those roles. For fans and the audience, this style grants seemingly intimate access into their lives, thinking, and joking. It allows them to speak freely. But this access is carefully constructed in that The Dixie Chicks own these feminine, domestic spaces and set the agendas for them. Kopple and Peck make no comments of their own on the film's events. The style allows The Dixie Chicks to continue their critique of country music from within its expectations (Griffiths 2015, 229) while at the same time subverting them and asserting their own issues. And while The Dixie Chicks retain this control, the observational approach allows audiences what appears to be an intimate look at their private lives.

References

Adolphson, Jeremy V. 2014. "'Mad as Hell': Democratic Dissent and the Unpatriotic Backlash on the Dixie Chicks." *Journal of Popular Music Studies* 26(1): 47–63.

Clarke, Betty. 2002. "The Dixie Chicks." *The Guardian*. <https://www.theguardian.com/music/2003/mar/12/artsfeatures.popandrock> (last accessed 30 January, 2019).

Edgar, Robert, Kirsty Fairclough-Isaacs, and Ben Halligan. 2014. "Introduction: Music Seen: The Formats and Functions of the Music Documentary." In *The Music Documentary: Acid Rock to Electropop*, eds Robert Edgar, Kirsty Fairclough-Isaacs, and Ben Halligan. New York and London: Routledge. 1–22.

Griffiths, Christian. 2015. "The Dixie Chicks 2001-2003: The Dissonances of Gender and Genre in War Culture." *Media, War & Conflict* 8(2): 229–43.

Hall, Jeanne. 2014. "'Don't You Ever Just Watch?': American Cinema Verité and *Dont Look Back*." In *Documenting the Documentary: Close Readings of Documentary Film and Video*, eds Barry Keith Grant and Jeanette Sloniowski. Detroit: Wayne State University Press. 237–54.

Jane, Emma A. 2017. *Misogyny Online: A Short (and Brutish) History*. Los Angeles: Sage.

Katz, Claire. 2008. "'The Eternal Irony of the Community': Prophecy, Patriotism and the Dixie Chicks." *Shofar: An Interdisciplinary Journal of Jewish Studies* 26(4): 139–60.

Keel, Beverly. 2004. "Between Riot Grrrl and Quiet Girl: The New Women's Movement in Country Music." In *Boy Named Sue: Gender and Country Music*, eds Kristine M. McCusker and Diane Pecknold. , Jackson, MS: University of Mississippi Press: 131–47.

Mamber, Stephen. 1974. *Cinema Verite in America: Studies in Uncontrolled Documentary*. Cambridge, MA: The MIT Press.

Marshall, P. David. 2014. *Celebrity and Power: Fame in Contemporary Culture*. Minneapolis: University of Minnesota Press.

Marwick, Alice, and dana boyd. 2011. "To See and Be Seen: Celebrity Practice on Twitter." *Convergence* 17(2): 139–58.

Nichols, Bill. 1991. *Representing Reality: Issues and Concepts in Documentary*. Bloomington and Indianapolis: Indiana University Press.

Plantinga, Carl. 2014. "Gender, Power, and a Cucumber: Satirizing Masculinity in *This Is Spinal Tap*." In *Documenting the Documentary: Close Readings of Documentary Film and Video*, eds Barry Keith Grant and Jeanette Sloniowski. Detroit: Wayne State University Press. 339–55.

Poey, Delia. 2010. "Striking Back without Missing a Beat: Radical Responses to Domestic Violence in Country Music's The Dixie Chicks and Salsa's Celia Cruz." *Studies in Popular Culture* 32(2), 1–15.

Pruitt, Lesley. 2007. "Real Men Kill and a Lady Never Talks Back: Gender Goes to War in Country Music." *International Journal of World Peace* 24(4): 85–106.

Rasmussen, Eric E., and Rebecca L. Densley. 2017. "Girl in a Country Song: Gender Roles and Objectification of Women in Popular Country Music Across 1990 to 2014." *Sex Roles* 76: 188–201.

Redmond, Sean. 2014. *Celebrity and the Media*. New York: Palgrave Macmillan.

RIAA. n.d. "Gold & Platinum." <https://www.riaa.com/gold-platinum/?tab_active=default-award&se=dixie+chicks+home#search_section> (last accessed 30 January, 2019).

Rojek, Chris. 2001. *Celebrity*. London: Reaktion.

Rossman, Gabriel. 2004. "Elites, Masses, and Media Blacklists: The Dixie Chicks Controversy." *Social Forces* 83(1): 61–79.

Taylor, Aaron. 2011. "Angels, Stones, Hunters: Murder, Celebrity and Direct Cinema." *Studies in Documentary Film* 5(1); 45–60.

Tolson, Andrew. 2001. "Being Yourself: The Pursuit of Authentic Celebrity." *Discourse Studies* 3(4): 443–57.

Turner, Graeme. 2014. *Understanding Celebrity*. 2nd edn. Thousand Oaks, CA: Sage.

Van Sickel, Robert W. 2005. "A World without Citizenship: On (the Absence of) Politics and Ideology in Country Music Lyrics, 1960-2000." *Popular Music and Society* 28(3): 313–31.

Watson, Jada, and Lori Burns. 2010. "Resisting Exile and Asserting Musical Voice: The Dixie Chicks Are 'Not Ready to Make Nice'." *Popular Music* 29(3): 325–50.

9. ROCK 'N' ROLL FAMILY ROMANCES: THE ROCKUMENTARY AS MALE MELODRAMA

Gunnar Iversen

Three men are sitting in a room quarrelling in the presence of a therapist, trying to work out their issues with each other. A big brother is scolding his little brother for his excessive and childish behavior, and the two try to work through their relationship. At first glance, scenes like these do not seem very rock 'n' roll, but rock music and the rockumentary genre are often about male bonding, masculinity, homosociality, and the rock band as a troubled family.

Numerous rockumentaries depict the pop or rock group as a kind of family unit. This is especially true when the band members themselves come from the same family, but also when the rock band functions as a chosen family. Perhaps the most important theme in *Oasis: Supersonic* (Mat Whitecross, UK, 2016) is the troubled family. The film foregrounds the disputes and rivalry of the Gallagher brothers as they constantly provoke each other throughout their career in the Britpop band Oasis. In another Britpop rockumentary, *Coldplay: A Head Full of Dreams* (Mat Whitecross, UK, 2018), the band Coldplay is depicted as the opposite of Oasis, a happy and caring chosen family. In a particularly emblematic scene, the guitarist Jonny Buckland says about the band: "It has evolved into much more than just friendship, we are more like a family now."

Many documentaries about pop or rock bands, and even concert documentaries, focus more on the band as a family unit than on the band's relationship to their audiences and fans. The Neil Young concert rockumentaries *Rust Never Sleeps* (Bernard Shakey, USA, 1979) and *Year of the Horse* (Jim

Jarmusch, USA, 1997) are good examples. They are either about the energy created by Young and his backing band Crazy Horse on-stage or their backstage homosocial bonding. The camera and the microphone almost never leave Young or the band to explore their relationship with the audience or depict the concert event itself. These two Young rockumentaries are all about the group as a chosen family of adult men.

These and numerous other rockumentaries focus on the band-as-family and discuss how relationships between men are strengthened or wither away in emotionally charged and melodramatic scenes. Often performing music together or dealing with the myth of rock 'n' roll, the band-as-family functions as a way to work through emotional troubles and homosocial relationships. The rock or pop band seen as a family unit is also an important trope in rock journalism, and writers frequently use the word divorce to discuss the breaking up of a band, like in the famous cases of The Beatles or Pink Floyd.

Two of the most interesting examples of the rockumentary as family romance and male melodrama are *Metallica: Some Kind of Monster* (Joe Berlinger and Bruce Sinofsky, USA, 2004), and *Mistaken for Strangers* (Tom Berninger, USA, 2013). Both films are about family ties, either between siblings or between the members of a chosen band-family, and in very different ways the two documentaries foreground the troubled relationships of the family members. In this chapter, I will analyze how *Metallica: Some Kind of Monster* and *Mistaken for Strangers* map the nervous system of rock 'n' roll through the depictions of homosociality, family ties, and the male melodrama.

Hybrid Forms and Rock 'n' Roll Myths

Documentary film historian Michael Brendan Baker has distinguished between five broad trends in the rockumentary genre (Baker 2011, 67; Baker 2014, 6). The first type of rockumentary is the biography. This rockumentary subgenre portrays an artist or a band and combines observational concert footage with interviews and archival material. Examples are *Amy* (Asif Kapadia, UK, 2015), a biography of singer Amy Winehouse, and *Joe Strummer: The Future is Unwritten* (Julien Temple, Ireland/UK, 2007). The second type of rockumentary is the concert or performance-based rockumentary. Examples of this form are Martin Scorsese's tribute to The Band in *The Last Waltz* (USA, 1978), or Jonathan Demme's *Stop Making Sense* (USA, 1984) featuring Talking Heads. A third type of rockumentary is the tour film or making-of documentary. The Beatles' *Let It Be* (Michael Lindsay-Hogg, UK, 1970) is an early example of this type. The fourth subgenre is an ethnographic study of rock or a music subculture. Wim Wenders' *Buena Vista Social Club* (Germany/USA/Cuba, 1999) is an example of this subgenre. The fifth and last type of rockumentary according to Baker is the compilation or archival project. These are most often rockumentaries made for TV, but there are also many examples of this type of rockumentary produced for theatrical release. *The Kids Are Alright* (Jeff Stein, USA/UK, 1979) is one early example.

Baker points out that many rockumentaries are hybrid forms, combining two or more of the proposed five main types (Baker 2014, 6). *Metallica: Some Kind of Monster* and *Mistaken for Strangers* are good examples of modern hybrid rockumentaries that combine different rockumentary types. *Metallica: Some Kind of Monster* combines a "making-of" documentary with biography, mostly depicting the personal problems and creative struggles writing and producing the band's eighth album *St. Anger* (2003) in the period from 2001 to 2003. *Mistaken for Strangers* is both a tour film, depicting the indie band The National on tour in Europe, and a biographical film, with a biographical approach to the portraits of singer Matt Berninger and his less successful little brother Tom.

A central theme in these two rockumentaries is the critique of the claims of rebellion and non-conformity in rock culture. Rebellion has been singled out as one of the most important aspects of rock culture. Rock historian David P. Szatmary states that rebellion defined rock 'n' roll, and other social historians of popular music have pointed out how rebelliousness and rebellion are at the heart of rock culture and history (Szatmary 1996, xiii; Doggett 2017, 252; Kearney 2017, xv). However, in the two rockumentaries discussed here the interplay between rock 'n' roll rebelliousness and the responsibilities of fatherhood and family ties are foregrounded, creating a critique of foundational rock 'n' roll myths.

The otherworldly mysteriousness of Metallica's music, its heaviness, is constantly undermined in *Metallica: Some Kind of Monster* by the representation of the band's petty quarrels, emotional outbreaks, and discussions "behind-the-scenes." The supreme importance of rebellion, an anti-establishment attitude, and non-conformity in rock culture is replaced by emotional expressions and the clichés of excess in modern rock culture. The global entertainment industry of rock is explicitly linked to the band members' branding as rebels and outsiders, especially in the last part of the documentary, where the band perform some of their new songs for an audience of inmates in the San Quentin prison, as a way of rebranding the group as dangerous outsiders and angry rebels in a music video.

Metallica: Some Kind of Monster and *Mistaken for Strangers* both use the behind-the-scenes form with its promise of tell-all of the life of rock 'n' roll stars. In different ways, the two rockumentaries present the rock 'n' rollers in complex ways, as popular stars but also as very ordinary men. Again, this trope of backstage or behind-the-scenes access is reversed and complicated by the film's use of a fall-and-rise structure rather than the opposite. We meet Metallica at their lowest in *Metallica: Some Kind of Monster*, a band-family in the process of disintegration. All the petty quarrels clog all the creative streams, as well as threatening the family with a painful "divorce." In *Mistaken for Strangers*, band leader Matt Berninger is depicted as a responsible big brother, while little brother Tom's experiment with rock 'n' roll excess goes bad and puts strains on family ties and brotherly love. However, Tom Berninger's rockumentary itself turns the experience into another fall-and-rise film. The film *is* the final proof that he finally managed to get his act together and did something with his life.

Both films depict family ties, relations, and emotional bonds between grown men. They have the same basic fall-and-rise structure, an inversion of the more common rise-and-fall structure of many rockumentaries, and they focus on the band as a family. The demystification of rock is important in the two films. In an age of endless self-promotion, the two films use the warts-and-all biopic or reality-TV-like behind-the-scenes approach to discuss both the artistic and the industrial aspects of rock 'n' roll. The main lens through which the rock 'n' roll myths are presented and discussed is the family romance.

Family Therapy: *Metallica: Some Kind of Monster*

The very last image in the more than two-hour-long *Metallica: Some Kind of Monster* is the image of the four men in the band standing together, with their arms around each others' backs, a happy "family" facing the crowd of fans in one of their first concerts in years and with new bass player Robert Trujillo as an integral part of the family. Trujillo's integration into the family is important in the last part of the film. However, the rest of the film is a close look at a process of making an album and, at the same time, a depiction of the band's successful attempt at patching up problematic emotional relationships and a history of antagonism.

When the filming of *Metallica: Some Kind of Monster* begins in April 2001, Metallica experiences a deep crisis, and the band is not a happy family. The relations between the band members have reached an all-time low. The bass player Jason Newsted has just quit the band. The band's lawsuit against the popular Internet file sharing service Napster has resulted in a fan backlash, and the band has not toured or released an album for several years. Before the recording sessions for a new album begin, the band's management Q-Prime hires Phil Towle, a therapist and performance enhancement coach, to help the band function and make new music. Towle's job is to help the band with their personal and emotional relationships. However, throughout the film, Towle's job resembles the work of a marriage counselor more than a performance coach.

Initially, making a rockumentary about the process of writing and recording an album was seen as a simple promotional tool. In 1992, the video *A Year and a Half in the Life of Metallica* (Adam Dubin, USA) had been made to accompany the release of the *Black Album* (Wall 2010, 398). The new film was meant to have the same function for a new album. However, *Metallica: Some Kind of Monster* ended up as a more ambitious and complex rockumentary. Early on in the process of making the film it is also clear that the film itself is used as a tool for making the band uncomfortable in order to get creative. The film ties in with Towle's provocative words early on in the film challenging the band as to whether they are "free enough to risk being seen by people." Here, the film echoes *Let It Be*, an early example of a rockumentary about a dysfunctional band-family, and Towle's words resemble Paul McCartney's argument in that film.

Many fans and writers have not been kind to *Metallica: Some Kind of Monster*. In his entertaining history of heavy metal, Andrew O'Neill calls the film "embarrassing" and writes: "It shows what used to be my heroes being petty and egotistical and at times really, really bad at making music." He sums up his feelings in the short and sharp sentence: "It's just not metal" (O'Neill 2017, 223). Mick Wall, author of a biography of the band, calls the documentary "a stupendously awkward film" (Wall 2010, 406). Guitarist Kerry King in thrash metal band Slayer is reported to have called the Metallica members "fragile old men" after seeing the film (Wall 2010, 437). However, other writers have been more positive and have seen specific qualities in the film. Philosopher Rachael Sotos has seen the film as "a tragic-comic revelation of the human condition," and she continues: "From the perspective of Metallica's journey as a band grounded in the quest for an *authentic* expression of freedom in music it is of particular significance, for it brings us full circle to the experience of the 'we' that came so spontaneously in the heady days of early speed metal" (Sotos 2007, 96).

The film starts with a number of texts informing us that Metallica was the top concert draw throughout the 1990s, and a band that has sold over 90,000,000 albums. However, the three years preceding the release of the album *St. Anger* and the film in 2003 were the most troubling in the history of the band. Power struggles, aggression, and big competing egos threatened to tear apart the love between the members. In April 2001, the band has not worked together for nine months, but this emblematic break does not produce a new album-child. Bass player Newsted has just quit the band, starting his new band Echobrain, and without a bass player the remaining members of Metallica hole up with producer Bob Rock for more than two years trying to make an album. After 715 days in crisis, the band can finally meet an audience for real again.

The band members have, in the words of therapist Towle, "lost touch with their personal relationships," and even if *Metallica: Some Kind of Monster* is a film about the "monster" of a metal mega-group, the group's relations to

9.1 Metallica working out their issues in *Metallica: Some Kind of Monster* (2004). Therapist Towle in the background.

industry and the commercial apparatus behind the band, and about the desperate fight to rekindle the artistic spirit of earlier days as rebel outsiders, the film is first and foremost a chronicle of the "monster" of damaging emotional relationships and family ties that nearly break.

When *Metallica: Some Kind of Monster* starts, the relationship between guitarist James Hetfield and drummer Lars Ulrich has reached a low point. Egos and machismo are getting in the way of artistic expression. The two old buddies can hardly be in the same room together. When Ulrich complains to Hetfield about the changes in their relationship, and uses the word "intimacy" to describe their friendship, James spits out the words: "What intimacy are you fuckin' talkin' about?" The therapy sessions with Towle, and the constant presence of a documentary film team, do not make matters better. Hetfield complains about having the microphone boom over him all the time and how it makes him self-conscious.

Soon Hetfield leaves the band for rehab, and with minimal communication stays away for nine months. When the band resumes work on the new album, relations between Hetfield and Ulrich seem to be even worse, with guitarist Kirk Hammett as silent bystander, but slowly the band starts working together for real and the finishing touches on the album *St. Anger* are made in 2003. The film ends with the beginning of Metallica's summer tour of 2003. With new bass player Robert Trujillo, and better relationships between all band members, Metallica seem to have overcome the many disputes and found a new common understanding. The family is healed and the homosocial bonds are rekindled.

The importance of the band-as-family is at the core of the film and the search for artistic inspiration. The film plays with the contrast between the band-family on the one hand and the families of the band members on the other hand. The film contains a few very brief scenes where children and wives visit the recording studio, or scenes with band members and their families. Drummer Lars Ulrich is depicted especially as a family man, in scenes with his father and his wife and children. These scenes of Hetfield and Ulrich as family men – fathers, husbands, and sons – are contrasted with the difficult internal struggles of what Hetfield in a poignant scene calls his "other family."

The theme of the band as a family is highlighted early in the film. An early sequence points to the main theme of the band's quest to become a family again and underlines the contrast between the collective and the individual. First, the band members discuss how they worked together earlier, and they decide that all three members should now contribute to writing lyrics and music. No rules or boundaries when it comes to artistic development should be established this time. That is what happened in the past and it has led them to the point of emotional aggression and an artistic impasse. Then, with the help of their family therapist, a new mission statement for the band is produced, in order to energize the band and heal the emotional wounds. This mission statement illustrates the emphasis on family: "We have discovered the true meaning of family. It is both our mission and our destiny to manifest this ideal. As we accomplish the ultimate togetherness we become healers of ourselves and the countless others who embrace us and our message." The directors cut from the discussion of collective artistic work and the mission statement to a brief scene where the families of Ulrich and Hetfield visit the studio to show the parallels between the biological families and the "other family." Immediately after this the band takes a short vacation from studio work, and the film focuses on how Hetfield, instead of spending the time with his wife and children, goes on a long hunting trip to shoot bears in Russia. Back in the studio with his "other family" the hyper-masculine guitar player nearly breaks down talking about how he missed his family and how he tragically missed his son's first birthday because of the hunting trip. Again, just not metal. Instead it is a family melodrama in a double sense, since both families are involved in the scene. However, by the end of the film, with counseling a "divorce" is avoided and the family ties are healed.

The constant contrast and comparison between the band-as-family and the band members' family life is important to the melodramatic tone of the film and the depiction of Metallica's troubles as a family unit. The biological families of Hetfield and Ulrich may not be present beyond very brief moments, but they are constantly alluded to, most clearly in a statement by Hetfield after rehab. Hetfield says: "I'm working hard to be the best father and husband." As a quick afterthought he also adds: "And, the best me." In the studio with his friends and members of his chosen "other" family, he is not yet his "best me," not even close, but they are all working on their emotional ties with the help of their therapist and the producer and bass player Bob Rock.

Male bonding and homosociality are important in rock culture and in numerous rockumentaries. Philosopher Judith Grant has pointed out that: "*Some Kind of Monster* is very crucially about the relationship between Lars Ulrich and James Hetfield. It is about the bond between rock brothers and the erotic nature of that bond" (Grant 2007, 219). In many ways, Hetfield is the constant troublemaker in the band-family, the hyper-masculine and aggressive macho man who loathes the word "intimacy," but both Ulrich and Hetfield are attention-seekers who are jealous of each other.

Since *Metallica: Some Kind of Monster* is all about masculinity and male bonding, fatherhood emerges as an important theme. Women are peripheral in the documentary and the family system that the film and much of rock culture embraces is built on male homosocial bonding. The therapist Towle is obviously some type of father figure, but more important is how the film foregrounds Hetfield and especially Ulrich's relationships to their own fathers. Ulrich's father is very present in an important scene early in the film.

In contrast to Hetfield's absent and dead father, who did not approve of his son's attraction to rock and metal, Ulrich's dad comes across as very present and an expert on nearly everything, and that obviously creates some emotional and personal problems for the drummer, who desperately tries to live up to his dad's high standards. Ulrich takes not only his real father, Torben Ulrich, to inspect a piece of land that he has bought, but also brings along his new father figure, the therapist Towle. With two fathers present, Lars Ulrich behaves like a little boy intimidated by the presence of his fathers, and to make matters worse, when he seeks approval from his biological father he is denied what he most wants. He first tells Towle how it sucks to have a father who is so knowledgeable about music that he can "see right through that in two seconds flat." In a scene right after this, in the recording studio, Ulrich asks his father what he thinks about some of the new music they have worked on. Torben Ulrich responds: "If you are asking for my advice I would say 'delete that.' For me that doesn't cut it." An hour later in the documentary, when manager Cliff Burnstein hears some new music, the same thing happens. The first song makes Burnstein enthusiastic, but soon the camera finds him looking at his watch or looking around the room bored. His comment is just as clear: "Maybe you're watering it down."

Interestingly, Torben Ulrich and Cliff Burnstein look quite similar, with wild grey beards and casual clothes. Together with therapist Towle, later characterized by Hetfield as both an "angel" and a "father figure," they are the many fathers who look down on the sons in *Metallica: Some Kind of Monster*. Motherhood and relationships to women or wives are peripheral, while masculinity, fatherhood, and homosocial relationships are foregrounded. Time and again the film focuses on the moments when the members of Metallica talk about family ties and emotions. The inclusion of Robert Trujillo as a band member is the symbolic resolution of the family's problems. In a poignant scene where Trujillo and the other band members go over the details of their contract, the lawyer first outlines a relationship where Trujillo has very little to say over financial matters compared to the original three band members, but suddenly Hetfield, Ulrich and Hammett cut off the lawyer, demanding that all four be treated equal. Eager not to make the same mistake that they had done with former bass player Newsted, they finally create an equal family. A moment later, Hetfield says to Trujillo how happy he is to be with his "new family."

By focusing on emotions, relationships, power struggles, and issues of family and fatherhood, *Metallica: Some Kind of Monster* subverts many of the codes of rock culture and especially heavy metal. Even though it describes a world of men, and different conceptions of masculinity play an important part in the relationships between the band members, the film catches the metal heroes with their guards, and maybe even pants, down. We experience a sort of "unplugged" version of the life as rock millionaires, alternating between the toxic hyper-masculinity of Hetfield – constantly depicted driving cars or motorcycles – and the softer masculinities of the Buddhist and surfer Hammett and the sensitive art collector Ulrich.

Metallica: Some Kind of Monster obviously owes a lot to the reality-TV success of *The Osbournes* on MTV between 2002 and 2005, but the clownish antics of Ozzy Osbourne and his family are replaced in the Metallica documentary by a focus on desperate group therapy, anger management, and jealousy in a high-octane drama of male bonding. The film also points to the inherent problem for a band with a reputation for youthful rebellion and anti-conformist attitudes becoming, literally, "the Man," policing its fans for downloading music through Napster. As rich members of a family of millionaires, so sensitive that they nearly cry when they talk about fatherhood or about selling a piece of art, and who try hard to please father figures like Towle, Burnstein, and Torben Ulrich, and whine about work rules and regulations, how can you keep up the facade of rock 'n' roll anger, non-conformity, and rebelliousness? Philosopher Judith Grant has written that: "*Some Kind of Monster* is the story of a middle-aged rock band whose members now have wives and children, but who lock themselves in a room to try and recapture the youthful rebelliousness that contributed to their iconic status as the monsters of metal. It is *Spinal Tap* meets *Survivor*" (Grant 2007, 220). Rock parody meets reality-TV, and that was exactly how many saw the rockumentary when it was first released.

In the end, *Metallica: Some Kind of Monster* is all about grown men being emotional and the troubled relationships between the members of a chosen family of men. When we go behind-the-scenes in the studio – and what could be more masculine than the former army barracks in the Presidio where Metallica start their work on the album *St. Anger* – we observe three men in a prolonged and very expensive family therapy. The film focuses not on rebellion but on rock excess in the form of wealth, suffering, emotionally-loaded family situations, and dramatic mood shifts. Many of the same themes and issues are important in Tom Berninger's *Mistaken for Strangers*.

IN THE SHADOW OF BIG BROTHER: *MISTAKEN FOR STRANGERS*

At the end of his film *Mistaken for Strangers*, director Tom Berninger films himself while talking about his older brother Matt, the lead singer of the indie rock band The National. "Having Matt as my older brother kind of sucks because he is a rock star and I am not," Tom says, and he continues with a lump in his throat: "And it's always been that way." *Mistaken for Strangers* is first and foremost a self-portrait, a portrait of the artist as an unsuccessful little brother, but the film is also a behind-the-scenes tour documentary about life on the road. More than anything, it is a film about rock 'n' roll myths and about rock as a family romance and male melodrama.

In the beginning of the film, Tom Berninger is invited by his nine years older brother to work as a crewmember and roadie when The National go on their long tour of Europe and the US, following the release of the album *High Violet* in 2010. An amateur horror filmmaker, Tom brings his DV-camera with him backstage. He wants to make a movie about the group and the tour. What sort of documentary he is making is unclear, and this uncertainty irritates his brother Matt and the band members of The National, who obviously only put up with him because of Matt.

On the road, Tom is surprised and disappointed by the fact that not enough "crazy stuff" is happening. He is obviously expecting to find the excesses of a wild rock lifestyle but instead he finds a hardworking and disciplined band about to experience big success. The one who is drinking too much and partying all the time is Tom. Matt is worried, and obviously embarrassed by the way his younger brother acts, and asks him over and over again to stop filming and to take his responsibilities as a member of the crew more seriously. Both Matt and the tour manager admit to him that the only reason he is there is because he is Matt's brother, but even that does not stop him from being fired. Matt continues with the tour, while Tom goes home to live with his parents in Cincinnati.

THE ROCKUMENTARY AS MALE MELODRAMA

9.2 Tom and Matt Berninger discussing the editing of *Mistaken for Strangers* (2013).

Six months later, when the tour is over and the band start working on their new album, Matt once more invites his little brother to stay with him. Tom lives with his brother's family – emblematically in the playroom of Matt's little daughter – while he is trying to edit his film.

Finishing the film turns out to be hard, and brings out a range of emotions in him and his big brother. When he is feeling depressed because a screening of a rough-cut of the film experiences technical problems, Matt at first scolds his little brother for not preparing the screening sufficiently to avoid the technical issues, and then when Tom tells him that he filmed himself crying the night before, Matt laughs and exclaims: "This is just a rock documentary." However, Tom finally manages to complete the editing of the film with the help of Matt's wife Carin Besser. The documentary ends with footage showing The National on stage, and how Matt starts walking into and through the audience in a concert hall, with Tom behind him holding the long electric cord to Matt's microphone.

Mistaken for Strangers is about brotherhood and the problems of male and family bonding. It is extra pertinent because the band The National is made up of two pairs of brothers plus the singer Matt Berninger. On tour, the fact that the other band members are brothers and that the Dessner and Devendorf brothers work together successfully and in harmony makes it even harder for Tom to succeed in the shadow of his big brother. When Tom complains about his brother not understanding him to one of the band members before he is fired as crewmember, guitarist Aaron Dessner answers briefly: "Maybe your relationship is suffering?"

Even though we do see The National on stage and on tour, and get a glimpse of tour life from behind-the-scenes, *Mistaken for Strangers* is mostly about the troubled relationship between Tom and his brother Matt. Tom is defined in the film as the "underdog" while Matt is the "alpha male." Matt helps his younger brother, first by getting him a job as a member of the crew and then later by inviting him to finish his movie in New York, but Tom seems bent on self-destruction. The film shows him as an eccentric metalhead who likes to draw and make short gory horror films but seems totally incompetent as a crewmember, and does not understand that performing rock is first and foremost a job. He has the rock attitude but seems to have no other qualities. His presence backstage on the road creates antagonism and irritation, and his constant childish clowning gets on his brother's nerves. Tom is the Michael Moore of rockumentary filmmakers, but he does not have any plan for his film other than using it to be closer to his big brother.

In a similar way as with *Metallica: Some Kind of Monster*, the film compares and contrasts the band-as-family with the Berninger family and the relationship between the two Berninger brothers. After he is fired as a roadie Tom returns home and talks to his mother and father. He needs some consolation, and both mother and father praise him for his creativity. The main reason why Tom is fired, and maybe does not have any direction in his life and filmmaking, is because he is unable to work as a real family member. The contrast between "we" and "I" that became so important in the Metallica rockumentary is also at the heart of *Mistaken for Strangers*. Tom embraces the individualism of rock rebellion and excess, missing the tour bus and disturbing the band members, when his job is to help make a collective of artists work better together. Tom is the stubborn individualist, while Matt and the band of brothers in The National have understood how the band must work together as a family to be successful. The connection between the band-as-family and larger social issues and ties is an important theme in the film, especially in scenes where The National play at rallies to re-elect Barack Obama as US president. It is highly emblematic that the band get to meet the president, because they are working together as a big family even beyond making music, while Tom is sent away by the Secret Service men and is even prohibited from seeing the meeting from a distance.

Mistaken for Strangers is first and foremost a film about Tom Berninger being a little brother in the shadow of his famous big rock star brother Matt. Early in the film Tom says about his brother and his relationship with his brother that: "I never get to see him." He sees the work as a roadie, and the work on the rockumentary about the band's tour, as a way to get closer to his brother. However, by being too much of an individualist, unable to work together with the crew and the band-as-family, and by being too eager to embrace the "crazy stuff" of rock excess, he is cast out of the big family and has to go home to mom and dad.

An especially poignant scene depicts the quarrel between Tom and Matt in New York. The two are sharing a hotel room on the tour and Matt complains that when he had to go to the bathroom the floor was covered with cereal and milk. Not only does Tom not understand that being a rock musician is a job that demands concentration, but his rock excess becomes an infantile parody. He is not trashing a hotel room in a reversal or subversion of expected social behaviour, like a real rock rebel, drinking and doing drugs, but rather is spilling cereal and milk on the bathroom floor. This scene shows how Tom's relationship to his big brother infantilizes him, and, at the same time, shows the wonderful ridiculousness of rock 'n' roll. Tom never manages to grow up, due to being in his big brother's shadow, and his unsuccessful attempts to work as a crewmember or pick up girls on the road by referring to himself as the brother of Matt Berninger illustrate some of the important themes of masculinity and male melodrama in the rockumentary form.

The Rockumentary as Male Melodrama

In a particularly emblematic and highly emotional scene in *Metallica: Some Kind of Monster*, Lars Ulrich paces back and forth in a small room and vents his frustration and aggression by complaining about how James Hetfield, fresh out of rehab and back in the studio after an absence of nine months, insists on keeping very specific work hours. "I realize that I barely knew you before," Ulrich says to Hetfield, "And all these rules and all this shit, man! This is a fucking rock and roll band! I don't want fucking rules." This scene not only shows how far from youthful rebelliousness Metallica have come, but also highlights the role of melodrama and emotions in modern rock culture.

Rules are also important in *Mistaken for Strangers*. By being unable to follow the rules and do what is specified in his job description while on the road, Tom Berninger does not get to be close to his famous big brother. His rebelliousness is too infantile and creates an environment where the band can't work as a harmonious family. Tom tries to work through his emotional frustrations in the rockumentary, but at the same time he exposes the many ridiculous ideas about rock culture and masculinity.

Both *Metallica: Some Kind of Monster* and *Mistaken for Strangers* expose the uncomfortable combination of authenticity and commerciality of rock culture by questioning rock 'n' roll myths. Masculinity and homosocial bonding are central to rock culture and many rock bands function as chosen families, but without women. It is symptomatic that Tom and Matt's sister Rachel is not in Tom's film, and that in the Metallica documentary the wives are only present for a few very brief moments. These two rockumentaries, as with much of rock culture, are about feelings between adult men. By focusing on emotions more than anything else, both films are melodramatic and the male bonding is given the form of male melodrama.

In his classic essay on the Hollywood family melodrama, film scholar Thomas Elsaesser points out how the plots of the family melodramas revolve around family relationships and focus on emotionally-loaded family situations that bring out the inner violence in these relationships (Elsaesser 1991). Both *Metallica: Some Kind of Monster* and *Mistaken for Strangers* discuss the band-as-family and focus on the highly emotionally charged relationships between either members of a chosen family or between actual family members. *Metallica: Some Kind of Monster* in particular depicts the aggression and inner violence in the relationships between the band members, either between Hetfield and Ulrich or between Newsted and both Hetfield and Ulrich. As in so many melodramas, the violence is also directed inward, towards the family members themselves, and results in self-destructive behavior. In *Mistaken for Strangers* Tom Berninger does not listen to his older brother or his new friends in the band, he does not stop filming when they tell him to concentrate on his job as a roadie and make sure the band can perform, and this threatens to damage his relationship to his brother. He seems set on irritating his older brother, showing how he is still a *little* brother, and his self-destructive behavior initially creates an even bigger distance between the two. Tom wants to get closer to Matt but only manages to drive him away.

Both rockumentaries are melodramas about male bonding, homosociality and masculinity. The melodramatic mode is characterized by emotional and dramatic excess. Literary scholar Peter Brooks points out how melodramas are characterized by an urge to tell all and leave nothing unsaid. The melodramatic style is highly expressive, and in melodrama relationships are heightened and polarized. Brooks writes that the people depicted in a melodrama "assume primary psychic roles, father, mother, child, and express basic psychic conditions" (Brooks 1976, 4). To this one could add the role of brothers. In the two rockumentaries analyzed here brotherhood is the most important, although the other primary psychic roles are also obviously important, like the many father figures in *Metallica: Some Kind of Monster*, or Tom Berninger's self-infantilization in *Mistaken for Strangers*.

The strong emotionalism of *Metallica: Some Kind of Monster* and *Mistaken for Strangers* makes the two films into fundamental dramas about life, and about rock life. As documentaries about rock culture the films are both typical, in the sense that they focus on rock music, homosociality, and different aspects of being in a band, but at the same time the films are atypical in their exposure of rock myths. By telling all, exposing metal gods and indie stars as fathers, brothers, and sons, in highly expressive and emotional situations where basic relationships are explored, the films also question central aspects of rock culture. Neither James Hetfield, Lars Ulrich, and Matt Berninger, nor the members of The National, are rebels in the old sense, and the two rockumentaries focus more on the internal emotional mechanisms of male rock-families than on non-conformity, rebelliousness, or the search for authenticity through rock music.

In his classic study of literary melodrama Peter Brooks writes that: "Melodrama handles its feelings and ideas virtually as plastic entities, visual and tactile models held out for all to see and to handle. Emotions are given a full acting-out, a full representation before our eyes" (Brooks 1976, 41). When watching these behind-the-scenes tell-all documentaries about rock families we, the audience, experience basic emotions in their most primal and unrepressed form. Primal screams are important in the films. Lars Ulrich screams "FUCK" to his old friend James Hetfield, who tries to control and manipulate the band, and Matt Berninger screams repeatedly to his little brother: "Put the camera down!"

Even though *Metallica: Some Kind of Monster* and *Mistaken for Strangers* are very different films aesthetically, they have much in common. The two films are important explorations of troubled rock families, masculinity, homosociality, and male bonding. In emotionally charged and melodramatic scenes the two rockumentaries question central rock myths and explore rock culture through the troubled relationships and emotional bonds between family members.

References

Baker, Michael Brendan. 2011. *Rockumentary: Style, Performance & Sound in a Documentary Genre*. Ph.D. thesis. Montréal: McGill University.

Baker, Michael Brendan. 2014. "Notes on the Rockumentary Renaissance." *Cinephile* 10(1): 5–10.

Brooks, Peter. 1976. *The Melodramatic Imagination: Balzac, Henry James, Melodrama, and the Mode of Excess*. New York: Columbia University Press.

Doggett, Peter. 2017. *Electric Shock: From the Gramophone to the iPhone: 125 Years of Pop Music*. New York: Vintage.

Elsaesser, Thomas. 1991. "Tales of Sound and Fury: Observations on the Family Melodrama." In *Imitations of Life: A Reader on Film and Television Melodrama*, ed. Marcia Landy. Detroit: Wayne State University Press: 68–91.

Grant, Judith. 2007. "Boys Interrupted: The Drama of Male Bonding in *Some Kind of Monster*." In *Metallica and Philosophy: A Crash Course in Brain Surgery*, ed. William Irwin. Oxford: Blackwell Publishing. 219–31.

Kearney, Mary Celeste. 2017. *Rock and Gender*. Oxford: Oxford University Press.

O'Neill, Andrew. 2017. *A History of Heavy Metal*. London: Headline.

Sotos, Rachael. 2007. "Metallica's Existential Freedom: From We to I and Back Again." In *Metallica and Philosophy: A Crash Course in Brain Surgery*, ed. William Irwin. Oxford: Blackwell Publishing: 85–97.

Szatmary, David P. 1996. *Rockin' in Time: A Social History of Rock-and-Roll*, 3rd edn. New York: Prentice-Hall.

Wall, Mick. 2010. *Enter Night: Metallica The Biography*. London: Orion.

10. PERFORMING DYLAN: THE MANY LIVES OF BOB DYLAN IN *I'M NOT THERE*

Magdalena Fürnkranz

Looking back on the career of Bob Dylan (*1941), which so far has lasted over five decades, it seems both an impossible and futile task to approach the notion of the real or the authentic artist. Following biographical chronology, a small boy called Robert Allen Zimmerman was born to middle-class Jewish parents and raised in Hibbing, a quintessential small-town in Minnesota. During his days at the University of Minnesota he began introducing himself as "Bob Dylan," and later legally changed his name to Robert Dylan in 1962 when already in New York City (Sounes 2001, 121). Dylan remarked on his change of name, "You're born, you know, the wrong names, wrong parents. I mean, that happens. You call yourself what you want to call yourself. This is the land of the free" (Bradley 2004). After dropping out of college and moving to New York in May 1960, Dylan became part of the folk music scene there and performed at clubs in Greenwich Village. He was signed to Columbia Records, released his first album *Bob Dylan* in 1962, beame a nationwide success with his second album *The Freewheelin' Bob Dylan*, and committed himself to the Civil Rights Movement in 1963. Two years later the musician performed his first electric set, headlining the Newport Folk Festival, and thus provoked a hostile response from the folk music establishment. In 1966, Dylan crashed his motorcycle near his home in Woodstock (New York) but was not hospitalized (Sounes 2001, 217; Scherman 2006). Biographers tend to interpret that the mysterious crash offered him the chance of escape (Sounes 2001, 217–19; Heylin 2000, 268) that was mentioned in his autobiography, "Truth was that

I wanted to get out of the rat race" (Dylan 2004a, 114). He stopped touring for almost eight years but appeared in a few TV Shows in the late 1960s and early 1970s, and in Sam Peckinpah's movie *Pat Garrett and Billy the Kid*. In the mid-1970s, Dylan returned to touring and converted for a short period to Evangelical Christianity (Gray 2006, 643; Heylin 2000, 480–1) undertaking a three-month discipleship course run by the Association of Vineyard Churches in the late 1970s (McCarron 2017; Heylin 2011, 494–6) until the release in 1983 of his twenty-second studio album *Infidels*, which is seen as his return to secular music. In 1988, Dylan started his touring schedule nicknamed the "Never Ending Tour" (Hann 2011), which he has been on to this day.

Even this very rudimentarily-sketched biography of Dylan reveals one thing: continuous inconsistency. These biographical and artistical incisions act as turning points in the film *I'm Not There* (Todd Haynes, 2007). The film therefore approaches the subgenre rockudrama as a field in which different identity representations can be discussed. As the official film poster advertises, "Christian Bale, Cate Blanchett, Marcus Carl Franklin, Richard Gere, Heath Ledger, Ben Whishaw are all Bob Dylan." Even though each actor and actress portrays different facets of the artist's public persona, every character embodies an episode of Dylan's biography. The "fake" Woody Guthrie, the "poet" Arthur Rimbaud, the "rock and roll martyr" Jude Quinn, the "star of electricity" Robbie Clark, the "prophet" Jack Rollins later named "Father John," and the "outlaw" Billy McCarty. The rockudrama tells its story by using non-traditional narrative techniques, shifting between the six different Dylan-inspired characters.

In this chapter I discuss *I'm Not There* not only in terms of Dylan's life narrative, but especially in the performance of sexual identities, focusing on the way Dylan's public persona is represented by using selected intersectional approaches. As David Muldoon states, "the film deconstructs the biopic genre and Dylan himself, but it does not deconstruct the masculinities that drive them" (2012: 53). The rockudrama features numerous songs written and performed by Dylan that work as a suture for Dylan's public persona and his private narrative. The White male characters who portray facets of the artist's public persona are associated with the concept of "hegemonic masculinity" (Connell 2005). However, two Dylan-inspired characters in the movie are not White heterosexual males. Apart from the focus on categories such as class, race, body, or sexual identities, I also reflect on Dylan's songs that work as a suture for Dylan's public persona in the movie, especially the eponymous song "I'm Not There."

Eat the Rockument: Bob Dylan in Film

The film genre biopic recreates an artist's biography, as a space of representation; it plays a role in the making of history in popular culture. Biopics are generally based on true events in the life of an artist, but they tend to dramatize facts and eventually contribute to the artist's mythification. If produced posthumously, a biopic has the ability to create or manipulate the historical memory of generations by using blurry lines of fact and fiction to (re-)write an artist in the narrative of his or her time. An alternative form of storytelling marks the rockumentary genre. The term rockumentary describes a television program or a film documentary that tells the stories of an artist's or a rock band's rise to fame in a retrospective manner and focuses on them as individuals and musicians on stage. Rockumentaries discuss the narrative identity of these musicians, the performance personae they have created, and how these concepts are perceived by society. Bill Drake first used the term in the radio show *The History of Rock & Roll* in 1969 (Landau 1973). From the 1970s rockumentaries became popular because they were "comparatively cheap to produce and conform easily to the promotional needs of the music recording industry" (Roscoe & Hight 2001, 119). They not only take a deeper look at the career of musicians, but also at the artists themselves and why they choose to perform the way they do. Since rockumentaries often have retrospective elements, the viewer is able to follow the notion of a star identity in progress. The first rockumentaries were *Dont Look Back* (D. A. Pennebaker, USA, 1967), *Woodstock* (Michael Wadleigh, USA, 1970), and *Gimme Shelter* (Albert Maysles, David Maysles, Charlotte Zwerin, USA, 1970). *Dont Look Back* was shot hand-held on black-and-white 16mm film during Bob Dylan's 1965 UK tour and documents his last acoustic solo tour. The opening scene of the film was used as a kind of music video for Dylan's song "Subterranean Homesick Blues," in which the singer displays a series of cue cards with selected words and phrases from the lyrics, including intentional misspellings and puns written on them. Pennebaker turned his camera to what happened backstage; his film shows Dylan during interviews with journalists, with fans and singing together with his former partner Joan Baez in a hotel room. By using the hand-held camera and recording the original film sound, the director introduced the French *cinéma vérité* to American pop culture. Dylan's second collaboration with D. A. Pennebaker was the rockumentary *Eat the Document*. It documents Dylan's 1966 UK tour with The Hawks, later to become The Band. Pennebaker shot the film under Dylan's direction; the musician edited the film himself. *Eat the Document* includes footage from the Manchester Free Trade Hall concert, with the infamous scene wherein an audience member shouted "Judas!" during the electric half of Dylan's set.

Martin Scorsese's acclaimed rockumentary, *No Direction Home* (2005), focuses on the period from Dylan's arrival in New York in 1961 to his motorcycle crash in 1966. The film traces not only the biography of Dylan, but primarily his impact on twentieth-century American popular music and culture. It features interviews with artists, friends, and partners like Suze Rotolo, Joan Baez, Allen Ginsberg, Pete Seeger, Mavis Staples, and Dylan himself; its accompanying soundtrack includes unreleased songs from his early career. *The Other Side of the Mirror: Bob Dylan at the Newport Folk Festival* (2007), directed by Murray Lerner, documents Bob Dylan's performances at the Newport Folk Festival in 1963, 1964, and 1965. By presenting previously unseen footage of Dylan's appearences at Newport in three successive years, the rockumentary chronicles the changes in Dylan's style. Additionally, it includes Dylan's controversial electric set from 1965. Martin Scorsese's second film on Dylan, *Rolling Thunder Revue: A Bob Dylan Story by Martin Scorsese*, was released in 2019. It is a pseudo-documentary, composed of both fictional and non-fictional material, focusing on Dylan's 1975 Rolling Thunder Revue concert tour. The film consists of outtakes from the film *Renaldo and Clara* (1978), directed by Dylan, that integrate the genres of the concert film, documentary interviews, and dramatic fictional vignettes reflective of Dylan's life and lyrics and starring himself. *Rolling Thunder Revue: A Bob Dylan Story by Martin Scorsese* also features contemporary interviews with prominent artists of the tour such as Dylan himself, Joan Baez, Sam Shepard, archival interviews with deceased artists like Allen Ginsberg, and fictional interviews of actors and actresses portraying characters who were not actually involved in the tour. The film mixes fictional and factual accounts; in his interviews even Dylan himself refers to the fictional characters.

Bob Dylan's Absent Presence in *I'm Not There*

The feeling of history that *I'm Not There* leaves the audience with through the music and life of Dylan may be extremely real. By using Dylan's songs, Todd Haynes's film tends to recreate the genre of 1960s documentaries in black-and-white. The film's soundtrack features only one recording by Dylan himself plus other artists' recordings of songs written by Dylan. Artists like Sonic Youth, Calexico, Cat Power, The Black Keys, Glen Hansard, and Markéta Irglová reinterpret less than half of the titles that are heard in the film, which features more of Dylan's own recordings. "Dylan's songs in the biopic are left almost untouched, if not slightly enhanced by the re-mastering of the music for the film" (Muldoon 2012, 58). Todd Haynes uses Dylan's songs to interweave Dylan's public and private persona. The cinematic connection of multiple facets of Dylan's personas concerning his private life, his public image, his on- and off-stage performances, and his acting career is enabled by the use of untouched Dylan songs to reconstruct the artist's myth. Dylan's approval to have the film produced, and the rights to use the artist's music in the soundtrack, were granted following the presentation of a one-page summary of Haynes's concept, starting with an Arthur Rimbaud quote to Jeff Rosen, Dylan's long-time manager. The poet Rimbaud was a subject Haynes figured he and Dylan were both familiar with (Sullivan 2007).

The film is named after a Dylan song recorded during *The Basement Tapes* sessions in 1967 with The Band, which circulated on bootlegs for four decades until its first official release on the film's soundtrack in 2007. The song's original title was "I'm Not There, I'm Gone" chosen by The Band's organist Garth Hudson. Even though the title was not Dylan's, it is an excellent, condensed commentary on Dylan's artistic persona. Whereas the title marks Dylan's absence in the movie, the artist is present through his songs.

Woody Guthrie: The "Fake"

The slogan "This machine kills fascists" is written on the guitar case of an eleven-year-old boy traveling in a boxcar through the Midwestern United States. It is 1959. The African American boy calls himself Woody Guthrie, referring to Dylan's youthful admiration of folk singer Woody Guthrie. The message on the guitar case is inspired by Woody Guthrie, who placed the same message on his guitar in 1941 (Weir 2007, 337). Playing the Blues and singing about topics such as trade unionism, he seems so outdated that a woman advises him to sing about his own time instead. After an attack by hobos, the boy is rescued by a couple who are impressed by his musical talents. The boy elopes when the couple receive a telephone call from a juvenile corrections center revealing that young Woody is an escaped fugitive. The boy escapes to New Jersey to visit the real Woody Guthrie, who is deathly ill, in a hospital.

The story of the character Woody Guthrie in Haynes's film symbolizes the nineteen-year-old singer Bob Dylan who arrived in "dead-on winter" (Dylan 2004a, 9) in Greenwich Village with a "determination to emulate his hero Woody Guthrie" (Bingham 2010, 387). The singer became popular by mystifying himself with a fictional life story and combining (folk) traditions with musical and poetic styles. The twelve-year-old Marcus Carl Franklin embodies the fictional journey Dylan took to New York City. Early on in his book *Chronicles, Vol. I*, Dylan describes his dialogue with Billy James, the head of publicity of Columbia Records, asking how he got to the city:

> Dylan: I rode a freight train.
> James: You mean like a passenger train?
> Dylan: No, a freight train.

James: You mean, like a boxcar?
Dylan: Yeah, like a boxcar. Like a freight train.
(Dylan 2004a, 8)

Later on that page he states "I hadn't come on a freight train at all. What I did was come across the country from Midwest in a four-door sedan . . . At last I was here, in New York City, a city like a web too intricate to understand and I wasn't going to try" (Dylan 2004a, 8–9). Young Woody Guthrie embodies that story, a character full of confidence but unable to do what he is expected to do: a subject that "is permeated with childlike enthusiasm and faith" (Bingham 2010, 387). Woody is the only one of Haynes's characters who sings in his own voice, although his voice isn't trained at all. Performances by the other "Dylans" are lip-synched cover versions. Marcus Carl Franklin's character is not only singing Dylan's Blues, he is also depicted as the young Dylan on the cover of his first LP *Bob Dylan*.

Franklin is the exception in Haynes's all-White cast. bell hooks states that all-White casts are usually regarded as a reflection of the producer's environment (hooks 1996, 69). However, White producers often cast a number of Black actors and actresses to prevent the accusation of racism (hooks 1996, 74). An African American child actor embodies a facet of Dylan's public persona that is named "the fake" as a character who transgresses the boundaries of race. Young Woody leaves his childhood behind and at the same time he represents the youth and freedom of young Dylan, who left his past behind by moving to New York: "His blackness is not alarming or symbolically controversial as intended. Neither is what his character represents so revolutionary: Dylan's reappearance in the form of an African American boy is a clear mask for his Jewishness" (Muldoon 2012, 66). The African American boy as an allegoric figure replaces the Jewish boy.

In compliance with dominant agencies, Black men have often been represented as yearning for a White hero's devotion. It is the lack of something important that justifies the need of the White man's friendship (hooks 1996, 84). The film needs the presence of the real Woody Guthrie to continue Haynes's storyline. Young Woody as dislocated character "takes to *running* the whole movie, running away from the white Jew inside him. The transferral of masculinities from Jewish to black and back reinforces a masculine framework of identity that has been part and parcel of American racism and capitalist opportunism" (Muldoon 2012, 67). Guthrie, one of the most significant figures in American folk music, represents the redeeming savior in Haynes's film. It becomes a trope of hegemonic masculinity as role model for an African American boy pushed into an allegorical version of the young Jewish Dylan.

Arthur Rimbaud: The "Poet"

Confronted only by a camera, a nineteen-year-old "Arthur Rimbaud" answers questions in a bare room. His cryptic responses to the invisible interrogators are interspersed throughout Haynes's film. As the only person in the scene, Arthur Rimbaud, "a teenage French symbolist poet Dylan" (Muldoon 2012, 55), embodies Dylan's and Haynes's passion for the eponymous artist "who seems to have inspired Dylan in his early days nearly as much as he inspired Todd Haynes" (Sullivan 2007). The poet's literary influence is believed to have affected Dylan's own writing, as Dylan wrote in his autobiography that he was influenced by Rimbaud's outlook (Dylan 2004a, 146).

The twenty-six-year-old Ben Whishaw depicts Arthur Rimbaud. Dressed in an old-fashioned suit, which the audience might recognize from nineteenth-century period dramas, he confronts the interrogators with his stoic answers. As the only person not dramatically interacting with other characters, Haynes's Rimbaud is depicted as a man who responds with quotes from Dylan's interviews and writings. His palpable androgyny is not comparable to normative ideas of masculinity. The character's link to the deceased poet elevates him to a non-human being that can act only as a fragment of Dylan's public persona.

The "Prophet" Jack Rollins Who Turns into "Father John"

The folk musician Jack Rollins's career is framed as a documentary film. In the film's narrative the story is told by interviewees, especially by the folk singer Alice Fabian; a story that could have simultaneously been told by the folk singer Joan Baez or the artist Suze Rotolo on Dylan's early career. This echoes the stylistic approach to the interviews with Joan Baez in Martin Scorsese's *No Direction Home*.

In the early 1960s, Jack Rollins is portrayed as the star of the Greenwich Village folk and protest scene. However, he stops singing protest songs when the Vietnam War escalates. His decision is caused by the disbelief in the power of music to influence social or political movements. Jack receives an award from a civil rights organization and states in his acceptance speech that he saw something of himself in John F. Kennedy's assassin Lee Harvey Oswald. This is an allusion to the speech given by Dylan in December 1963 upon receiving the Tom Paine Prize from the National Committee on Civil Rights Violations (Shelton 1986, 200–5). Turned off by the audience, the singer backs out from public life. In 1974 he enters a Bible study course in Stockton (California), from which he emerges a born-again Christian. Reborn as "Father John," he denounces his past and becomes an ordained minister performing gospel music.

THE MANY LIVES OF BOB DYLAN IN *I'M NOT THERE*

10.1 Civil Rights March on Washington, DC. Close-up view of vocalists Joan Baez and Bob Dylan, 28 August 1963 by Rowland Scherman.

The actor Christian Bale impersonates two facets of Dylan's public persona. The character of Jack Rollins embodies Dylan during his acoustic career, which turned from "protest songs" into a "protest phase" ending in a temporary retreat from the public eye: "Christian Bale seeks to impersonate Bob Dylan during his years as a beginner singer/songwriter and voice of the American folk generation" (Muldoon 2012, 62). At this stage of his career Dylan released *The Freewheelin' Bob Dylan* and *The Times They Are A-Changin'*. Jack Rollins, as the "voice of a generation," appears in 1963's "March on Washington" together with the young performer Alice Fabian (played by Julianne Moore). He embodies Dylan's voice, which had a direct connection to society and was dubbed "the voice of the generation." The darling of the Newport Folk Festival in 1963, the singer of protest songs like "Masters of War" dressed in denim could be associated with the album cover of *The Times They Are A-Changin'* (1964).

The character of Pastor John embodies Dylan's "born-again" period recording his Christian trilogy. Consisting of *Slow Train Coming* (1979), *Saved* (1980), and *Shot of Love* (1981), the songs not only deal with Christian topics but are gospel arrangements. The parallel to his old life becomes apparent when Jack, who had disappeared for fifteen years, re-emerges on-stage in

1979, and is opposed to "Pastor John," who fights for Jesus Christ just as "Jack" fought against racism and war.

Significantly, it is Alice Fabian who tells the story of Rollins and Pastor John. Fabian's memories construct the masculinity of Jack Rollins told by a female voice. She distances herself from her influence on the musician's career and focuses on Rollins as the voice of a generation: "This way of acting seems to be part of the intention of the script as Bale's character is part of the documentary style of the film" (Muldoon 2012, 62). Even though Rollins's performance is associated with Connell's concept of "hegemonic masculinity" in the particular scene where he is interviewed on a television program, the character seems to be emotionally insecure, talking about the uncertainty he feels regarding humankind.

Robbie Clark: The "Star of Electricity"

Twenty-two-year-old actor Robbie Clark embodies Jack Rollins in the biographical film *Grain of Sand* in 1965. Like a storyline taken out of a romance film, he falls in love with French artist Claire during filming in Greenwich Village. The film becomes a hit and its star Robbie marries Claire. When the couple have an argument over whether the evils of the world can be changed, Robbie states that women can never be poets. The couple separate; Claire gains custody of their children. Robbie shoots a thriller in London and starts an affair with his female co-star. In the last scene of the Robbie Clark episode the actor takes his daughters on a boating trip.

The couple Robbie and Claire romantically wandering the streets of New York is a re-enactment of the album cover of *The Freewheelin' Bob Dylan* in 1963. The photo depicts Dylan and his then-girlfriend Suze Rotolo strolling around Greenwich Village (Mitchell 2016; Carlson 2006). By showing a disintegrating marriage, Haynes reflects on Dylan's personal life around the release of the album *Blood on the Tracks* in 1975. The album has been interpreted as Dylan's artistic process of separation from his wife Sara. Dylan has always denied a direct connection. However, Dylan was divorced from his wife in June 1977, involving court battles over the custody of their children (Gray 2006, 198–200).

Robbie Clark was Heath Ledger's last role in a film to be released during his lifetime. He embodies an actor who portrays the fictive folk star Rollins in a biopic shot in a certain style of cinematography. "At some point, Haynes would sit you down and show you that ... Ledger's rock-star Dylan would feature the wide shots and close ups of objects that characterize Godard" (Sullivan 2007). With Rollins as a facet of Dylan's public persona, a film's character becomes as famous as the person he portrays, that is also a character embodying another facet of the same persona in the film. As a trope of hegem-

10.2 Allen Ginsberg and Bob Dylan by Elsa Dorfman in 1975.

onic masculinity, the Robbie Clark episode is not shot in the documentary style, although its narrative is told by the character in a low toned-off voice.

Jude Quinn: The "Rock 'n' Roll Martyr"

Performing with a full electric band at a folk festival outrages the fans of popular folk singer Jude Quinn. The musician is booed and accused of being a sell-out. He travels to London, where he has to answer critical questions by journalist Keenan Jones. The journalist later reveals on television that Jude, who claimed that he had had a vagabond past, is in fact the well-educated son of a suburban, middle-class department store owner. Jude hangs out in The Beatles' hotel room and is attacked by a hotel employee. He repeatedly encounters his former lover Coco Rivington and meets the poet Allen Ginsberg, who is suggesting that Jude Quinn has "sold out to God."

While performing "Ballad of a Thin Man" on stage, Jude is called a "Judas" by an enraged fan. Although his European tour is upcoming, the musician gives in to his drug addiction and dies in a motorcycle accident.

I'm Not There begins with the autopsy and funeral of Jude Quinn depicting the mid-60s Dylan, the dandy with big hair and sunglasses, an allegoric figure for "the frizzy-haired speed freak who, went electric" (Bingham 2007, 369). By killing his persona "the folk star," Dylan creates a new public persona.

Quinn embodies Dylan's controversial performance playing electric guitar at the Newport Folk Festival, and his 1966 UK tour with The Hawks, which was booed (Shelton 1986: 301). The musician performed a rock version of "Maggie's Farm" followed by provoked booing of outraged folk music fans. Dylan performed this song at the Newport Folk Festival in 1965 (see *The Other Side of the Mirror: Bob Dylan at the Newport Folk Festival*). Jude Quinn's answers at the London press conference are quotes from Dylan's press conference in the studios of KQED, the educational television station, in December 1965 (Dylan 2004b, 51–8). With no other Dylan character in the movie, so many documented Dylan quotes are used. "How can I answer that if you've got the nerve to ask me?" is Quinn's reply to the character of Bruce Greenwood. It emerges out of a similar response Dylan made to a reporter in Pennebaker's documentary of Dylan's 1965 UK tour *Dont Look Back*. Even the audience member calling Quinn "Judas" is based on the concert in Manchester (17 May 1966) and captured on the Bootleg Series album *Live 1966*, while the death of the character could reflect Dylan's motorcycle accident (Sounes 2001, 217; Scherman 2006).

Cate Blanchett portrays the character of Jude Quinn, in a trouser role. The actress was praised for her performance and awarded a Golden Globe for Best Supporting Actress, along with an Academy Award nomination for Best Supporting Actress. Haynes states that Blanchett's performance was received successfully because the actress uses all her body when embodying a character: "The psychical transformations that occur in her roles ... she really does have to find the equivalent body parts to throw herself into the role" (Haynes at IFC 2007). Anthony DeCurtis states that "... Blanchett's translucent skin, delicate fingers, slight build, and pleading eyes all suggest the previously invisible vulnerability and fear that fueled Dylan's lacerating anger. It's hard to imagine that any male actor, or any less-gifted female actor for that matter, could have lent such rich texture to the role" (DeCurtis 2007, 6). However, it is the female body "that reinforces the stereotype of women as hysterical" (Muldoon 2012, 68). Blanchett's embodiment of a facet of Dylan's public persona supports masculine ideas of stereotypical feminine behavior as *hysterical*. The "Rock 'n' Roll Martyr" is insomniac by taking all kinds of pharmaceutical pills: "The loss of gender norms would have the effect of proliferating gender configuration, destabilizing substantive identity and depriving the naturalizing narrative of compulsory heterosexuality of the central protagonists: 'man' and 'woman'" (Butler 1990, 54). Like Arthur Rimbaud, Jude Quinn faces interrogators in *I'm Not There*. While Arthur is less affected by their questions, Jude is distracted by them. Jude takes refuge in the hysterical behavior that terminates the character's appearance with a motorcycle accident.

Billy McCarty: The "Outlaw"

Billy McCarty's narrative is staged as a Western. A man who is believed to be dead lives in hiding as an outlaw, with his dog. His alleged killer, commissioner Pat Garrett, plans to build a highway, causing several inhabitants of the affected town to commit suicide. Confronted with McCarty, the commissioner recognizes him as Billy the Kid. The outlaw is thrown in jail but breaks out with the help of his friend Homer. Hopping on a freight train passing by, he finds Woody Guthrie's guitar in a boxcar. When riding away in the train, he says farewell to his dog while simultaneously reflecting on the nature of freedom and identity.

The endless touring habit of Dylan imbues the ghostly figure of Billy McCarty, haunting the landscape with indelible poetry. Richard Gere embodies Billy the Kid, a reference to Dylan's role as "Alias" in the Western *Pat Garrett and Billy the Kid*, directed by Sam Peckinpah, from 1973. Gere doesn't approach Dylan through a physical transformation but as Robert Sullivan (2007) states, "Richard Gere's Billy the Kid Dylan would be shot like a late-'60s, early-'70s Western." Sullivan mentions *Butch Cassidy and the Sundance Kid* or *McCabe and Mrs. Miller*; Haynes's technique could be a visual reference to *Pat Garrett and Billy the Kid*. Concerning the concept of "hegemonic masculinity" (Connell 2005), Billy McCarty embodies the outlaw who acts in a powerless manner in Haynes's film. He does not have the ability to break out of jail but needs the support of his friend Homer (Paul Spence), who resembles Dylan's appearance in *Pat Garrett and Billy the Kid*. Billy's final monologue in *I'm Not There* is an allusion to Dylan's *Newsweek* interview from 1997: "I wake and I'm one person, and when I go to sleep I know for certain I'm somebody else. I don't know who I am most of the time. It doesn't even matter to me" (Gates 1997). By using Woody's guitar in a boxcar as the film's MacGuffin, Haynes refers back to the opening episode of the movie.

I'm Not There, I'm Gone

Todd Haynes's main characters can be seen more as themes than characters. Never called Bob Dylan, they fall down, rise up, and appear in or as different stages of the artist's career. *I'm Not There* tries to cover Dylan's juvenile search for his personal role model Woody Guthrie, the start of his career in the late 1950s, his motorcycle accident, and the separation from his first wife Sara in the mid-1970s, his Christian phase in the early 1980s, and his Never Ending Tour. The film's title refers to the denial of authenticity in portraying characters that seem to be inspired by the musician's biography, but appear to be anyone other than Dylan the artist. Haynes deconstructs the classic narrative cinema in *I'm Not There* by combining extra- and introspection, close-up and panoramic view. The director's concept underlines the impossibility of telling the true story of the authentic artist. *I'm Not There* doesn't follow a straight line; contrariwise it takes turns, jumps, repeats, and moves in circles. The film begins with the death of the Dylan-inspired character Jude Queen. "There he lay: poet, prophet, outlaw, fake, star of electricity. Nailed by a peeping tom, who would soon discover: even the ghost was more than one person," a voice-over tells the audience. The text is a variation of the two epitaphs Dylan wrote in *Tarantula* in 1966 (published in 1971), the year of his and Quinn's motorcycle accident. The metaphorical death of the film's embodiment of Dylan's Rock 'n' Roll spirit marks the limited lifespan of the different facets of the artist's public persona. The variety of actors that portray Dylan in *I'm Not There* is evidence for the artist's absence in the film. Neither the single portrayal nor the sum of portrayals tends to capture the "orginal" Bob Dylan.

None of the characters explicitly bear Dylan's name, nor is the artist verbally mentioned. Only at the beginning of the film do the credits show the words "Inspired by the music and many lives of Bob Dylan." All six characters embody different creative phases or aspects inspired by Dylan. Jude (Cate Blanchett) personifies the electrified Dylan, who hits his fans with his rock sound. This part is based mostly on the rockumentaries *Dont Look Back* and *Eat The Document*. The character looks like Dylan in *Dont Look Back* and cites interview passages from this rockumentary, as well as from *Eat The Document*. Arthur (Ben Whishaw) is the poet. Jack (Christian Bale) represents the folk icon Dylan. Jack's part is staged as a classic documentary, wherein Haynes uses "Super 8" shots and imitated pictures of Dylan's record covers. Billy (Richard Gere) refers to Dylan on his Never Ending Tour. The setting of Billy's episode is inspired by the revival of Western movies in the late sixties. Woody (Marcus Carl Franklin), a twelve-year-old boy, represents the roots of Dylan's music, a time when he was very strongly oriented towards his idols, such as Woody Guthrie. Robbie (Heath Ledger) is the only character to cover the private life of Dylan, showing him as a failing family man; his episode is meant to recall the early films of Godard.

Analyzing the performance of sexual identities focusing on the way Dylan's public persona is represented by using selected intersectional approaches, the film depicts the musician's life as a collection of anecdotes consisting of stereotypes of class, race, body, or sexuality: "Stereotypes, however inaccurate, are one form of representation. Like fictions, they are created to serve as substitutions, standing in for what is real. They are there not to tell it like it is but to invite and encourage pretense" (hooks 1992, 341). In the genre of the biopic, an actual theme is turned into a character. *I'm Not There* has several stereotypical characters searching for a subject that is not there. By reformulating an artist's myth that is too tremendous for one character, Haynes uses Dylan's quotes as common thread for his film. These quotations come from Dylan's songs, statements in interviews and press conferences. The film ends with footage of Dylan playing a harmonica solo during a live performance in 1966. Breath becomes a tool of self-creation; Dylan's music played by himself with all the associations that we hear through the harmonica in his non-voice-performance. Thus *I'm Not There* presents the apotheosis of Bob Dylan, a conclusion that would not be any different if the performing subject was no longer among us.

References

Banauch, Eugen, ed. 2015. *Refractions of Bob Dylan. Cultural Appropriations of an American Icon*. Manchester: Manchester University Press.

Barkham, Patrick 2007. "The Power and the Glory." *The Guardian*, 26 October 2007. <https://www.theguardian.com/culture/2007/oct/26/awardsandprizes> (last accessed 29 May, 2018).

Bingham, Dennis. 2010. *Whose Lives Are They Anyway? The Biopic as Contemporary Film Genre*. New Brunswick, NJ, and London: Rutgers University Press.

Bradley, Ed. 2004. "Bob Dylan Gives Rare Interview." *CBS News*, 5 December 2004. <https://www.cbsnews.com/news/60-minutes-bob-dylan-rare-interview-2004/> (last accessed 25 May, 2018).

Butler, Judith. 1990. *Gender Trouble. Feminism and the Subversion of Identity*. New York and London: Routledge.

Carlson, Jen. 2004. "NYC Album Art: The Freewheelin' Bob Dylan." *Gothamist*, 18 April 2006. <http://gothamist.com/2006/04/18/nyc_album_art_t.php> (last accessed 29 May, 2018).

Connell, R. W. 2005. *Masculinities*, 2nd edn. Berkeley, CA: University of California Press.

DeCurtis, Anthony. 2007. "6 Characters in Search of an Artist." *The Chronicle of Higher Education*, 23 November 2007. <https://www.chronicle.com/article/6-Characters-in-Search-of-an/2360> (last accessed 30 May, 2018).

Dylan, Bob. 1963. *Transcript of Bob Dylan's Remarks at the Bill of Rights Dinner at the Americana Hotel on 12/13/63*. <http://ilovemuggsy.tripod.com/BobDylan/id23.html> (last accessed 23 May, 2018).

Dylan, Bob. 1971. *Tarantula*. New York: Scribner.

Dylan, Bob. 2004a. *Chronicles. Vol. One*. New York: Simon & Schuster.

Dylan, Bob. 2004b. "Excerpt from the KQED Press Conference, December 3, 1965." In *Studio A: The Bob Dylan Reader*, ed.Benjamin Hedin. New York: W. W. Norton & Company. 51–8.

Gates, David. 1997. "Dylan Revisited." *Newsweek*, 6 October 1997. <http://www.newsweek.com/dylan-revisited-174056> (last accessed 29 May, 2018).

Gates, David. 2007. "'Full-on Rave' for Dylan Film." *Newsweek*, 17 November 2007. <http://www.newsweek.com/full-rave-dylan-film-96961> (last accessed 29 May, 2018).

Gray, Michael. 2006. *The Bob Dylan Encyclopedia*. London and New York: Continuum International.

Greene, Andy. 2011. "The Evolution of Bob Dylan." *Rolling Stone Magazine*, 10 May 2011. <https://www.rollingstone.com/music/pictures/the-evolution-of-bob-dylan-20110509> (last accessed 28 May, 2018).

Hann, Michael. 2011. "Bob Dylan Begins his 'Never-Ending' Tour." *The Guardian*, 12 June 2011. <https://www.theguardian.com/music/2011/jun/12/bob-dylan-never-ending-tour> (last accessed 28 May, 2018).

Hans, Simran. 2018. "Where to Begin with Todd Haynes." *British Film Institute*, 2 January 2018. <http://www.bfi.org.uk/news-opinion/news-bfi/features/fast-track-fandom-where-begin-todd-haynes> (last accessed 24 May, 2018).
Hedin, Benjamin, ed. 2004. *Studio A: The Bob Dylan Reader*. New York: W. W. Norton & Company.
Heylin, Clinton. 2000. *Bob Dylan: Behind the Shades: Take Two*. London: Viking.
Heylin, Clinton. 2011. *Behind the Shades: The 20th Anniversary Edition*. London: Faber & Faber.
hooks, bell. 1992. "Representing Whiteness in the Black Imagination." In *Cultural Studies*, eds Lawrence Grossberg, Cary Nelson, and Paula A. Treichler. London, New York: Routledge. 338–46.
hooks, bell. 1996. *Reel to Real: Race, Sex, and Class at the Movies*. New York: Routledge.
IFC News. 2007. *New York Film Festival Press Conference with Todd Haynes*, 3 October 2007. <http://www.youtube.com/watch?v=HBAsheMKyos> (last accessed 25 May, 2018).
Landau, Jon. 1973. "'Let the Good Times Roll' indeed." *Rolling Stone*, 19 July 1973: 62–3.
Lee, Christopher Paul. 2000. *Like a Bullet of Light: The Films of Bob Dylan*. London: Helter Skelter.
McCarron, Andrew. 2017. "The Year Bob Dylan Was Born Again: A Timeline." *Oxford University Press's Academic Insights for the Thinking World*, 21 January 2017. <https://blog.oup.com/2017/01/bob-dylan-christianity/> (last accessed 28 May, 2018).
Mitchell, Elizabeth. 2016. "The Freewheelin' Bob Dylan cover immortalizes a budding Greenwich Village love story." *New York Daily News*, 27 August 2016. <https://www.goodreads.com/author_blog_posts/14324805-new-york-stories-the-freewheelin-bob-dylan-cover-immortalizes-a-budd> (last accessed 18 May, 2018).
Muldoon, David. 2013. "The Postmodern Gender Divide in the Bob Dylan Biopic 'I'm Not There'." *Miscelánea: A Journal of English and American Studies* 46(1): 53–70. <http://www.miscelaneajournal.net/index.php/misc/article/view/133/61> (last accessed 4 May, 2018).
Roscoe, Jane and Craig Hight. 2001. *Faking it. Mock-documentary and the Subversion of Factuality*. Manchester: Manchester University Press.
Scherman, Tony. 2006. "The Bob Dylan Motorcycle-Crash Mystery." *American Heritage*, 6 November 2006. <http://www.freerepublic.com/focus/f-chat/1674242/posts> (last accessed 1 June, 2018).
Shelton, Robert. 1986. *No Direction Home: The Life and Music of Bob Dylan*. New York: Da Capo Press.
Sounes, Howard. 2001. *Down the Highway: The Life Of Bob Dylan*. New York: Grove Press.
Sullivan, Robert. 2007. "This Is Not a Bob Dylan Movie." *The New York Times*, 7 October 2007. <https://www.nytimes.com/2007/10/07/magazine/07Haynes.html> (last accessed 28 May, 2018).
Turner, Kyle. 2015. "The Films of Todd Haynes: Performance, Desire, and Identity." *The Film Stage*, 24 November 2015. <https://thefilmstage.com/features/the-films-of-todd-haynes-performance-desire-and-identity/> (last accessed 14 May, 2018).
Weir, Robert, ed. 2007. *Class in America: An Encyclopedia*. Santa Barbara, CA: Greenwood Publishing Group.

The publication of this chapter was supported by the mdw – University of Music and Performing Arts Vienna.

PART III

AESTHETICS AND POLITICS

11. U2'S *RATTLE AND HUM*: GOD, SEX, ROCK 'N' ROLL AND GOD AGAIN

Karine Bertrand

The 1980s were a defining decade for the Irish rock group U2, who became, with the release of *The Joshua Tree* (1987), the biggest band in the world. From its beginnings in mid-70s Dublin, the band cultivated the image of a sullen group of Irish men interested in religion, politics and social activism, all the while pursuing their own personal vision of the American Dream, promoting the values of freedom and opportunity they associated with the USA. Shot just before what would become a major turning point for the band (the production of *Achtung Baby* in 1990, and a move towards postmodern irony), the rockumentary *Rattle and Hum* (Phil Joanou, USA, 1988) portrays the band pushing the very limits of the sincere image they had carefully crafted for themselves, before religion turned into sex, and earnestness turned into irony. Produced with the help of American iconography and musical styles (blues, gospel, Dylan), and using an aesthetic infused with (false) humility, Irish martyrdom and gospel choirs, *Rattle and Hum* is alternatively described either "as a stunning work of art or a misguided, pretentious, self-serving snapshot of stardom." In this vein, this chapter explores the ways in which *Rattle and Hum* represents U2's fall from innocence, their attempt at exporting and incorporating the American Dream, and how the band avoids re-addressing political issues raised throughout the 1980s (except perhaps in their live rendition of "Sunday Bloody Sunday"). Moreover, shot at a time when cinema – and the rockumentary, in films such as *Stop Making Sense* (Jonathan Demme, USA, 1984) – was embracing postmodern concerns such as the loss of meaning and the fragmentation of community and communication, I explore how this quite conservative rockumentary shied away from developing a postmodern commentary on *contemporary* music and politics, choosing instead to focus on nostalgia (both musical and political) and the power of faith. Finally, because so many articles, reviews and essays have been written about *Rattle and Hum*, this chapter will take on a more personal approach to the analysis of the rockumentary, inspired by Roland Barthes' work on photography and more specifically on the *studium* and the *punctum*. In Barthes' iconic study of photography, *Camera Lucida* (1981), the phenomenologist elaborates a distinction between two planes of the image. The *studium* refers to the meaning, context (historical context, for example) and the general information that is given to us by an image or a photograph, in front of which we, the viewers, keep a certain emotional distance. In contrast, the *punctum* refers to the elements in the image that punctures us, that reach our sensibilities and affect us in a more personal way. Written at a moment when the author was grieving the death of his mother, *Camera Lucida* is Barthes' attempt to find her again and again through piercing elements found in various photos. Looking at *Rattle and Hum* as a chapter in U2's history, it is safe to say that the *studium* and the *punctum* are omnipresent in different ways, whether through the treatment of the image or through the music and lyrics themselves. As a long-time fan, it would be very hard to pretend to write an objective chapter on a movie made by a very famous music group; instead I opt to acknowledge my subjectivity towards the subject and reveal how and why *Rattle and Hum* is not only a testament to U2's eternal search for belonging and rediscovering the American Dream (which I address in the first part of the chapter) but also a poetic work of art revealing more nuanced contours of the band's journey, beliefs, and their music.

Silver and Gold: Looking for the American Dream

In *U2 by U2*, lead singer Bono explains how *Rattle and Hum* is about "our journey through America" as well as a desire to "mythologize the tour" (191–2). Creating the band in 1976 out of a sheer desire to make music and have fun, the four Irish boys coming from modest families were, like millions of others, looking to America from their isolated island, feeding themselves with American music (Elvis Presley, The Ramones, Bob Dylan) and the dreams that accompanied it. Moreover, because the Dubliners were heavily exposed to American culture and landscapes through television and cinema, and because many Irish families had relatives who emigrated to America in search of a better life, the symbolic connection between the Irish and the promised land was fed and imbricated into the city's music, history and storytelling (Stockman 2001, 86). Bono explains this connection through historic reasons – "the Irish had lost to the British crown its self-esteem and a lot of its land whereas in America, Irish people were actually in some odd way reversing that" – and through a shared love of folk music and the ballad tradition, which drew the Irish to singers such as Bob Dylan and Johnny Cash (Assayas 2005, 162). Looking at the social context in Dublin in the 1960s and 1970s, with the ongoing violence in Northern Ireland, the high unemployment rate and a city drained of its talents by emigration, it is no surprise that the band developed into a political, social, and spiritual group, conscious of the world around them, and anxious to set out and conquer it, at the heart of which lay the USA. Beyond these reasons, it is perhaps as part of their spiritual journey that America most appealed to the band whose singer, drummer, and guitarist had once been part of a non-denominational religious group, the Shalom Fellowship, which was almost the end of the road for the band who eventually – and thankfully – decided that God and Rock 'n' Roll were not incompatible. In fact, when they first came to America at the beginning of the 1980s, the country's obsession with religion and its promotion of "Bible bashing televangelists that are knock-off salesmen for God" heightened Bono and his mates' fascination and curiosity for a nation united and torn apart by Christianity (Bono, quoted in in Assayas 2005, 167). To this end, even though the band members have somewhat distanced themselves from the Church over the years, the band, and more specifically Bono, have never shied away from speaking of God, the Scriptures or of their faith, their music "inhabiting that dangerous and exhilarating space that connects spiritual and physical, mortal and divine" (Stockman 2001, 5). In the short film *Bono and Eugene Peterson: The Psalms* (David Taylor, USA, 2016), which documents Bono's meeting with Eugene Peterson – author of the book *The Message*, a modern-day transcription of The Bible – the singer/activist talks of the stories of The Bible as metaphor, citing Peterson's interpretations of the Holy Book as the thing that helped him stay sane in the last few years:

> I had never thought of Jeremiah as a performance artist. Why do we need art? Why do we need the lyric poetry of the psalms? Because the only way we can approach God, is if we're honest. Through metaphor, through symbol. So arts become essential, not decorative. I learned about art, I learned about the prophet Jeremiah, through that book, and that really changed me.

Metaphors are indeed present in songs – such as "Gloria" from *October* (1982), "40" from *War* (1983), "I Still Haven't Found What I'm Looking For" from *The Joshua Tree* (1987), "Until the End of the World" from *Achtung Baby* (1991), and "Yahweh" from *How to Dismantle an Atomic Bomb* (2004) – which respectively speak of the glory of God, the search for meaning, the dialogue between Jesus and Judas, of the necessity of rejoicing, and generally of God as being love and light. Biblical passages are present in at least a few songs from each of their fourteen studio albums, the messages underlying those compositions being ones of hope, humility, surrender, gratitude, light, and grace. For example, in the song "Love Rescue Me," from the *Rattle and Hum* soundtrack (1988) album, the lyrics "*Yeah though I walk through the valley of the shadow/Yet I will fear no evil/I have cursed thy rod and staff/They no longer comfort me*" are a direct reference to Psalm 23: "Even though I walk in the dark valley I fear no evil; for you are at my side with your rod and your staff that give me courage" (@U2 2018). This sense of connection to a higher power is palpable from the very start of the creation process; the band have stated a few times that something quite *magical* can happen when they are in a room making music together – up to the performance of their work in concert. Journalists, artists and fans alike have been earnest whilst speaking about the experiences they have had going to a U2 show, describing it as "a collective emotional and spiritual surrender of epic proportions," a deep spiritual experience which leaves people "cleansed" and a place where individuals are able to "free their souls at the altar of U2" (Maynard 151). Music videos such as "Song for Someone" (2011), "Original of the Species" (2004), and "Stay" (2003) all evoke the mystery, grace and light inherent to the spiritual world. The contrast between light and darkness in the "Stay" and "Song for Someone" videos, as well as the demonstration of growth and creation in "Original of the Species," illustrate the profound, illuminated place where the band is coming from. The same kind of spirited glow is present in the many rockumentaries made about and with the band, including of course *Rattle and Hum*.

It is safe to say that the American part of the journey leading to the *Rattle and Hum* film thus started way before the 1987–8 shooting of the film; U2's curiosity, hunger and obsession with the USA having been fed throughout the 1980s, with the band, and particularly Bono's, investment in God. But this obsession also emerged through reading the Beats, particularly Ginsberg's *Howl* (1956) and Kerouac's *On the Road* (1957); the exploration of the southern landscapes during the Joshua Tree tour; Larry Mullen's love of Elvis Presley and their collaboration with many American musicians, including B. B. King and Bob Dylan.[1] Dylan suggested to Bono at the time *The Unforgettable Fire* album came out that the band should return to the roots of American music: "If I'm honest, this was the end of a journey that Bob Dylan had sent us on." Bono continues: "In 1985, sitting backstage at his concert in Slane Castle, he said to me, 'You've got to look back. You've got to go back. You've got to understand the roots'" (Deriso 2015). Therefore, I turn to how *Rattle and Hum* is not, as has often been written, the end of an era for U2, or the last step before their fall from innocence (with the advent of the postmodern *Achtung Baby*), but rather the continuation of their spiritual journey of self-discovery, a journey through which they start looking for God in the 1990s in shadowy alleys and corrupted mass media culture, rather than in deserted landscapes and the American soul.

Rattle and Hum:
U2 Still Haven't Found What They Were Looking For

The band's fifth studio album, *The Joshua Tree*, was about the discovery of America and more specifically about the wide, empty spaces that came into existence to be loved and conquered. In the song "In God's Country" for example, the lyrics describe America as a place of beauty and contradiction, where "crooked crosses" and "desert roses" speak to soul searching, desire and freedom.

The poetic landscapes described in this song correspond to both a physical, symbolic and cultural place, as if the desert is both a place of perdition and of salvation. For these Irish lads coming from an emerald green island surrounded by the sea, the desert is also a place of escape. Moreover, in the American consciousness, the western landscape has always been a complex construct, representing "the romantic dream of a pure, unsullied wilderness where communion with nature can transpire without technological mediation [and at the same time] it can be viewed as the repository of the vestiges of the Frontier, with its mythical freedom from the rules and structures of urban social contracts" (Bright 130). Questioned on this subject, lead guitarist The Edge explains how the Joshua Tree "is a reference to that whole desert southwest and the experience of being out there. The desert is a transitional place ... For us it was like a journey through this neutral ground to get to where we were going" (*U2 by U2* 186). Shot in the western landscape of the Joshua Tree Park in California by the Dutch photographer Anton Corbjin, the album cover and subsequent black-and-white promo images reveal a band alone in a deserted space, a band reflecting on itself, the serious faces on the photographs looking intently at the camera (Adam Clayton, Larry Mullen Jr., and The Edge) or towards the horizon (Bono).

The landscape is stripped of any superfluous elements, and the use of black-and-white photos adds to the symbolism of the image, where simplicity, unity and space present the band as a united front. Moreover, *The Joshua Tree* came forth at a time when road movies were emerging as a serious genre, with films such as Wim Wenders' *Paris, Texas* (West Germany/France, 1984) and Jim Jarmusch's *Stranger Than Paradise* (USA, 1984) indicating the need for people to break free of the system and rediscover themselves on open roads. In 1987–8 the band went on their own road trip through America, Bono and Adam Clayton taking time off to absorb the essence of the American South, renting a Jeep Cherokee and driving from LA to New Orleans. Bono states:

11.1 U2, *The Joshua Tree* press photo, 2007.

> We started the drive on highway 10, a road that links the west coast to the east. You drive out of L.A. and you leave one America and enter the other. It is the real America, an America I love. We filled up the car with Johnny Cash and set off, headed out through the Painted Desert ... through New Mexico, Arizona, Texas, diverted to Tennessee. We didn't know exactly where we were going, we were making it up as we went along. It was an adventure. (*U2 on U2*, 203)

The Joshua Tree album, which sold more than 1,000,000 copies on CD in the USA in the first year of its release, and an impressive number throughout the world, propelled the band to world-wide stardom, and left them pondering what to do next. Riding high from the popularity they had found in America, the band decided to incorporate various elements of their trips and discoveries into a new album, an homage to American music and the musicians who remained important symbols of the land and country. Adam Clayton and Bono's road trip allowed them to wander into little bars, often unrecognized, and meet incredible singers such as Blues artist Junior Kimbrough, Cowboy Jack Clements, John Prine, The Neville Brothers and Johnny Cash, all of whom fed their hunger and inspiration for the album to come. It has been described as an "angry, always argumentative, absolutely restless, sometimes sprawling and curiously contradictory hybrid of an album" by *Hot Press* music critic Bill Graham (2001, 1), and as "carrying forward U2's near obsession with the brave new world of America" by *Rolling Stone* critic Anthony

DeCurtis (1988, 1). It is perhaps true that the *Rattle and Hum* album is first and foremost a soundtrack and "a document of events that often were staged and arranged for the express purpose of being filmed and recorded" (DeCurtis, 1). On this subject, even the band admits to being to some extent held hostage by the movie, as noted by Mark Brown:

> 'The first night, there was a disconnect. They couldn't tell if they were doing a concert or a TV show,' Brown recalls. 'Cameramen were onstage following them around. Bono was getting irritated. They had a few equipment malfunctions.' He finally said: "(Screw) the cameras. These people paid to see us. I gotta play to them and hope the cameras get it." He had a great quote that night: "I feel like a book that shouldn't be made into a movie." The second night was much better, but the first was a disaster' (Brown: 1)

Whilst the majority of UK and US reviews of the album are rather harsh, pointing to the self-indulgent tones and to the arrogance of a band "trying to show it is the natural heir to rock's most prized legacy" others do not fail to notice how U2 positioned themselves as fans of great music, delivering a dynamic if not coherent record, whose intent was "to dramatize U2 in motion and transition and to exult in the barrage of influences the band had just begun to admit on *The Joshua Tree*" (DeCurtis, 1).

The heterogeneous double album thus evokes The Beatles ("Helter Skelter"), John Lennon ("God Part II"), and Jimi Hendrix ("All Along the Watchtower"), and includes collaborations with B.B. King ("When Love Comes to Town"), Keith Richards ("Silver and Gold"), and Bob Dylan ("Love Rescue Me"). Songs such as "Angel of Harlem," a tribute to the Blues singer Billie Holliday, "Heartland," a picture of America as seen through Bono's eyes, "Hawkmoon 269," whose title refers to a place in Rapid City, Dakota, and "I Still Haven't Found what I'm Looking For," recorded with Harlem's New Voices of Freedom Choir, all reflect the band's investment in American music, culture and landscapes; an ambition they partially succeeded in accomplishing through the *Rattle and Hum* rockumentary.

Rattling and Humming at the Sound of U2: Roland Barthes and the Puncture of Light

Rattle and Hum started out as a rather modest (if that is a word can be applied to U2) project, the band wanting to make a low-budget film on the road, and have it released in a small number of theaters. However, as with most of the band's ideas, the project rapidly became "a monster" in the hands of Paramount Pictures. As with the album, the movie was also harshly criticized for its grandeur, lack of modesty and for the fact that it left the fans hungry for more information, as interviews in the movie are scarce, with most of the footage focusing on the live performances. Shot partly in Ireland, at Hanover Quays, and mostly in the USA while the band was on tour in 1987, the movie presents itself as a poetic artwork. Created at a time when the film image reflected the beginnings of the postmodern media era, with its taste for pastiche, kitsch and rapidly moving images and very short shots, *Rattle and Hum* can be seen either as an alien creation or as a timeless piece of art, with its black-and-white footage, poetic shots and emphasis on lights and shadows. For most writers who revisited the rockumentary twenty-five years after its release, the sentence "love the music, hate the vanity of the project" remains true. For an academic who has been a fan of the band since *The Joshua Tree* came out in 1987, and whose memories of the *Rattle and Hum* era mark the beginning of her teenage years, it is quite a different experience watching it (and watching it and watching it again) through a different lens; that of a film scholar whose knowledge and love of the band certainly taints what we might call *objectivity*. In my eyes, it is relevant to analyze the *Rattle and Hum* rockumentary based on the fans' and critics' judgments of the singer's megalomania, or the fact that Paramount tried to transform a humble project into a cash cow. It is also relevant to classify a "before and after" *Rattle and Hum*, even if Bono himself often qualified their following album, *Achtung Baby*, as "the sound of three men chopping down the Joshua Tree" because the album and movie insert themselves into a continuity that goes well beyond U2's changing sounds and images, when they momentarily embraced the over-mediatized postmodern world of the 1990s. Yet, it is a much more interesting exercise to look at the rockumentary using what Barthes calls the *studium* (the classical body of information present in an image) and *punctum* (the quality which breaks or punctuates the *studium*) and applying these photographic terms to a continuously moving image (Barthes 1981, 26–7). What if, in a moving image, the repetition of the *studium* allowed for the same elements to become *punctum*, the thing that 'bruises me, that is poignant to me' (Ibid., 27)? What if, to paraphrase Walter Benjamin, the loss of the aura through the reproduction of a work of art and through absence and instantaneity could be partly recuperated through this *punctum* that is only the creation of the spectator, and whom, by taking possession of said images, imputes a new meaning upon them? Moreover, when Benjamin (1935) writes about the transformation of the spectator from a position of distanced contemplation – possible when in the presence of an original work of art – to a position of consumption, when the work becomes a mechanical reproduction of itself, he perhaps forgets to take into consideration the power of the spectator who possesses the will to engage in more than a simple experience of distraction. If ultimately, as Barthes writes, "Photography is subversive not when it frightens, repels, or even stigmatizes, but when it is *pensive*, when it thinks," why not allow this contemplative dialogue between the image and its receiver, a dialogue based on a variety of factors including the spectator's cultural background and knowledge of the band, become a constituent part of the analytic frame (Barthes 1981, 38)? Following this train of thought, the *Rattle and Hum* rockumentary can be analyzed through various spectrums.

The very first shots of *Rattle and Hum* are significant, as they show the band live in concert, reprising the infamous Beatles song "Helter Skelter." Shot in velvety tones of black-and-white, this particular scene brings us on stage with the four musicians, the soft, slow circular movement of the camera transporting us in front of the singer and then abruptly cutting to another shot, where the camera is positioned behind Bono, who stands tall, arms wide open in front of a cheering crowd of thousands of human bodies with their arms raised over their heads, joined together in pure joy. The camera continues its circular movement to present the other members of the band playing their instruments. Following the live footage, the next scene shows U2 at home, with shots of the Irish Sea, the camera quickly gliding over the body of water and on to Point Depot Dublin, where U2 are recording a new song. The music and lyrics of "Van Diemen's Land," about the Irish famine and uprising as lived by its leader John Boyle O'Reilly, situates the audience in relation to U2's position as an Irish band coming from a place of historical poverty and upheaval. We are then introduced to the band through an attempted (and failed) interview with Joanou asking the members to explain the film's journey, but to no avail. Right from the start we are to understand that *Rattle and Hum* is about the music, the music's message and the way it carries this message through live shows and interactions with the audience. The circular and fluid camera movements add to the constant flickering of a discreet but ever-present light lurking in the background or standing above the singer's head, illuminating his face and creating a bright aura around his body. These elements, conjugated with vast panoramas and the forceful contrasts between black and white, light and darkness, and the numerous slick close-ups of the band members' faces and facial expressions, thus set the tone for the first half of the rockumentary. The aesthetics prescribed by Joanou thus emphasize the spiritual nature of the musical quest while at the same time showing the band as being bigger than life, which renders them inaccessible to the audience. Moreover, because the movie is lacking any shots that are meant to show unity between the concert crowd and the band up on stage, there remains a feeling of disconnection from the individuals and their work. Ironically, one of the particularities of a U2 concert is that willingness from the band, and more specifically from Bono, to reduce the space that exists between him and the crowd. Before technology was used to abridge that distance through the use of numerous screens (*Zoo TV* tour, 1992–3), stage extensions (*Elevation* and *Vertigo* tours 1999, 2005), and giant movable bridges that circulated close above the crowd (*360* tour, 2011), the singer would use strategies such as stage diving, cutting across physical barriers, bringing fans on stage with him, or climbing up scaffoldings to get closer to people. It is perhaps this missing element in Joanou's rockumentary that helped fuel the critics' negative responses to a movie that kept the fans wanting more connection, more intimacy, more contact. Through scenes that show the band performing the songs "Exit," "In God's Country," and "Bad," there is a distinct cut between the shots showing the band and the very rare ones in which we can actually see the crowd responding to the performance. The camera thus becomes the main (and only) spectator of a show that seems to be put together for the pleasure of the lens only. The lighting contributes to that separation by wrapping itself around the musicians, leaving the crowd in shadow. A constant reminder of the fact that the band's egos have become too big for their boots it is through lighting and through one particular light – the one illuminating the band members from the back – wherein lies what at first glance could be described as the images' *studium*, the object that generates a *polite* interest becomes the *punctum*, the thing that "fills the whole picture" even if it is a more discreet or partial presence in the image (Barthes 1981, 27). In Bono's passionate rendition of "Bad," it is those evanescent rays of light, coming from a perpendicular angle, that make us believe the Heavens are watching over and guiding the singer, as he tells us "*to let it go*" with the recurrent actions of surrendering, kneeling and letting go being a constant in U2 songs. During the song "Exit," the entire stage is plunged into darkness, while the four musicians bask in a soft glowing light. In the scenes showing the band's rendition of "Helter Skelter" and "In God's Country," the nervous, flashing lights add a hint of drama to lyrics that bear a political or social message, i.e. Bono's statement at the beginning of "Helter Skelter": "This song Charles Manson stole from The Beatles, we're stealing it back."

In this respect, the first part of the rockumentary also highlights the band's discovery of American roots music through a visit to Graceland – with U2 channeling Spinal Tap and their own visit to the King's house – and the recording of three songs at the famous Sun Studios, where artists such as Elvis Presley, Johnny Cash, and Jerry Lee Lewis recorded their albums at a time when rock 'n' roll was being born. As the faint light of the sun comes down on the city of Memphis, letting the streetlights shine bright like artificial stars, the song "Heartland" announces the impending arrival of a new dawn. Once again, it is the artificial and natural lighting that "punctures" the musical and visual landscape, through the symbolism it brings when connected to the lyrics, which invoke the light and darkness of the American South. It is that "belief" that is shown through the rockumentary's lighting, the obvious symbolism shining through of the light of God, the light of Heaven. It is a belief that is also interconnected with the soul and Blues music of the South, the visceral sounds of its African roots standing not too far away from Irish music, as

Bono explains: "Oddly enough, Irish music has more than a little in common with African music or Middle eastern music . . . Its musical scale is pentatonic, not chromatic, i.e. quarter notes, bent notes. The *sean no* singers, for example, their melodies they sing unaccompanied can be traced to Northwest Africa" (Bono, quoted in in Assayas 2005, 225). Moreover, as the Irish were called the "white Negroes of America" or "Negroes turned inside out" when they landed in the mid-nineteenth century USA and joined in the oppression of the African Americans, U2's spiritual and political journey to the heart and soul of America comes as no surprise (McKenna 2013, 1) as this *LA Times* critic sums up:

> These ballads, poignant meeting grounds, briefly confirm those cultural or psychic similarities John Ford saw between the Irish and the American blacks: a common pain and persecution, a common unity, a common strength. And in U2's hands, a common song. Black as rage, white as faith, soft as hope and sharp as pain, it's a song that surges out, stabs you with its eloquence and fire. 'Rattle and Hum' (MPAA rated PG-13 for language) preserves it beautifully. (Wilmington 1988, 1)

Indeed, two of the most applauded parts of the rockumentary are the ones showing the band performing "I Still Haven't Found What I'm Looking For" with the New Voices of Freedom gospel choir of Harlem, and U2's collaboration with B. B. King. In the first sequence, the voices of the choir are visually accompanied by a camera that makes the most out of the bright, blinding sunlight coming through the naked windows, flooding the space with a white, incandescent light, while the angelic, powerful voices of the singers fill the room and the screen with warmth. But perhaps the most symbolic of all the lights found in *Rattle and Hum* is the one emanating from Blues legend B. B. King, for whom Bono and the band wrote a song, "When Love Comes To Town," whose lyrics talk about "the soldiers rolling the dice for Christ's robes." The five-minute sequence, showing different stages of the musical relationship built mainly between B. B. and Bono, lets us discover a singer humbled by the presence of a great man and musician, and expresses the sincerity of the undertaking, beyond the megalomania, the messianic complex and the economic aspects of the filmmaking endeavor.

The rehearsal scene, however, contributes to the disconnection of the band from its audience, as it is shot in an empty arena, the wayward camera reminding us that the filmmaker is the one leading the show and the spectators are not truly invited backstage, except as distant guests. A short sequence at the beginning of the scene briefly invites us to participate in the performance, as we hear the crowd cheering on, but that moment is rapidly cut short, the camera transporting us elsewhere without visually showing us the audience. It is,

11.2 Bono and B. B. King performing on stage during Love Town Tour.

however, the "big-hearted character" of B. B. King that transcends part of the distance between us and the band through his monumental presence on screen and his warm interactions with Bono.

In the second part of the movie, Joanou temporarily leaves behind the black-and-white footage that gives the rockumentary an eerie look to incorporate colors, and more specifically, red, white, and dark blue lights, perhaps representing the colors of the American flag. Four stadium performances are shot in explosive colors, which support at least one of the songs – "Bullet the Blue Sky" – that holds a political message of peace and tolerance, at the same time constituting a very direct denunciation of the American military interventions in Nicaragua and El Salvador. The *punctum* here is the blood red light that flashes like a police car siren to the sound of guitarist The Edge's screeching and wailing guitar, painting the portrait of a country ripped apart by its desire to conquer and reign over the world. At the very beginning of the song, a melting flag of red, white, and blue stands amongst a stormy sky filled with 1,000 (artificial) stars. Inspired by the Scriptures, the lyrics express the fear and pain associated with violence, and the singer's disbelief that such interventions were not being discouraged by American Christians. In this instance, Joanou brilliantly uses colored lighting to illustrate how the damning fires of hell have materialized in those regions of South America taken over by American military forces, the crimson red drowning the band in a bloodbath of searchlights. At one point in the song, Bono spontaneously takes one of the white spotlights and maneuvers it in such a way as to put the emphasis on The Edge's passionate guitar solo, the light moving in sync with the movements of the guitar rhythm. Opting for a dramatic ending, the singer ends the song with the lyric *"into the arms of America,"* as he points the giant spotlight towards the audience, making them witnesses and culprits of their country's unconscious. The three other "color" performances do not project the same intensity or coherence found in the "Bullet the Blue Sky" sequence, and the rockumentary goes back to its black-and-white roots for its final acts.

Perhaps the most talked about sequence of the film is the "Sunday Bloody Sunday" performance, as it relates to the Enniskillen bombing that had just happened the very same day the band was recording a live show in Denver, Colorado.[2] Bono's angry diatribe, telling a frantic crowd that he's had enough "of Irish Americans who haven't been back to their country in 20 or 30 years come up and talk about the resistance and the glory of the revolution" is soon followed by a heartfelt interpretation of the band's signature song. Shadows and darkness take over the stage, a soft, pale halo light contouring the singer's body as he is seen kneeling in front of an invisible crowd. It is only halfway through the song that the bright overhead spotlight re-appears, the camera carefully moving in half-circles around Bono, as he condemns the IRA's actions and the Irish immigrants' support of violence. "Fuck the revolution," Bono says, as the second part of the song is belted out with passion, ending with the singer once again bending down in a posture of prayer, inviting the audience to share a moment of silence and communion. Because of this "dedication to bringing justice issues onstage," some aspects of a U2 show "have been poorly integrated or over explained verbally" instead of the symbolic act being recognized for "carrying a performative power that stays with listeners much longer than a lecture" (Maynard 159). In *Rattle and Hum*, it is the musical journey (as Larry Mullen Jr. describes it) through live performances that should speak louder than words (i.e. interviews), something fans and critics alike did not seem to understand.

On this note (no pun intended) the rockumentary ends with another political song, "Pride (In the Name of Love)" written this time for Reverend Martin Luther King, Jr., the leader of the Black Civil Rights movements in the USA who was brutally murdered on 4 April 1968 in Memphis, Tennessee. The lyrics evoke Judas's betrayal of Jesus (*"one man betrayed with a kiss"*) and advocate peaceful activism and love (*"One man come in the name of love/ One man come and go/One man come, he to justify/One man to overthrow"*). For this last performance, the audience is clearly invited in by the camera, as the stadium is flooded in light and the singing crowd – also invited to join in by Bono – becomes a visible entity that could be seen as an extension of the stage. Coming full circle, with a black-and-white musical opening and ending sequence, the camera bids us goodbye while panning over the ecstatic crowd, as the stage fades to black and the band, far away on the solid ground, is illuminated by three distinct spotlights.

Conclusion

In his celebrated first feature-length film, *Black Girl* (France/Senegal, 1966), Senegalese filmmaker Ousmane Sembene uses black-and-white to show the discrepancies in economic relations between the colonizers (the French employers) and the colonized (the Black Senegalese girl hired to work for them in Europe). Indeed, the overwhelmingly white decor of the apartment where the young woman works, heavily contrasting with the colors of her homeland, highlights her position of apparent inferiority, as she is drowned in real and symbolic Whiteness. Although Joanou's use of black-and-white remains first and foremost an artistic choice – perhaps having nothing to do with symbols and metaphors – it is interesting to think of it otherwise. After all, U2's journey through the American South, their interest in blues, soul, rock 'n' roll and other African American or African-inspired music, the country's history with the USA (nineteenth-century immigration and the *métissage* of the Irish and African Americans), and the religious ties that unite Irish and African American Christians, are all elements that could be connected to the movie's color scheme. In the same way, the ever-present lights puncturing the screen can be considered through various (spiritual, technical) lenses, whether they are piercing through and illuminating places of darkness, forming a halo around the singer's body, making the crowd partially or fully visible, or alternately creating an atmosphere to bring awareness, to celebrate joy and hope, or to join the band and audience in a communal prayer. Whatever the perspective, when looking at the group's musical and spiritual journey – which I argue are one and the same – through rockumentaries made before and after *Rattle and Hum*, it is clear that U2's journey is one that has never suffered from ruptures, as their "holy quest" has simply had them visiting, investigating, and discovering new spaces, landscapes, and ways of expressing their unique musical identity. In this sense, Joanou succeeds in capturing a key moment in the foursome's career, i.e. the inevitable road trip through a Black and White America, a land filled and fulfilled with its own contradictions and desire to "*dream it all up again,*"[3] as expressed in the song "In God's Country":

> "*Desert sky*
> *Dream beneath a desert sky*
> *The rivers run but soon run dry*
> *We need new dreams tonight.*"
>
> (U2, "In God's Country," 1987)

Notes

1. On this subject, Bono credits Ginsberg's *Howl* with helping him see the poetry of The Bible (Stockham 1986).
2. The Enniskillen bombing, also known as the Poppy Day Massacre or the Remembrance Day Bombing, refers to an IRA intervention near a Remembrance Day parade in Northern Ireland, on 8 November 1987. The bombing killed twelve civilians and injured more than seventy people.
3. These are also the words pronounced by Bono at their pre-New Year's Eve concert in Dublin, 30 December 1989: "This is just the end of something for U2. And that's why we're playing these concerts – and we're throwing a party for ourselves and you. It's no big deal, it's just – we have to go away and . . . and dream it all up again" (Bono @U2.com 1).

References

[anon.] 2017. "Hundreds Gather On Anniversary Of Enniskillen Bombing As Memorial To Victims Unveiled." *The Irish News*, November 6. <https://www.irishnews.com/news/northernirelandnews/2017/11/09/news/hundreds-gather-on-anniversary-of-enniskillen-bombing-as-memorial-to-victims-unveiled-1182948/> (last accessed 11 October, 2018).

Assayas, Michka. 2005. *Bono: In Conversation with Michka Assayas*. New York: Riverhead Books.

Barthes, Roland. 1981. *Camera Lucida: Reflections on Photography*. New York: Hill and Wang.

Bono. n.d. "Dreaming It All Up Again." <https://www.atu2.com/news/dream-it-all-up-again.html> (last accessed 1 October, 2018).

Bright, Deborah. 1992. "Of Mother Nature and Marlboro Men, an Inquiry into the Cultural Meanings of Landscape Photography." In *The Contest Of Meaning: Critical Histories Of Photography*, ed. Richard Bolton, Richard. Cambridge, MA: MIT Press. 125–44.

Brown, Mark. n.d. "Rattle and Hum Also Shot at Denver Concerts." <https://www.atu2.com/news/rattle-and-hum-also-shot-at-denver-concerts.html> (last accessed 3 October, 2018).

Calhoun, Scott. 2012. *Exploring U2. Essays on the Music, Work and Influence of U2*. Lanham, Toronto, Plymouth: The Scarecrow Press.

DeCurtis, Anthony. 1988. "'Rattle and Hum' *Rolling Stone* movie review." <https://www.rollingstone.com/music/music-album-reviews/rattle-and-hum-251583/> (last accessed 2 October, 2018).

Deriso, Nick. n.d. "That Time U2 Dug up Some American Roots on Rattle and Hum." <http://ultimateclassicrock.com/u2-cover-dylan-and-the-beatles-on-rattle-and-hum/> (last accessed 29 August, 2018).

Graham, Bill. 2001. "'Rattle and Hum' movie review in *Hot Press* magazine." <https://www.hotpress.com/music/rattle-and-hum-551874> (last accessed 20 September, 2018).

Hilburne, Robert. 1988. "The First Temptation of U2: Will the Biting Criticism of 'Rattle and Hum' Cause the Band to Weaken Its Vision?" *Los Angeles Times*. <http://articles.latimes.com/1988-11-20/entertainment/ca-441_1_rock-band> (last accessed 23 September, 2018).

Kokkoris, Tassoula E. n.d. "Rattle and Reminisce: Critics Revisit Their Reviews 25

Years Later." <https://www.atu2.com/news/rattle-and-reminisce-critics-revisit-their-reviews-25-years-later.html> (last accessed 1 October, 2018).

Maynard, Beth. 2012. "Where Leitourgia has no name: U2 Live." In *Exploring U2: Essays on the Music, Work and Influence of U2*, ed. Scott Calhoun. Lanham, Toronto, Plymouth: The Scarecrow Press. 151–64.

McKenna, Patrick. 2013. "When the Irish Became White: Immigrants in Mid-19th Century US." In *The Irish Times*, February 12. <https://www.irishtimes.com/blogs/generationemigration/2013/02/12/when-the-irish-became-white-immigrants-in-mid-19th-century-us/> (last accessed 11 October, 2018).

Newfeld, Tim. n.d. "Bible References in U2 Lyrics. Drawing their Fish in the Sand." <https://www.atu2.com/lyrics/biblerefs.html> (last accessed 24 August, 2018).

Stockman, Steve. 2001. *Walk On. The Spiritual Journey of U2*. Lake Mary, FL: Relevant Books.

U2. 2005. *U2 on U2*. London: HarperCollins.

Wilmington, Michael. 1988. "Movie Reviews: 'Rattle and Hum' Catches U2's Music and Message." In *The Los Angeles Times*, November 4. <http://articles.latimes.com/1988-11-04/entertainment/ca-1284_1_u2-rattle-and-hum> (last accessed 11 October, 2018).

12. PUNK CITY SYMPHONY: THE CLASH AND *RUDE BOY*

Celine Bell

In London, England in the late 1970s, the punk rock movement was at its height. London-based bands like the Sex Pistols, The Damned, and The Clash sang about the alienation and frustration of urban youth, capturing a vivid snapshot of a city that was decaying, degenerating, and, in the words of The Clash's most famous song, drowning. The urban landscape evoked in the lyrics of punk songs was also captured in a number of punk rockumentaries made during this era, such as *The Great Rock 'n' Roll Swindle* (Julian Temple, UK, 1980) and *The Punk Rock Movie* (Don Letts, UK, 1978). In this chapter, I will focus on Jack Hazan's and David Mingay's 1980 film *Rude Boy* featuring The Clash. I examine the film's presentation of British youth and their relationship to the urban metropolis at the end of the 1970s. The film aligns the fascist and racist impulses of late 1970s London with the government and the police, two interconnected institutions that are presented as simultaneously oppressive and ripe for mockery. The tension between the police and the youth of Britain is largely manifested in a stylistic tension within the film, created by the uneasy juxtaposition of documentary footage with a fictional narrative. On the one hand, footage of contemporary Britain in conjunction with the socially conscious lyrics of The Clash's songs seems designed as a call to arms, urging the young punks to take action against the oppressive forces of the government. On the other hand, the somewhat cynical portrayal of the film's fictional protagonist, who frequently comes across as apathetic, ignorant, and thoroughly unsympathetic, suggests that the promise of punk politics is dead on arrival.

Initial reaction to the film was largely negative and, even today, most critics see its main value as lying in the performance footage that captures The Clash in their prime. Stacey Thompson, in his book *Punk Productions: Unfinished Business* (2004), is one of the few critics to attempt to reinterpret *Rude Boy*'s seemingly obvious defects as triumphs of punk filmmaking. For Thompson, the film's meandering pace, rejection of traditional narrative, and lack of closure force the spectator to become an active interpreter of the text, creating their own meaning out of the film's loosely connected images (Thompson 2004, 166). While I would agree with Thompson's move to reassess the seeming weaknesses of *Rude Boy* as key elements of its punk form, I would argue that he is too quick to suggest that the film is wide open to viewer interpretation. While it is true that many of the images are not provided with the kind of historical, social, and political framing that one would expect from a traditional documentary, there is one element of the film that is clearly deployed to "explain" the images contained in the film – the songs of The Clash.

"He's in love with Rock 'n' Roll"

Although not released until 1980, Hazan's and Mingay's *Rude Boy* was primarily shot in 1978, capturing the final glory days of the British punk scene in the shadow of Margaret Thatcher's rise to power. While the film was originally conceived with no clear purpose, Hazan and Mingay knew that they wanted to include footage of a punk band and eventually chose to collaborate with The Clash (Gray 2009, 230). The decision to collaborate with The Clash fundamentally shaped the direction that the film then took. As Hazan told the *New Musical Express* in 1980, "The ultimate structure was not known to us until very late in the movie" (Gray 1995, 341). The film's rather sparse narrative focuses on a London punk named Ray who roadies for The Clash at various gigs in and around London. At the time the film was shot, The Clash were riding high on the success of their self-titled debut album and were in the process of recording their second record, *Give 'Em Enough Rope* (1978), a process that is partially documented in the film.

Rude Boy co-director David Mingay has stated that the filmmakers' goal was to create a film more akin to a Hollywood musical (where the songs are intended to relate to the plot) rather than being a typical concert film (Gray 2009, 233). To this end, the performance footage is interspersed with scenes that are either wholly or partially scripted, including conversations between Ray and various members of The Clash that were inspired by real conversations with the band (Ibid., 231). Although the film does not feature formal interviews, these conversations between Ray and the members of The Clash often play out as pseudo-interviews with Ray prompting the band members to elaborate on various topics, often by playing devil's advocate. According to

12.1 Police officers prepare to face off against British youth in *Rude Boy* (1980).

Mingay, these conversations were meant to provide an opportunity for Ray and the band members to debate the thematic content of the songs featured in the film with a particular emphasis on the political and racial tensions highlighted therein (Ibid., 231). Many of the film's other scripted sequences draw on and illustrate the lyrical content of the Clash songs used in the film, including an extended thematic thread exploring the unequal treatment of White youth and Black youth by the London police.

While punk bands like the Sex Pistols were known for an outright rejection of all aspects of polite society, a stance that included dabbling in Nazi imagery, The Clash were a more progressive and socially conscious band, known for speaking out against injustice and discrimination. The film thus tries to take up this urge to expose inequality, but with somewhat mixed results. Towards the end of filming, the band fell out with the filmmakers, which likely accounts for the often fragmented, disjointed nature of the film. Rather than being a serious defect, however, the fractured nature of the film seems to mirror the directionless existence of its protagonist, who moves from one arbitrary episode to the next over the film's two-hour-plus running time.

Music is presented as the only form in which the generally inarticulate youth of London can express their dissatisfaction with urban life. The music in the film is overwhelmingly by The Clash. The few non-Clash songs heard are largely by Jamaican reggae artists, underlining the connection between London punks and Jamaican rude boys established by the film's title. The original Jamaican rude boys were young men who came from rural areas to the capital in search of work (Gray 2009, 217). While the term "rude" originally designated the rude boy as "unsophisticated," it later took on the connotations of "antisocial" and "offensive" as the unemployed rude boys formed violent gangs (Ibid., 217). This second meaning seems most apt for understanding the appeal of the rude boy in the punk context, where boredom and unemployment led to the formation of "gangs," often in the form of punk bands. The Clash's music emphasizes the association between the punk band and the urban street gang in such songs as "Last Gang in Town," "All the Young Punks," and "Garageland" (the latter two of which are featured in *Rude Boy*).

"The towers of London, these crumbling blocks"

An examination of the opening sequence of the film demonstrates the way in which the film combines documentary, fiction, and the music of The Clash. In a subversion of expectations like those celebrated by Thompson, The Clash do not appear until nearly fifteen minutes into the film. Their first song, however, provides a strong thematic summary of the opening section of the film. The film opens with two images that quickly establish the film's setting as well as providing a visual representation of the film's central thematic preoccupations of the panoptic, surveying gaze of the police versus the street level, mobile gaze of the punk. The film opens with an image of London's high-rise tower blocks that served as cheap housing for many of the urban working-class (as well as a repeated symbol of urban alienation in punk songs and discourse). We cut to a shot of a police helicopter circling in the sky, presumably patrolling the frequently rowdy housing estates. While the estates as a visual presence figure most prominently in this opening sequence, the image of the helicopter (or the sound of its rotating blades) will be repeated throughout the film, typically associated with the presence of the police and their capabilities of surveillance. After several shots of the estates, Ray is introduced staring out of a window in one of the towers. As he gazes upon a cheering crowd waving Union Jack flags, Ray spits out the window, demonstrating his contempt for the patriotic display. As Ray leaves the building, the camera lingers on the graffiti that covers the walls. Most of the graffiti points to the urban racial tensions that form a subplot in the film: "Get out you dirty black barstards [sic]," "white power," and a drawing of a Ku Klux Klan member are all seen, as well as multiple "NF" logos (for the right-wing National Front political party). The camera follows Ray from the housing estate to another location celebrated in many punk songs – the unemployment office.

The sight of the police helicopter sets up an exploration of the simultaneously oppressive and incompetent nature of the London police force that runs throughout the film, receiving both documentary and fictional treatment. Following the opening credits, the film unspools a lengthy sequence on the police, weaving together documentary, fiction, and music. An extended sequence of what appears to be documentary footage shows the police observing two rallies – one held by the National Front, followed by one held by an anti-fascist group. Although the police officers actually do very little, they are the subjects of lingering shots showing them standing in groups and observing their surroundings with unreadable expressions. To explicate the film's stance towards the police, the film thus shifts to a clearly scripted interlude. After leaving his job at a sex shop, Ray is stopped by the police while wandering through the neighbourhood of Westminster. Although the officer warns Ray not to "get lippy," the two soon start swearing at each other and the police end up arresting Ray, claiming he's drunk. While Ray is being willfully belligerent, the effect of the scene is to make the police officer look simultaneously ridiculous and oppressive, prone to easy anger and an abuse of his power. The scene is followed by more documentary footage that underlines these elements of the police. On a London street, masses of police face off against a group of youths (with the camera singling out a number who are Black). Although the police appear imposing, they prove to be no match for the crowd of young people, who begin throwing bricks at the assembled cops. The sequence abruptly cuts off mid-riot, leaving the viewer with a somewhat dim view of the police's ability to control the streets. At this point, nearly fifteen minutes into the film, we are finally treated to the first appearance of The Clash. The Clash are shown performing "Police and Thieves," a song that appears to both respond to the action thus far and foreshadow events still to come. The chorus of the song, a cover of a track by reggae artist Junior Murvin, references the "police and thieves in the street" who are "scaring the nation with their guns and ammunition."

"Police on my back"

Personal run-ins with the police are a frequent occurrence for the punk characters of *Rude Boy*, and here we see a stark division between how the White characters and the Black characters are treated. Two encounters between the (White) members of The Clash and the police are related in the film. Bassist Paul Simonon and drummer Topper Headon's arrest for shooting at pigeons from the roof of their recording studio is a key piece of Clash lore, while Paul and frontman Joe Strummer's later arrest for starting a fight during a gig was a standard part of early punk shows. While both arrests were real, the filmmakers appear to have been present for neither and thus they utilize a specific narrative pattern to tell the story of the arrests. Both arrests are introduced with a short narrative sequence. For the pigeon arrest, this narrative sequence is linked only thematically, showing Paul stealing money from his girlfriend to highlight his criminal credentials. For the fight arrest, the narrative sequence shows Ray attempting to break up a fight between a young Clash fan and two bouncers before road manager Johnny Green arrives to tell him that Joe and Paul have been arrested (lest the film become too narrative-driven, this sequence also includes an unrelated scene in which Ray vomits in the toilets.) These narrative scenes are followed by documentary footage of the band and various hangers-on milling about outside a courthouse. In both cases, the group is vaguely discussing the recent arrests, but the sound quality is generally quite poor and thus the sequences are significant more for the symbolic value of the courthouse as a location.

Because of the poor sound quality, these documentary sequences are augmented by semi-scripted sequences in which a member of the band (Topper in the first case and Paul in the second) explains the details of the arrests to Ray. In these sequences, Ray assumes his interviewer-like mode as he offers the band members prompts to guide their stories. These semi-scripted sequences play up the outlaw mystique of the band. Topper sports a replica of the yellow and black tracksuit worn by Bruce Lee in *Game of Death* (Robert Clouse, Hong Kong, 1978) and spars with a punching bag while Paul listens to The Slickers' 1970 reggae song "Johnny Too Bad" (sample lyric: "*You're just robbing and you're stabbing and you're shooting and you're looting/Boy, you're too bad*") while reclining shirtless on a hotel bed. While "Johnny Too Bad" clearly has a thematic connection to The Clash's lawless antics, this sequence also features a performance of a Clash song that comments on the action. In between the documentary footage outside the courthouse and Paul and Ray's discussion of the arrest, The Clash are shown performing "The Prisoner." The song's repeated refrain of "*I don't want to be the prisoner*" clearly resonates with the band's predicament at this juncture in the film. The song also mentions dodging the cops as well as name-checking the song Paul will listen to in the proceeding scene ("*Johnny Too Bad meets Johnny B. Goode*"). Ultimately, the band manages to escape the life of the prisoner. Both arrests (as well as Ray's arrest early in the film) ultimately end with the punks paying a fine and being released. As well, these arrests end up serving as dramatic fodder for The Clash's songs. The pigeon incident and its subsequent media coverage inspired a song called "Guns on the Roof" while guitarist Mick Jones is shown recording a song titled "Stay Free" about a childhood friend who served prison time for armed robbery before becoming a roadie for The Clash. In general, these encounters with the police are viewed as being alternately ridiculous or glamorous, enhancing the rebellious, anti-establishment credentials of the punks while simultaneously devaluing the power of the police.

About mid-way through the film, a fictional subplot is introduced involving a group of suspected Black pickpockets who the police are shown observing via surveillance camera as they attempt to ply their trade at a bus stop. These scenes are notable in that they have no overt connection to the main plot (there is no implication, for instance, that the pickpockets know Ray or any of the members of The Clash). Instead, these scenes serve as another indication of the ways in which the narrative is meant to serve as an illustration of the songs. "(White Man) in Hammersmith Palais" advocates solidarity between the White and Black youth of London in lyrics such as "*White youth, black youth – you better find another solution.*" What is most notable in this sequence, however, is the way in which it exposes the radically different circumstances of the Black youth. Even though the police are unable to obtain actual photographic proof of them committing a crime, they pick up the various members of the group on the streets of London in a sequence that is shot alternately through the window of the police car and from a bird's eye view shot of the street. While the White punks all escape with fines, the Black pickpockets are beaten and deemed likely to serve jail time despite the lack of concrete evidence that they have committed a crime. The Clash songs used in the scenes with the pickpockets typically serve as an ironic counterpoint to the narrative. Mick's performance of "Stay Free" (which ends with the line "*Go easy, step lightly, stay free*") is followed by a series of brief scenes of the police rounding up and arresting the pickpockets. Similarly, the scene in which one of the accused pickpockets learns he will likely serve jail time is ironically preceded by a brief snippet of the song "Rudie Can't Fail." In these sequences, the film thus uses an able blend of fiction, documentary, and music to create a clear argument about the racist and oppressive nature of the London police.

"How you get a-rude and a-reckless?"

The sequences exploring the interaction between the police and the youth of London also succeed by sidelining Ray, the film's nominal protagonist. When the film's focus shifts to Ray, the tensions and contradictions between the film's documentary mode and its narrative mode bubble to the surface. Ray spends much of his time wandering the streets of London, seemingly without a specific destination. The fragmented structure of the film enhances the impression that Ray's wanderings are largely directionless. After the first Clash performance, a shot of Ray in the audience abruptly cuts to a shot of Ray walking through the Brixton market. As Ray is now wearing different clothing, this is clearly not intended to show Ray's trip home from the concert. Yet this sequence also does not follow Ray to any particular destination, ending instead with an abrupt cut to Ray at home, looking as though he just woke up. Ray's walk therefore appears entirely unmotivated. Bored, directionless, and either unwilling or unable to find a steady job, Ray drifts through London's urban wasteland. "London's Burning," performed at the Rock Against Racism concert, encapsulates the punks' relationship to the urban streets. The repeated refrain "*London's burning with boredom now*" emphasizes the urban ennui of the punk who wanders the London streets searching for kicks. The song's lyrics appear to speak directly to Ray's late night walks around the city: "*The wind howls through the empty blocks looking for a home/I run through the empty stone 'cause I'm all alone."*

Ray is only briefly shown in his flat, where he drinks beer, listens to a Clash record, and receives his dole cheque. The connection between punk and the dole is brilliantly expressed in the Clash song Ray listens to in this sequence. "Career Opportunities" speaks to the difficulty of finding work, particularly meaningful work. The song's narrator is advised to take any job he can get, but the narrator dismisses all the jobs, which are either too mundane (bus driver, ticket inspector) or too dangerous (fighting in the army or opening letter bombs). Without a job, the punk has little to do but wander the streets and go to gigs. In *Rude Boy*, the punk is overwhelmingly associated with the public spaces of urban life. With most of his time spent at pubs, clubs, and simply wandering, Ray is far more at home on the city streets than he is in his own flat.

The song "All the Young Punks" is similarly used to point up Ray's dead-end existence. Late in the film, Joe is shown recording his vocals for the song. The verse he is recording speaks to the difficult employment situation of British youth:

> *Face front you got the future shining like a piece of gold*
> *But I swear as we get closer, it looks more like a lump of coal*
> *But it's better than some factory*
> *Now that's no place to waste your youth*
>
> (The Clash, "All the Young Punks," 1978)

This is followed by a brief scene featuring Ray at his sex shop job, staring blankly at a tally of the day's sales. A cut brings Ray to the studio where The Clash are recording. He chats with another roadie and describes his sex shop job as "boring as all shit." He expresses his desire to get back to work as a roadie, stating that "hard works pays off" when "you get some enjoyment out of it." While this statement is certainly in line with the Clash ethos, this is not really borne out by the portrayal of Ray himself, who continues to be generally useless in his roadie work for The Clash.

In the scenes showing Ray performing his roadie duties, he is depicted as generally inept. He naps rather than helping move equipment, he steals beer from the band's dressing room, and he misses the tour bus after oversleeping. Beyond his poor job performance, Ray is generally an unsympathetic character, culminating in a scene late in the film in which he casually drops several racial slurs. The choice to feature such an unsavory protagonist seems almost perverse. While the songs featured in the film seem designed to bolster sympathy for directionless British youth, Ray's unappealing behaviour undermines this goal at every turn. The character of Ray thus embodies the film's funda-

THE CLASH AND *RUDE BOY*

mentally conflicted nature, presenting both a celebration of punk principles and a questioning of those principles.

"Back in the garage with my bullshit detector"

The film's contradictory nature becomes even more apparent in the scenes in which Ray interacts with the members of The Clash. Over the course of the film, there are three sequences in which Ray and Joe "debate" various political issues. As mentioned earlier, the directors intended this to be an opportunity for The Clash to clearly outline their progressive political stance, but the band seem either unable or unwilling to do so outside of their song lyrics. In one exemplary sequence, Ray visits Joe in his hotel room and asks about the meaning of the t-shirt he wore to the Rock Against Racism gig.

Joe shows off the t-shirt, which is emblazoned with the words BRIGADE ROSSE and RAF, the names of two far-left terrorist groups active during the 1970s. Rather than taking this opportunity to explain who these groups are and why he chose to wear the shirt, Joe jokes that Brigade Rosse is a pizza restaurant and claims he does not know anything about the RAF. Instead, the explanation comes in the next scene, in which Joe and the rest of The Clash perform their song "Tommy Gun," a song that takes a sardonic look at terrorism and hero worship, featuring the line, "*I'm gonna get a jacket just like yours/An' give my false support to your phony cause.*" Perhaps more so than in any other scene in the film, the music here becomes crucial for providing any kind of explanation of the dialogue sequence. At the same time, the music

12.2 Joe Strummer (left) and Ray Gange debate contemporary political issues in *Rude Boy* (1980).

illuminates at a relatively general thematic level only. If the viewer, like Ray, is unaware of the Brigade Rosse or the RAF, they are similarly clueless after viewing the film. Indeed, by the film's end, there is no sense that Ray has gleaned even the vaguest sense of political awareness from the band's songs. In his final scene with Joe, Ray tells him, "I don't think you should mix your music with politics anymore."

While Joe often goes out of his way to be forgiving of Ray (including pretending to mishear the racial slurs he drops in their last scene together), Mick is often openly hostile towards Ray. Compared to the other band members, Ray shares relatively few one-on-one scenes with Mick. One of these scenes occurs when Ray watches Mick record his vocals for "Stay Free." In an odd moment, Ray approaches Mick after he finishes recording and speaks passionately (or as passionately as the inarticulate Ray can muster) about how emotional and meaningful he finds the song. Mick, who has already been shown to be the most resistant to Ray's limited charms, responds with a blank stare before nicking Ray's can of beer. This moment is particularly fascinating since it seems to blur the line between documentary and fiction. It is hard to tell whether Mick's lack of reaction is scripted or whether he has "failed" (presumably deliberately) to pick up on his cue to engage Ray in conversation, using Ray's comments to expand on the meaning of the song. Mick's hostility towards Ray also features in another moment that cleverly blends documentary and fiction. During a performance of "I'm So Bored with the USA," an obviously exasperated Mick yells directly into the camera, "Get off the fucking stage!" This is often reported to have been a moment of genuine annoyance with the camera crew, who must indeed have been an obstacle on the relatively small stages of the clubs The Clash were playing in this era. The moment is cleverly inserted into the film by intercutting shots of Mick with shots of Ray rushing on-stage to detangle the band's guitar cords.

Even the performance sequences are not free of contradiction. The first footage of The Clash shot for the project was their appearance at the Rock Against Racism carnival organized by the Anti-Nazi League, at which they perform "London's Burning" and "White Riot." "White Riot" is intended to be a laudatory tribute to the Black youth who Strummer sees as being unafraid to stand up for themselves, a quality that he wants to see White youth imitating, but based on its title and chorus ("*White riot/I wanna riot/A riot of my own*") the song was occasionally misunderstood as advocating a kind of race war. In the context of the film, this impression is not helped by the presence of Sham 69 frontman Jimmy Pursey (whose band was known for its right-wing following) and the fact that the crowd appears to be predominantly White. This song resurfaces in similarly ironic contexts later in the film. At two different concerts, the members of The Clash are shown admonishing the concertgoers for fighting before immediately launching into "White Riot."

The contradictions of the film are encapsulated in a decidedly un-punk footnote about the film's production. Due to the limited resources of the filmmakers, the sound quality of many of the live performances was too poor to include in the finished film and the band were thus required to overdub their performances in the studio (Gray 1995, 341). Gray notes that the film was later praised chiefly for capturing the live Clash in their prime, a fact that becomes somewhat ironic when one learns that these performances were in fact "fake" (Ibid., 343). The portions of the film that appear to have the greatest claim to documentary authenticity (the concert performances) are thus revealed to actually involve significant manipulation.

"Death or glory becomes just another story"

As I have argued throughout this chapter, the film's uneasy juxtaposition of documentary footage with a fictional narrative is elucidated through the music and lyrics of The Clash. The film ultimately ends on a markedly pessimistic note. Our last look at Ray shows him aimlessly wandering down a dark street past a poster for a Clash gig, underlining the loss of both his job and the community he found through punk music. The film then segues to a scripted sequence revealing the fate of the Black pickpockets. Their incarceration once again underlines the futility of fighting the law. The fictional narratives thus resolved, the film cuts to documentary footage showing newly-elected prime minister Margaret Thatcher arriving at 10 Downing Street. Although the filmmakers could not have known it at the time, the beginning of Thatcher's term is generally viewed as the end of the punk era (Savage 1991, 541). By 1980, punk was clearly on the decline following the implosion of the Sex Pistols, the splintering of the scene into various subgenres, and the increasing mainstream assimilation of the punk look and sound.

Still, although the film seems to point towards defeat, the film continues to sizzle with tension from its many contradictions. In this final section, it is ultimately the music of The Clash that underlines and amplifies the film's contradictory desires to serve as both a call to arms and a cynical takedown. In the final appearance, The Clash perform "I Fought the Law," a song that speaks to both the defeatism of the film's ending (*"I fought the law and the law won"*), but also makes clear that the punks will not go down without a fight. As the end credits roll, "Rudie Can't Fail" plays. This final song choice reads as simultaneously ironic (Rudie *has* failed) and optimistic (but he can always bounce back!). Indeed, at the time of the film's release, the band were riding high on the critical acclaim for their third album *London Calling* (1979), an album that moved their sound ever further away from the stripped-down punk sound showcased both on their first record and in *Rude Boy*. The stylistic and narrative tensions of *Rude Boy* thus embody the contradictions of The Clash itself. While punk was dying out and losing its way (just like Ray), The Clash was moving onward and upward.

REFERENCES

Gray, Marcus. 1995. *Last Gang in Town: The Story and the Myth of the Clash*. New York: Henry Holt and Company.
Gray, Marcus. 2009. *Route 19 Revisited: The Clash and London Calling*. London: Jonathan Cape.
Savage, Jon. 1991. *England's Dreaming: Anarchy, Sex Pistols, Punk Rock and Beyond*. New York: St. Martin's Press.
Thompson, Stacy. 2004. *Punk Productions: Unfinished Business*. Albany: State University of New York Press.

13. LISTENING FROM THE EMPTY BOOTH: PERFORMING THE GRATEFUL DEAD COMMUNITY IN *LONG STRANGE TRIP*

Randolph Jordan

In Act III of Amir Bar-Lev's six-part Grateful Dead documentary *Long Strange Trip: The Untold Story of the Grateful Dead* (USA, 2017), recording engineer Dennis "The Wiz" Leonard recounts a story from the last night of the European tour at the Lyceum Theatre in London. He left his post in the studio truck, the first mobile unit to employ 16-track recording for live performance, to reposition a microphone on stage inside the venue. On his way back out, the band started to play what would come to be known as one of its best renditions of "Morning Dew," and Leonard decided to stay and experience the performance first-hand. Teary-eyed at the memory of the emotional impact of this moment, Leonard describes being "caught" by frontman Jerry Garcia in mid-performance, who saw him listening and gave a look that Leonard interpreted as "I know what you're doing, and it's okay." Leonard took Garcia's expression as a gesture of the band's larger philosophy: what the Grateful Dead wanted most was for everybody to be there, with them, in the moment, no concern for the roles that everyone was supposed to play in the relationship between the band, its crew, and its audience. In the end, Leonard got to have his cake and eat it too: the track came out just exactly perfect[1] enough to be selected for inclusion on the *Europe '72* live album release. "And there was no one in the truck!" Garcia reminded him on his way out of the mixing studio the day they decided that it had made the cut.

The figure of the empty recording booth capturing a live performance evokes one of the central tensions in the Grateful Dead imaginary: capturing their notoriously ephemeral performances on tape seems anathema to what they were about as live performers, while being essential to forming the Deadhead community experience that made the continuing performances possible. As such, Leonard's story highlights the main discursive thrust of the film: that to understand the Grateful Dead, we have to understand the unique relationship they forged with their audience. Now, this is not news to anybody versed in Dead lore. But Bar-Lev takes things off the beaten path by tying the film's conventional rise and fall narrative arc, culminating in the final act's in-depth analysis of Jerry Garcia's demise, to the connection between the band's famous community environment and their relationship to media documentation. In this chapter I argue that the most productive way to address Bar-Lev's film, often critiqued for its historical gaps, overemphasis on Garcia's death, and lack of attention to the music itself, is as a meditation on what the band's relationship to the larger community known as the Grateful Dead can say about the nature of documentary media itself. *Long Strange Trip* is self-consciously about the act of performing the history of the Grateful Dead on film while it reports on the band's history of performance. As such, it offers productive pathways into thinking about core issues in the discourse of the rockumentary.

Vanishing Acts

Documentaries live at the intersection of faith in the ability of recording technologies to provide a window onto the world as it exists outside of networks of representation, and knowledge that the filmmaking process always intervenes in the events being documented. I begin by charting two intersecting threads in documentary media theory that are activated by Dennis Leonard's story of the empty booth: the goal of "transparency" in certain sectors of media culture, and the "performative" nature of media-makers bringing these events into being by the act of recording.

The figure of the recording engineer moving from the recording booth to a spot in the audience recalls the "Is it live? Or is it Memorex?" advertizing campaign. The conceit of these ads, popular in the hi-fi industry at large to this day, is that some stereo equipment is so good that you can't tell the difference between a recording and "the real thing." As sound technology historian Jonathan Sterne puts it, this promotional thrust was based on the impossible notion of "vanishing mediation ... where the medium produces a perfect symmetry between copy and original and, thereby, erases itself" (2003, 285), an idea commonly expressed as "transparency." Of course, media cannot vanish from processes in which they are embedded, and a recording of a live sound event will always bear the markers of the recording process, what Rick Altman calls "the material heterogeneity of recorded sound". (1992). A "Betty Board" tape by the band's long-time recordist Betty Cantor Jackson will always sound different from a tape made by their sound engineer and LSD chemist Owsley Stanley, which will always sound different from a recording made by an amateur in the audience.

Of course, nobody was more aware of the material heterogeneity of recorded sound than Dennis Leonard, who enacted his own vanishing mediation by getting out of the truck and into the performance space that night in London. He was in a privileged position to be able to do so. But this very act points to an unusual situation with respect to the Grateful Dead's relationship to recording: the tapes that have circulated so prolifically through the networks of the Deadhead community, more than for any other band in history, had tremendous power to get people out of their living rooms and into the shows. In a way, the relationship that the tapes fostered between band and audience managed to enact a very real form of vanishing mediation, not on the level of technological fidelity, but on the practical level of personal motivation. It was one piece of the puzzle in how the Dead performed the relationship between band, audience, and even crew like Leonard. This is the most consistently recurring theme across Bar-Lev's film: the band continually sought to render invisible any practical line between the different facets of the Grateful Dead community, however many difficulties this ideal engendered in practice. Here I argue that Bar-Lev lays new ground for documenting the Dead in the way he ties questions of the vanishing mediation between band and surrounding community to issues of authenticity in media documentation itself.

The critique of the fiction of vanishing mediation in sound theory is part of a larger movement in documentary theory that has long abandoned the notion that you could ever use film to provide unmediated access to the world before the cameras and microphones. The technology, and the filmmakers' hand in the use of that technology, are always present in the material, and only convention shapes the level to which we are meant to be aware of these mediating factors. This fundamental skepticism about documentary media's potential to provide access to something called "reality," or the "truth," has led to the popularization of increasingly reflexive modes of documentary filmmaking. Here we find the notion of the "performative documentary," which Stella Bruzzi defines as any non-fiction film that uses performance, "whether built around the intrusive presence of the filmmaker or self-conscious performances by its subjects," to enact "the notion that a documentary only comes into being as it is performed" (2006, 186). Bruzzi's formulation considers how "real" people perform their lives when in front of the camera and addresses the ways in which filmmakers bring the worlds they document into existence through the act of making their films. Yet this way of recognizing the performative quality of documentary filmmaking is troubled by the tradition – as old as the cinema itself – of filming subjects like theater actors or musicians who engage in acts conventionally understood as performance whether they are being documented or not.

Michael Chanan frames the issue like this: when filmed musicians are already performing for an audience, "the camera can adopt the same role as any other listener" (2013, 341). Performance in a case like this is less likely to serve as the distanciating device that premises Bruzzi's formulation of the "performative" mode. Michael Brendan Baker raises a similar issue when theorizing the role of documentary film music more generally. Defusing the staple critique of music in documentary as marker of biased editorial comment, Baker points out that if the subject of the documentary is musical performance, then "the soundtrack is internally motivated and thus preemptively rationalized for the viewer" (2011, 234). So, a film about performing musicians is prone to deflect attention away from the act of "performing" the film itself, thus deflecting the film's ability to use its own performance of the material as a reflexive move to distance the audience from claims to authenticity.

Yet, as Baker rightly notes, "to have people perform for machines fundamentally changes the process of representation and the event's subsequent reproduction" (246), necessarily binding filmmaker and subject together in the performative act of filmmaking. This harkens back to Jonathan Sterne's essential argument about sound reproduction in general: that sonic events are always transformed during the act of recording, not only by the recording itself but also in its staging *for* the recording process (2013, 290). Here there is no room for an *a priori* performance act to be documented without affecting the act itself, a discursive position increasingly popular with documentary filmmakers and theorists alike.

Long Strange Trip sits uneasily across the intersecting discourses of vanishing mediation and performativity. On its face, the film is a rather conventional music documentary, recounting the history of a band with a combination of historical footage and a range of interviews. It's not a performance film, so it doesn't fall easily into the construct articulated by Baker and Chanan that allows for the filmmakers to occupy the position of the audience without affecting the performance. As some have pointed out, the film contains relatively little footage of the band performing at all. So, the film isn't an obvious candidate for considering the relationship between performative documentary modes and musical performance in documentary. What I will demonstrate, however, is that Bar-Lev and his team constructed a film that is very much a performance of Grateful Dead history, while making that performance clear through the way in which it structures its path through a vast collection of archival material around one single recurring issue: how the Grateful Dead performed its relationship to the larger community of family, crew, and fans that, collectively, is what constitutes the Grateful Dead. As such, Bar-Lev's goal is not to re-inscribe his documentary about performing musicians with distanciating techniques that suggest the impossibility of accessing the reality of the Grateful Dead through the media, but rather to emphasize how his performance of documentary media about the Grateful Dead can invite the audience into the community, just as the band used the media to do back in the day. Here the issue of vanishing mediation becomes vital. The film knows that its historical footage cannot provide transparent access to the realities of the world that it captures. At the same time, the band's own documentation practices often enabled something like this transparency. Bar-Lev structures the film around stories about the band's relationship to its own documentation that intersect with the mythology of its invisible boundaries between stage, crew, and audience. The empty booth becomes a loaded image for the idea that the band required a paradoxical presence and absence to make its magic happen.

Transparent Contradiction

Let's see where the film's structure can be read as a deliberate performance of the material on hand for the sake of demonstrating the band's own performative nature. Dennis Leonard's story about leaving his post in the recording truck sits smack in the middle of Act III, titled "Let's Go Get In The Band" after a line from the interview with Donna Jean Godchaux, singer with the Grateful Dead from 1971 to 1979. It's a segment that might feel particularly disjointed if one is hoping for a linear trajectory through the history of the band, but this is where the segment shows its strength: a dramatic shift, by way of Leonard's story, from the band's triumphant communalism with its audience to a lengthy meditation on the death of many members within this community.

The segment begins with Godchaux relaying the story of how she and her husband Keith joined the band as singer and keyboard player respectively in 1971. Keith Godchaux was a classically-trained pianist who fell in love with the music of the Grateful Dead across several live experiences and decided he wanted to play that music. Donna Godchaux boldly approached Garcia after the next show that she attended and told him that her husband would like to be their next keyboard player. "And just like that we were in the band!"

Grateful Dead aficionados might get their backs up at the beginning of this segment when Donna Jean Godchaux's story seems to run callously past the sad details about why the band was in the market for a new singer and keyboardist to begin with: because their other keyboardist and frontman, Ron "Pigpen" McKernan, was drinking himself to death. Bar-Lev knows this, of course, and he turns the easy breezy view of the band's communal nature, such that fans could turn into band members "just like that," into a revelation of how costly membership in this community had been for so many, even early on, and a harbinger of what costs there would be yet to come.

Bar-Lev makes the shift from Keith and Donna to Pigpen masterfully, passing us through the story of Dennis Leonard leaving his post to watch "Morning Dew" live, a story that begins in fun about his little escapade and what it meant for the band's notion of family that his actions here would be considered acceptable, to a darker meditation on the nature of that particular performance of that particular song, a post-apocalyptic requiem for humankind, Garcia soloing with his back to the audience, tears streaming down his face. These darker details are then taken up in a moving interview with lyricist John Parry Barlow about how Pigpen's soft soul was slowly ejected from the band, and from life. As we ride with Barlow in his car en route to Pigpen's grave, he tells us that there's much sadness in the Dead's history, "and it hasn't properly been wept over." Barlow laments the scene in the early 1970s that he describes as overtly macho and frequently misogynistic, such that nobody in the "family" would dare cry over the passing of one of their own. Yet less than two minutes after, the film cuts to an interview with road manager Steve Parish, who recalls that there wasn't a dry eye in the house when news of Pigpen's passing broke.

This conclusion to Act III is important on two fronts. The section's celebratory opening turns into critique, offering one layer of contradiction present in the scene. Then two historical accounts of one critical event contradict each other, highlighting the impossibility of history being written coherently even by those who lived it. Bar-Lev hangs the shift in tone, and these contradictions, on the back of Leonard's story about the relationship between the band as both performers and documentarians. The image of the empty recording booth functions to evoke the absence at the core of any process of media documentation, a contradiction inherent to the very idea that recording can provide access to the live experience. The empty booth also signals the absences that sit at the core of the band itself, not only through those that have been lost from the community but in the way that the band attempted to organize itself without a centre, without a leader, and without internal borders. Act III is wonderfully organized in and of itself, but it's useful also to consider how Act III fits into the full set of the film as a whole, and in particular how it serves as a hinge for prior and subsequent discussions of the idea of the band's community as a performance of vanishing mediation within its own organization.

Immediacy

Let's go back to Act II: "This is Now," the film's golden nugget of lost footage found. The section begins with percussionist Mickey Hart telling us that "drums give their life in the playing." They degrade and decay. This is a poignant segue out of Act I, which begins with a lengthy rendition of "Death Don't Have No Mercy" over a credit sequence lushly illustrated with images of death, and ends with a story of the Watts Towers in Los Angeles, work of sculptor Simon Rodia and symbol of artistic longevity. The Watts Towers are framed as the antithesis of what Jerry Garcia hoped for his own life's work, explaining in one of the film's many interviews that he did not want to build something that couldn't be torn down after he's gone, but to live in the moment and produce the ephemeral, that which is subject to change, effectively to give his life in the playing and leave nothing behind. Yet Mickey Hart's rumination is also a setup for Act II's remarkable meditation on the nature of media documentation. Recording, of course, is an attempt to defeat the natural decay of the live performance, but also a medium subject to decay itself. Hart is busy sampling every drum in his collection so that these instruments can transcend time and space. A fraught project since tapes, films, and hard drives give their lives in the playing too. Again, we find the central tension between the life of performance and its artificial extension on record. Yet in this section of the film, this tension is put in service of detailing the very particular way in which the band performed its own relationship to documentary media.

Rhythm guitarist Bob Weir and his wife are in the Grateful Dead vaults pulling out a film reel that he refers to as the "Holy Grail," saying that this has never been seen and that he doesn't know why. An elaborate visual setup ties Hart's gestural strumming of his famous Beam instrument with the ignition of a film projector, and suddenly we pass through a portal in time to see an early 1970s Jerry staring at us right down a wide-angle lens, making self-conscious peering gestures through his glasses augmented by the vignette distortions inherent to this focal length.

What is this footage? Former Grateful Dead tour manager Sam Cutler tells us that he knows, and of course Bar-Lev makes sure that we take the scenic route to the answer, as if by way of a quick "Playing in the Band" intro verse before dropping into a lengthy improvisational section common to the tune in this period and then re-emerging for the chorus quite some time later. It's around two thirds of the way into the act when we finally see the image of Garcia again and proceed to learn about the Warner Bros. film crew that had been assigned to make a film about the band's arrival in Europe for their 1972 tour. The band, Cutler explains, didn't like promotion, and they didn't like to be photographed. So, they dosed the filmmakers with LSD who, inexperienced on the scene, fell apart as Garcia talked them through their highs and lows, often on camera. The footage they returned was not professionally viable, and so the film was packed up and locked away. More than just self-sabotage or self-defense, two terms used by Cutler to explain this behavior, this episode also points explicitly to the long-running theme throughout the entirety of the film: the dissolution of the boundary between band and audience. In Cutler's words, they didn't like to be filmed because being filmed relegates you to one side of the band/audience divide.

Here the film emphasizes the idea that the band wanted to be in charge of their own trip, no distinction from those they brought along with them. That's why, earlier in this act, we're told the story of how they commandeered the Warner Bros. studio on the early records and ran costs through the roof while they tinkered with childlike naïveté. That's why this act also covers their poor financial management skills, returning from tours as broke as when they left. They didn't want to run music like a business. They just wanted to be in the now, with their people. "This is now." Most remarkable about this segment, however, is how Bar-Lev positions these aspects of the band in the context of a new documentary film form in the making: the rockumentary, born in the 1960s with early peaks like *Woodstock* (Michael Wadleigh, USA, 1969) and *Monterey Pop* (D. A. Pennebaker, USA, 1968) which, as Cutler reminds us, gave major boosts to the careers of many of the Grateful Dead's contemporaries, most notably Jimi Hendrix and Janis Joplin. The Grateful Dead performed at both events, but opted out of appearing in either film, signing away their share of major box office successes and industry awards for both (Richardson 2014, 133). It was in this milieu, now assigned a film crew of their very own to assist with promotion of a tour that many argue stands as their very best, they decided to remain in shadow. The 16-track recording truck was enough, and the engineer was free to leave his post and join the show anytime (or so the story goes).

More than any other segment, Act II is where we learn about how the band wanted to manage their own media documentation, and how this related to the organizational structure of their community. The reason why Donna Jean and Keith Godchaux could just go and get in the band, the reason why Dennis Leonard could leave his post to join the audience, and the reason why Pigpen could be left by the wayside, all have to do with the notion that the band did not want to construct any ideological barriers between themselves as performers and the larger community that made their performance possible. If you wanted in, you got in. And nobody would stop you on your way out.

Revealing this footage is one of the film's clearest objectives. It's a real find and is amazing to watch regardless of rhetorical context. However, it's also a goldmine in terms of positioning the band in relation to media, a demonstration of how they performed for the cameras while OFF the stage. Cutler's version of the story of this footage seems tailor-made for the issues raised by Bruzzi, Baker, and Chanan around the ways in which filming performers changes how the idea of "performative" filmmaking can work. Hyper-aware of the ways in which being filmed creates a division between the band and their audience, the band worked to disarm the process in this particular case by inviting the filmmakers across the divide to participate in the band's world, marked most notably by the use of LSD. This is the off-stage version of the idea that camera crew at a concert can become part of the audience and capture the staged performance without affecting the performance itself. Here, the band similarly dissolved the boundary line by inviting the camera crew to become part of the scene backstage.

Walls Go Up

The psychedelic experience occupied a similar position to technologies of recording and transmission in the dissolution of boundaries between the band and its community. Grateful Dead studies abound in the exegesis of the role that psychedelic drugs played in the band's musical strategies and the relationship they fostered with their fans. Ideas about the loss of boundaries between self and world feature importantly in the ideology driving the band (Silverman 2010, 222). "Just as there was little distinction made between band members and the rest of the organization (the 'family'), the line between 'fan' and 'family' was often a blurry one, as well," a relationship assisted by the use of psychedelics that "quickly dissolved boundaries and unmasked anyone entering this realm" (Dierderich-Hirsch 2010, 300). It is not at all surprising, then, that the band's most ambitious technological experiment, the PA system known as the Wall of Sound, was devised by Owsley Stanley, the same person who also made their acid and engineered the recordings of many of their early shows. Acts IV and V include substantial discussions of the Wall of Sound and the taping community respectively, extending the setup of the first three acts around the band's conscious performance of their presence off-stage, and laying the foundation for the focus in Act VI on how the whole thing got away from them in the end.

The premise of the Wall of Sound was to create a PA system that could fill very large outdoor venues without distorting, thus creating a tighter bond between stage and audience. Michael Brendan Baker has pointed out that live sound in the 1960s and 1970s was frequently dreadful, a reality disguised by the trend in rockumentary films to produce the soundtracks according to the high standards of the music recording industry (2011, 192–3). In addition to making the listening experience better for the audience, especially as the Grateful Dead began playing stadium environments in the early 1970s, the system allowed for the removal of the stage monitors that continue to be the norm for allowing band members to hear each other properly while playing. With the Wall of Sound PA system behind the band instead of in front, the band heard itself through the same system as the audience, removing another level of separation between stage and dancefloor. The desire for a system like this highlights one of the key problems in subscribing to the myth of vanishing mediation: the live event itself is heavily mediated, so the idea that a recording can provide access to some pre-mediated event is impossible given that there is no such originary event. At the same time, the Wall of Sound was put in service of dissolving the mediation between band and audience so that they were bound up within the very same process. They were all on the same drugs, and they all heard the music through the same speakers.

The goal of the Wall of Sound maps neatly onto the idea of "acoustic community" from the field of acoustic ecology. Starting with the idea of the "acoustic profile" to define the area over which any given sound can be heard (Truax 1978, 5), people within these spatial boundaries bound together by common experience of the same sounds, as in the way parishes of old have been defined by the auditory limits of the church bell (Truax 2001, 66). The Wall of Sound, then, might be understood as a tool for extending the acoustic profile of the band's sound and thus expanding their community. At the same time, the technological nature of this community evokes R. Murray Schafer's notion of "schizophonia" as a negative consequence of the electroacoustic transmission of sound (1977, 90–1). While the term has been roundly critiqued for its failure to account for the medial nature of human engagement with the world and its negative representation of mental disability, it is interesting in this context to consider how schizophonia is bound up with Schafer's notion of the "hi-fi soundscape," equating fidelity not only with a strong signal-to-noise ratio, but also with the ability of sounds to travel a long way in an environment without being masked by density (Ibid., 43). The greater the distance from which we can hear any given sound, the greater the fidelity of the sound environment. This is an instructive conflation of fidelity and geographical range when considering the value of the acoustic profile concept: fidelity, in this construction, maps community. Embracing the role of sound technology in fostering community while enacting a particular model of vanishing mediation is a major component of understanding the Grateful Dead experience, and *Long Strange Trip* demonstrates this.

The Wall of Sound, while effective in establishing an acoustic community within any given venue, was famously impractical, requiring massive setup and tear-down times that strained the crew and cost a great deal in transportation. As bassist Phil Lesh puts it in the film: "We didn't give a shit. We were going to do it, and we were going to blow it out until we couldn't do it anymore." When the road weighed heavily enough on the band for them to call an indefinite hiatus in 1974, the PA was retired permanently. Metaphorically, the impracticality of sustaining these technologies of boundary dissolution and community development served as a foreshadowing of how the scene as a whole would implode over the next twenty years.

Walls Come Down

Act V dives into the emergence of the audience taping community, which functioned as a very effective extension of the Wall of Sound in allowing the sounds generated at live performances to reach far beyond the spatial and temporal specificity of these events. While the band is often given credit for progressive thinking in allowing taping to take place, they have made clear in interviews that, in fact, they simply didn't want to be responsible for policing the scene. Born of their lack of desire to take a position of authority over their audience, the acceptance of taping at shows had an enormous role in building their community network, often compared with the practice of file sharing in the BitTorrent era and engaging in community monitoring practices that "anticipated mechanisms like seller ratings on eBay, Amazon, and other websites" (Cummings 2013, 164). In 1984, the band officially sanctioned the practice by selling "tapers tickets" for the first time, a practice that continued until the end. While professional documentarians needed to be disarmed and brought into the space of the audience, amateur documentarians needed to be allowed the freedom associated with all activities at a Dead show.

While the Wall of Sound dramatically improved the quality of the band's sound while it improved its range, taping was at the mercy of how well any given rigs for recording and playback could deliver this sound to listeners in other spaces and times. As such, taping also demonstrated how a recording that stands at a remove from the live event proves the impossibility of vanishing mediation – one can never forget that it's a recording – while also proving the role that mediation can play in establishing an acoustic community well beyond the boundaries of the performance locale. In turn, this reflects back on key issues in the discourse of documentary media themselves. This is a dichotomy that fidelity discourse frequently posits between the world and its media representations, and a way out of debilitating arguments about authenticity in documentation is to change the dominant notion of "mediation" from something that separates us from the world in which we live to something that is a function of that world. Jonathan Sterne identifies a problem with conflating the term *media* with *mediation*, asserting that "[m]ediation is not necessarily intercession, filtering, or representation" (2012, 9). He uses the term *mediality* to address the reality "that communication technologies are a fundamental part of what it means to speak, to hear, or to do anything with sound. Mediality simply points to a collectively embodied process of cross-reference" (Ibid., 10). In short, sound is always of the world, regardless of the medium through which it travels. Addressing mediality is not about assessing distances between source and copy, but rather acknowledging the ways in which our various methods for experiencing the world – technological and otherwise – interact with one another as a function of our engagement with the world.

The twin developments of live sound and its documentation in the story of the Grateful Dead are fertile ground for Bar-Lev to structure his film. Hanging Acts IV and V on these parallel developments in the relationship between technology and the band/audience relationship puts a particular spin on the final act, charting the downfall of Jerry Garcia as the community of fans exploded beyond the limits of sustainability, Garcia ultimately retreating too far into the refuge of his drug habits. The scene grew to the point where the division between band and audience began to materialize through their need to act as moderators, issuing letters to fans pleading for civility outside venues after a series of gate-crashing events in the late 1980s and 1990s. The irony is that the act of gate-crashing is one of attempted vanishing mediation. Remove the barrier between the inside and outside of the venue and extend the acoustic community to encompass the growing parking lot scene that lived outside the venue at these later shows. But these fan-driven attempts at dissolving the boundary between band and audience led the band to resort to affirming their separation, an act that is simply not sustainable according to the logic of their development.

The mediator became visible, in other words, and this is emphasized in the film's final Act, when we learn of Garcia's view that he lived in a world without the Grateful Dead, for the band no longer served him in the way that it served his community. He had become isolated. As drummer Bill Kreutzmann puts it, playing stadiums was like playing in the studio: no connection to the audience. Garcia's daughter Trixie echoes this sentiment through her own experience at these later shows, wherein she felt she was not able to cross the line over into the community and thus couldn't understand what all the fuss was about. The Grateful Dead family was being isolated by the borders that their success in building community had fostered. The power of the live performance experience had been inverted to its contrived private equivalent, ironically one of the reasons why the scene exploded in the late 1980s: the "Touch of Grey" radio single gave the band their first Top Ten hit on the Billboard charts. Dennis Leonard's empty booth as a metaphor for Grateful Dead community and its relationship to recording became its opposite: the band became trapped in the booth of their own making. Finally, they came to embody the emptiness at the core of their live experience, the sense of loss that Nicholas Meriwether argues was essential to their music from the beginning (2010, 203).

Conclusion

In the details of the relationship between the band, their community, and their technologies of documentation, I see a metaphor for the problem of documentary truth itself: revealing the mediator becomes a distanciating device, a severance of the possibility of connection between reality and recording. But like the Grateful Dead themselves, Bar-Lev is attempting to shift the notion of vanishing mediation away from the stuff of technological fantasy and towards the reality that the band fostered through their use of the media to perform a sense of inclusion amongst their larger community. In this film, performative documentary strategies are a way of pulling people into the scene, not pushing them away. The idea that documentary media can reveal unmediated truth is just as impossible as the magical Memorex tape. Yet in making a film that finds a way to perform archival material that highlights the performative qualities of the band's own relationship to its community, the attention shifts from questions of historical accuracy or completism towards an appreciation of how the band's relationship to recording technologies allowed them to perform the community that ultimately made, and broke, the band. This is what Bar-Lev's documentary does best. It allows us to listen from the empty booth: that place where vanishing mediation is possible if we know how to maneuver ourselves just exactly perfect.

Note

1. The phrase "just exactly perfect" was a favourite of rhythm guitarist Bob Weir on stage to describe their goal during extended mid-set pauses to adjust their equipment, a marker of the regularly imperfect nature of the Grateful Dead performance style and the band's never-ending quest to get it just right.

References

Altman, Rick. 1992. "The Material Heterogeneity of Recorded Sound." In *Sound Theory, Sound Practice*, ed. Rick Altman. New York: Routledge. 15–31.
Baker, Michael Brendan. 2011. "Rockumentary: Style, Performance & Sound in a Documentary Genre." Ph.D. Dissertation. Montréal, Quebec: McGill University.
Bruzzi, Stella. 2006. *New Documentary*, 2nd edn. New York: Routledge.
Chanan, Michael. 2013. "Music, Documentary, Music Documentary." In *The Documentary Film Book*, ed. Brian Winston London: British Film Institute. 337–44.
Cummings, Alex Sayf. 2013. *Democracy of Sound: Music Piracy and the Remaking of American Copyright in the Twentieth Century*. New York: Oxford University Press.
Dierderich-Hirsch, Amanda. 2010. "Examining Grateful Dead Improvisation as a Catalyst for Creating Sustained *Communitas*." In *The Grateful Dead in Concert: Essays on Live Improvisation*, eds Jim Tuedio and Stan Spector. Jefferson, NC: McFarland. 294–309.
Meriwether, Nicholas. 2010. "Innocence and Experience in the Grateful Dead: A Reading of Stuart Hampshire." In *The Grateful Dead in Concert: Essays on Live Improvisation*, eds Jim Tuedio and Stan Spector. Jefferson, NC: McFarland. 200–10.
Richardson, Peter. 2014. *No Simple Highway: A Cultural History of the Grateful Dead*. New York: St. Martin's Press.
Schafer, R. Murray. 1977. *The Tuning of the World*. Toronto: McClelland and Stewart.
Silverman, Eric K. 2010. "'Mysteries Dark and Vast': Grateful Dead Concerts and Initiation into the Sublime." In *The Grateful Dead in Concert: Essays on Live Improvisation*, eds Jim Tuedio and Stan Spector. Jefferson, NC: McFarland. 214–31.
Sterne, Jonathan. 2003. *The Audible Past: Cultural Origins of Sound Reproduction*. Durham, NC: Duke University Press.
Sterne, Jonathan. 2012. *MP3: The Meaning of a Format*. Durham, NC: Duke University Press.
Truax, Barry, ed. 1978. *Handbook for Acoustic Ecology*. Vancouver: A. R. C. Publications.
Truax, Barry. 2001. *Acoustic Communication*, 2nd edn, Westport, CT: Alex Publishing.

14. MINIMUM AND MAXIMUM ROCK 'N' ROLL: NICK CAVE AND THE BAD SEEDS AND ROCKUMENTARY FORM

Anthony Kinik

A Brief History of Time

In the opening moments of Iain Forsyth and Jane Pollard's film *20,000 Days on Earth* (UK, 2014) – their ambitious portrait of the Australian ex-pat singer/songwriter/composer, novelist, poet, screenwriter, sometime actor, and occasional mixed-media artist Nick Cave, and his band, The Bad Seeds – the audience is subjected to a breathtaking showcase of multimedia and split-screen montage. As the film's title suggests, Cave was in his late fifties at the time and somehow, against all odds, for an artist as infamously nihilistic as he, not only had he managed to survive "20,000 days on Earth," but, in fact, he seemed to be thriving (J. H. Baker 2013, 3). Cave has been described as a "restless creator, skipping blithely across genres and forms," and the last decade had seen him produce a torrent of albums with the Bad Seeds and Grinderman, his fuzzed-out hard rock outfit; numerous scores and soundtracks, many of which had been composed with his bandmate and fellow countryman Warren Ellis; and two major books – *Complete Lyrics: 1978–2006* (2007) and *The Death of Bunny Munro* (2009), Cave's second novel – among other projects. The film caught a reunited Nick Cave and the Bad Seeds as they worked on their 2013 recording *Push the Sky Away* (Dominik 2013).

The sequence begins with a head-on shot of a bank of three rows of five television screens, all of them dark, all of them standing against a black wall in a moodily lit space of some kind. The audience hears the sound of a newborn baby wailing, and the televisions suddenly light up with the very same image carried across all fifteen screens: a birth scene in a hospital. Immediately afterward a five-digit counter appears, superimposed upon the second row of television sets, and as the doctor raises a baby up into the air, its umbilical cord still attached, the counter begins to count at breakneck speed, as a flurry of images attempts to keep pace. What follows over the course of the next ninety seconds is an audio-visual assault – part expanded cinema, part installation art – summing up a life from Day 1: the life of Nick Cave. Cliché images of childhood (a toddler's first steps) and Australia (a koala) are interspersed with more disturbing material (a scene from a film depicting Christ crucified); pop cultural references are introduced (Vladimir Nabokov's *Lolita*, Johnny Cash, Elvis Presley's 1968 comeback special); allusions to drug use and abuse are made (the needle and the spoon); and, finally, Nick Cave, the public persona, appears on the scene. From this point on, geographical indicators (images of London, Berlin, Brazil) get added to the mix of pop cultural icons and violent and upsetting imagery, but Forsyth and Pollard's montage is focused primarily on Nick Cave's career as a singer/songwriter/author/actor, his various musical projects (The Boys Next Door, The Birthday Party, The Bad Seeds, and Grinderman, primarily), and, to a lesser extent, his personal life (his marriage to his wife Susie, the birth of his sons), until the counter reaches 19999 and the images on the screens go dead quite abruptly.

Forsyth and Pollard's barrage of clips captures the chaos and cacophony of Cave's personal history in a clever and highly compressed form. It constitutes a brief but powerful experiment in expanded cinema, and because of the biography involved, this archive of images spans 19,999 days of a life that bridges the late twentieth century and the early twenty-first, from the mid- to late-1950s (Cave was born in 1957), to the 2010s. After a brief respite, the screen lights up again, and the audience is presented with a short, highly stylized sequence that captures Cave's early morning routine, as well as his anxiety and world-weariness (Kermode 2014). Cave's voice-over narration makes the film's conceit plain: "This is my 20,000th day on earth." There is perhaps some documentary truth to this sequence – it features Cave, his wife, and a room that may very well be his master bedroom – and the scene calls to mind similar ones in classic observational documentaries of the 1960s, such as Jean Rouch and Edgar Morin's *Chronique d'un été* (France, 1961), with its famous sequence depicting a day in the life of Angelo, a Parisian auto worker, and, more relevantly, Donald Brittain's *Ladies and Gentlemen... Mr. Leonard Cohen* (Canada, 1965), his revealing and highly ironic portrait of the poet just before he became a pop star. But like *Ladies and Gentlemen*, with its warnings of *caveat emptor*, this is a film that takes pains to alert its audience to its constructedness, and one that problematizes its status as a documentary, in any kind of "pure" sense, right from its opening seconds. As more than one critic has noted, Cave may be playing himself in this film, but it's quite clear he's playing a version of himself, a character of some kind (Kermode 2014). In fact, the film's opening minutes establish *20,000 Days on Earth* as a rather striking example of what Barry W. Sarchett once referred to as the "'rockumentary' as metadocumentary" (1994, 28).

Though it leans heavily on concert footage, music videos, and film appearances by Nick Cave and his bands quite specifically, the film's blistering opening montage also captures an entire history of popular culture (musical acts, television shows, advertisements, educational films, etc.) at a particularly significant juncture, one that's evident in the nature of the images presented, as well as in their shifting production values. What's maybe not as obvious and is something that Forsyth and Pollard don't explicitly draw attention to, is that the time period represented coincides almost exactly with the history of the rockumentary, which, as many scholars have pointed out, got its start in the years between 1958 and 1960, when Bert Stern shot the 1958 Newport Jazz Festival for his feature film *Jazz on a Summer's Day* (USA, 1959), before it coalesced into a recognizable genre over the course of the 1960s (Baker 2014, 6; James 2016, 188–91). Already by the early 1970s, when Cave was still a teenager, this genre – the popular music documentary – had become one of the most important developments in pop music, its visibility, and its increasingly sophisticated marketing and promotion, as well as in the development of documentary form. And by the 1980s, as Cave became something of an international icon due to his distinctive body of work and some impactful on-screen appearances (most notably with the Bad Seeds in Wim Wenders' *Wings of Desire* (West Germany/France, 1987)), the genre had become a fixture of documentary, and the name "rockumentary" had officially taken hold. Perhaps not surprisingly, it was late in the 1980s that Nick Cave and the Bad Seeds first became the subject of a rockumentary themselves. Taking into account two rockumentary projects associated with Nick Cave and the Bad Seeds – Uli M. Schüppel's film *The Road to God Knows Where* (Germany, 1990) and Forsyth and Pollard's *20,000 Days on Earth* – this chapter explores Cave's shifting engagement with the rockumentary over a quarter century, examining these films as a manifestation of post-punk's response to the history of popular music (including the rockumentary), it will elucidate two tendencies that have helped determine the parameters of the rockumentary since its early history but have taken on new significance in recent decades – minimalism and maximalism. As we shall see, these two Nick Cave rockumentaries represent remarkable examples of each.

The Rockumentary and the Early Post-Punk Era

In some ways, although its history dates back to the late 1950s, the rockumentary was a product of the post-punk era. Though the term "rockumentary" had first been coined in the late 1960s, it was not originally applied to the pop music documentary film, but rather to radio documentaries on the topic of rock 'n' roll and the culture that surrounded it (Baker 2011, 2). If there remains some confusion surrounding the precise moment of its crystallization, it appears as though the term "rockumentary" only began to be applied to documentary films about popular music in the early 1980s – first, with the publication of David Ehrenstein and Bill Reed's *Rock on Film* in 1982, a book that covered the topic and used the term repeatedly, as though it was already in common usage, and, secondly, with the release of Rob Reiner's *This is Spinal Tap* (USA, 1984), a parodic mockumentary whose form, whose underlying assumptions, and whose subtitle – "a rockumentary by Martin DiBergi™" – helped to further cement the notion of the rockumentary, as well as its clichés (Baker 2011, 2, 66). While the history of punk is obviously a contentious topic, one can safely state that punk rock as a major disruptive force, one that shook up the music industry on both sides of the Atlantic and beyond, was at its peak between 1976 and 1980, and the first wave of punk rockumentaries had effectively come to a close by the early 1980s, with the release of films like Penelope Spheeris's *The Decline of Western Civilization* (USA, 1981) and Lech Kowalski's *D.O.A.: A Right of Passage* (USA, 1981). In other words, though the popular music documentary had already been around for well over twenty years, the formal and established conceptualization of the rockumentary was a product of the immediate post-punk era.

Of course, Nick Cave too was a product of this transitional period, as well as one of its most provocative instigators. Formed in Melbourne, Australia in 1976, Cave's band The Boys Next Door relocated to London in 1980, bringing their Reign of Terror right to the very heart of the music industry. Soon afterwards they rechristened themselves The Birthday Party, a name whose wholesomeness belied the band's dedication to lyrical, sonic, and performative violence, and to a lifestyle that was utterly and seemingly gleefully self-destructive. Indeed, in an era where nihilism and chaos were rampant across many facets of popular culture, The Birthday Party somehow managed to distinguish themselves as "the world's most dangerous band" in the eyes of many. Not surprisingly, this philosophy of life and its accompanying pressures proved unsustainable, and The Birthday Party imploded in 1983. Out of the ruins emerged Nick Cave's next musical outfit, The Bad Seeds, a band that has shifted and changed over time, both in terms of personnel and in terms of its sound and its approach to music, but one that has nevertheless maintained a remarkable coherence and proven itself to be a lasting and surprisingly nimble proposition since its formation in 1984. By the time of their 1989 North American tour, Nick Cave and the Bad Seeds had reached a new level of recognition due to their star turn in the international art house hit *Wings of Desire*, followed by the release of their 1988 album *Tender Prey*, which

14.1 Uli M. Schüppel's *The Road to God Knows Where* (1990) as it appears in the opening montage of Iain Forsyth and Jane Pollard's *20,000 Days on Earth* (2014), roughly 12,152 days into the life of Nick Cave.

contained two singles – "The Mercy Seat" and "Deanna" – that would become staples, and it was precisely at that moment that Uli M. Schüppel initiated the band's engagement with the rockumentary when he shot the tour diary that would become *The Road to God Knows Where*.

Of course, the post-punk era coincided with the launch of MTV, and thus the very pinnacle of the music video era. Music videos didn't wipe out the rockumentary, but the concert film no longer held the central place in the culture that it had in the 1960s and 1970s, and this turn of events coincided with a shift away from theatrical exhibition and towards the rise of cable television and home video, most relevantly. Notably, when *The Road to God Knows Where* was released, it received minimal theatrical distribution and was circulated primarily in the form of a videocassette produced by Mute Film, the short-lived video arm of Mute Records, Nick Cave and the Bad Seeds' longtime label. The band was not of the stature that might have generated a rockumentary event of the likes of *Pink Floyd: Live at Pompeii* (Adrian Maben, France/Belgium/West Germany, 1972) or *The Song Remains the Same* (Peter Clifton and Joe Massot, UK/USA, 1976), even if they'd wanted to, but there's no question that 1990 amounted to a very different era in the distribution and exhibition of audio-visual media, and part of what *The Road to God Knows Where* deals with is the fate of a musical outfit like Nick Cave and the Bad Seeds in this new media culture.

Interestingly, when one looks at the body of literature that has emerged on the rockumentary and the popular music film more generally, one finds that the post-punk era has been largely overlooked. Virtually all of the major accounts on the topic have focused almost exclusively on the genre's classical period, 1960–78, and especially on the eleven-year period between the theatrical release of D. A. Pennebaker's landmark *Dont Look Back* (USA, 1967) and Martin Scorsese's *The Last Waltz* (USA, 1978), a film which is commonly seen as marking the end of an era, and one that roughly coincides with the advent of the punk rockumentary (e.g., Plasketes 1989 and Sarchett 1994). Some recent works like David E. James' *Rock 'n' Film: Cinema's Dance With Popular Music* (2016) can hardly be faulted for having chosen to focus on a historical span – essentially the mid-1950s to the late 1970s – that excludes later developments. What's surprising is that even studies committed to pushing beyond the classical rockumentary canon have often concentrated their analysis on the canonical works to a high degree. Thus, Keith Beattie's 2005 essay "It's Not Only Rock and Roll: 'Rockumentary,' Direct Cinema, and Performative Display" states quite clearly that its purview extends beyond a study of the rockumentary's origins and its classical era to encompass much later films – including Jem Cohen's *Instrument* (USA, 1999) and Joe Berlinger and Bruce Sinofsky's *Metallica: Some Kind of Monster* (USA, 2004) – but perhaps because of its focus on the direct cinema form, its most in-depth analyses are devoted to *Dont Look Back* and *The Last Waltz*. Similarly, even though Michael Brendan Baker's highly ambitious *Rockumentary Style, Performance, and Sound* (2011) points out that the only rockumentaries that have received "any sustained consideration" from scholars are *Dont Look Back* and *The Last Waltz*, and his study "seeks to correct this limited treatment of rockumentary," it is only in its conclusion that this study begins to address "The Third Wave" – punk and beyond – in any detail, and his closest readings are devoted to classical rockumentaries like *Woodstock* (72, 221). It was only in a later essay, "Notes on the Rockumentary Renaissance" (2014), that Baker really broke free of the canon, and redirected the conversation to cover a whole body of work that has emerged since the turn of the century and that has seized upon the advent of digital technologies in notable ways, including everything from Jonathan Caouette's *All Tomorrow's Parties* (UK, 2009) to the video game *The Beatles: Rock Band* (2009). So, while a number of twenty-first-century studies of the rockumentary and its development have made great strides when it comes to creating a fuller, more nuanced account of the genre's characteristics and its overall trajectory, they have also pointed towards how much work needs to be done to make the picture more inclusive, far-reaching, and complete. In many ways, that is the very task that the current volume is trying to address. A consideration of the rockumentaries devoted to Nick Cave and the Bad Seeds can help shift the focus of "rockumentary studies" well beyond the canonical films of the classical era, while, at the same time, maintaining an engagement with the genre's past precisely because Nick Cave's body of work has displayed a studious awareness of the history of popular music, and of pop culture more generally.

ANTHONY KINIK

Minimum Rock 'n' Roll: the Anti-Rockumentary

In a sense, the hyper-minimalist "anti-rockumentary" has its roots in the early history of the rockumentary, and, quite specifically, in a film that is often said to typify the classical rockumentary and its connection to the American direct cinema tradition: D. A. Pennebaker's *Dont Look Back*. Not only is *Dont Look Back* a rockumentary whose primary focus is not on rock, but on folk music – or more accurately, on Bob Dylan's hesitant and highly contentious transition from being a folk icon, to re-embracing rock 'n' roll and becoming a full-blown pop icon – but the film is famously frustrating when it comes to delivering the kind of triumphant musical performances that the rockumentary would later become synonymous with. The 1965 UK tour documented in the film was hugely successful and hugely momentous – not only did it mark a turning point in Dylan's career, but it also marked a turning point in the history of rock 'n' roll: one where the dominance of the three-minute pop song began to break down, one where pop musicians began to be taken with a higher degree of seriousness, and one where a vast and sophisticated pop-oriented media and publicity apparatus would begin to replace the hastily assembled one that is still in evidence in *Dont Look Back*. The influence of this tour is hard to underestimate, but the film itself is not much of a celebration. As David E. James has pointed out, the film has a very unusual structure to it: "fragments of Dylan's performance are set in a matrix of off-stage activities: traveling by car and train to engagements, jamming or bantering backstage; visits by friends, musicians, and fans; parties in hotel rooms, and interviews in which he is questioned about the meaning of his music" (202). *Dont Look Back* doesn't present its audience with the hagiographic portrait of Bob Dylan one would expect for a film about the Voice of the Generation. In fact, sometimes the proceedings are downright laughable – as in the famous scene where Dylan takes the stage and begins to perform into a dead PA system. Backstage, the venue's personnel scramble to figure out what the problem is, only to discover that they hadn't actually *plugged it in*. Instead, the film's focus has more to do with tedium and frustration, with the absurdities of Dylan's transformation into a pop icon, and with the fleeting moments of grace that sometimes occur behind-the-scenes, off-stage, and beyond the hungry eyes of his fans.

In many ways, *The Road to God Knows Where* is the film that took the logic and approach of *Dont Look Back*, and pushed it to its hyper-minimalist extremes. It did so almost a quarter of a century after Pennebaker's classic was released, and therefore at an entirely different point in the history of rock 'n' roll and the development of the pop music industry, which helps to explain why the film remains so obscure, even among fans of Nick Cave. Simply put, Nick Cave in 1989 was not Bob Dylan in 1965, and, similarly, Uli M. Schüppel was not D. A. Pennebaker. Nick Cave was not recording for Columbia Records, his songs weren't appearing on *Top of the Pops*, he didn't have a manager of the stature of Albert Grossman, and he wasn't playing venues along the lines of the Royal Albert Hall. In fact, in one notable sequence, Schüppel uses a clever pan of a scene of outright urban demolition just outside the door of one show space in order to comment on the kind of venues the Bad Seeds were playing on their North American tour.

But perhaps the most important reason for the film's obscurity goes beyond issues of name value and distribution and has to do with its willful renunciation of pleasure and its anti-rockumentary form. Like *Dont Look Back* before it, this is a film that is part tour film and part concert film, but if its predecessor was largely a study of tedium and frustration, here those qualities are emphasized to an even greater extent. Some of this has to do with the expanse of North America and the huge distances between gigs. Some of it has to do with the relative obscurity of Nick Cave and the Bad Seeds, an act whose great claim to fame at the time was that they'd had a memorable turn as themselves in Wenders' *Wings of Desire*. But much of it has to do with the fact that Schüppel goes out of his way to drain the drama and showmanship from the proceedings, which is quite a feat given that Nick Cave and the Bad Seeds had forged a career based on tales of blood melodrama and legendary showmanship. Like Pennebaker's 1967 film, this is a highly fragmented film and one that refuses to feature concert songs performed in their entirety, even though it is ostensibly a tour film. Instead, most of the film's attention is placed on backstage scenes, soundchecks, post-show green room parties, and life on the tour bus. And although the music industry now featured a vast and sophisticated media and publicity apparatus, the routine of photo shoots and interviews has not become any less tedious since the days of Dylan's 1965 UK tour. Every time the film indicates that it might provide a full and satisfying taste of the Nick Cave and the Bad Seeds experience, the moment is cut short – usually very abruptly – and Schüppel, like Pennebaker, displays an interest in highlighting the artifice of the life of the performer within a film whose minimalist form suggests notions of authenticity and fidelity. Thus, in the film's opening minutes, at the first show of the band's US tour – in Philadelphia – we witness the spectacle of Cave working himself up for his performance with the words, "Three things! I'm Nick Cave, I love you, and . . ." – quoting the opening line from "From Her to Eternity," the band's opening song – "I want to tell you about a girl." The audience could be forgiven for thinking that Cave and the band are just having fun backstage, making light of the ritual of on-stage banter, but, in fact, it turns out the singer was actually rehearsing the exact spiel he was about to use on-stage, as the film's audience discovers when the band takes the stage, Cave addresses the audience, and they launch into their set. Like virtually every performance in the film, Schüppel cuts from the song sharply, indicating that the significance of the scene has more to do with the fakery behind a seemingly impromptu opening monologue, and less to do with the song, the musicianship, or the other aspects of the performance.

Similarly, in true anti-rockumentary fashion, the film's few moments of grace do not occur on-stage, they occur behind-the-scenes, such as a seemingly impromptu rendition of Hank Williams' "Lost Highway," a song that Dylan had also performed behind-the-scenes in Dont Look Back. Here, however, the song takes on even greater meaning because it refers back to the early history of the rockumentary, because it's actually performed in a moving vehicle – the tour bus – *on* the highway, because of the map of the US that partially frames Cave's rendition, and because the impression one gets of this tour is often so bleak. Ultimately, if Dont Look Back is surprisingly anti-triumphalist in its orientation, The Road to God Knows Where is absolutely so – it's also incredibly nihilistic. Just the title of the film alone suggests as much.

Tellingly, the only time Schüppel's editing allows Cave and company to perform a song in its entirety is when they visit a Los Angeles radio station and perform a stripped, unplugged version of "The Mercy Seat." This is significant because although there is presumably an audience of thousands listening to the show over the airwaves, the nature of radio is such that the band is essentially performing solely for the show's DJ and the station's small crew. Consequently, there isn't nearly the boisterous reaction one would expect the song to receive if the band was on-stage – the song ends not with a bang but with a whimper. Furthermore, because the band has visited this radio station as part of an LA publicity tour to promote their album and their concert, the song takes on new meaning. A song that is ostensibly about capital punishment and one man's nearly unrepentant execution in the electric chair ("the mercy seat") becomes a song about the seat Cave occupies when he sits down with rock journalists, and the interviews he (like Dylan before him) finds so excruciating.

Maximum Rock 'n' Roll: the Meta-Documentary

Almost a quarter of a century later, Iain Forsyth and Jane Pollard released *20,000 Days on Earth* (2014), a documentary that not only deals with a very different version of Nick Cave and the Bad Seeds, at a very different point in the band's trajectory, but reflects a very different moment in the history of popular music, as well as the history of the rockumentary. So even though the band at the center of this film is ostensibly the very same one that appeared in The Road to God Knows Where, these films could hardly be more different. And, indeed, if Schüppel's film represented an exercise in extreme minimalism, Forsyth and Pollard's is grandiose, extravagant, and 'fantasia-like' (Elson), a prime example of what we might call maximalism in rockumentary form. Whereas Schüppel's film was a record of a transcontinental tour and a study of the drudgery of life on the road – a brutal demystification of the myth of the rock 'n' roll lifestyle – *20,000 Days on Earth* is a much more ambitious undertaking: part 'making-of' film, part concert-based film, part archival project, part tour film, and, as the film's title suggests, part biographical film, as much of the film's focus has to do with Nick Cave, his life story, his artistry, and his creative process. What makes this undertaking not only tolerable, but fascinating, has to do with its formal qualities and with the great liberties the filmmakers took on this project, in collaboration with Cave – with their willingness to dispense with many of the conventions of the rockumentary and vastly expand its potential.

In the opening portions of this chapter, we explored Forsyth and Pollard's introductory montage and its basis in expanded cinema and even in installation art. We then saw how the filmmakers followed up this multimedia barrage with a scene that established the one-day-in-the-life-of-Nick Cave conceit that gives form to most of the rest of the film, and that shifts the film into seemingly conventional rockumentary territory, while suggesting a sense of fabrication and fabulation that is both unsettling and highly intriguing. And while there are scenes in the film that appear to be straightforward and hold a great deal of documentary value to them – some of the recording session scenes, for instance – what makes the film so captivating is that this is clearly *not* one-day-in-the-life-of-Nick Cave, the film isn't trying to convince its audience otherwise, and the film is constantly and openly fluctuating between modes of representation, playfully asking its viewers to sift out what is truth and what is fiction, challenging them to construct the meaning of Nick Cave themselves. In the end, the film is less of a biography than a rumination *on* biography – on how one makes sense of a life, and how one reconstructs it.

Thus, later in the film, the filmmakers follow Cave as he pays a visit to an archive facility that appears to be in Brighton and that is devoted to Cave's life and to the ephemera that helps to piece together this story. Does this facility actually exist? Is it populated by a team of archivists dedicated to collecting and making sense of photographs, film and video clips, diaries, and other artifacts the way they do in this film? It seems highly unlikely, but by this point in the text the audience's sense of what is truth and what is not has been unsettled to such an extent that it's hard to tell. In fact, this archive *does* exist, but it's not located in Brighton, as the film leads its audience to believe – it's located in Melbourne. And the scene provides an opportunity for yet another plunge into Cave's past – this time driven by some of the material elements that have constituted Cave's life, and his sense of a multifaceted *oeuvre* – and this time focused on Cave's early history as a performer.

What's refreshing about these scenes is just how casually and effortlessly Cave's early history, and the histories of his first two bands, are crafted out of seemingly random artifacts. "Who knows their own story?," Cave asks in voice-over as he first enters the archive. "Certainly it makes no sense when we are living in the midst of it. It's all just clamour and confusion" – exactly the way Cave's life was presented in Forsyth and Pollard's opening montage. One's life, according to Cave, "only becomes a story when we tell it and retell it," which is precisely what he and his collaborators have been doing in this film all along; but here, in this archival space, a new approach is taken, and through Cave's intervention, seemingly random bits of ephemera are transformed into a story before our eyes.[1] The scene's initial premise is that the archive has just received a new batch of photographs from Cave's mother, and that the archivists require his assistance to make sense of them. By sifting through old school photographs, answering questions, and providing observations, Cave simultaneously presents the earliest history of The Boys Next Door, and how the band was formed. Soon Cave is looking at photographs documenting the band's transformation into The Birthday Party, and he performs a fascinating forensic investigation of a series of photographs of a particularly anarchic gig that took place in Cologne in 1981 to illustrate the pressures – internal and external – that would eventually rip the group apart. In short, Cave's analysis reveals a great deal about the deranged fans the band was attracting (one fan can be seen urinating on-stage), and about bassist Tracy Pew's particular role in the band (he acted as their enforcer), and he even definitively identifies the song that was being played at the time the shots were taken ("King Ink"). As Cave explains, "We were billed by some promoter as the most violent live band in the world," and this reputation turned The Birthday Party's performances into a dangerous and unsavory carnival. Towards the end, the band was so fed up with the routine that they quite literally turned their backs on their audience.

The other thing that's refreshing about these scenes is Cave's self-deprecating humor, and there's no better example of this than when the archivists bring a copy of his last will and testament, which he penned in 1987, to his attention and get him to read it aloud before the camera: "Okay, it seems like I wanted all my money – which was nothing, I would say, at the time – to go to the Nick Cave Memorial Museum. 'A small but adequate room or rooms will serve as the Nick Cave Memorial Museum.'" Cave and the team of archivists burst out in laughter, but the grim arrangements he made as a thirty-year-old man have proven to be prescient – that's exactly where we are as he reads this document. It might not be open to the public, but this archive occupying a series of "small but adequate ... rooms" *is*, for all intents and purposes, the Nick Cave Memorial Museum. "Yeah, I was always a kind of ostentatious bastard," Cave quips after reading the will, as if that was some kind of phase he went through, but this archive, *this film*, are both evidence of the ostentatiousness that has defined his entire career, and much of his life. And here, yet again, is another thing that Cave shares in common with Dylan: a profound interest in collecting practices, and in preserving and cataloging one's own legacy. Of course, the Nick Cave archive in Melbourne is not the University of Tulsa's

14.2 Nick Cave reads his last will & testament from 1987 to two archivists (and to the camera) in Forsyth and Pollard's *20,000 Days on Earth* (2014).

state-of-the-art Bob Dylan Archive, but, as we've determined, Nick Cave is not Bob Dylan (Sisario 2016).

CONCLUSION: THE MINIMALIST/MAXIMALIST ROCKUMENTARY

If Cave had flirted with expanded cinema in his collaboration with Forsyth and Pollard, on his most recent experiment with the rockumentary, 2016's *One More Time With Feeling*, directed by the Australian filmmaker Andrew Dominik, Cave and company embraced expanded cinema wholeheartedly. Shot in black-and-white and in color, and in both 3D and 2D digital video, Dominik's film began as a relatively straightforward "making of" documentary, a film that was meant to capture the recording sessions that would become the Bad Seeds' sixteenth studio album, *Skeleton Tree* (2016), and to celebrate its release. The twist was going to be the use of 3D. The idea was to use a digital 3D camera to shoot the film in a trippy, meditative style inspired in part by Alfonso Cuarón's *Gravity*, thus returning the rockumentary to the "head film" tradition of films like *Live at Pompeii* from the genre's 1970s heyday. What no one could have imagined is that tragedy would strike during the recording sessions – Cave's fifteen-year-old son Arthur died accidentally, plunging off one of Brighton's famous cliffs while under the influence of LSD. In a sense, a project that was meant to be an expanded cinema novelty turned into something that fluctuated between maximalism and minimalism, one that made great use of multiple cameras, elaborate setups, long, meandering traveling shots, and elaborate digital special effects, but one whose greatest impact came from its highly reflexive demystification of direct cinema aesthetics, as well as a series of brutally honest and painful reflections upon "the event" by Cave in particular, shot in plain, unflinching long takes. In other words, the film's significance had less to do with expanded cinema, and more to do with expanded emotions, one that took this latest Nick Cave and the Bad Seeds rockumentary to places the nihilistic minimalism of *The Road to God Knows Where* and the arch maximalism of *20,000 Days on Earth* had only hinted at.

Note

1. Cave's narration here is remarkably similar to a passage from Margaret Atwood's *Alias Grace* (1996), one that also served as the epigraph for another extremely inventive documentary, Sarah Polley's *Stories We Tell* (Canada, 2012): "When you are in the middle of a story it isn't a story at all, but only a confusion ... It's only afterwards that it becomes anything like a story at all. When you are telling it, to yourself or to someone else." This set of resonances is fitting. Atwood's novel is also a study in unreliable narration, and Polley's film is a similarly profound reckoning with personal history and the nature of the artistic process.

References

Baker, John H., ed. 2013. *The Art of Nick Cave: New Critical Essays*. Bristol and Chicago, IL: Intellect.
Baker, Michael Brendan. 2014. "Notes on the Rockumentary Renaissance." *Cinephile* 10(1): 5–10.
Baker, Michael Brendan. 2011 *Rockumentary: Style, Performance & Sound in a Documentary Genre*. Ph.D. thesis. Montréal, Quebec: McGill University.
Beattie, Keith. 2005. "It's Not Only Rock and Roll: 'Rockumentary,' Direct Cinema, and Performative Display." *Australasian Journal of American Studies* 24(2): 21–41.
Dominik, Andrew. 2013. "Nick Cave." *Interview*, 30 May 2013. <https://www.interviewmagazine.com/music/nick-cave> (last accessed 15 October, 2019).Ehrenstein, David and Bill Reed. 1982. *Rock on Film*. New York, NY: Putnam Publishing Group.
Elson, Gerard. 2015. "Conversation with Nick Cave." *Kill Your Darlings*, 22 July 2015.
James, David E. 2016. *Rock 'n' Film: Cinema's Dance With Popular Music*. New York: Oxford University Press.
Kermode, Mark. 2014), "*20,000 Days on Earth* Review: A Day in the Life of the 'Real' Nick Cave." *The Guardian*, 21 September 2014 <https://www.theguardian.com/film/2014/sep/21/20000-days-on-earth-nick-cave-review> (last accessed 15 October, 2019).
Plasketes, George M. 1989. "Rock on Reel: The Rise and Fall of the Rock Culture in America Reflected in a Decade of 'Rockumentaries'." *Qualitative Sociology* 12(1): 55–71.
Sarchett, Barry W. 1994. "'Rockumentary' As Metadocumentary: Martin Scorsese's *The Last Waltz*." *Literature/Film Quarterly* 22(1): 28–35.
Sisario, Ben. 2016. "Bob Dylan's Secret Archive,' *The New York Times*, 2 March

2016<https://www.nytimes.com/2016/03/06/arts/music/bob-dylans-secret-archive.html> (last accessed 15 October, 2019).

Wood, Mikael. 2016. "Interpreter of Pain: How Andrew Dominik Relays Nick Cave's Trauma in 'One More Time With Feeling'." *Los Angeles Times*, September 12, 2016. <http://www.latimes.com/.../la-et-ms-nick-cave-andrew-dominik-20160912-snap-story.html> (last accessed 15 October, 2019).

15. "EVERYTHING WAS STORIES": THE AESTHETIC IMAGINARIES OF *SEARCHING FOR THE WRONG-EYED JESUS*

Asbjørn Grønstad and Øyvind Vågnes

INTRODUCTION

In this chapter, we examine Andrew Douglas's documentary *Searching for the Wrong-Eyed Jesus* (UK, 2003), a film about the elusive identity of Southern music and culture, in the context of the notion of an *aesthetic imaginary*. Finely balancing the anecdotal with the mythological, Douglas's energetically idiosyncratic and unruly film, we propose, shares a notable affinity with the cultural narratives that Greil Marcus subsumes under the master trope of the *Old Weird America*, "the catacombed archives of utopia and morbidity beneath American highways of practical enterprise and manifest destiny" (Marcus 1997, 179). *Searching for the Wrong-Eyed Jesus* combines highly stylized and staged musical performances (The Handsome Family, Cat Power, David Eugene Edwards, Johnny Dowd) with tall-tale storytelling (Harry Crews, Jim White), carefully situated at various sites and locations in the natural and cultural landscape of the South. We want to argue that the film departs both from the dominant observational modes of classic rockumentaries like *Dont Look Back* (D. A. Pennebaker, USA, 1967), *Woodstock* (Michael Wadleigh, USA, 1970), and *Gimme Shelter* (Albert Maysles, David Maysles, and Charlotte Zwerin, USA, 1970), as well as from modern "behind-the-scenes" rockumentaries like *I Am Trying to Break Your Heart: A Film About Wilco* (Sam Jones, USA, 2002), *Metallica: Some Kind of Monster* (Joe Berlinger and Bruce Sinofsky, USA, 2004), and *Mistaken For Strangers* (Tom Berninger, USA, 2013). No less importantly, we would like to suggest that there are in fact several different aesthetic imaginaries of the South in literature, film, and television, a claim to which Douglas's documentary attests.

While indisputably a part of the diverse genre of rockumentary media, *Searching for the Wrong-Eyed Jesus* bears a pronounced family resemblance to the artefacts and concepts of the particular tradition Marcus alludes to, a tradition the cartography of which features key intersections such as Carl Sandburg's *American Songbag* (1927), Harry Smith's *Anthology of American Folk Music* (1952), Bob Dylan and The Band's *The Basement Tapes* (1975), the magazine *No Depression* (1995–), and Marcus's own *Invisible Republic* (1997), not to mention the multitude of recordings made under the Americana moniker over the last few decades. Taken together, these artefacts, we suggest, comprise an aesthetic imaginary. Put to productive conceptual use by Ranjan Ghosh and others, the idea of an aesthetic imaginary is complex and layered, and has been understood, for instance, in terms of "entangled figurations" (Ghosh 2015, 134). These figurations find many forms in scriptwriter Steve Haisman's suggestive narrative, which can be read as a performative engagement with the oral tradition on many levels. Our chapter considers the film's difficult yet productive tension between performativity and authenticity, proposing two distinct frames of reference to contextualize its narrative: the literary and aesthetic trope of the *Southern Gothic* and the inter-aesthetic trope of the *Old Weird America*.

Southern Gothic

By the middle of the twentieth century, three distinct representational tropes – all crucially informed by popular culture, and Hollywood cinema in particular – had started to accrue about the ways in which the American public imagined the South. These tropes could be delineated as the Old South, the South as Other, and the South of the burgeoning Civil Rights Movement (Williams 2011). The first of these is closely aligned with the Gothic tradition in American art and letters, metonymized in the image of derelict mansions and Spanish moss and painstakingly described in the fiction of writers such as William Faulkner, Flannery O'Connor, and Carson McCullers. The depiction of the South as an opportune scapegoat constitutes the second of these tropes and may have originated with the Baltimore-born satirist and scholar H. L. Mencken's essay "The Sahara of the Bozart" (1917), a derisive jibe at the supposed intellectual poverty of the Southern states. Essentially a long diatribe, the essay encapsulates the condition of the South as a "curious and pathological estrangement from everything that makes for a civilized culture" (Mencken 1977, 161). While this diagnosis was soon to be refuted by writers such as Katherine Ann Porter, Thomas Wolfe, James Branch Cabell, and

Tennessee Williams, the image of the South as the nation's scapegoat would inform depictions of the region in much post-war American cinema (Pinkerton 2015: 44). The latter's description of Southern Gothic literature as streaked by a sense of "underlying dreadfulness" would seem to apply also to films set in the South – formally and politically disparate as they may be – from *Thunder Road* (Arthur Ripley, USA, 1958) and *Wild River* (Elia Kazan, USA, 1960) to *The Beguiled* (Don Siegel, USA, 1971), *Deliverance* (John Boorman, USA, 1972), *White Lightning* (Joseph Sargent, USA, 1973), *Macon County Line* (Richard Compton, USA, 1974), *Wise Blood* (John Huston, USA, 1979), *Mississippi Burning* (Alan Parker, USA, 1988), and *Midnight in the Garden of Good and Evil* (Clint Eastwood, USA, 1997), to name just a few (Williams 1978: 42). The playwright's characterization seems to apply also to fictional representations of the South in the medium of television; a case in point would be the HBO's mini-series *True Detective* (created by Southern native Nic Pizzolatto, 2014), the web television series *Ozark* (Bill Dubuque, 2017–18), and the HBO mini-series *Sharp Objects* (Jean-Marc Vallée, 2018). Rather than forming a genre or an expressive modality, the American Gothic may more fruitfully be considered as a "discursive practice," one that, as Travis Stimeling maintains, is typically embraced by "disenfranchised populations" to confront "the notion of the American dream by focusing on the people who have failed to adapt to cultural progress and who have been left behind as a result" (Stimeling 2013, 20). Manifesting this evolutionary stasis are two archetypes familiar to us from popular culture, what Margie Burns terms "the decaying aristocracy" and "a primitive peasantry" (Burns 1991, 105–6).

The representations of the South as a place of existential dread, violence, and the kind of cultural backwardness discussed by Mencken comprise what might be termed an *aesthetic imaginary*. There are several conceptualizations of this phenomenon (Castoriadis 1987; Ghosh 2015; Grønstad 2015), all in various ways attuned to the figural basis of cultural perceptions, but here we would like to turn to the work of the French sociologist, philosopher, and filmmaker Edgar Morin and his influential book *The Cinema, or the Imaginary Man* (1956, English translation 2005). "The psyche of the cinema," Morin argues in his intellectually fecund study, "not only elaborates our perception of the real" but it also "secretes the imaginary" (Morin 2005, 202). This somewhat strange turn of phrase suggests that cinema as a technological and signifying apparatus is capable not only of *conveying* someone's imaginary (that of the filmmaker, for instance) but also of actually *engendering* imaginaries through its very dispositif. The cinematic image, according to Morin,

> is the strict reflection of reality, and its objectivity is contradictory to imaginary extravagance. But at the very same time, this reflection is a 'double.' The image is already imbued with subjective powers that

displace it, deform it, project it into fantasy and dream. The imaginary enchants the image because the image is already a potential sorcerer. The imaginary proliferates on the image like its own natural cancer. It crystallizes and deploys human needs, but always in images (quoted in Penley 1989, 11)

The aesthetic imaginary, in both Morin's account and that of the critics alluded to above, is a generative rather than a reflective device. Even if Morin perhaps somewhat confusingly states that the film image is a 'strict reflection' of the real, the larger point is that cinema – through the specificity of its technological and formal affordances – inevitably transforms this profilmic material into an object that is singularly aesthetic. What should also be pointed out here is that an aesthetic imaginary cannot simply ensue from just one lone artefact or text, such as a film or a novel; it is by nature cumulative, the epistemological outcome of a larger array of representations connected by a complex tissue of intertextual, thematic, and stylistic relations.

Can there then, in literature, film, and television, be not just one but several different aesthetic imaginaries of the South? And where exactly in this representational landscape does Douglas's documentary fit in? How does the film inscribe itself into the discursive practices already established by the narrative tropes referred to above? Caroline Williams notes that from the 1980s and onward, with the availability of new filmmaking technologies, Southerners themselves increasingly started to contribute to the portrayal of their region, sometimes commenting on the Hollywood versions. Films such as *Sherman's March* (Ross McElwee, USA, 1985), *Waking in Mississippi* (Christie Herring and Andre Robinson, USA, 1998), *Stranger With a Camera* (Elizabeth Barrett, USA, 1999), *Homecoming... Sometimes I am Haunted by Memories of Red Dirt Clay* (Charlene Gilbert, USA, 1999), and indeed *Searching for the Wrong-Eyed Jesus* have been seen as "auto-ethnographic" interventions contesting established tropes and aiming to generate new imaginaries for the South (Williams 2011). Roughly the same period saw the emergence of feature film directors whose roots were in the South, chief among them David Gordon Green, who has been called "the defining figure of indigenous Southern cinema in the 21st century" (Pinkerton 2015, 47). The inclusion of *Searching for the Wrong-Eyed Jesus* in this small auto-ethnographic tradition might seem incongruous, as the film's director is British, but conceivably the key presence of musician Jim White as narrator and guide explains why Williams sees an affinity with the work of the other documentarists (the film's title also references White's first album *(The Mysterious Tale of How I Shouted) Wrong-Eyed Jesus!*, released by Warner Bros. in 1997).

As reviewers were quick to pick up on, however, Douglas's film nonetheless displays a pronounced European sensibility. Writing for *Variety*, Leslie

Felperin detects in Douglas's approach a similarity to that of Austrian filmmaker Ulrich Seidl and his penchant for the freakish and the grotesque, as well as for his ambiguous stance vis-à-vis his filmed subjects, maintaining a precarious balance between affection and disparagement. Douglas's position, Felperin finds, represents "a romanticized, outsider's view of the South that willfully seeks out the culture's strangest, most weirdo aspects for other outsiders' gleeful delectation; the one place the film might not play well is the American South itself" (Felperin 2004). Later research largely affirms this appraisal. In their analysis of the film, Daniel Chapman and Jeremy McClain develop the thesis that *Searching for the Wrong-Eyed Jesus* is governed by what they call "a gaze of hipness" (Chapman and McClain 2011, 154). Framing the film as an "art documentary" and White as an "ethnographic informant" (Ibid., 153; 154), Chapman and McClain critique the political indifference that they see as fundamental to Douglas's project. That the film is more attracted to myth and the archetypal than to material specificity is evidenced, for instance in the evasion of geographical location in favor of generic places such as the church, the trailer park, the prison, the honky-tonk bar, and the coal mine. Furthermore, Chapman and McClain argue, the primary mode of communication in the film is based on affect, which is what unites the filmmakers and their subjects. Their stories and memories are relayed without any "political or cultural judgment" (Ibid., 154), which evidently could also be construed as an accomplishment (their description here would be apt for the work of the aforementioned Seidl), but in the present context it is intended as criticism. On Chapman and McClain's reading, Douglas's film attempts to "redeem" the image of Southern poverty through a set of representational techniques that produce this gaze of hipness; chief among them, the conception of the film as a road movie, White's role as our chaperon, the use of a soundtrack consisting of critically esteemed indie Americana, the allusions to the Southern Gothic, and the reliance on affective interviews. This gaze, according to Chapman and McClain, can be "refreshing" and "startling," but is still, in the final instance, "vacuous" and unable to recognize power structures (Ibid., 154; 155). "Through hip glasses," they claim, "oppression is experienced aesthetically and affectively, rather than politically" (Ibid., 155). The lens through which Douglas views the characters and their environment is tainted by this sensibility, which by nature is at odds with the political. Some of the hallmarks of hip, which in the US historically is tied to Black experience, are a proclivity for the outsider, for style over narrative, and for ambiguity over certainty. Political activism, due to its favoring of the collective and of material needs over cultural expression, is anathema to the aesthetics of hip that Chapman and McClain claim permeates Douglas's movie (Ibid., 156). Berating the patronizing attitude that occasionally surfaces in the film, the critics hold that the filmmakers "get caught up in the mythology of the South" and that they celebrate "the stereotypical White Southerner without engaging him like an adult" (Ibid., 159; 158). Another bone of contention, finally, is what these scholars see as a regrettable omission – the absence of any discussion of race in the film.

A question that remains to be answered is whether such interpretations of *Searching for the Wrong-Eyed Jesus* mostly serve to align the film with the conventional aesthetic imaginary of the South previously considered, or if Douglas brings something different to the table. While Chapman and McClain's critique is justified for the most part, it also functions within an interpretive frame that perhaps unduly reduces the scope and meanings of what is clearly a complex and multilayered endeavor. What is missing from Felperin's as well as Chapman and McClain's readings of the film, we want to argue, is a sense of additional interpretive frames that might be equally significant to those discussed above. *Searching for the Wrong-Eyed Jesus* is not just an ethnographic documentary *about* the South; it is also a performative rockumentary about a particular genre of music and the multiple relations – historical, cultural, and artistic – that this genre entertains *with* the South.

Strange Maps

Rather than seeing Douglas's film as contributing to the ongoing creation of what has been referred to as a "mechanically reproduced South," threateningly "indistinct and simulated" (Bone, Link, and Ward 2015, 2), we consider Haisman's cartographic orientations, drawn out on a piece of paper torn out of a notebook, as something of a roadmap for the territory into which protagonist White invites the viewer to join him. In the center of the sketch are the words "the South," around which six suggestive concepts are caught in a spinning wheel: "Church," "Honky Tonk," "Backwaters," "Truck Stop," "Mountains," and "Jail." Combining institutions of authority and non-specific but evocative locations and landscapes with a concept of musical culture, the drawing can be said to conjure up a set of interrelated ideas of "the South," rather than any concrete manifestation of the region as a geographical or sociopolitical place. Although the circular movement of the picture hints at connections and patterns, it leaves questions of causality unsettled, at the same time gesturing towards the interrelation between new conceptual constellations, including "religion," "landscape," and "music."

In stirring such associations Haisman's idiosyncratic map is reminiscent of a very specific project that might very well have inspired the search in *Searching for the Wrong-Eyed Jesus*, namely Harry Smith's *Anthology of American Folk Music* (1952), issued on Folkways Records. Consisting of previously released music, the collection was remarkable for its resonant assemblage of material, which in effect enabled a new generation of artists to discover seminal, but not easily locatable artists of the 1920s and 1930s. According to Greil Marcus, who convincingly traces the genealogy of *The Basement Tapes* (recorded in 1967-8 and released in 1975) back to Smith's influential compendium, it served as Bob Dylan's "first true map of a republic that was still a hunch to him" (Marcus 1997, 88).

Borrowing a phrase from the poet Kenneth Rexroth – "the old free America," originally intended to evoke the country that "lay behind Carl Sandburg's work" – Marcus finds that a distinct aesthetic imaginary informs Smith's collection, and in turn Dylan and The Band's late 1960s reimagination of its contents, and he calls it "the old, weird America" (Ibid., 89). A compilation of American folk songs, Sandburg's *The American Songbag* (1927) was immensely influential, greatly impacting, for instance, Pete Seeger's commitment to the folk tradition. Furthermore, the intellectual effort of Sandburg's engagement with the material he collected suggested a combination of seriousness and playfulness that opened a whole new avenue of inquiry to listeners who wanted to respond to it analytically. In the very act of curating a set of songs lay the possibility to say something about their shared origins and their distinctive qualities. The organization of the *Anthology*, with three sets of two long players in each, is conceptual, rather than historical, chronological, or generic, and reflected Smith's fabulistic approach, with sections titled "Ballads," "Social Music," and "Songs," in effect constructing "internal narratives and orchestrated continuities": "Linking one performance to another," Marcus writes, "he ultimately linked each to all" (Ibid., 104). Smith's aim was not to present an all-encompassing introduction to folk music so much as to curate the selected songs according to a very distinct notion of a shared landscape from which their characters and stories grew – "a perfectly, absolutely metaphorical America," in the words of Marcus (Ibid., 124). Drawing a comparison between the illustrations Smith selected for the *Anthology* with the cut-outs that appear in his animation film *Heaven and Earth Magic* (1957–62), Marcus suggests that "every image was less a representation of the real than the symbol of the imaginary, of the notion that the imaginary could become real at any time" (Ibid., 109).

The South, as it appears in *Searching for the Wrong-Eyed Jesus*, belongs in this cartography, "an arena of rights and obligations, freedoms and restraints, crime and punishment, love and death, humor and tragedy, speech and silence" (Ibid., 124). Like a Virgil to Jim White's Dante, writer Harry Crews leads the way down a gravel road surrounded by swamps and kudzu, sharing memorable passages from his memoir *A Childhood: The Biography of a Place*:

> I first became fascinated with the Sears catalogue because all the people in its pages were perfect. Nearly everybody I knew had something missing, a finger cut off, a toe split, an ear half-chewed away, an eye clouded with blindness from a glancing fence staple. And if they didn't have something

missing, they were carrying scars from barbed wire, or knives, or fish-hooks. But the people in the catalogue had no such hurts. They were not only whole, had all their arms and legs and eyes on their unscarred bodies, but they were also beautiful (Crews 1995, 58)

Born in 1935 in Bacon County, Georgia, Crews' earliest years were shaped by the Great Depression. He shares with Smith a fascination with the imagery of the Sears catalogues, which appears in several cut-outs in *Heaven and Earth Magic*. Emblems of the promise of perfection, the 1950s advertisements provide the *Old Weird America* with its counter-image, an illusion against which to rub the harsh realities of its stories and songs. This relationship between conflicting imaginaries runs through Smith's imagery, Crews' imaginative recollections, and their juxtaposition in *Searching for the Wrong-Eyed Jesus*.

Whereas in the *Anthology* the assemblage is presented in the form of an issued collection of previously recorded material, the songs come alive in a different way altogether in Douglas's film, namely in the form of a series of carefully orchestrated site-specific performances. Much more than a gimmick, this live rendering enables a form of hauntological evocation of traditional song that is instrumental to the film's engagement with the past. Rather than inviting the artists to sing and play at points of historical or cultural interest, such as heritage sites of various kinds, Haisman and Douglas are predominantly looking for situated experiences of a more general kind, in alignment with their scribbled roadmap. David Eugene Edwards sings and plays the banjo surrounded by trees, placing us in the forested wilderness into which several characters in folk balladry escape and seek refuge. Likewise, Melissa Swingle plays "Amazing Grace" on a saw, seated on the hood of a car, while the sounds of animal life are faintly audible in the background. All along, oral storytelling seems inextricably connected with musical performance, often resulting in a new contextualization of both. After having played the saw, Swingle shares some reflections on death, spurned by a family funeral she recently attended, a recollection that places the hymn she has just performed simultaneously in history and in the contemporary moment. Seated in a Southern barbershop, Johnny Dowd sings his own "First There Was" in a duet with one of the hairdressers in the salon, while hair is being cut and conversation plays out. When Dowd returns to perform "One Way" in front of a gas station at night an hour into *Searching for the Wrong-Eyed Jesus*, it is obvious that the site-specific nature of these live renditions is indicative of the film's vision of the South, which appears to us in a way that echoes Marcus's sentiments, so that "every image was less a representation of the real than the symbol of the imaginary, of the notion that the imaginary could become real at any time" (Ibid., 109).

In a couple of instances, a song will hum from White's car stereo – memorably

"The Coo Coo Bird," one of the cornerstones of the *Anthology*'s "Songs" section – but for the most part, this form of site-specific live performance ties a specific song to the timbre of an individual voice, or to the sound of an individual instrument, and simultaneously the essential qualities of a specific locale that throws new light over the song in question. The Handsome Family appear one moment in a rough bar behind a pool table, in the next performing "When That Helicopter Comes" at a crossroad, with a wide-eyed boy watching and listening attentively. David Johansen – one of the artists most intensely engaged with the *Anthology*, naming a band "the Harry Smiths" and recording and performing songs from the compilation – plays "Last Kind Word Blues" (Geeshie Wiley) in a motel room, images of Elvis Presley from the mid-1950s suddenly shining into the room from the television set.

The forest, the hood of the car, the barbershop, the gas station, the crossroad, the motel room: all these sites, and more, are reflective of the engagement with the South that is at the centre of *Searching for the Wrong-Eyed Jesus*. "If one accepts the proposition that the meanings of utterances, actions and events are affected by their 'local position,' by the *situation* of which they are a part, then a work of art, too, will be defined in relation to its place and position," Nick Kaye suggests in the opening pages of *Site-Specific Art: Performance, Place and Documentation* (Kaye 2000, 1). Although the musical performances of Douglas's film hardly belong in the world of art that Kaye engages with, the principle of what he calls "site-specifics" is relevant in the context of their situatedness in a distinct cultural landscape. When the very positioning matters in relation to political, aesthetic, geographical, institutional, or other discourses, the location will necessarily inform our reading of an image, object, or event, Kaye argues, and thus shape our thinking about "what 'it' can be said to *be*" (Ibid., 1). If all the artists that appear in *Searching for the Wrong-Eyed Jesus* shared a stage and performed live in concert, they would have been removed from, rather than situated in the midst of, the aesthetic imaginary that informs the songwriting. When The Handsome Family perform "When That Helicopter Comes" live at a crossroads for an audience of one – excluding Douglas's crew, and, of course, future spectators of his film – they are well aware of the mythical reverberations of the site, which place it in a relationship with both Greek mythology and Blues culture (Robert Johnson).

It is this very situatedness of the musical performance which allows the evocation of the aesthetic imaginary of the South in *Searching for the Wrong-Eyed Jesus*. Producer Martin Rosenbaum describes how Douglas was very determined to bring high production values to the film, using camera dollies, tracks and lights at the locations selected for each song. In staging each performance carefully, he made sure that they "grew organically out of their experience of being in that environment ... The musicians infused the locations they inhabited with a special atmosphere that motivated the way the film came together" (Shadow Distribution 2003, 7–8). Eleven people contributed on set, a relatively large crew for a documentary of this kind, reflecting how its aesthetic ambitions were closely tied with its philosophical underpinnings. In this respect, *Searching for the Wrong-Eyed Jesus* is also indicative of a distinct, but more general tendency in the production of contemporary musical documentary, one in which "music has been radically altered by its incorporation of screen media . . . , and screen media has been deprived of its old assumptions about documentary form and techniques of documentary-making through its encounters with music" (Edgar et al. 2013, xvi). The film's artful refiguration and recombination of the tropes of Southern Gothic and the *Old Weird America*, finally, also demonstrate the extent to which aesthetic imaginaries are always embedded within and made possible by the specific affordances of any given medium.

References

Burns, Margie. 1991. "A Good Rose is Hard to Find: Southern Gothic as Signs of Social Dislocation in Faulkner and O'Connor." In *Image and Ideology in Modern/Postmodern Discourse*, eds David B. Downing and Susan Bazarzan. Albany, NY: SUNY Press. 105–24.
Butler, Mike. 1999. "'Luther King was a Good Ole Boy': The Southern Rock Movement and White Male Identity in the Post-Civil Rights South." *Popular Music and Society* 23(2): 41–62.
Castoriadis, Cornelius. 1987. *The Imaginary Institution of Society*. trans. Kathleen Blamey. Cambridge: Polity Press.
Chapman, Daniel and Jeremy McClain. 2011. "Documenting the Discourse of a Hip Dixie, or, How Do We Speak of the South?" *Power and Education* 3(2): 150–63.
Crews, Harry. 1995. *A Childhood: The Biography of a Place*. Athens, GA: University of Georgia Press.
Edgar, Robert, Kirsty Fairclough-Isaacs, and Benjamin Halligan, eds. 2013. *The Music Documentary: Acid Rock to Electropop*. New York: Routledge.
Felperin, Leslie. 2004. "Searching For the Wrong-Eyed Jesus." *Variety*, January 12–18.
Ghosh, Ranjan. 2015. "The Figure that Robert Frost's Poetics Make: Singularity and Sanskrit Poetic Theory." In *Singularity and Transnational Poetics*, ed. Birgit Kaiser. London: Routledge. 134–54.
Grønstad, Asbjørn. 2015. "Here is a Picture of No Country: The Image between Fiction and Politics in Eric Baudelaire's *Lost Letters to Max*." In *Socioaesthetics: Ambience – Imaginary*, eds Anders Michelsen and Frederik Tygstrup. Leiden: Brill. 119–28.
Kaye, Nick, ed. 2000. *Site-Specific Art: Performance, Place and Documentation*. London and New York: Routledge.
Marcus, Greil. 1997. *Invisible Republic: Bob Dylan's Basement Tapes*. New York: Henry Holt and Company.
Mencken, H. L. 1977. "The Sahara of the Bozart." In *The American Scene: A Reader*, ed. Huntington Cairns. New York: Alfred A. Knopf. 157–68.
Morin, Edgar. 2005. *The Cinema, or The Imaginary Man*. trans. Lorraine Mortimer, Minneapolis: University of Minnesota Press.
Penley, Constance. 1989. *The Future of an Illusion: Film, Feminism, and Psychoanalysis*. Minneapolis: University of Minnesota Press.

Pinkerton, Nick. 2015. "Southern Gothic." *Sight and Sound* 25(5): 44–50.
Shadow Distribution 2003. Press Kit. <http://www.shadowdistribution.com/searching/> (last accessed 17 September, 2018).
Stimeling, Travis D. 2013. "'Stay Out of the Way of the Southern Thing': The Drive-By Truckers' Southern Gothic Soundscape." *Popular Music and Society* 36(1): 19–29.
Williams, Caroline. 2011. *Capturing Southern Identities: Auto-ethnographic Documentaries of the Southern United States*. ProQuest Dissertations and Theses.
Williams, Tennessee. 1978. *Where I Live: Selected Essays*. New York: New Directions.

PART IV

COUNTER-CULTURES

16. CHILE: THE ROCK OF POLITICAL CULTURE AND THE HARD PLACE OF CULTURAL POLICY

Jorge Saavedra Utman and Toby Miller

INTRODUCTION

Documentary films about popular music are quite new to Latin America. In the case of Chile, our focus here, they emerged in the late 1990s, made by directors who were more concerned with political culture than celebrity lifestyles, show-business glamor, or bravura stadium footage. Their work engaged the political culture of rock through ways of life and stories that are classically disregarded by hegemonic narratives of mainstream culture. Instead, they focused on marginal bands and solo artists in the context of art more generally, treating rock music as a platform to exemplify and debate the cultural politics of social identity.

Inevitably, tension emerged at such an intersection of memory and recognition, art and politics; for documentaries about popular music represent a component and commentary on Chile's long and turbulent history of social and political art. They shed light on a wide spectrum of cases, stories, and issues across generations. At the same time, they incarnate the weakness of a film industry in which the increasing production of movies has encountered difficulty reaching large audiences.

This chapter argues that Chilean rockumentaries have their roots in the 1960s work of filmmakers who addressed the temporary rise of the popular classes to power;[1] that their increased production since the late 1990s is characterized by questioning of national identity, recovering collective memory, and recognizing non-hegemonic lifestyles; and that they have endured restricted circulation due to the absence of cultural policies challenging the power of a distribution system ruled by Hollywood, and a local media industry that is neither interested in, nor supportive of, critical filmmaking.

From the Edges to the Center

The first non-fiction Chilean films were mostly newsreels or picturesque insights about life in regions far-flung from the country's metropolitan areas. But the sheer fact of professionals' continuous involvement with filmmaking, as well as an interest in neorealism and a critical cinema and democratic desires that were starting to mobilize demands across Latin America, impelled a group of students based at the Universidad de Chile (Vega 2006). From the 1960s, documentary film in Chile tended to concentrate on the popular classes – people typically left behind by development models – and the political, social, and cultural contexts surrounding the rise and fall of Salvador Allende's 1970–3 socialist government, ousted by a fascist *coup* under the approving eye of DC (Dittus and Ulloa 2017).

Among these young students active in the 1950s, Pedro Chaskel and Sergio Bravo embraced the prospect of an observational cinema that could, ironically, be facilitated by the right's fetishization of the countryside. Their work was far-distant from picturesque portraits and languorous laments for Arcady, focusing instead on the material conditions of life. The seminal films of this era did not resemble "planned" newsreels. They were more akin to cinematic and experimental journeys into the lives of those who had not previously been considered filmic material: artisans from peripheral areas, Indigenous people, the poorer classes, and others who occupied an obscure place in the mainstream lights of Chilean institutions. This focus was later transferred onto political campaigns in which filmmakers portrayed leftist parties' quest for the presidency (Alberdi et al. 2007).

The rise of the left in the 1960s across Latin America, with Cuba as an icon, gave filmmakers a sense of purpose to their role in the wave of changes underway (Chanan 1976). *La Marcha del Carbón* (*The Coal March*, Sergio Bravo, Chile, 1963) and *Las Banderas del Pueblo* (*The Flags of the People*, Sergio Bravo, Chile, 1964) criticized the conditions of workers, forwarded their claims for better life conditions, and favoured Allende's 1964 presidential campaign (Mouesca 2005). That coverage was banned from being used in the campaign by the then-government of Jorge Alessandri. With Allende's 1970 victory came Patricio Guzmán's landmark trilogy *La Batalla de Chile* (*The Battle of Chile*, 1974–9), a monumental four-and-a-half hour epic that portrayed life and politics during the life of the popular-front government. Observing the elite and union workers alike, as well as life in shantytowns, marches, and demonstrations, the film carries a political mission:

La Batalla de Chile shows for the first time – day by day, step by step – a revolution in Latin America filmed by an independent crew. We started working in Santiago (Chile) on October 15th, 1972, and we ended on September 11th, 1973 (the day of the coup). It is a documentary movie made at the same time events were happening. It is not a film made from archives ... but the direct shooting of a political experience that shocked the world (Guzmán, interview)

Music was not a central theme in this tradition, but nor was it absent – *La Batalla* featured a mass singing of Sergio Ortega's inspirational "Venceremos" [We Shall Overcome].[2] And consider the folk composer, musician, and singer Violeta Parra in Bravo's work, such as the short documentary *Mimbre* [*Wicker*] (1957) (Escobar 2018). Nevertheless, filmmakers of the 1960s and early 1970s did not pay particular attention to bands, singers, or the growing music industry, despite the enormous popularity of pop, romantic, and tropical Chilean music, and the folk and Andean tradition that came to be known as *La Nueva Canción Chilena* [The New Chilean Song] (Fairley 1985). While contributors to *La Nueva Canción Chilena*, such as Parra, Patricio Manns, Rolando Alarcón, Inti Illimani, and Quilapayún played, the world and the country were changing. Cultural expression came to be deeply embedded in politics, to the point where culture *meant* politics. There was no politics without a cultural foundation in the "new men" who were supposed to grow from the Popular Unity bloc (Bowen 2013; Morris 1986). It can be no surprise that the world's most famous weapon against cultural imperialism, Ariel Dorfman and Armand Mattelart's *Para leer al pato Donald* [*How to Read Donald Duck*] (1971), emerged from this febrile context (Dorfman 2018).

But Popular Unity ended abruptly with the criminal conspirators' *coup*. That initiated seventeen years of military dictatorship ordered around detention, persecution, torture, murder, exile, and censorship (the *apagón cultural* [cultural blackout]). The disappearance and imprisonment of thousands of people, along with attempts to reform the nation in every single aspect of life, took culture as a major target (Errázuriz 2009). It is telling that Allende's moving, monumental last broadcast on Radio Magallanes, as he saw, heard, and felt treasonous, treacherous assaults from the cowardly armed forces, referred to the *Nueva Canción* as a crucial formation of the popular classes and his own commitments and passions. But once Allende had fallen, the next sound coming from TV and radio was Nazi marching music (Vilches 2004, 195; Neustadt 2004, 129).

Chilean society rapidly came to be characterized by omnipresent surveillance. Everything was under military control. People's entire lives were scrutinized, from the way they dressed, looked, and moved to the songs they were allowed to hear on radio and the films they could watch. The new fascist state examined all cultural content and authorship for "suspicious" themes – anything resembling the heyday of Popular Unity. Filmmakers and musicians alike were tortured, killed, or fled the country (in Guzmán's case, postproduction of *La Batalla de Chile* concluded in Cuba, after he clandestinely boarded a ship to the Caribbean). Torturers would interrogate prisoners about their musical preferences as a means of identifying their politics, and play loud music while beating, taunting, and raping their victims (Chornik 2018).[3]

Music, literature, and other forms of cultural expression connected to Allende, whether intimately or not, were outlawed by the new military authorities, who raided houses looking for anything they deemed subversive. Ordinary people destroyed or hid records, books, magazines, and pieces of celluloid. The Franco-Spanish filmmaker Jose María Berzosa's documentary series *Chile: Impressions* (1976) shows the military publicly building bonfires of books by Mario Vargas Llosa and Gabriel García Márquez, *inter alios* (including Dorfman and Mattelart's *Para leel al pato Donald*). Unique material held at the state film institution Chilefilms was eliminated in a wave of cultural destruction that was designed to build a new nation in ways that denied or decried the ashes of the previous epoch (Power 2015).

These erasures of past and present cultural forms were designed to eliminate any Marxist imprint from Chilean society and undo the legacy of Popular Unity. The new state's cultural policy document, published in 1974, sought to "eradicate from its roots, and forever, the infection that developed and can develop in the moral fibre of our country" (Junta Militar de Gobierno 1974, 37). The new nationalist culture would restore and re-emphasize conservative, authoritarian, and elitist elements, signaling who was entitled to have a say in the public sphere, what Chile and Chilean culture was, and which historical memories were allowable. As the dictatorship became an ongoing government, the state accreted powers to arrest people in their homes, move them from one side of the nation to distant regions, otherwise restrict freedom of movement, ban people from entering or exiting the country, prohibit the right to gather in public spaces, suspend the freedom of speech, impede the right of association, and impose censorship even on mail services (Fuenzalida 2003).

Songs of Freedom

The *junta*'s omnipresent control of radio, theater, and urban spaces placed restrictions on music, but it nevertheless played a big role in opposing the dictatorship. Songs from *La Nueva Canción Chilena*, mostly by artists living in exile, such as Inti Illimani, Quilapayún, and Manns, or assassinated by the military, in the case of Víctor Jara, were not played on radio. Citizens who owned vinyl records of such music ran serious risks in so doing, because ownership amounted to a threat to national security in the eyes of the *junta*.

CHILE: THE ROCK OF POLITICAL CULTURE

Music was dangerous. Audiocassettes became vital means of listening, sharing, and copying music, attracting less attention than bulkier LPs (Jordán 2009).

Little by little, resistance to the dictatorship grew. Music associated with the left, such as the Cuban singer Silvio Rodríguez, became a centerpiece of the resistance through its intimate recreation of folk *peñas* [clubs] (Bravo and González, 2008). For although the military showed no sign of paving the way for a return to democracy, and developed a strategy to appeal to young people (Sierra 2014) as the 1980s began, poverty and unemployment were rapidly rising in a country whose people had no voice in politics. Shantytowns grew, extending metropolitan areas (Schneider 1995). Intimate spaces of everyday resistive gathering and encounter flourished across the country. General Augusto Pinochet's *junta* unsuccessfully sought to incite violent rebellion as a means of justifying further repression so it could cling to power despite catastrophic economic failure and horrific oppression (Huneeus 2009).

Meanwhile, FM radio played pop and rock in English and AM focused on Latin American ballads, romantic songs, and Mexican *corridos* [story songs]. But cracks were emerging in this banal fascist facade. The music magazine *La Bicicleta* (1978–90) and the record label Sello Alerce (1975 until today) played a big role in covering and publishing bands that otherwise would not have seen the light of day, and promoted the idea of *Canto Nuevo* [New Chant] an electrified successor to the banned *Nueva Canción* that resisted Pinochet's violence. A new breed of musicians took elements from *La Nueva Canción Chilena*, but used more poetic, less vehement lyrics. Bands like *Santiago del Nuevo Extremo* [Santiago of the New Extreme] and *Schwenke y Nilo* helped birth the *Canto* (Salas 1993).

By the mid-1980s, the musical matrix available to young people was more diverse, thanks to new genres that became available on radio and in record stores or were brought home by people returning from abroad. Pirate cassettes provided a means to access "subversive" material from the USA and Britain. A new generation, not necessarily attached to the emotional rhetoric of the 1960s, grew up feeling real repression day by day, developing the urge to have a say – and soon – in subtle ways. As per other Latin American countries suffering under dictatorships, music started to flow, with artists synthesizing bits and pieces from varying influences. Bands like *Los Prisioneros* [The Prisoners], *Pinochet Boys*, *Emociones Clandestinas* [Clandestine Emotions], and *Electrodomésticos* [Home Appliances] formed a spectrum that offered everything from easy listening to critical pop, rock, and punk rock. They spoke to the experience of living within a dictatorship, about marginality, deceit, and love, and in a way that was more energetic and danceable than *Canto Nuevo* had been (Party 2010). Eventually, spaces and opportunities to get together became more common in different cities, though they could be shut down at any minute. The popularity of pop and rock bands despite a radio system reluctant to play Chilean music also meant the recovery of Spanish as a musical language for a new generation imbued with "frustration and rebellion" (González 1991, 68).

After peaceful mass mobilization by social democrats and radicals alike, ongoing critiques from the Catholic Church, trade unions, and local and international non-government organizations, the population, tired of the financial disasters bought on by neoclassical economists in alliance with fascists, finally turned against the regime, denying Pinochet re-endorsement in 1988 via what was effectively a plebiscite on his continuing (Huneeus 2009). The deadly dictatorship ended in 1990.

Its democratic successor was welcomed in part with hopes for a renaissance of a local music industry that could become successful across Latin America. Record companies signed more local bands and solo artists; traditional labels supported new music; radio stations expanded their playlists (Fortuño 1995); and concerts of local and international figures became part of the new era. Even at an institutional level, there were spaces for learning rock poetry, performance arts, and so on, in such places as *Balmaceda 1215* (which started in 1992), and the project *Escuelas de Rock* [Schools of Rock] from 1994. By the end of the decade, this progressive presence of rock, pop, hip hop, punk, and heavy metal in Chilean society stimulated music documentary to reinterpret the country's recent past by uncovering cultural actors who had been silenced by the dictatorship and the mainstream music industry, and to encourage a new national narrative of peace, democracy, and justice.

Memory, Recognition, and Critique

The first rockumentary of the 1990s is actually not about a rock figure *per se*, but Jara. One of the nation's most important popular folk singers, and a hero of the international cultural left, he was assassinated in the first days of the dictatorship, as noted above. Jara's legacy – seemingly erased under military rule – has been rediscovered and valorised by younger generations and musicians, from hip hop to rock and solo artists. Jara even provides an eponym for the very sports stadium in which he passed away, about which he wrote his last words and where thousands more were detained, tortured, and murdered (San Francisco et al. 2010).

"It happened almost by chance," says journalist Carmen Luz Parot in describing *El Derecho de Vivir en Paz* [*The Right to Live in Peace*] (1999), her documentary about Jara. Following his detention, imprisonment, torture, and murder by the military in the immediate aftermath of the coup, Jara's music was withdrawn from radio, television, record stores, and schools. After Pinochet's seventeen years in power ended, the new democratic regime did little to commemorate, or even mention, figures like Jara, or the wider history and critical legacy of Chilean music, drama, dance, film, and the arts in general.

In the second half of the 1990s, Parot was working at the recently created Rock and Pop Channel, a TV subsidiary of the homonymous radio station that was launched in 1992. Targeting an audience ranging from adolescents to young adults, the station started in precarious conditions but had a less restricted agenda than more established channels. Part of that autonomy was evident in the attention it paid to Chilean popular music and culture – not as a rejection of what was coming from abroad, but as a way to level the field. Parot, who studied filmmaking with Héctor Ríos, a key figure of 1960s cinema, understood that the mere expression of an interest in Chilean music was a political gesture in a country that "has an overwhelming taste for what comes from other regions as something valuable, like high culture, and an enormous disdain for the local culture, labelled as unworthy." But to make such a gesture via the figure of Jara was a major leap. As she remembers it:

> In the 1990s, Víctor Jara's music was not on the radio, not on television; there was a decade of censorship against Jara in democracy ... video recordings of his life and music were gone, disappeared. But I obtained some files from a presentation by Jara in Peru. That tape was restored by the channel. When we hit play and saw him giving that concert, with high-quality image and sound, we realised we had to follow the story of his songs and his life. And we ended up making a documentary. The day we broadcast the film, one day at 4pm, the channel's switchboard collapsed. People could not believe they were watching Víctor Jara on TV – and we are talking about 1999.

Although the channel was not available across the entire nation, this screening vividly expressed what was possible through filmmaking: the impact of recuperating images from an obscured past and posing questions about a culture that had been silenced for more than two decades. With decreases in the cost of recording and filming, the growth of journalism and film schools at universities and professional institutes, and the boom in Chilean history and popular culture, music documentaries after *El Derecho de Vivir* kept on coming. Three areas of interest define these films over the last twenty years.

The first area is expressed in two ways. One thread is in films like *Los Angeles Negros* [*Black Angels*] (2007), *Los Blue Splendor* [*The Great Blues*] (2007), *Piedra Roja* [*Red Rock*] (2011), *Los Jaivas, La Vorágine* [*The Crabs, The Maelstrom*] (2011), and *O'Brien: Las Edades del Hombre* [*O'Brien: The Ages of Man*] (2016), which reconstruct the history of important musicians and events from the 1960s through the 1990s. They draw on archival and live sources and testimonies to document the social and cultural context in which music thrived or survived to show their popularity, impact, and legacy for Chilean popular culture. These works counterbalance elitist culture's disregard for the local, and the institutional avoidance of recent history, initiated under the dictatorship and carried on by the new democratic regime (until 2015, radio stations were not obliged to play more than 5 per cent of Chilean music each day).[4] For Gonzalo Planet, a member of the band *Matorral*, a musical researcher, and a crew member on *O'Brien: Las Edades del Hombre*, this interest in the history of local bands and solo careers arose from a question that became unavoidable at the dawn of the new century: "who are we, Chileans? What is Chilean music? Our identity always seems to be in tension; the Chilean music documentary helps us understand who we are through diverse stories and points of view shaping a major history – our history."

The second thread came from the observation of local scenes beyond metropolitan areas. *Ruidos Molestos* [*Annoying Noises*] (2007) is set in the Valparaíso region, known as the nest of Chilean rock. *Gritos de Fin de Siglo* [*Cries at the End of the Century*] is about Concepción, a source of important rock bands since the 1980s. This subgenre makes a statement about local stories versus grand narratives and a history built from below. For instance, in *Ruidos Molestos*, such insights emphasize the connection between neighborhood and community centers in the hills of Valparaíso, with the evolution of rock and metal.

A second area of rockumentary interest emerged as the inscription of this music as part of Chile's cultural history, not just a mere footnote. Consider the attention given to a generation of bands, solo artists, scenes, and events, because filmmakers wanted to make this music central to the nation's popular music heritage. They did so across genres, from contemporary pop (*Al Unísono* [*At the Same Time*], 2007), to metal (*Herreros de Chile* [*Blacksmiths of Chile*], 2014), and hardcore punk (*Hardcore, La Revolución Inconclusa* [*Hardcore, The Unfinished Revolution*], 2009). There were also more personal films, dedicated to the punk singer *Pogo, El Peor de Chile* [*Pogo, The Worst of Chile*, 2009]; or *Unfinished Plan, El Camino de Alain Johannes* [*Unfinished Plan, the Journey of Alain Johannes*, 2016]; and also films devoted to bands like *Matorral, Emociones Clandestinas, Fulano*, and *Electrodomésticos* in *Estamos Bien* [*We're Fine*, 2009], *Mi Nuevo Estilo de Baile* [*My New Dance Style*, 2012], *Animal en Extinción* [*Endangered Species*, 2014], and *El Frío Misterio* [*The Cold Mystery*, 2010], respectively.

The third area of interest is decidedly more political. It finds expression in three ways. One looks back to the role of musicians in the Popular Unity government and the struggles of the left as expressed in songs of resistance by solo artists and rock bands. These rockumentaries include the aforementioned *El Derecho de Vivir en Paz* (1999), *Gringo Rojo* [*Red Gringo*, 2016], and *Quilapayún, Más Allá de la Canción* [*Quilapayún, Beyond the Music*, 2015].

A second form sets music against the strictures of institutional politics, especially in the aftermath of dictatorship and the first years of democracy. A key film in this trend is *Malditos: La Historia de Fiskales Ad-Hok* [*Damned: The Story of Fiskales Ad-Hok*, 2004]. Focused on the punk rock group *Fiskales Ad Hok* from Santiago, which had formed in the late 1980s, the film is a dialogue with band members, supporters, and media critics. The film highlights middle- and working-class youth's experience of the transition from dictatorship to democracy. This tendency also pays attention to less overtly political music, such as the rock of the 1980s, which expressed anger and joy in a context in which the mere act of saying something passionate was forbidden. That was the story underlying Tomás Achurra's *Toque de Queda* [*Curfew*, 2014]: "Chilean rock of the 1980s has always been labelled as just amusement, an alienating movement, and I think the film does justice to a bunch of young people who are not so different from us."

A third way in which rockumentaries have embraced a political stance is in constructing the history of women in rock music. *Frontwoman, La Historia de Denise de Aguaturbia* [*Frontwoman, the History of Denise, from Aguaturbia*, 2009], tells the story of the nation's first female lead rock singer as "a gender issue ... we wanted to know the influence of women in the rock scene," says Stephanie Servello, one of the filmmakers. Similar perspectives animate *Femme Rock* (2009). Director Denise Elphick explains that "in 2008, there was a heavy macho attitude in the rock scene but there was also something happening with music made by women and the kind of sound coming from them. It was different."

Who Are We?

Today, the increased production of rockumentary films in Chile has seen a body of work that questions recognition, identity, creativity, and daily life. As per Gonzalo Planet's question cited above, the United Nations Development Programme (PNUD, 2002) published *We the Chileans: A Cultural Problem*, an observation about this curious malaise of identity in a country whose macroeconomic figures indicated consistent growth. The report underlined that after twelve years of recovered democracy, in a postmodern atmosphere crossed by global fluxes of finance and culture, the topic of what was Chilean – and who were the Chileans – had become impoverished and blurry. Among the challenges of the country, according to the report, was the need to articulate diverse identities, experiences, and representations with culture and government. The report was followed by the enunciation of the first National Cultural Policy since the dictatorship, designed "to sustain the cultural identity and diversity of the country" (CNCA 2005, 12), where the Chilean state manifests a commitment to "create and promote the best possible conditions for art and cultural expressions to emerge, promote and be appreciated by the public" (2005, 13).

But this has not been the experience of the filmmakers behind the continuous growth of rockumentaries, which generally do not benefit from exposure in commercial movie theaters or television stations. Chilean cinema in general has a marginal presence in local cinemas; in 2014 and 2015, just 4 per cent of movies screened in 2014 were made by local production companies (CNCA 2017). Cinema exhibition is colored by the dominance of Hollywood. Documentary filmmaking represents 23 per cent of the overall film production in Chile but an insignificant percentage of the national audience. Mainstream cinema chains – such as Hoyts – attract 99 per cent of cinemagoers nationwide. They screen just over 3 per cent of Chilean national films per year; 90 per cent of cinema comes from the US (Ministry of Culture 2018). In the case of television, there is a bias against programming that could represent a political problem with advertizers, owners, or other stakeholders, in a landscape dominated by private media interests that abjure films that dig into the painful past (Traverso 2017). So, *La Batalla de Chile* has never been seen on free-to-air or cable TV in Chile. Non-fiction series touching on the dictatorship are generally funded by the National Council of Television (CNTV), a state institution, the Ministry of Culture, and grants given to selected projects.[5] These funds are limited and hard to get. Commercial networks also refuse to screen such topics.

Distribution is the key *lacuna*. Most of these films are only screened in small circles, a few independent theaters, and some festivals. There is one crucial festival: In-edit. Part of an international organization, the Chilean version started in 2004 with the intention of forging "a bridge between usually disconnected audiences and getting our country closer to the best international premieres of the genre" (http://www.inedit.cl). Held mainly in Santiago, the festival takes place in six rooms across the city, featuring documentaries of rock, pop, and alternative music from different regions of the world, including many Chilean productions. The four awards given acknowledge Best National Film, Best International Film, People's Award, and Best Sound. Funded initially by Javiera Undurraga and Carlos Mora (general director and program director, respectively) and later by a coffee company, the Cinema Fund of the National Council of Culture and Arts, and private companies encouraged by tax incentives, the Festival has become enormously popular with attendees.

Nevertheless, the ultimate goal of the festival – to "offer a valuable showcase for new Chilean filmmakers, allowing to put them in touch with each other and expand their promotional chances" – is just a small step towards what filmmakers need. In-edit Festival happens but one week a year. It is no answer to the restricted exhibition opportunities for rock documentaries. Achurra says:

> Musical documentaries in Chile have little room. It should not be the case that the whole year revolves around the In-Edit festival, which is the

only national instance to show these films. The team of that festival has made a tremendous effort to install the musical documentary in Chile, and they have achieved it, but the festival ends and then you enter a tremendous colander in the other film festivals nationwide, because they don't understand it, because they prefer fiction, because they have everything cooked before, etc. It is difficult. Many directors end up releasing content on YouTube or make a small commercial sale; in my case, I do all that independently. *Toque de Queda* is a documentary that due to its historical content could enter other festivals here in Chile. It has also been to festivals in Colombia and Mexico. But the musical documentary has little space here.

The overarching dominance of market logics, political constraints, and cultural disdain towards non-hegemonic arts and collective identities discourages a strong connection between independent cinema and the people.

Is the Internet a solution, given that it has the potential to reach large audiences at minimal cost? It seems a good option for circulation, but success still necessitates promotional budgets and returns – if there are any – do not meet the costs of production or marketing. That said, exposure on YouTube or Vimeo may attract the attention of festival programmers or those interested in collaborative work. Against that, the comparatively open architecture of the web means that documentaries can be uploaded without permission. "Yes, the main distribution was via the Internet, on YouTube, the film has like thirty thousand visits, but it was uploaded by a guy we do not know," says *Al Unísono*'s director Rosario González.

Conclusion: The Future

The short life of rockumentary filmmaking in Chile revolves around three elements: recognition, filling in the gaps in collective memory, and contributing to an ongoing reflection about identity and the constituent elements of a possible "we" in Chilean history; the inscription of musical genres and their creative processes as part of national culture and arts, and not as something to look at with disdain by contrast with other art expressions; and finally, as a political exercise, in terms of how rock music, and popular music in general, has something to say, has particular ways of conveying its artistry, and records the reality of playing a guitar, giving a concert, or following a band. Since the late 1990s, rock documentaries have portrayed and helped to form a political culture seeking to connect with the mainstream media, but held back by cultural policies that have failed to take them beyond niche groups.

The power relationship exerted by two actors emerges as fundamental. One is a film industry largely shaped by market logics, where Hollywood dominates the scene thanks to free-trade agreements and its general influence across Latin America. The second actor is the Chilean media, especially television, which is largely owned by private companies and evinces little interest in national cinema, and even less in supporting filmmaking. These two actors make for a powerful barrier to Chilean rockumentaries. Nevertheless, the latter hold onto their rebellious role of digging into the past, bothering the post-dictatorship status quo, thinking who and what we are, and presenting a permanent challenge to what Parot calls "the eternal self-loathing of our own culture."

Notes

1. The concept of "the popular" in Spanish refers specifically to people and practices that Anglos tend to categorize as the peasantry, proletariat, native/Indigenous, or underclasses.
2. Guzmán's *Chile, Memoria Obstinada* (*Chile, Stubborn Memory*, 1997) recorded the first time that "Venceremos" was openly sung by marchers in Chile since Allende's time (Neustadt 2004, 132).
3. The *Cantos Cautivos* [*Captive Songs*] project records the music of torture, both as produced by victims and used by torturers (https://www.cantoscautivos.org/en/index.php).
4. After ten years of debate, Congress passed law 20810 in 2015. It set a quota of 20 per cent for Chilean music on radio stations (www.leychile.cl/Navegar?idNorma=1076447).
5. A recent case shows the reluctance of Chilean TV to broadcast programs connected to memory, human rights and politics: one of the short films in the series *A Necessary History*. Winner of the Short-Form Series award in the 2018 Emmy Awards, the series was only distributed through YouTube, in spite of its high-quality production and funding from CNTV. As Antonio Ballestrazzi, the series' executive producer, said after receiving the award, "over 40 years after the genocide in Chile and they still have fear," explaining why television companies did not buy the programs (quoted in "Productor").

References

"Productor de 'Una Historia Necesaria' recordó que la TV abierta rechazó emitir la serie." 2018. *Cooperativa* 20 November. <http://www.cooperativa.cl/noticias/entretencion/television/series/productor-de-una-historia-necesaria-recordo-que-la-tv-abierta-rechazo/2018-11-20/034819.html> (last accessed 12 Jan, 2019).
Alberdi, Maite, Carolina Larraín, Camila Van Diest, and Pablo Corro. 2007. *Teorías del Cine Documental Chileno, 1957–1973*. Santiago: Pontificia Universidad Católica de Chile.
Bravo, Gabriela, and Cristian Yáñez Aguilar. 2009. *Ecos del tiempo subterráneo: Las peñas en Santiago durante el régimen militar (1973–1983)*. Santiago: Lom.
Chanan, Michael. 1976. *Chilean Cinema*. London: BFI.
Chornik, Katia. 2018. "Memories of Music in Political Detention in Chile Under Pinochet." *Journal of Latin American Cultural Studies* 27(2): 157–73.
CNCA, Consejo Nacional de la Cultura y las Artes. 2017. *Oferta y Consumo de Cine en Chile*.<http://chileaudiovisual.cl/documentos/infografia/Infografia%20Cine%20DICIEMBRE%202017.pdf> (last accessed 12 Jan, 2019).

CNCA, Consejo Nacional de la Cultura y las Artes. 2005. *Chile quiere más cultura: Definiciones de política cultural 2005–2010*. Valparaíso: Consejo Nacional de la Cultura y las Artes.
Dittus, Rubén, and Ema Ulloa Castillo. 2017. "Cartografía del cine documental político chileno: Entre el discurso político y la retórica audiovisual." *Anàlisi: Quaderns de Comunicació i Cultura* 56. 33–47.
Dorfman, Ariel. 2018. "How We Roasted Donald Duck, Disney's Agent of Imperialism." *The Guardian*. <https://www.theguardian.com/books/2018/oct/05/ariel-dorfman-how-we-roasted-donald-duck-disney-agent-of-imperialism-chile-coup> (last accessed 12 Jan, 2019).
Errázuriz, Luis Hernán. 2009. "Dictadura militar en Chile: Antecedentes del golpe estético cultural." *Latin American Research Review* 44(2): 136–57.
Escobar Mundaca, Alejandro. 2018. "I Don't Play the Guitar for Applause: Turning the World Upside Down." In *Mapping Violeta Parra's Cultural Landscapes*, ed. Patricia Vilches. Cham: Palgrave Macmillan. 57–71.
Fairley, Jan. 1985. "Annotated Bibliography of Latin-American Popular Music with Particular Reference to Chile and to nueva canción." *Popular Music* 5. 305–56.
Fortuño, Sergio. 2005. "Esperando Nada." *Rock and Pop* 12: 7–13.
Fuenzalida Faifovich, Edmundo. 2003. "Derecho y cultura jurídica en Chile (1974-1999)." In *Culturas jurídicas latinas de Europa y América en tiempos de globalización*, eds Hector Fix-Fierro, Lawrence M. Friedman and Rogelio Pérez Perdomo. México D. F: Universidad Nacional Autónoma de México. 195–230.
González, Juan-Pablo. 1991. "Hegemony and Counter-Hegemony of Music in Latin-America: The Chilean *Pop*." *Popular Music & Society* 15(2): 63–78.
Huneeus, Carlos. 2009. "Political Mass Mobilization Against Authoritarian Rule: Pinochet's Chile, 1983–88." In *Civil Resistance and Power Politics: The Experience of Non-Violent Action from Gandhi to the Present*, eds Adam Roberts and Timothy Garton Ash Oxford: Oxford University Press. 197–212.
Jordán, Laura. 2009. "Música y clandestinidad en dictadura: La represión, la circulación de músicas de resistencia y el casete clandestino." *Revista Musical Chilena* 63(212). 77–102.
Junta Militar de Gobierno. 1974. *Política Cultural del Gobierno de Chile*. Santiago: Asesoría Cultural de la Junta de Gobierno y Departamento Cultural de la Secretaría General de Gobierno.
Morris, Nancy. 1986. "Canto porque es necesario cantar: The New Song Movement in Chile, 1973-1983." *Latin American Research Review* 21(2): 117–36.
Mouesca, Jacqueline. 2005. *El documental chileno*. Santiago: Lom.
Neustadt, Robert. 2004. "Music as Memory and Torture: Sounds of Repression and Protest in Chile and Argentina." *Chasqui* 33(1): 128–37.
PNUD, Programa de Naciones Unidas para el Desarrollo. 2002. *Nosotros los Chilenos: Un Desafío Cultural*. Santiago: Programa de Naciones Unidas para el Desarrollo.
Power, M. 2015. "Chile: Film." in *Censorship*, ed. D. Jones. Abingdon: Routledge.
Rist, Peter H. 2014. *Historical Dictionary of South American Cinema*. Plymouth: Rowman & Littlefield.
Salas, Fabio. 1993. *La primavera terrestre: Cartografía del rock chileno y la nueva canción chilena*. Santiago de Chile: Cuarto Propio.
San Francisco, Alexander, Miguel Fuentes, and Jairo Sepúlveda. 2010. "Hacia una arqueología del estadio Víctor Jara: Campo de detención y rotura masiva de la dictadura en Chile (1973–1974)." *Revista de Arqueología Histórica Argentina y Latinoamericana* 4. 91–116.
Silva, M. Bowen. n.d. "El proyecto sociocultural de la izquierda chilena durante la Unidad Popular: Crítica, verdad e inmunología política." *Nuevo Mundo Mundos*

Nuevos, <http://journals.openedition.org/nuevomundo/13732> (last accessed 12 Jan, 2019).
Traverso, Antonio. 2017. "La 'Flaca' Alejandra: Post-Dictatorship Documentary and (No) Reconciliation in Chile." *Critical Arts* 31(5): 95–106.
Vega, Alicia. 2006. *Itinerario del Cine Documental Chileno: 1900–1990*. Santiago: Universidad Alberto Hurtado. <https://www.patricioguzman.com/es/peliculas/la-batalla-de-chile-i-ii-iii> (last accessed 12 Jan, 2019).
Vilches, Patricia. 2004. "De Violeta Parra a Víctor Jara y Los Prisioneros: Recuperación de la memoria colectiva e identidad cultural a través de la música comprometida." *Latin American Music Review/Revista de Música Latinoamericana* 25(2): 195–215.

INTERVIEWS

Carmen Luz Parot, October 15, 2018
Denise Elphick, October 1, 2018
Stephanie Servello, October 9, 2018
Gonzalo Planet, October 5, 2018
Rosario González, October 22, 2018
Tomás Achurra, October 31, 2018

17. PSYCHEDELIA AND REBELLIOUSNESS IN TIMES OF DICTATORSHIP: ARGENTINIAN ROCKUMENTARIES (1973–1983)

Javier Campo and Tomás Crowder-Taraborrelli

Over the last ten years, we have witnessed a veritable explosion of the production of documentaries about music (see Boffard 2014; Deutsch 2014). This cinematic momentum seems to confirm Thomas F. Cohen's suggestion that "cinema may provide valuable information about the physical dynamics of musical performance" (2012, 11). In particular, rock music and documentary film have formed a somewhat controversial duet, characterized by occasional tensions and crises. Rockumentaries, the product of this union, have given high visibility to rock bands and brought a large number of spectators to the theaters to watch their performances on film. The popularity of rockumentaries in Argentina would be non-existent, were it not for the rebelliousness of the music genre; rock music was used sonically and poetically to express opposition to the repression of the dictatorship. Between 1971 and 1986, there were numerous major political events in Argentina: the return of Juan Domingo Perón from his eighteen-year exile after having been overthrown by the coup in 1955, the appearance of guerrilla groups, as well as paramilitaries from the extreme right; the military coup of 1976, which established the bloodiest dictatorship in South America; and the fall of it in 1983, marking an end of the dictatorship cycle and the beginning of the democratic transition.

Although rockumentary has not become a widespread phenomenon in South America, we can trace a handful of films made in this corner of the world that are in tune with the parameters of rockumentaries produced under the watchful eye of the Hollywood industry. Using conceptual tools from music theory, we analyze documentary films about rock made in Argentina between 1971 and 1986. In particular, we focus on two of the most representative films of the genre: *Rock hasta que se ponga el sol* [*Rock until the Sun Sets*] (Aníbal Uset, 1973), and *Buenos Aires Rock* (Héctor Olivera, 1983).

Direct cinema developed around the time rock was exploding on the world scene, and some of the earliest filmmakers interested in filming music concerts and festivals have been associated with the genre. It should come as no surprise that direct cinema forerunners were interested in recording rock concerts, since recitals contain inherent narrative structures (Altman 1992, 218). Thus, these filmmakers contributed "to the emergence of the rock star" (Cohen 2012, 55). On a graph, direct cinema could be plotted at one end and rock music at the other. At the central convergence point, they both come out winners during this period: rock garners images that ratify the musical genre as a pop-cultural landmark, while the observational documentary gains a degree of public visibility it has never had before and will never have again. In short, it would not be an exaggeration to classify the period between the Maysles Brothers' films *What's Happening!: The Beatles in the USA* (USA, 1964) and *Gimme Shelter* (USA, 1970) as canonical of rockumentary (Cohen 2012, 59–60). And it would not be an exaggeration to describe this period as one that saw the rise and fall of the counter-cultural movement. Counter-culture was the clay with which rockumentaries were moulded. This perspective helps us to understand what happened, musically and politically, in Argentina during the same period.

Music documentaries have the power to crystalize the memory of events/concerts/festivals; in short, they can embody a moment in time in a visceral manner.[1] According to Julie Lobalzo Wright (2013), the popular memory of the iconic Woodstock and Altamont rock festivals can be understood as a pair of diametrically-opposed moments in terms of the rise and fall of counter-culture. This memory "is shaped by the nature of the aesthetic structures" of rockumentaries like *Woodstock* (Michael Wadleigh, USA, 1970) and *Gimme Shelter* (Albert Maysles, David Maysles, and Charlotte Zwerin, USA, 1970) (Wright 2013, 84). According to Richard Altman (1992), the significance of documentaries about rock stems from a combination of documentary film methodologies and the fact that cinema has the ability to turn its protagonists into stars (Altman 1992, 227).

For filmmakers, rock captured the spirit of the times. For audiences, these films uncovered the secrets of rock stars (Strachan and Leonard 2009, 289). Diego Bruno (2000) stresses how significant it was for a rock artist to be featured in a film: "Despite the connotations of massive glorification attached to TV, the 'establishing reputation' system of any artist, singer, or musical group is definitely still the cinema. All we have to do is think of *Woodstock* to prove that from that film, many of the musicians who participated in it were strengthened or swiftly launched into a popularity, that, otherwise, would have required them years of work" (Bruno 2000, 9).

Concert Film or Rockumentary?

Donn Alan Pennebaker defended his pioneering leadership taking up the standard of "his" creation – the *concert film* – as a "new genre within the documentary" (Cohen 2012, 43). Although it is true that *Monterey Pop* (USA, 1968) is the most prominent film of a music festival, this documentary is a recorded performance rather than documentation of the off-stage lives of its featured artists. *Woodstock* is the most canonical representation of rock as a social movement in the 60s. The film features music as a force that unites people, encouraging participation instead of passive contemplation: "rather than being seen as entertainment, music was considered to say things of cultural and political importance" (Edgar et al. 2013, 3). According to Christopher Small (1998), *Woodstock* demonstrated what this generation already knew: that music is "not a thing at all but an activity, something that people do" (10).

Considering the literature on rock and documentary films, we are able to tease out the following typology:

1) Documentaries narrating the career of a singer, a band, a music genre, a time, or a subculture.
2) Concert documentaries (concert films). These documentaries focus mainly on the audio-visual record of the concert (Deutsch 2014; Cohen 2012).
3) Other films that include parts of concerts but are characterized differently: performance documentaries, or, as Brian Winston suggests, the *rock performance documentary* (Cohen 2012, 19). According to Winston, this is one of the most truly popular forms of documentary; Chanan (2013) identifies the main characteristics of this type of film as: use of hand-held cameras, scenes shot off-stage, takes of fans, interviews in cars, streets, theatres, and homes (339).
4) Finally, we must mention other types that will not be analyzed in detail in this work: ethnomusicological documentaries (Chanan 2013, 340), the visualized album (Chanan 2013, 341), anti-musical documentaries, that is, those that, according to Chanan, disdain the genre conventions and are identified with avant-garde experimental approaches.

The music documentary, understood here as the rockumentary subgenre, is a by-product of popular culture. The genre uses different conventions now than it did during the more artisanal times of *Woodstock*; today it falls within the path of celebrity culture (Edgar et al. 2013, 16–19). There are also other cases in which productions are independent and provide alternative perspectives, ones that are not contaminated by the rock stars' points of view (naturally, in this case, we are talking about low-budget films in which the most famous bands rarely participate). In Argentina, RCA financed the film *El extraño de pelo largo* [The Long-haired Stranger] (1970) to promote signed artists such as Litto Nebbia, the film's protagonist, and groups such as La Joven Guardia, Pintura Fresca and Trocha Angosta, among others (Bruno 2000, 9).

Rock hasta que se ponga el sol (Aníbal Uset, 1973)

When Perón finally returned to Argentina in 1973, there were times of revelry that had already begun in the so-called "Camporist spring" (the return facilitated by the government of Héctor José Campora). *Rock hasta que se ponga el sol*, directed by Aníbal Uset, is a documentary of great historical value to the history of Latin American popular music. When the film came out, the rock magazine *Pelo* anticipated how important Uset's film would become: "What is filmed there will be the first significant visual document of rock development in Argentina" (Bruno 2000, 7).[2] Produced by Héctor Olivera and Fernando Ayala, two distinguished directors in the media industry, the documentary showcases performances in the B. A. Rock festival (in its third year), as well as performances of pioneering artists and bands in other locations: Color Humano, Vox Dei, Pescado Rabioso, Pappo, Leon Gieco, Litto Nebbia, Sui Generis, Arco Iris, Billy Bond, and Gabriela, among others. Many of the musicians who were members of these groups continued their careers in other important bands or as solo artists, as in the case of Luis Alberto Spinetta and Charly García, two of Argentina's most beloved artists. Despite the limited resources with which this documentary was made, the film reveals the urgency of registering the growing strength of the most important popular urban music movement of Argentina's history after tango. Uset's movie represents the first steps in a rebellious cultural movement that sought funding to represent itself during a time marked by political turbulence. Juan Domingo Perón had just returned to the country after an eighteen-year period of exile: "There was a mild opening-up but there was also a severe repression," Uset recalls in an interview (Pereyra 2016, 1). The film was accompanied by a soundtrack: the second LP recorded live and edited in Argentina, which featured artists who performed at the festival. Some artists were left out because they were signed to other record companies (Bruno 2000, 2). Jorge Álvarez and Daniel Ripoll (editor of *Pelo*) came up with the idea of the film in order to organize an "Argentinean Woodstock" (Bruno 2000, 2). Uset was able to film the performances thanks to remaining film stock from a Jorge Porcel comedy he was working on at the time: "It was all very crude; during the part where León

(Gieco) is featured, for instance, you can see how all the cameramen cross each other on the stage" (Pereyra 2016, 2).

Qualitative comparisons between national and foreign bands are rather trivial, even as they can be a pet hobby for fans of the genre. But Uset's documentary proves that as early as the 1970s, Argentinean groups had already achieved a high quality of technical and lyrical production. *Rock hasta que se ponga el sol* is an essential document for understanding the creation of a social movement that celebrated rock and its most representative bands. On the other hand, the film allows for an understanding of the discourse of relations between a band's performance, its lyricism, its musical expressions, and audience reception, giving cultural context to a period (Berger 1999, 241). Uset commented as follows: ". . . I wanted to reflect the reality of an entire Argentinean generation, expressing itself through music, and managing to imprint their own characteristics on music" (Bruno 2000, 6).

The first sequence of *Rock hasta que se ponga el sol* alternates between shots of a dawn in the port of Buenos Aires with shots of the festival.[3] The message for the audience is clear: the sun comes up with music. Edelmiro Molinari, singer of Color Humano, joins the celebration: "In sorrow my dreams with no destiny, long live the sun." The four cameramen, under the direction of Víctor Hugo Caula and Uset, move freely on the stage, vigorously recording the group's performance. The editing counterpoints the refrain of the song with short takes of streets, squares, buildings, and the sky of Buenos Aires. In a rhythmic interlude from the song in which the drummer Oscar Moro is featured, Uset cuts to an extradiegetic image of a young man browsing psychedelic patterned fabrics in a hippie store in *La Recoleta* (one of the patterns evokes a shining star). In a wall surrounding the park, graffiti reads: "Against censorship." There are few explicit references in the film to the political context, since many rock musicians felt awkward about the role of activists: "The left thought of us as bloody stupid hippies . . . alienated. And the right, more or less the same, that we were like beggars. No one took notice of you. They only repressed you in order to hide you, because you were ruining the view. You were tarnishing the picture. 'You can't have long hair'; 'you're a poof.' That kind of stuff, you know?" (Billy Bond in Rodríguez 2016, 216).

The titles introduce the bands while the audience is captured on an empty plot of land next to the Argentinos Juniors soccer stadium. The editing of these close-ups reminds us of *Woodstock* and presents a romantic portrait of the youth as creative, caring people attracted by the social causes championed by Gieco's lyrics: "Boy, let go of your thoughts, as the wind is loose, you are the hope and the voice that will bloom in the new land."

Rock hasta que se ponga el sol is a hybrid documentary where performances of the festival are combined with acted scenes, filmed in a studio and on location. These resources make the material less authentic, but allow Uset to surround some of the acted out sequences with ambitious cinematographic aesthetics. For instance, the performance of the hit "Las guerras" [Wars], by Vox Dei, was filmed in a Methodist Church on Corrientes Street. Ricardo Soulé's voice, one of the finest voices of Argentinean rock, defies the reactionary sectors of society from his post in a traditional building: "Weapons, force ... What's the point in it? This story isn't over, no, no, no ..." Nebbia's performance was shot in a film studio. The former singer of the famed band, Los Gatos, plays "Si no son más de la tres" [It's only past three] on guitar, accompanied on the Argentine bass drum by folklorist Domingo Cura.

The documentary has no narrative axis, only the brief appearances of the presenter and organizer, Ripoll, who names the artists that follow each other. Some appearances are clearly filmed outside of the festival. A noteworthy moment from the film is the performance of a raga (a traditional melodic mode from South Asia) by guitarist Claudio Gabis (accompanied by Isa Portugheis on percussion). Ripoll points out, by way of an introduction, that this music is favorable "... precisely to meditate on the many things that are going on in the world." Uset follows with the insertion of a photograph of a nuclear explosion, photographs of prisoners of war in Vietnam, and of nurses caring for starving children.

There are two legendary sequences in *Rock hasta que se ponga el sol* which beckon an archive of Argentinean rock: "Tontos" [Idiots] by Billy Bond y la Pesada and the mini-recital of Pescado Rabioso, shot in the Olympia Theater. At the beginning of the sequence, the screen is split into three frames: one of them portrays the band (Jorge Pinchevsky on the violin, Claudio Gabis on the guitar, and the bassist Alejandro Medina), and the other two depict images of the audience as they move around the stage's perimeter. Giuliano Canterini (a native of Italy who was baptized by the director of EMI Records with the stage name Billy Bond) sings in a raspy voice: "There are idiots, idiots, whether hippies, hippies, or blokes with thick vests ..." Uset chooses a rhythmic style of editing for "Tontos," alternating medium shots with close-ups of Bond's shoes dancing about the stage, accompanied by the microphone stand. The syncopated strumming on the guitars lends itself to these contra-punctual rhythmic breaks. Uset inserts a scene filmed in the studio, lending a humorous and bizarre tone to the performance. Utilizing a psychedelic, counter-cultural visual vocabulary (James 2012, 27), Billy Bond, portrayed in drag, is received along with other guests in a mansion complete with imitation marble columns and a steamy pool. A young faun devours a bunch of grapes nearby. In Bond's opinion, this scene should be remembered as the first video clip of Argentinean rock (Pereyra 2016, 3). But, as we have mentioned, Cosentino is the first director to produce a proto-clip of Argentinean rock, in *Buenos Aires Beat* (1971). Another bizarre scene from *Rock hasta que se ponga el sol*, involving Pescado Rabioso, would soon become one of the most memorable clips of

Argentinean rockumentary (there are thousands of reproductions of the clip on YouTube). The band, headed by Luis Alberto Spinetta, are walking down a street when they are blocked by two vehicles. An aggressor gets out of a car with a shotgun, confronts the band and shoots David Lebón, the other guitarist of Pescado. Lebón's reaction is comical: with his stomach covered in blood he faces the murderer and tells him that if he were a policeman he would put him in prison. This scene would have fallen into oblivion if it were not for the next scene. Uset moves his crew to the Olympia theater to film Spinetta and his band playing songs such as "Despiértate nena" [Wake up, babe] and "Post-Crucifixión" [Post-Crucifixion]. The latter is one of the greatest compositions of Argentinean rock; as early as 1973 Spinetta stands out as one of the significant leaders and composers of the genre.

Buenos Aires Rock (Héctor Olivera, 1983)

The fourth and final Buenos Aires Rock festival was celebrated on November 6, 13, 20, and 27, 1982 (a few days before the premiere of *Prima Rock*). *Buenos Aires Rock* (Héctor Olivera, 1983) was filmed in the wake of a dictatorship that was in retreat, following a defeat in the Malvinas War. This rockumentary, which premiered in January 1983, recorded the festival, but that was not all. *Buenos Aires Rock* turned out to be the most political Argentinean rockumentary, not only because of the editing methods employed but also because of what actually happened on stage. The musical performances reveal a shift from the symphonic stylings of progressive rock towards the more traditional troubadour song style (as shown by León Gieco) or the protest style (the case of Miguel Cantilo). The result of this shift saw the style of Argentinean rock move towards realistic poetry, more or less metaphoric, depending on the songwriter. From the first editions of B. A. Rock, when "Progressive Music Festival" was added to its title, until its last edition in 1982, the Argentinean rock scene had changed. It seemed that the progressive rock movement was beginning to lose its audience appeal, as shorter song compositions with an emphasis on repetitive catchy lyrics came into vogue. Performances abandoned the virtuosity of long musical passages in favor of eliciting greater public participation, as audiences were encouraged to sing along with the songs. This transition is perceptible in Olivera's film in an outstanding sequence at the beginning: Gieco, Cantilo, Raúl Porchetto, and Piero are jamming and alternately singing medleys of different songs in an interspersed manner, and they laugh at the ease with which they can reproduce and mix up each others' lyrics. This simple display of musical popularity shows that, at the time, there already was an Argentinean rock history, which in *Rock hasta que se ponga el sol* is introduced in a pedagogical manner.

Olivera, along with his company *Aries Cinematográfica*, was the producer of Uset's film and he would also produce *Que sea rock* [May it be Rock] (Sebastián Schindel, 2006), rounding out a sort of rockumentary trilogy. For *Buenos Aires Rock*, which was also produced by Daniel Ripoll, the festival's organizer, Olivera used more cameras as well as higher quality synchronized sound recordings, to enhance the sense of live performance. However, there are also passages with post-synchronized sound inserted in the musicians' performances with non-diegetic music, as well as the significant presence of backstage images and occasional interviews with musicians, technicians, and organizers.

The editing, performed by a team led by Eduardo López, reveals the film's ideological choices. After La Torre singer, Patricia Sosa, finishes saying, "[the] rock audience is sexist," V8's performance rolls out: leather jackets, aggressive lyrics, and fully overdriven riffs mingle with images of sweaty men both on stage and in the audience. Here, the film editing presents a political comment. During a sequence featuring audience opinions about what rock means, we hear: "it's the bomb, man!" A policeman replies: "it's just another kind of music." These fragments are repeated on three consecutive occasions. Then, two young men are shown reading "History of the Argentine Federal Police" while they cover their noses and while Gieco's song "Pensar en nada" [Thinking about Nothing] begins. Fragments of lyrics *"this country set free shall be,"* which make reference to the political context, are included among the images, while Piero sings "Coplas de mi país" [Folk Songs of my Country]. Alternately, the lyric *"when our men feel free, more free shall be our culture"* plays over the performance of "Los sueños de la cultura" [Culture's Dreams] by Cantilo. Lastly, we see another editing method, rich in political explicitness, in the insertion of photographs of John Lennon, shortly after his murder. These photos appear during a performance of "Algo de paz" [Some Peace] by Porchetto; and accompany the use of images from the Malvinas War at the end of the film when Gieco, Cantilo, Piero, and Porchetto sing "Sólo le pido a Dios" [I Only Ask of God].

The most ardently political moments from the festival are matched with images of the recording, in synchronized sound, of the performances of Piero, and of Pedro y Pablo (Cantilo and Jorge Durietz's band) who sing *"How many voices were silenced, oh, my country."* Piero rehearses on stage alone, while he receives cascades of carnations from the audience. The song "Coplas de mi país" is presented as an anti-war statement and an argument against the military regime. The lyrics *"this country was finished off/give to the people what belongs to the people"* play over the clamor of the spectators. Finally, any discussion of political commentary and rock should not fail to mention the performance of "Marcha de la bronca" [The Fury March], by Pedro y Pablo. On a stage illuminated by artificial light, Cantilo and Durietz shout *"fury because they shamelessly kill and nothing is ever made clear,"* while the Obras Sanitarias stadium pulsates with audience response.

Buenos Aires Rock is a hybrid rockumentary that cannot be placed within the direct cinema tradition of the Maysles' or Pennebaker's films, as there is no follow-up with the protagonist in different public and private spheres. And when backstage images are introduced, they are done so in an interview setting. This type of interview setting is not in keeping with what direct cinema promotes. On the other hand, as film scholars often say, this is just a "festival" film, like *Monterey Pop* or *Woodstock*. In this film there are images of the November 1982 performances, as well as scenes recreated with actors. The live performance is simulated with the insertion of music taken from the band's albums, as was the case in the Argentinean rockumentaries analyzed above. The director's images reflected the "spirit of a time" that, through rock, profoundly influenced the culture of a generation navigating politically rough waters.

By Way of Conclusion

The first Argentinean documentaries about rock provided a wide arena for recording live performances. However, there were additional resources at the time that prompt us to analyze the way in which rockumentaries were more than simple *concert films*. For instance, they featured fictionalizations, interviews, recordings of the audiences, observational scenes from the organization of concerts, archival images, etc. From *Rock hasta que se ponga el sol* to *Buenos Aires Rock*, the variation of cinematographic resources presented a musical scene in transformation: from hippie movement, to a rock informed by psychedelia and an ethos of virtuosity, to music and songs about reality, characterized by easily-memorizable refrains.

The musician who most readily embodies these stages of Argentinean rock is Luis Alberto Spinetta. Likewise, Spinetta is the only artist featured in both of the films analyzed herein (and in several other films from the period, such as *Prima Rock* [Osvaldo Andéchaga, 1982]). His career moves from a progressive period, characterized by aggressive performances with Pescado Rabioso in Uset's film, to the more melodic (jazz-rock fusion) performances with his band, Spinetta Jade, found in Olivera's and Andéchaga's documentaries. Nevertheless, Spinetta was reluctant to make explicit political comments, often associated with the type of troubador or folk rock in vogue during the democratic transition. His gradual abandonment of the progressive and symphonic in his compositions did not necessarily bring him closer to songs with simple poetic style, or easily recognizable choruses.

The first fifteen years of Argentine rockumentaries accompanied and documented the Argentinean music scene, observing rather than critiquing, interpreting or offering commentary; and operating in close relation with the record labels, production studios, and the organizers of major festivals. These films should be considered treasured archives of popular memory, whose origins point to a time of repression when large gatherings of people bonded over the enjoyment of live music.

Notes

1. Edgar et al. stress that there are many non-western music documentaries still to be explored (2013, 14), and we would add Latin American music documentaries to that estimation.
2. Two years earlier, the short film *Buenos Aires Beat* by Néstor Cosentino was made. The film is based on a revision of different landmarks of Argentine rock's brief history. Live performances (with post-synchronized sound) of Manal, Almendra and Vox Dei follow each other in the setting of an interview with a rock musician (simulated by the voices of actors). The film ends with what we could consider to be the first video clip, or a rough outline of a clip, based on the song, *Muchacha* [Girl] by Luis Alberto Spinetta and interpreted by two actors who represent being in love through their gazes and gestures as they walk along the Río de la Plata. As suggested in another work: "The large buildings provide the setting for the film that, with low-angle shots devoted to the skyscrapers and the images of construction workers demolishing old buildings, seems to round off one of Cosentino's main ideas: rock is the new thing that, whether the established order likes it or not, comes to take the place of the genres and customs already outdated among young people" (Campo 2012, 53). The origin of the Argentinean Beat movement is analyzed with greater detail in the feature film *Argentina Beat* (Hernán Gaffet, 2006).
3. The first edition of the festival was in November 1970.

References

Altman, Rick. 1992. "Conventions of Sound in Documentary." *Sound Theory/Sound Practice*. New York: Routledge. 217–34.
Berger, Harris M. 1999. *Metal, Rock, and Jazz: Perception and the Musical Phenomenology of Musical Experience*. Hanover & London: Wesleyan University Press.
Boffard, Rob. 2014. "Documenting Musicians." *Aesthetica* 56: 120–2.
Bruno, Diego. 2000. "Rock hasta que se ponga el sol." *Rebelde*. <http://www.dospotencias.com.ar/rebelde/esp_rock.htm> (last accessed 14 March, 2016).
Campo, Javier. 2012. *Cine documental argentino. Entre el arte, la cultura y la política*. Buenos Aires: Imago Mundi.
Chanan, Michael. 2013. "Music, Documentary, Music Documentary." In *The Documentary Film Book*, ed. Brian Winston. Basingstoke: Palgrave Macmillan/British Film Institute. 337–44.
Cohen, Thomas F. 2012. *Playing to the Camera: Musicians and Musical Performance in Documentary Cinema*. London: Wallflower.
Deutsch, Ron. 2014. "Docs That Really Rock: Music Documentaries Go Beyond the Performance." *Ida*, Winter. <http://www.documentary.org/magazine/docs-really-rock-music-documentaries-go-beyond-performance> (last accessed 7 December, 2015.)
Edgar, Robert, Kirsty Fairclough-Isaacs and Benjamin Halligan. 2013. "Introduction: Music Seen: The Formats and Functions of the Music Documentary." *The Music Documentary: Acid Rock to Electropop*. New York: Routledge: 1–21.

James, David E. 2012 "Rock 'n' Film: Generic Permutations in Three Feature Films from 1964." *Grey Room* 49: 7–31.

Lobalzo Wright, Julie. 2013. "The Good, The Bad and The Ugly '60s: The Opposing Gazes of *Woodstock* and *Gimme Shelter*." In *The Music Documentary Acid Rock to Electropop*, eds Robert Edgar, Kirsty Fairclough-Isaacs, and Benjamin Halligan. New York: Routledge. 89–104.

Pereyra, Daniela. 2016. "Entrevista a Anibal Uset." *La nave de los Sueños*, October 3. <http://lanavedelossuenos.blogspot.com/2012/10/entrevista-anibal-uset.html> (last accessed 16 March, 2016).

Rodríguez, Tomás. 2016. "Billy Bond: Historias Extraordinarias." *Playboy*. <http://www.playboyrevista.com/billy-bond-arquitectura-del-rock-nacional> (last accessed 16 March, 2016).

Small, Christopher. 1998. *Musicking: The Meaning of Performing and Listening*. Hannover: The University Press of New England.

Strachan, Robert and Marion Leonard 2009. "Rockumentary." In *Sound and Music in Film and Visual Media*, ed. Graeme Harper. New York: Bloomsbury Academic. 284–99.

18. *HARMONIUM IN CALIFORNIA*: MUSICALLY IMAGINED COMMUNITIES AND THE ROCKUMENTARY FORM

Eric Fillion

In September 1978, the progressive rock band Harmonium accompanied Quebec Premier René Lévesque on a cultural mission to San Francisco. Elected two years earlier, the Parti Québécois (PQ) intended to lead the predominantly French-speaking province on the path to independence. Its Opération-Amérique aimed to nurture goodwill in the USA by presenting a positive and engaging image of Quebec. Based in Montréal, Harmonium had lent support to Lévesque in the past, but this was the group's first excursion south of the 49th parallel. Serge Fiori and his bandmates were to perform *L'Heptade* (1976), a platinum album acclaimed as a masterpiece of *québécois* rock, in their efforts to both break into a new market and help sell the idea of an independent Quebec in the USA. As an exercise in musical diplomacy, the tour would help highlight the cultural attributes that Quebeckers shared with the rest of North America (their *américanité*) and those that made them different (their *québécité*).

This "musical nation branding" (Gienow-Hecht 2018, 272) centered on sound as much as it did on performance and image. News of the project caught the eye and ear of National Film Board of Canada/Office national du film (NFB/ONF) director Robert Fortier, who perceived the pertinence and urgency of capturing the event on film. *Harmonium in California* (Robert Fortier, Canada, 1979) negotiated this tension between *américanité* and *québécité* – between sameness and difference – using a "journalistic representational strategy" (Baker 2011, 115) that allowed for the making of multiple "musically imagined communities" (Born 2011, 383) without decentering Quebec's national project. Recognizing that musical experiences influence people's self-perception and sense of belonging, Fortier used the rockumentary form to communicate Harmonium's twofold objectives to broader audiences (from Quebec nationalists to Canadian youths and apolitical progressive rock fans throughout the world), thereby amplifying the representations and emotions conveyed through the group's on-camera performances.

This chapter situates *Harmonium in California* alongside *À soir on fait peur au monde* ("Tonight We Scare People," François Brault and Jean Dansereau, Canada, 1969) and *Tabarnac* ("Fuck!," Claude Faraldo, France, 1975) to demonstrate how rockumentaries in Quebec operate on the plane of collective self-representation through their foregrounding of national performance and their reliance on music's mediating potential. It explores the genre's malleability as a prism through which the nation can be both enacted and commodified. It does so using Erin Hurley's work on representational labors (the staging of mimesis) and emotional labors (the harnessing of affective appeals), which outlines new approaches for "thinking the performance-nation relationship" (Hurley 2011, 11). This chapter begins with a discussion of the conceptual framework deployed to situate and analyze *Harmonium in California*. It then explores the broader context within which the above rockumentaries were made before turning to the 1978 tour and Fortier's retelling of it.

Music, Mediation and the Rockumentary Form

One of *Harmonium in California*'s distinctive features as a tour film is that its main protagonists perform the roles of musicians and impromptu ambassadors simultaneously. It is therefore impossible to dissociate the film's object, a progressive rock band from Quebec, from the cultural diplomacy that made the tour possible. Cultural diplomacy is when nation-states (or nations striving for statehood, as in the case of Quebec) mobilize their cultural resources to shape elite or mass public opinions in other countries to create a climate conducive to reciprocal understanding. Music's seemingly apolitical and universal qualities, its affective and mediating potential, make it an effective tool for fostering conversations and promoting people-to-people interactions (Gienow-Hecht 2015, 20). Although musical diplomacy is most effective when it is bidirectional, it is also a potent vehicle for national projection and national self-representation. Nation branding, Jessica C. E. Gienow-Hecht contends, is central to the practice of musical diplomacy (Gienow-Hecht 2018, 266). As a type of information campaign, it is about constructing narratives and disseminating them widely to achieve desired political, economic or cultural ends. Musical nation branding, by its nature, lends itself easily to the rockumentary form.

Musicians who partake in national performance deploy a variety of strategies to engage audiences and elicit desired responses from them. On the one hand, they rely on mimesis and metonymy to evoke – or speak to – attributes that represent the nation (whether real or imagined). Hurley refers to these strategies as representational labors; that is, "representations that have a referential relation to an existing . . . idea of nation; they may support or contest that idea and they are decoded through analysis of signifier (the representation) and signified (the nation)" (Hurley 2011, 3). On the other hand, artists may seek to establish connections among themselves and with audiences using strategies that Hurley groups under the category of emotional labors. She explains:

> Emotional labour makes, manages, and distributes relationships through affective appeals; it draws people and objects . . . into affective webs. By allying audiences emotionally with the on-stage action, or providing vicarious experience – often of emotionality itself – or prompting thrill responses, for instance, emotional labour creates . . . 'national sentiment'. (Hurley 2011, 28)

This chapter argues that the intermediality of the rockumentary form (Fillion and Sirois-Trahan 2015) provides amplitude to representational and emotional labors.

It follows, then, that projects such as *Harmonium in California* can establish musically imagined communities. The concept builds on Benedict Anderson's work on nationalism, which demonstrates the centrality of media and expressive cultures (including the unison singing of national anthems) in the constitution and endurance, across time and space, of collective identities (Anderson 2006 [1983], 145). Damien Mahiet and his co-editors, in their introduction to *Music and Diplomacy*, broaden the scope of the concept by arguing that "sonorous coexistence" also generates "sonorous community" in transnational contexts (Mahiet, Ferraguto and Ahrendt 2014, 10). Conversely, Georgina Born approaches the idea of musically imagined communities through the lens of music scenes, which she describes as "aggregations of the affected" (Born 2011, 384). In all three cases, music is mediation and it engenders relationships between and among artists, audiences, producers and media. Rockumentaries that call attention to one of the above three types of musically-imagined communities bolster the sense of identity and belonging that musical experiences create.

Filmmakers accomplish this, in part, by using a "journalistic representational strategy" (Baker 2011, 115). Such an approach requires adequate lighting, sharp focus and a stable camera to convey detailed and realistic representations of the live event. "It foregrounds the act of witnessing the musical performance," explains Michael Brendan Baker (Ibid., 115). Directors who choose this strategy employ a wide range of shots – from the close-up to the wide shot – to offer intimate, but also enwrapping group portraits of the musicians both on-stage and backstage. Distinguishing between the two – on-stage versus backstage – is a "master trope" (Beattie 2008, 62) of the rockumentary form, which purports to demystify. Protagonists, in other words, are performing irrespective of where the camera is pointing. Jonathan Romney concurs: "Backstage ... is no less a space of display than the stage itself" (Romney 1995, 86). The evidential weight of visual elements, including those captured backstage and on the road, is a function of the importance accorded to authenticity and musicianship in rock culture, especially among progressive rock fans (Donnelly 2013, 172). Keith Beattie observes: "In the rockumentary, the provision of information ... operates within and through a mode which emphasises and exploits the representational capacities of the visual register" (Beattie 2008, 60). He adds: "The form of knowledge produced within this mode is subjective, affective, visceral and sensuous" (Ibid., 60). It therefore facilitates the establishment of musically imagined communities through the interplay of representational and emotional labors.

Quebec Nationalism on Stage and on Screen

The pace of change was spectacular in 1960s Quebec. At the beginning of the decade, the Liberal government of Jean Lesage sparked a Quiet Revolution [*la Révolution tranquille*] with a series of reforms that ranged from the increasing secularization of social services to the nationalization of electricity and a revamping of the education system to help French Canadians play leading roles in the political and economic life of their province. The Liberals' efforts to modernize Quebec and advance its interests within the Canadian federation signaled a departure from the so-called Great Darkness [*la Grande noirceur*], a term that described the previous government's antipathy towards progressive forces and its support of Christian corporatism. Yet to many, national independence was the only way to ensure the survival and continued development of the French fact in North America. Formerly Minister of National Resources, Lévesque broke with Lesage's Liberals in 1967 to create the Mouvement Souveraineté-Association, which became the PQ the following year. After two unsuccessful campaigns, his party won a majority government in 1976. For the first time in its history, Quebec had a government that saw itself mandated to work towards political independence. The first step was to prepare the terrain for what the PQ hoped would be a successful referendum in support of its national project.

Preparing the terrain meant, among other things, telling those who would be voting that the project was economically viable and that the transition to political sovereignty would be brisk and friendly. Hence Opération-Amérique, a seduction enterprise whose objective was to reassure American investors while convincing decision makers in the USA to maintain an attitude of goodwill and neutrality towards Quebec (Québec 1978a, 2). One of Lévesque's priorities was to reclaim control of the province's image south of the border in light of the "bad press" (Ibid., 2) given to Quebeckers' "nationalist aspirations" (Giniger 1977, 56). The PQ therefore sought to project the image of a "modern, dynamic and civilized Quebec, characterized by a high standard of living and, therefore, well-integrated within its North American context" (Québec 1978a, 9). In its White Paper on cultural development, the party had underlined Quebeckers' historical dynamism and their ability to creatively engage with other cultures (Québec 1978b, 333). It intended to spotlight those traits in California with Harmonium.

Formed in 1972 by Fiori and Michel Normandeau, Harmonium expanded into a trio the following year with the addition of Louis Valois. The group first explored the boundaries of folk rock before recruiting more members and venturing into the realm of progressive rock. Its self-titled debut (1974) was followed by *Si on avait besoin d'une cinquième saison* (1975) and then *L'Heptade*, an expansively-produced conceptual double album that featured musical interludes by composer Neil Chotem. In a stroke of synchronicity, Harmonium's opus hit the shelves on the day of the election that brought the PQ to power. Fiori and his bandmates had shared the stage with Lévesque on numerous occasions ahead of the party's successful political campaign. Yves LaDouceur, the group's first manager, recalls how the musicians and the PQ were traveling the same upward path (LaDouceur 2000, 231). Harmonium was therefore the obvious choice to kick-start the festivities surrounding Lévesque's diplomatic mission in San Francisco. Normandeau having left the group, Fiori and Valois took *L'Heptade* on the road with bandmates Libert Subirana, Jeff Fisher, Denis Farmer, Robert Stanley, and Monique Fauteux. Fortier accompanied them to document the encounter.

The NFB/ONF filmmaker was not the first to use the rockumentary form to examine the encounter between Quebec musicians and foreign publics. In *À soir on fait peur au monde*, Brault and Dansereau traveled to France, where pop singers Robert Charlebois and Louise Forestier, supported by the iconoclastic Rock libre du Québec, managed to get expelled from one of Paris's most prestigious venues: Olympia Hall. The film centered on the confrontation between the group and French audiences, between the New World and the Old World, to underline the capacity of individual actors to enact the nation and give resonance to its *américanité* and its *québécité*. Dansereau and Brault did so by using representational strategies that sharpened the markers of differentiation highlighted by the musicians' made-in-Quebec rock in their attempt to conquer – even if only culturally – their former imperial metropole. The two directors juxtaposed what appeared like a distant and ossifying France to images that evoked the vast and uncharted territories of Quebec, the proximity that characterized the performer-audience relationship at home, the musicians' combative posture as well as their resilience and self-confidence (Fillion 2015). The filmmakers also underlined the group's ability to creatively appropriate other expressive cultures through "cannibalistic" gestures (Sirois-Trahan 2016, 71). *À soir on fait peur au monde* thus helped turn an act of national projection (and musical self-promotion) into a vehicle for national self-representation for Quebec audiences in the closing years of the 1960s.

Likewise, Faraldo employed the trope of confrontation in *Tabarnac*, a rockumentary about the blues-rock band Offenbach and its 1974 stay in France. The French filmmaker had traveled to Montréal to meet the musicians after having discovered their music through a friend. He sold them on the idea of a tour that would be the basis for a film on *québécois* rock and its capacity to both awaken and mobilize people. Back in France, Faraldo rented a former convent in Malesherbes, which served as the home base for the group's on-stage and off-stage excesses. Cameras tracked Offenbach, day and night, as it disarmed and enlivened hostile crowds. Although he borrowed from direct cinema, Faraldo chose to end *Tabarnac* with actors disguised as police officers who, after a lengthy confrontation with the defiant musicians, joined the party to the sound of Offenbach playing Edith Piaf's "L'Hymne à l'amour." The film's *mise en scène* of the musicians' raw authenticity and spontaneity was a celebration of Quebeckers' resilience, their *prise de parole* (i.e. the act of finding one's voice) and their ability to reinvent themselves despite their minority status as francophones in North America. Directing with Quebec audiences and France's youth in mind, Faraldo used representational strategies to amplify the mediating potential of music while rendering more vivid – and broadening the reach of – Offenbach's national performance (Fillion 2015).

Harmonium in California

Harmonium in California began as one chapter in a three-part project tentatively titled *Musiculture*, whose objective was to "explore the significance of the Quebec music scene ... as an important expression of Quebec's culture and how it relates to the rest of North America" (Fortier 1978, 1). Submitted to the NFB/ONF on 11 September 1978, the proposal was quickly forwarded to a program committee for approval since the cultural diplomacy that inspired it was about to be deployed. Born in Nova Scotia, Fortier had made Montréal his home after moving there in 1963. Fifteen years later, he intended to explore (1) how one sells Quebec culture to the USA; (2) the economics of making it as a musician in Quebec; and (3) the origins as well as the future of music in the province. Thinking that the NFB/ONF wished to make a film on Lévesque's mission to California, the PQ agreed to invest $30,000 in the project, but it withdrew its offer when it realized that Fortier was more interested in filming

Harmonium for *Musiculture* than in documenting Lévesque's cultural diplomacy (Thibaudeau 1978).

Although the PQ backed out of the project, Fortier planned to discuss Harmonium using terms similar to those used for Opération-Amérique. He explained:

> The main idea behind the film is how does one go about selling Quebec as an independent nation. Let's start with California, the hot bed for the new music of the sixties, the place where the hippy generation was born. What better place and what better way to sell Quebec than through the most progressive sound in Quebec. Harmonium! Grab the arty people and convert them to your cause and they will help you in the future. (Fortier 1978, 3)

With contract in hand, Fortier began focusing on the musicians' role as cultural ambassadors while the broader ideas of *Musiculture* dwindled away. It is revealing that he also saw himself as playing a role in explaining the politico-cultural significance of the septet's music to English-speaking Canadians outside Quebec. Fiori and his bandmates had played in Ontario before. The press had praised their efforts to "charm Anglophones" (McGrath 1977, 19) while also aiming "for a more universal chord" (Johnson 1977, A10). However, the fact that Harmonium chose to rehearse its California set in Ontario was an indication that English Canada and the USA remained equally foreign to Quebec. Fortier, who went on the road with the group in Ontario, thought he could enhance the impact of the PQ's musical diplomacy by translating it through the rockumentary form for English-speaking audiences in Canada.

Harmonium's September 29 concert was to be the highlight of the PQ's information campaign in San Francisco. The organizers hoped that it would set the tone by displaying Quebec's culture as distinct, yet in harmony with the rest of North America. Earlier that day, Lévesque had told members of the city's Commonwealth Club that Quebeckers' roots ran deep in North America and that they shared with Americans a "continental outlook" (Lévesque 1978). He then invited the audience to enjoy the "wind of change" that was making "the traditionally boring neighbour to the North somewhat more interesting". Harmonium's musicians were apt envoys to project the image of a "happy, cheerful people, disposed to multiply opportunities to have fun" (Québec 1978a, 9). With a seating capacity of 2,000, University of California-Berkeley's Zellerbach Hall represented a formidable opportunity to connect with a receptive audience. The Montréal-born actress Geneviève Bujold, who lived in California, was expected to join the fifty-six-year-old premier to help him project a youthful and vibrant image. The septet would do its part by

18.1 Harmonium on stage at the Starwood in Los Angeles, California.
Source: National Film Board of Canada.

embodying a dynamic and modern image of Quebec. The group would then continue on to Belmont and Los Angeles.

Unfortunately, the van transporting Harmonium's equipment failed to arrive on time for the San Francisco concert. Delayed at the border, the driver then got lost around Salt Lake City. Fiori and his bandmates would not entertain the idea of performing *L'Heptade* with rented gear. They felt that they could not do justice to the rich intricacies of their music without their own instruments. The group thus canceled its San Francisco and Belmont concerts. It then headed to Los Angeles for a two-night engagement at the Starwood. Disappointed and bemused, the Quebec press lamented this "missed cultural encounter" (Petrowski 1978, 1). As for the PQ, it promptly sought compensation in the amount of $37,547 from Harmonium (Samson 1978). There was tension in the air, but little of this found its way into *Harmonium in California*. Rather than commenting on the crisis, Fortier sided with the musicians by minimizing, even obscuring, the seriousness of the situation. He remained undeterred in his efforts to champion the group's mission and amplify both its representational and emotional labors through the rockumentary form. Watching the film forty years after the events, Valois and Fauteux remarked that the director had indeed been especially empathetic (Valois 2018; Fauteux 2018).

In portraying Harmonium as being on par with other successful acts, Fortier sought to add substance to the idea that Quebeckers had caught up with the rest of North America and that they could hold their own on the international stage. He provided an indication of this *parti pris* in his proposal to the NFB/ONF when he mentioned wanting to shoot in the mobile recording studio that had been reserved for the tour: "To prove to everyone that the technical expertise in Quebec is as good or better than anywhere else in the world" (Fortier 1978, 4). To emphasize that point, Fortier showed the group arriving at the Starwood with a semi-trailer that contained more equipment and instruments than what the venue's power supply and stage could handle. The footage from the October 3 concert revealed a group in full control of the situation, with the seven musicians occupying the stage in a dense, but dynamic formation that allowed Fiori to move freely from his percussion set to the piano. The wide shot depicted an intricate and tightly woven collective that shone without any artifice. Close-ups emphasized complicity and coherence with musicians exchanging smiles and non-verbal cues as they progressed through their set. The minimal stage lighting created a perfect environment for cameras to move in and capture the dexterous playing of Fisher and Farmer on keyboards and drums, respectively. To complement the film's visual register, Fortier used a crisp soundtrack provided by the mobile studio's technicians. The story he told through sound and image was that of resilience, adaptability, self-assurance and expertise. It was a story that worked equally well for the progressive rock musicians and the nation that they were tasked with embodying.

Québécité was central to the musical nation branding that so enthralled Fortier. The filmmaker chose to begin the film with Fiori's opening remarks on the night of Harmonium's Los Angeles debut: "I don't know if you heard, but we sing in French," he told concertgoers.[1] He then indicated that the group would begin its set with "Aujourd'hui, je dis bonjour à la vie," at which point the crowd screamed in approval. Astounded, Fiori smiled, let out a friendly curse word – "damn" – and confided: "I didn't expect that really." These first few seconds set the tone by foregrounding the group's difference while indicating that it would be an asset, not a liability, in the USA. Officials at the Quebec government office in California had posited that French-language artists would appeal to Americans' taste for the exotic. Fortier thought the same. In his film proposal, he noted that students who listened to the "Peruvian guitar players" and the "African drummers" that played on Berkeley's campus would be drawn to Harmonium's music (Fortier 1978, 3). Fortier built on this essentializing association by inserting footage of some of these impromptu performers in the film. The idea of an encounter with a foreign other also informed depictions of the Starwood, a club that hosted "raw punk rock groups" and stood sturdily in the "land of Hollywood and hard sell." Difference was an asset and it sold, Fortier suggested. This play of opposition helped position *québécité* as a complementary counterweight to *américanité*.

Displaying Harmonium's difference made it possible to harness the affective appeal of made-in-Quebec rock. It also lent legitimacy to the authenticity of Fiori and his bandmates' performance as both progressive rock musicians and cultural ambassadors. Fortier's journalistic representational strategy provided glimpses of the group's life on the road – on board an Air Canada flight and in hotel rooms as well as on-stage and backstage at the Starwood – in a continuum that underlined continuity between public and private personas. Similarly, the images captured at KALX Radio and during an autograph-signing session at Rather Ripped Records demystified the musicians' iconic status to stress their unassuming professionalism and depict them as approachable, authentic ambassadors for *québécois* rock. At the end of one concert, an emotional Fiori confided to the camera: "I'm sure now that . . . a lot of things can happen with these people, it's just a question of being yourself, now we didn't do any funny compromise or anything." Fortier returned to this play of opposition at

18.2 Limited theatrical release of *Harmonium in California* on October 19–24, 1979. Source: *La Presse*.

the very end of the film with Fiori further explaining: "Just the fact of being there, with American people and singing what we are ... it just showed us what we are even more." That the director chose to end with this intervention revealed how important authenticity was in the efforts to sell Harmonium and Quebec to the USA, but also *Harmonium in California* to French-speaking and English-speaking audiences in Canada.

In this rockumentary, Fortier placed a variety of musically-imagined communities in relation to one another. Quebeckers who wished to follow Harmonium and Lévesque's adventure found themselves pulled into the film. They recognized themselves in the music, but also in the on-screen display of *québécité*. In the same way that Fortier emphasized camaraderie between the musicians, he showed Lévesque and Fiori exchanging friendly, encouraging remarks the night of the canceled concert in San Francisco. The image of the premier and the singer tapping each other on the shoulder told viewers in Quebec that their nation branding efforts remained unscathed despite emerging tensions between the group and the PQ. As for progressive rock fans outside Quebec, *Harmonium in California* reassured them that music was ultimately a universal language that transcended French-English divides. The insertion of interviews with various protagonists – from audience members to the Starwood's David Knight – served to substantiate the argument that Harmonium could bring together people from all over into a larger community of progressive rock enthusiasts. That message was evidently also destined for English-speaking Canadians who formed a third musically-imagined community in the film. Fortier invited his compatriots to claim Harmonium as their own in the opening minutes by superimposing the title of the film on an image of an Air Canada flight; a crown corporation, which like the NFB/ONF, owed its existence to the Canadian government. In the background, the group sang:

> *Like a sage*
> *Climb into the clouds*
> *Come to the floor above*
> *Come see the landscape*
> *Let me see your face*

Although Fortier foregrounded Quebec's distinctiveness, he also channeled the mediating potential of music to foster dialogue between Canada's so-called two solitudes. In Los Angeles, he interviewed an anglophone woman who did not feel "nationalistic" about Harmonium's music because of a "deep crevasse between the two cultures." Another young man retorted at the end of the film: "This is one of the few Canadian bands that I can come see and admit to other people in the audience that I'm Canadian." No doubt, Fortier sided with the latter.

CONCLUSION

The persuasiveness of *Harmonium in California* lay in its ability to engage different constituencies by providing amplitude to the septet's representational and emotional labors. Through its visual register and narrative circularity, the film gave additional resonance to music's mediating role. The interplay between sameness (*américanité*) and difference (*québécité*) put divergent musically-imagined communities in relation with each other in ways that revealed how attuned Fortier was to the socio-cultural and political context of the time. Although completed in 1979, *Harmonium in California* premiered on national television on 29 June 1980, a month after the PQ's referendum, which ended with 59.56 per cent of Quebeckers rejecting the party's proposal to negotiate secession from Canada.[2] Had the film been televized earlier, it would have brought Lévesque's musical diplomacy into Canadian homes from coast to coast. Coming out as it did in the charged emotional climate of post-referendum Canada, it aimed to heal differences and promote dialogue while displaying other modes of thinking about collective self-representation. Today, the film is a reminder that rockumentaries in Quebec are never exclusively about selling music.

NOTES

1. Unless otherwise indicated, all quotations are from *Harmonium in California*. Note also that French quotations have been translated to make the text more readable.
2. The film received a limited theatrical release in Montréal in October of 1979. The NFB/ONF completed a French version titled *Harmonium en Californie* (Robert Fortier, Canada, 1980) the following spring.

REFERENCES

Anderson, Benedict. [1983] 2006. *Imagined Communities*. London: Verso.
Baker, Michael Brendan. 2011. "Rockumentary: Style, Performance & Sound in a Documentary Genre." Doctoral thesis. Montréal, Quebec: McGill University.
Beattie, Keith. 2008. *Documentary Display: Re-Viewing Nonfiction Film and Video*. New York: Wallflower.
Born, Georgina. 2011. "Music and the Materialization of Identities." *Journal of Material Culture* 16(4): 376–88.
Donnelly, K. J. 2013. "Visualizing Live Albums: Progressive Rock and the British Concert Film in the 1970s." In *The Music Documentary: Acid Rock to Electropop*, eds Benjamin Halligan, Robert Edgar and Kirsty Fairclough-Isaacs. New York: Routledge. 171–82.
Fauteux, Monique. 2018. Interview with the author. Montréal, 14 March 2018.
Fillion, Eric. 2015. "Le rock québécois débarque en France. *À soir on fait peur au monde, Tabarnac*, ou: le retour par le rockumentaire." *Nouvelles Vues* 16, <http://www.nouvellesvues.ulaval.ca/index.php?id=2719> (last accessed 20 January, 2020).
Fillion, Eric and Jean-Pierre Sirois-Trahan. 2015. "Intermédialité(s): le cinéma rock

au Québec." *Nouvelles Vues* 16, <http://www.nouvellesvues.ulaval.ca/index.php?id=2714> (last accessed 20 January, 2020).

Fortier, Robert. 1978. "*Musiculture*: Film Proposal." *Harmonium in California* Production File, National Film Board of Canada.

Gienow-Hecht, Jessica C. E. 2018. "Of Dreams and Desire: Diplomacy and Musical Nation Branding Since the Early Modern Period." In *International Relations, Music and Diplomacy: Sounds and Voices on the International Stage*, eds Frédéric Ramel and Cécile Prévost-Thomas. Cham: Springer/Palgrave Macmillan. 259–74.

Gienow-Hecht, Jessica C. E. 2015. "Sonic History, or Why Music Matters in International History." In *Music and International History in the Twentieth Century*, ed. Jessica C. E. Gienow-Hecht. New York and Oxford: Berghahn Books. 1–28.

Giniger, Henry. 1977. "Quebecers Discern an Uphill Struggle to Win American Understanding for their Nationalist Aspirations." *The New York Times*, 25 September 1977: 56.

Hurley, Erin. 2011. *National Performance: Representing Quebec from Expo 67 to Céline Dion*. Toronto: University of Toronto Press.

Johnson, B. D. 1977. "Harmonium: A Celebration." *The Globe and Mail*, 1 June 1977: A10.

LaDouceur, Yves. 2000. *Harmonium: une histoire à raconter*. Prévost: Édition 12e Art.

Lévesque, René. 1978. "Quebec and Canada: A New Relationship." Fonds René Lévesque, Bibliothèque et Archives nationales du Québec, 1992-02-005\14.

Mahiet, Damien, Mark Ferraguto, and Rebekah Ahrendt. 2014 "Introduction." In *Music and Diplomacy from the Early Modern Era to the Present*, eds Damien Mahiet, Mark Ferraguto and Rebekah Ahrendt. New York: Palgrave Macmillan. 1–16.

McGrath, Paul. 1977. "Quebec Musicians Charm Anglophones," *The Globe and Mail*, 4 April 1977: 19.

Petrowski, Nathalie. 1978. "Un rendez-vous culturel manqué." *Le Devoir*, 2 October 1978: 1.

Québec 1978a. "Opération-Amérique: orientation et objectifs." Fonds Ministère de la Culture et des communications, Bibliothèque et Archives nationales du Québec. 1989-11-004\60.

Québec. 1978b. *La politique québécoise du développement culturel – volume 2*. Québec: Éditeur officiel.

Romney, Jonathan. 1995. "Access All Areas: The Real Space of Rock Documentary." In *Celluloid Jukebox: Popular Music and the Movies since the 50s*, eds Jonathan Romney and Adrian Wootton. London: British Film Institute. 83–93.

Samson, Jean K. 1978. Letter to Paul Dupont-Hébert, 21 December 1978, Fonds Ministère de la Culture et des communications, Bibliothèque et Archives nationales du Québec. 1995-02-001\131.

Sirois-Trahan, Jean-Pierre. 2016. "L'évolution intranquille: multiplicité et rock québécois." In *La contre-culture au Québec*, eds Karim Larose and Frédéric Rondeau. Montréal: Les Presses de l'Université de Montréal. 55–97.

Thibaudeau, Serge. 1978. Letter to Pierrette Arseneault, 27 September 1978, Fonds Ministère de la Culture et des communications, Bibliothèque et Archives nationales du Québec. 1995-02-001\131.

Valois, Louis. 2018. Interview with the author. Montréal, 14 March 2018.

19. STATIONS OF THE CRASS: COUNTER-CULTURE AND THE ANARCHO-PUNK MOVEMENT

Asbjørn Tiller

The Sex Pistols created an upheaval when they cursed live on the *Today* show on Thames TV in 1976, their behavior making headlines in the British press (Berger 2006: 4). The band were perceived as upstarts, conducting themselves in ways that were not only unheard of on public television, but that ran counter to all tradition, convention, and the conservative British establishment. The incident in many ways marked the start of the English punk scene, and it clearly expressed the rebellion against authority and the establishment which would become a trademark of the punk attitude.

Typically, the history of punk centers on seminal bands like the Sex Pistols, The Clash, and The Damned, while less commercially-accepted punk movements have been left out of the tale. This is also true of the anarcho-punk movement emerging in 1977, pushed forward by the band Crass (Cross 2010; Grimes 2015; Berger 2006). While the first wave of punk bands soon became parts of the very establishment and music industry they had initially rejected, Crass, throughout their short but intensive career from 1977 to 1984, constantly attacked the political system, the traditional family, the church, state, police, and courts. They also railed against what they considered the first wave of punk rock's failure to confront the established music industry. The anarcho-punk movement surfaced soon after the above-mentioned first wave. Based on the anti-establishment ethos of the initial punks, the bands within this movement took rebellion against the establishment to a new level in their lyrics, their artwork, and attempts to live off the grid. The anarcho-punk movement was initiated by Crass, who were based in the art collective Dial House in Epping Forest, UK.

This chapter will discuss the politics and aesthetics of this movement mainly through a case study of Crass and their commitment to do-it-yourself (DIY) principles – in their writing, recording, performance, distribution, and artwork – and how this had an impact on both the anarcho-punk movement and the UK establishment. An outset for this discussion will be Dutch filmmaker Alexander Oey's documentary *There is No Authority but Yourself* (The Netherlands, 2006), which itself also includes discussions of the band's artwork, especially the films made by Crass members Gee Vaucher and Mike Duffield. Their films are to some extent used as archival material in Oey's documentary. Six of Vaucher's films are compiled in the film *Semi-Detached* (UK, 2001; see Vaucher 2015), while three of Duffield's are compiled in *Christ – The Movie* (UK, 1990; see Duffield 2016). They were all produced in the period 1978–84 and screened during the band's live performances.

There is no Authority but Yourself (2006) offers a retrospective look at a specific phenomenon within the punk scene in the late 1970s – the band-collective Crass. The film opens with their song "White Punks On Hope," from the album *Stations Of The Crass*. While this is played, we see rapid images of the Crass logo, some of their cover artwork and stencils, and then archival still images of the band during live performances. While these images play, Steve Ignorant's voice recounts what a typical Crass gig was like. He describes feeling the tension between different gangs in the crowd, always being on the alert for potential attacks by National Front skinheads. In short: Crass gigs were a rather hostile environment.

Crass was formed in Dial House in Epping Forrest, north of London. As an artists' collective, Dial House had been a place for alternative cultural expression since the mid-1960s (Berger 2006, 12). The house was run by artist and writer Jeremy John Ratter, known as Penny Rimbaud, and Gee Vaucher. Ratter got the inspiration for his stage name from disreputed French poet Arthur Rimbaud, and from the fact that his brother felt he could be characterized as a "toilet-seat philosopher." A visit to a public toilet cost one penny at the time, and thus, this became his moniker (Burrows 2010).

Through interviews with selected band members Penny Rimbaud, Steve Ignorant (Steven Williams) and Gee Vaucher, the documentary presents their story of the band, the ideas that formed them, and how they put those ideas into action. Rimbaud's initial idea for the house was based on the traditional Chinese guesthouse, where one could pay to spend a night by performing a poem or a story. It had an open-door policy, and a general openness to alternative culture with roots in the hippie movement, as Rimbaud and Vaucher both confirm in the film. The interviews take place at Dial House, where they both still live.

Steve Ignorant is interviewed in front of his townhouse in Epping, and he shares how he was introduced to Dial House by his brother:

> [What] I realised about Penny Rimbaud and Gee was that for the first time in my life if they asked me a question or if I said something, they would treat me as an equal. That's the first time I ever had that, so I kept coming back to visit. (Steve Ignorant)

A young Steve Ignorant came to Dial House from a poor, working-class background, but instantly got on with Rimbaud, who had grown up as part of the upper middle-class. The much older Rimbaud and Vaucher displayed a welcoming nature and way of living that inspired the disillusioned boy, and he formed Crass along with them:

> So when it was Crass it was the same thing, we were just friends. I've always respected him for that, and he's always respected me for that. We really did blow away that upper class working class divide, and we were just two guys doing it. (Steve Ignorant)

Like so many others, Ignorant was also inspired by the first wave of punk. He saw The Clash in Colston Hall in Bristol in early 1977, when frontman Joe Strummer ended the concert by shouting "If you think you can do this better than this then start you own fucking band!" Rimbaud, at his side, listened to artists like Patti Smith. When Ignorant turned up at Dial House suggesting they form a band, Rimbaud was immediately on board. Eventually, more members joined too. These were strangers passing through Dial House, and musicality was not a criterion for joining Crass.

> Someone said 'can I join the band' and there wasn't any question of 'yes' or 'no'. There was an automatic 'of course you can, what can you do?' And it didn't matter if they could do anything at all. (Penny Rimbaud)

The all-important requirement for being a member of the band was attitude. In this sense, Crass became a band who more than others followed the punk ethos of not having to know how to play an instrument. Guitarist Andy Palmer became a member because he *owned* a guitar. He had no knowledge of how to play it, and according to Ignorant never learned how to do so in any conventional sense in the seven years the band existed. Some of the more well-known punk bands from this period unquestionably could actually play their instruments quite well, and were in fact musically competent rock 'n' roll bands (Berger 2006, 5)

Eventually, all members of Crass lived in Dial House, and it became the headquarters for all band activities. It functioned as a rehearsal space and a workshop for all their artwork, record label work, letter writing and so on. The rent was extremely cheap, and as they were almost entirely self-supporting, they lived on a minimum of money, self-sufficiency being a major goal in itself. The band soon became the inspiration for a new movement within punk called anarcho-punk, which eventually grew to consist of a lot of bands both in England and throughout Europe.

The most extensive overview of the British anarcho-punk scene is found in Ian Glasper's book *The Day the Country Died* (2006). Here, around eighty bands are presented, through interviews with former band members. There were, however, also several bands that were not included in this book, most notably Poison Girls. The movement grew large during the first part of the 1980s – in addition to the bands themselves, there were numerous people organizing gigs and events, not to mention all the followers and fans of the acts. The interviews in the book leave no doubt that Crass were the main inspiration for their activity, especially when it came to politics. While Crass rebelled against the system in general, some of these bands "specialized" in certain areas for their activities, like animal rights, vegetarianism and anti-vivisection. This was promoted in particular by bands like Conflict who, contrary to Crass's pacifist stance, took a more militant approach in their actions (Glasper 2006, 104).

Another major way in which Crass inspired other bands was with their DIY approach, expressed particularly through the organization of gigs, writing of fanzines, and running of their own record companies. An example of this is the band Flux of Pink Indians who, in addition to touring with Crass, set up their own record company to release their own and others' music. This was also a major activity for Crass, who released records by a lot of bands within the British anarcho-punk movement, and even the Icelandic band KUKL, featuring young vocalist Björk. Flux of Pink Indians took the same approach with their Spiderleg Records, releasing both their own records and those of other bands. In this respect, the record companies, along with all the people arranging events and following the bands, worked as networks for the anarcho-punk movement.

There is No Authority but Yourself

Oey's documentary about Crass is based around some of the three featured members' activities today, following them in their daily lives. It soon becomes apparent that they have chosen differing paths since Crass. Rimbaud and Vaucher are still living in Dial House, running different experimental projects, while Ignorant lives a more conventional life – going to the pub, watching football, and so on. Throughout the film, we are shown a band that – in the seven years they existed – stood in opposition and contrast to, while simultaneously strengthening the central politics of, the early wave of punk. In this way, director Oey presents a part of British music history which in many ways is left out of most of the tales told of punk as music and as a movement. More often than not, these tales tell the story of the most commercially successful bands from this period. Grimes (2015), in an analysis of the film, points to several aspects that both separate it from conventional rockumentary forms and place it within some of the conventions of documentary modes. It is especially interesting to compare this film to others with an outset in the punk movement, like *The Punk Rock Movie* (Don Letts, UK, 1978) and *The Filth and the Fury* (Julien Temple, UK, 2000). These films often utilize aesthetics that reflect the mood and style of punk (Grimes 2015, 190). The films are created with low production values and extended use of bricolage techniques.

Some of these techniques are seen in *There is No Authority but Yourself* too, as the rockumentary appropriates some archival footage of this kind through the use of Vaucher and Duffield's Crass films, which I will return to. Apart from this, however, Oey's film does not visualize the punk and DIY aesthetics, opting instead to make use of "other forms of mediation that seems to invite us, as an audience, to look, listen, contemplate, reflect and question the subjects he documents" (op.cit. 2015, 199).

These forms are connected to more conventional documentary modes, like the observational or expository modes proposed by Bill Nichols. Grimes connects this to the director taking the role of an observer, letting the band members speak directly to the camera and tell their story, even though the different stories at some points contradict each other, meaning that the film "challenges the notion of a singular truth" (op.cit. 2015, 198). In this manner, the mode of *There is No Authority but Yourself* makes it stand out from most rockumentaries, and punk films in general.

I will argue, however, that the form used in this film and the engagement of the filmmaker with his subjects are in precise accordance with some specific aspects of the activities in Dial House, both today and during the Crass period. This is closely connected to it being an open house. All of the interviewed members point to how, during the Crass years, large numbers of fans travelled to Dial House and stayed there to explore the band's ideas, how they worked, how the house was run, how they lived, and so on – seeking inspiration for their own rebellions. These anarcho-punks and fans stayed there as observers, to the point where the band felt these people were merely sitting there, waiting for their next move.

Oey now visits Dial House with, in many ways, a similar purpose. Large parts of his film depict how life continues in the house today, and the current situation closely resembles that of the band's active years. We get an impression of this in the opening scenes of the film, where Rimbaud sits in the house with a group of people, explaining how the house is run today, with some of his visitors also wanting to hear the story of Crass. We see it again later on in the film, where we follow a workshop on permaculture at Dial House. I would argue that Oey in the making of this film takes on a role resembling that of the visiting fans, during the band's active years and today, as an observer. Oey observes the activities that went on, and are still going on, albeit through different means and to a different end. The documentary presents the band and activities then and today in a way that is based on the members' own stories and the way they tell them. The film includes some archival footage and pictures from the band's career, as well as inserts of their music, underlined with some of the lyrics from their songs. It takes its title from what became their most prominent slogan. This is emphasized by Rimbaud in one of the interviews. Crass rebelled against everything and everyone. From the start, some of this rebellion was directly aimed at the first wave of punk.

DIY in Counter-Culture

> Within anarcho-punk, DIY activity was seen as indivisible from the political-cultural project by which the movement was enthused. (Cross 2010, 6)

The first wave of punk bands soon became their own industries. Sex Pistols, The Clash, The Jam, and similar bands continued their careers within the very industry and establishment they had originally rebelled against, with varying degrees of success. Moreover, punk aesthetics soon became fashion. This should not come as a surprise, as the Sex Pistols themselves began as an extension of the style launched by manager Malcolm McLaren and designer Vivienne Westwood, in their fashion boutiques in the Chelsea area of London (Berger 2006, 2). The Sex Pistols were rebellious in the sense that they promoted anarchy and chaos as a counterpart to the established and streamlined music industry, and the conformity of society as a whole. However, it is hard to see them as strictly political. They preached anarchy and chaos purely as a way to provoke the establishment. For Crass, the slogan "There is no authority but yourself" was a way of saying that every individual had the power to actually stand up against the establishment, whether that be family values, society, or the church.

> We kind of got very excited about the punk scene. The first wave of it. At last there was a youth culture growing just saying 'fuck off'. But then it sort of started to sour for us. The idea of 'no future' was really not in our realm. We were accused of being old hippies. Well fine. They had a dream and we were still dreaming. Still aim for that. And that is just coming

together. We took up that area of music and expression because none of us were musicians particularly, and the whole ethos was 'Just get up and do it! Just express it!' (Gee Vaucher)

The documentary shows that Crass was not a band in the conventional sense. It was more than that. Being a member of Crass was just as much about fronting a certain lifestyle, characterized by political and social consciousness based on an anarchist and pacifist approach to the freedom of the individual, as it was about playing in a band. The aim was to overthrow the capitalist system (Cross 2010, 1). This political and social consciousness was promoted through their music and, first and foremost, their lyrics. But it was also expressed through the way they lived in Dial House, and their political activism and art output. Life at Dial House was an experiment, an attempt to live outside the laws and regulations of normal society, and act in stark opposition to its framework. The members of Crass were not merely the people actually playing instruments, but included those who made the visual materials and artwork used by the band, underlining their identity. Oey has included Crass's songs on the film's soundtrack, as a means of underlining the stories told in the interviews. Indeed, the documentary has a strong focus on the lyrics. They are typed out on the screen – white on black – as we hear them, and although the film does not utilize punk aesthetics, these intertitles resemble the band's own.

The overall legacy of Crass is just as much tied to the aesthetic presentation of the band and the DIY approach as to the music produced. They were equally interested in how the music was presented as in the lyrics and tunes themselves: "Crass began from an assumption that the music was a delivery mechanism for the ideas" (Cross 2010, 2). The artistic presentation underlined and amplified the musical expression and its content. The whole band lived together as a collective in Dial House, from where they conducted their business in a self-sustaining manner. That was where they made the music, rehearsed it, recorded it, and created the cover art for their releases, and stage artwork for their concerts. They also established their own record label, which included distribution. All of this to circumvent the control of the traditional music industry. Every aspect of Crass's work followed the DIY principle, working outside of, and in opposition to, the established music industry. This kind of strategy can be seen as a prolongation of the counter-culture of the hippie movement. Rimbaud and Vaucher had been connected to this movement, partly through their membership of the performance group EXIT at the beginning of the 1970s. EXIT utilized multimedia means in its performances (Berger 2006, 30). Much of this approach was continued in Crass.

Another central point in Crass's activities was the neglect of profit. All of their work was based on the principle of non-profit, meaning their records were sold with close to none. Most of their concerts were benefit performances

19.1 Crass art.

for projects aligned with their political agenda. If they earned money from their records, this was immediately channeled into new creative and social projects. These projects were conducted by the band themselves, or by others they wished to support, be they local organizations or musicians at the different places they toured. All in all, everything Crass did was based on their ideological principles, to the extent that they never stayed in hotels when they were traveling for gigs, preferring to stay with private individuals. Anything to avoid capitalist mechanisms.

This adherence to the DIY principle led to a coherent and specific aesthetic seen in their records, their stage performances, and in the symbols the band used. They also wore all black at all times, the intention of which was to act as anonymously as possible, and to demonstrate opposition to the extremely expensive punk fashions being sold in Kings Road, London. Most specifically, the band created a distinct aesthetic for their record releases. Even before they released any music, they started using a special logo developed by designer Dave King, which was used by Penny Rimbaud on a pre-Crass pamphlet called *Christ's Reality Asylum*. Even at this early point, the power of the church, family, and state are central themes, and are described by Rimbaud as fascist tendencies. King's design was a circular logo, inspired by the circle and the cross. It also includes a snake biting its own tail, symbolizing the ruling order destroying itself. It was designed in such a way that none of the parts touched, so it could be cut out and used as a template for spray painting.

Both Gee Vaucher and Mick Duffield were members of Crass despite having next to nothing to do with the musical side of the band. Their contribution was towards the presentation of the band's aesthetic and style. Vaucher was responsible for the design of all the cover art on the band's records, and from the very first release, they had unique designs. All of the first releases, be they 7 inch singles or 12 inch LPs, were created as huge posters, which could be folded out to a size six times the original cover size. Aside from all the lyrics (a necessity, as Ignorant spat out the words so fast, it was nearly impossible to catch them all without reading them), the covers included large collages created by Vaucher. They underlined the anarchistic political messages in the lyrics. Vaucher and Duffield also made collage-like films, which were screened at Crass gigs. All of this can be seen as a continuation of the aesthetics they had already developed with EXIT. The films were also closely connected to DIY principles. They were all created to be used at Crass gigs and events, and they all used the technique of bricolage. Vaucher's films consist of recordings made on a VHS camera, filming directly from television sets (Vaucher 2001/2015). Duffield's are partly filmed on super 8, but also include found footage (Duffield 1990/2016). They were screened while the band played, using simple DIY techniques like "two video machines linked so that one could override the other" (Vaucher 2001/2015). All of the material used in these films was edited to highlight and underline the political ideas and lyrics of the band. In Oey's film, some of the archival material from these films is intercut to give an impression of how the films align with the rest of the artwork from the band.

All of the record sleeves were black-and-white, and the writing used a military font template, encouraging cut-outs for spray painting. Many other bands released their records on Crass Records, and as Penny Rimbaud produced them all, their sound was formed by the Crass aesthetics, and their cover designs were in the same style, with the same foldout cover size.

Vaucher's collages were perhaps the aspect of the Crass expression that stood out the most, becoming a unique part of the overall expression. One collage that effectively sums up the aggressive political stance of the band, both towards the first wave of punk and the establishment as a whole, can be found in in the 1980 release *Bloody Revolutions*. This split single with the band Poison Girls has a cover image based on a picture of the Sex Pistols, but with their heads torn out and replaced with images of Queen Elizabeth, Pope John Paul II, The Statue of Liberty, and Margaret Thatcher. The initial political ideas of the band, their musical style, and their artwork were all seminal for the rest of the anarcho-punk movement, which spread throughout both the UK and other parts of Europe. This fact is barely touched upon in Oey's film. As noted earlier, the film does not utilize classic punk aesthetics. However, one can note the presence of some DIY principles, as Oey directed, filmed, and edited the film himself.

Punk Is Dead

Already on their first release, *The Feeding Of The 5000* (1978), the band attacked the commercialization and conformity of the first wave of the punk rebellion.

> *Yes that's right, punk is dead,*
> *It's just another cheap product for the consumer's head.*
> *Bubblegum rock on plastic transistors,*
> *Schoolboy sedition backed by big time promoters.*
> *CBS promote the Clash,*
> *But it ain't for revolution, it's just for cash.*
> *Punk became a fashion just like hippie used to be*
> *And it ain't got a thing to do with you or me*
> (Punk Is Dead, The Feeding of the 5000, 1978)

Ignorant's initial inspiration, The Clash, are criticized here for having sold out to a major record label. Later in the same lyric, Rimbaud's inspiration Patti Smith gets it in the line "*Patti Smith you're napalm/You write with your hand but it's Rimbaud's arm.*" Smith was highly inspired by and a great admirer of the French poet.

In Oey's conventionally-created documentary – but perhaps more unconventional rockumentary – we get an impression of how the lifestyle and initial ideas of Crass have been continued by members Rimbaud and Vaucher in Dial House. Remaining self-sufficient still appears to be a major goal, along with not being part of the capitalist social framework. Dial House is still run as an open house, where anyone who wants can visit and take part in activities like workshops in permaculture, sustainability, and self-sufficient settlements. Against this backdrop, the slogan "There is No Authority but Yourself" still appears to be a guideline for the remaining settlers.

The documentary was made in 2006, and though much of the Crass philosophy is still embraced, it seems that life in Dial House these days is much more relaxed and less aggressive than during the Crass days. The film highlights some of the problems that occurred within the band, both because of their uncompromising behavior and the amount of time spent trying to achieve their goals and live up to their own standards. In the end, the members of the band were all exhausted.

This was clearly related to their principle of doing everything themselves and doing it without any profits at all. The film accentuates both the impact the band had with their music and lyrics, and how this impact in fact became a problem for the band in the end. The extremely intensive period of activity, during the seven years the band existed, wore the members out. The individualism that they advocated for was based in selflessness, and in the end this selflessness led to a kind of self-destruction. Rimbaud states in the film that their career was like living in a play, where the members were scripted parts, and not actually independent individuals. "You became an idea of yourself, and not yourself."

Additionally, towards the end of their career, the band became entangled in the political game they opposed. In this period, Margaret Thatcher became their main target, and they released the single "How Does it Feel to be the Mother of 1000 Dead." This was a direct comment on the prime minister's role in the Falklands War, and led to several statements of support for the band from central members of the Labour Party.

It is ironic to witness how the band in retrospect became victims of the society and industries they opposed. This is especially true in the case of their economic principles. Their attempts to do everything in a non-profit manner left nothing for the band members; everything was channeled into new projects. But in later years, we find several examples of how their logos and symbols have been exploited within the fashion industry. This has been especially noted by Steve Ignorant when he speaks about how multimillionaires and celebrities like David Beckham have been depicted in magazines wearing t-shirts with the Crass logo, together with clothes designed by Jean Paul Gaultier and the like.

The film in many ways clarifies the break between the members of the band, especially through the interviews with Steve Ignorant and Penny Rimbaud. While Rimbaud continues, along with Vaucher, to run Dial House in a liberated eco-philosophical manner, based on ideological principles, Ignorant, who is interviewed in a pub while watching a football match, lives his life in stark contrast to this. This amplifies the feeling one gets of Rimbaud being the ideological force in the band, while Ignorant represented its aggression, youthfulness and bloody-mindedness. The break between the members is additionally accentuated in this film through the fact that only three out of an original ten members were interviewed.

There is No Authority but Yourself gives an in-depth and detailed description of the work done by the band. However, it barely touches upon the influence the band had on the contemporary punk scene in England and elsewhere in Europe, and how the band involuntarily became the frontmen of the anarcho-punk movement. In the case of Britain, this is well-documented and discussed in Ian Glasper's book *The Day the Country Died* (2006). Within the anarcho-punk movement, Crass in many ways became the authority they opposed, an institution of their own.

> *Movements are systems and systems kill.*
> *Movements are expressions of the public will.*
> (*Punk Is Dead. The Feeding of the 5000*, 1978)

Very few elements in the film show the influence the band had on the DIY movement internationally. "Crass's work helped to inspire the creation of a diverse network of bands, activists, publishers and organizers, committed in one way or another to the movements' creative and political priorities" (Cross 2010, 5) *There is No Authority but Yourself* barely touches upon these aspects, and how the band has inspired later movements within music, both in Europe, and equally, if in a slightly different manner, in the USA, where Dead Kennedys, with their frontman Jello Biafra, in many ways represented the same ethos. This is especially evident in how later independent bands and musical networks have adopted the DIY approach to distributing and promoting music. In this respect, Crass paved the way for underground musical networks throughout Europe, some of which have managed to survive and keep on going even today, based on the DIY ethos.

In retrospect Crass appear as the most uncompromising band of the anarcho-punk movement, where the power of the individual was central, although it seems like the individuals in the band Crass actually lost their individuality precisely because of the way they acted. The power and framework of society was attacked no matter what political directions they came from.

> *Left wing, right wing, you can stuff the lot.*
> *Keep your petty prejudice, I don't see the point,*
> ANARCHY AND FREEDOM IS WHAT I WANT
> ("White Punks on Hope. Stations of the Crass," 1980)

References

Berger, George. 2006. *The Story of Crass*. London: Omnibus Books.
Burrows, Alex. 2010. Penny Rimbaud on Crass & the Poets of Transcedentalism & Modernism. <http://thequietus.com/articles/05258-penny-rimbaud-crass-interview> (last accessed 28 June, 2019).
Cross, Rich. 2010. "'There is No Authority but Yourself': The Individual as Collective in British Anarcho-Punk." *Music & Politics* 4(2): 1–20.
Duffield, Mike. [1990] 2016. Liner notes, *Christ – The Movie*. ExitstencilPress.
Glasper, Ian. 2006. *The Day the Country Died – A History of Anarcho-Punk 1980–1984*. London: Cherry Red Books.
Grimes, Matt. 2015. "Call it Crass but 'There is No Authority but Yourself': De-canonizing Punk's Underbelly." *Punk & Post-Punk* 4.2(3): 189–204.
MOCAtv. 2013. The Art of Punk – Crass – The Art of Dave King and Gee Vaucher. <https://www.youtube.com/watch?v=ubzKiomuUB0> (last accessed 28 June, 2019).
PanCrack Productions. 2007. Penny Rimbaud Talks – Crass DIY Punk Jazz Politics

Art & Activism, at the NEXNE Music Convention. <https://www.youtube.com/watch?v=mADo_8D8nmc> (last accessed 28 June, 2019).

UVP Productions. 1998. An Interview with Steve Ignorant on Crass at Dial House. <https://www.youtube.com/watch?v=IgNToZnyslE> (last accessed 28 June, 2019).

Vaucher, Gee. [2001] 2015. Liner notes, *Semi – Detached*. Exitstencil Press.

20. CARS AND GUITARS, OR, DETROIT AND THE MC5: ON REPRESENTATIONS OF MUSIC AND PLACE IN *MC5: A TRUE TESTIMONIAL*

Lindsey Eckenroth

Preamble: Psychogeography and the Situated Rockumentary

Rockumentaries tell stories about bands, but frequently, they also tell stories about cities. In other words, their stories are often situated, involving representations of a city's built landscape, sonic ecology, and history, alongside portrayals of everyday urban life, venues, fan communities, performances, and the processes of popular music's production and consumption in specific places.[1] Through their assemblage of these place-based materials, situated rockumentaries engender ideas about what life in cities is like, stage encounters between urban spaces and popular music, and structure our stance towards the music being documented. In order to understand the functions of these rockumentary representations of city life, we should depart from the premise that these films do psychogeographical work: they make arguments about how the emotional, behavioral, and musical lives of urban subjects are regulated by their experiences within the built environment and its social history.

My main point of entry into psychogeography, and the psychogeographical ideas that have most informed my approach to situated rockumentaries, are those put forward by Guy Debord and the Situationist International. Debord offered the following definition in his 1955 article "Introduction to a Critique of Urban Geography":

> *Psychogeography* could set for itself the study of the precise laws and specific effects of the geographical environment, consciously organized or not, on the emotions and behaviour of individuals. The adjective *psychogeographical*, retaining a rather pleasing vagueness, can thus be applied to the findings arrived at by this type of investigation, to their influence on human feelings, and even more generally to any situation or conduct that seems to reflect the same spirit of discovery. (Debord 2006, 5)

Though the "pleasing vagueness" of the term psychogeographical is highlighted here, it becomes clear that for Debord, psychogeography exists at the intersection of materialist geographical inquiry and a conscious consideration of an individual's psychological state (Debord 2006; see also Plant 1992, 58–9; Coverley 2006, 10). Debord goes on to describe how psychogeographers should strive for awareness of everyday urban realities that are only vaguely recognized, rarely articulated, and certainly not interrogated. Floating through daily life, urban subjects take well-worn, habitual paths for granted and fail to recognize how the "zones of distinct psychic atmospheres" in cities manipulate their movements and condition their emotional responses (Debord 2006, 6). Having become aware of how the city conditions their experiences, psychogeographers could then begin to expose, subvert, and ultimately transform their everyday lives.

Situated rockumentaries, particularly through their inquiries into the interactions among sounds, acoustic spaces, and urban subjects, can also promote such an awareness. Frequently, these films remediate and thicken city/music relationships that are already apprehensible in the music – meaning, more accurately, already available in the network of images, star texts, reception history, and musical production surrounding the rockumentary's subject. But rockumentaries further ground musical production both geographically and historically, valorizing the culturally generative potential of cities by instigating considerations of how urban life structures – and might be transformed by – musical creation.

In doing this kind of psychogeographical work, it becomes clear that situated rockumentaries contribute to what Adam Krims has called the urban ethos: a "regime of representation" that encompasses all of the possible representations of the urban in cultural production at any given historical moment (2007, 9). Krims describes the urban ethos as heterogeneous in that contemporaneous cultural products may represent the same city in vastly different ways. The logic behind this heterogeneity becomes transparent when we understand the urban ethos "as a set of representations detailing which subjects move through the urban landscape, which parts of that landscape they traverse, and the extent to which that landscape imposes its constraints on those subjects" (Krims 2007, 13). So, for instance, an urban subject's race, class, and gender structure the possibilities of life in cities (Krims 2007, xxvi–xxxi). These possibilities of life speak to an urban subject's spatial agency, or their "ability to be in, act on or exert control over a desired part of the built- and natural- environment" (Montgomery 2016, 777). As such, the representations of cities in situated rockumentaries should be considered not as statements of fact about the historical world outside the film, but rather as mediated constructions participating in a system of signification that can promote arguments about what is physically and sonically possible for musicians as urban subjects. The following analysis of *MC5: A True Testimonial* demonstrates how relationships between musical production and urban development can be expressed and commodified in the situated rockumentary, and further illustrates the necessity of critically assessing how filmic representations of spatial and sonic agency interact with the geographical and social history of cities.

> "GTO baby, the sound of liberation"
> – MC5 guitarist Wayne Kramer in *MC5: A True Testimonial*

> "The dictatorship of the automobile, the pilot product of the first stage of commodity abundance, has left its mark on the landscape in the dominance of freeways that bypass the old urban centers and promote an ever greater dispersal."
> – Guy Debord, *The Society of the Spectacle*

MC5: A True Testimonial (David C. Thomas, USA, 2002) opens as we might expect of a twenty-first-century rockumentary situated in Detroit: with footage of an empty, crumbling building.[2] We are later informed that the subject of these shots is the Grande Ballroom, a venue on Detroit's West Side where the MC5 were, during the late 1960s, the crowd-drawing house band. This footage is remarkable in that it provides a glimpse into the contemporary deterioration of Detroit's urban landscape, which is otherwise avoided through *Testimonial*'s nostalgic stance. As a hand-held camera is walked up the stairs and into the main floor of the venue, the reverberating, plaintive guitar arpeggios from the slow closing section of the MC5's "Future/Now" provide a sonic pathos that both affectively and acoustically conforms to the space being filmed. Amid the light streaming in from broken windows and the walls that seem to be peeling away from themselves, the camera finds moments to focus on details that reveal the Grande's past splendor, as both a 1930s ballroom and a 1960s rock venue: the delicate archways that flank the dancefloor, an intricate carving in the ceiling, and finally the proscenium arch of the stage. But as a final guitar gesture fades out and MC5 frontman Rob Tyner's signature rallying command – "kick out the jams, motherfuckers!" – arrives on the soundtrack, we find this glimpse into the present of the Grande short-lived.

The rest of *Testimonial*'s opening credits reach back to the past through a montage of the MC5 performing live at the Grande, candid videos of the band members, footage of laborers in automobile factories, and a dramatic, black-and-white shot of the US flag being unfurled on the edifice of Hudson's department store. In its audio-visual assemblage of car manufacturing imagery and the power-chord driven MC5 track "Kick Out the Jams," which is played in its entirety, the remainder of *Testimonial*'s credit sequence begins to construct an argument about the relationship between the MC5 and Detroit.

Testimonial's representation of Detroit contextualizes, and is contextualized by, the MC5's musical praxis; the city is used to explain why the band sounds like it does. This psychogeographical argument works throughout the film to represent the MC5 as having a high degree of spatial agency, which is expressed primarily as *sonic* agency. For instance, the band is seen and heard freely impacting Detroit's sonic ecology with outdoor concerts – a feat especially significant given the MC5's exploitation of crowd-gathering noise as a means for resisting separation and establishing an alternative lifestyle. But more specifically, cars and guitars are mobilized as sonic signifiers of the MC5's spatial agency, and these signifiers operate through their situation in a version of Detroit seemingly dominated by Fordist industrialization. Through frequent audio-visual reference to Detroit's industrial landscape, *Testimonial* positions the MC5's music as not only a response to that landscape's products, but also as a subversive harnessing of their technological power. Substantiating the importance of technology to the MC5's musical project, critics and scholars alike have noted the band's affective use of maximally amplified sound. Whiteley (2013, 22) asserts, "Above all, the MC5 celebrate subversion through their manipulation of electronic noise," and Waksman (2009, 230) has argued that the MC5's "politics cannot be understood apart from their use of amplification." And, as Waksman further notes in describing an MC5 show at the Grosse Point Hideout, "amplification was a useful weapon" for the MC5 during encounters with law enforcement, as they could use it to rally crowd support (2009, 212–3). Yet in furthering a celebratory view of the MC5's electric assault on the status quo, *Testimonial* relies on a glaringly partial representation of Detroit. In other words, the psychogeographical perspective constructed by the film excludes crucial aspects of Detroit's social and economic history, including the impacts of deindustrialization and racial segregation on the possibilities for life in the Motor City during the MC5's active years (1964–72). Though the decline of Detroit has been well-ingrained into the urban ethos, *Testimonial* nostalgically promotes the Detroit of the 1960s and 70s as a thriving industrial metropolis marred by only vague racial tensions. In what follows, I consider how the film's expression of the connection between cars and guitars promotes a desire to believe in the MC5's musical power; I will also problematize the representation of Detroit that is implicated in the construction of that power, especially in relation to the MC5's political associations and the film's assertion of the band's spatial agency.

The MC5 and Radical Politics: "Cultural revolution by any means necessary"?

Throughout *Testimonial*, archival and interview documentation verifies the MC5's involvement with multiple radical, counter-cultural, and anti-capitalist organizations throughout their career. Related activities included supporting the Civil Rights Movement, the end of the Vietnam War, and, in a proto-punk fashion consistent with their musical style, an assault on White, working-class norms and morality. The film provides testimonial evidence of these activities resulting in harassment from the Detroit and Ann Arbor Police Departments and as being unequally valued by the band's members. The latter point is a tension frequented in discourse surrounding the MC5: namely, that generated by the band members' uneven commitment to social change, especially in relation to their aspirations for mainstream commercial success. As Bartkowiak (2007) has extensively documented, there simply never was a consensus among the MC5's members regarding what their political intentions were or how those intentions might inform, or be actualized through, their music. Yet the rhetoric of rebellion has been embedded in the band's reception: "Whether a radical cultural and politically subversive threat, or a sellable form of counter-culture in a time of counter-cultural power and presence, the MC5 continues to be an object of attention for those focused on dissent, corporate power, the power of the mass media, and American radicalism" (Bartkowiak 2007, 60). Whiteley similarly questions whether the MC5's project was more about "sonic anarchy" than "revolutionary zeal," meanwhile noting that their political affiliations "and the often revolutionary rhetoric that accompanied the band through its career was sufficient for the Federal State Authorities to recognize them as a politically subversive threat" (Whiteley 2013, 22; 19).

In many respects, the film *appears* to remain ambiguous in its evaluation of the MC5's engagement with radical politics. The interviews – both archival and contemporary – included in *Testimonial* do nothing to clarify the band's ideological stance, and at times humorously highlight its lack of cohesion. Take, for example, the film's introduction of the White Panther Party (WPP). At the time of the WPP's formation in 1968, co-founder John Sinclair was acting as the MC5's manager, and the band was serving as the ostensible mouthpiece for the organization. Sinclair, against a black background and looking directly into the camera, expounds upon the tenets of the WPP in archival footage: "The White Panther program is cultural revolution by any means necessary. We've drawn up a ten-point program. The first point is the full endorsement and support for the Black Panther Party's ten-point program. Point two is a total assault on the culture by any means necessary, including rock 'n' roll, dope, and fucking in the streets." At first, a contemporary interview with MC5 guitarist Wayne Kramer seems to confirm the band's commitment to Sinclair and the WPP: "The White Panther Party was an expression of our frustration with the slow pace of change. We needed to carry on the revolutionary work of the Black Panther Party in the white counterculture." But then Sinclair, contradicting his 1968 self in a contemporary interview, asserts: "It was the farthest thing from a political organization you could ever possibly imagine." Then, in a series of hard-cut interviews, the contradictions continue:

> *Kramer, standing on the band shell stage in West Park, Ann Arbor:* "... everybody went shooting guns; everybody went, you know, everybody had a Red Book; I mean, everybody believed."
> *Drummer Dennis Thompson in his home:* "The MC5 wasn't a part of that. All we wanted to do was to play great music ... be the best performing, live act, there was. Ever. Fuck the political baggage."
> *Bassist Michael Davis, outside his home in Tucson, Arizona:* "I don't care if they live in a commune or if they vote for republicans."
> *Back to Kramer:* "Maybe the rhythm section looked at it a little differently in terms of just the rock and roll end of it."

Clearly, the band's ideological stance was neither unanimous nor static, and *Testimonial* here verges on mocking this lack of clarity, framing it as a crisis of authenticity: was the band's association with radical politics merely an effort to hit the sweet spot where you can take your subversion to the bank? But ultimately, *Testimonial* smoothes over this discrepancy in intentions by promoting an understanding of the MC5's agency in Detroit, which in turn valorizes the potential of their music – as amplified in specific spatial and temporal contexts – to oppose sonic and spatial domination. In other words, the film's psychogeographical perspective and projection of the MC5's agency serves as a partial solution to the problem of the band's ambivalent investment in, to recall Sinclair's words, "cultural revolution by any means necessary." This solution relies on the well-established association of the MC5 with Detroit (Carson 2005; Bartkowiak 2009; Waksman 2009) as well as a projection of the symbolic power of Detroit's automotive industry.

Escaping the Car, or Escaping *By* Car?

It would be difficult to overstate the automotive industry's impact on Detroit's urban landscape, and, in psychogeographical terms, on its populace. For instance, the spatial logic of Detroit's manufacturing industries was based, in part, on proximity to transportation infrastructure. As Detroit's industrial neighborhoods expanded during the first half of the twentieth century, they were placed strategically along railway lines (Ryan and Campo 2012, 103). This urban geographical feature is visualized at the closing of *Testimonial*'s credits, when a car-carrying train rolls by to the feedback-laden ending of "Kick Out the Jams." In the post-war years, the city's highway system expanded, providing increased access to the growing suburbs and facilitating industrial decentralization. Detroit's freeways also appear multiple times in *Testimonial*. One such instance occurs directly after the credit sequence, when the relationship between cars and guitars continues to be negotiated. Kramer, being interviewed while driving his Pontiac GTO on the highway, gestures towards a passing automotive plant on the horizon and says: "You grow up in Detroit, that's your birthright: a shop-rat. I had to face the prospect of working there for the rest of my life. That wouldn't be too cool, so I found some guys that wanted to start a band." Though this comment positions the blue-collar everyday as a dismal fate, Kramer also indicates the aesthetically productive aspects of the Motor City's industry: "There seemed to be a parallel between a loud electric guitar, and a 400-horsepower hotrod car. It was all the same thing ... hotrods, rock 'n' roll, all fits together." This interview sequence with Kramer further substantiates the relationship posited during the credit sequence, namely that between the MC5's music and Detroit's signature commodity. In addition to Kramer's words, sound design also persuades us of this connection. As "Kick Out the Jams" and the final shot of the credit sequence fade out, they are immediately replaced with the sound of Kramer revving his GTO's engine. Then, as Kramer monologues and drives through Detroit, his words are spoken into a sound bath of the engine's rumbling, the wind coming through the open windows, and eventually, the MC5 track "Gotta Keep Movin'" piping through the car radio.

Of course, drawing musical inspiration from the production and use of automobiles – and, for that matter, critical assertions about the relationship between cars and rock – are not unique to the MC5. Don McLeese, for instance, writes that the "high-energy, high-octane approach" of Detroit's rock 'n' roll "suggested the musical equivalent of a muscle car, with a sound as hard as the steel forged for the city's auto plants" (2005, 32). But this paradigm of sonic borrowing is complicated in *Testimonial*'s opening credit sequence and the subsequent interview with Kramer, which, taken together, are ambivalent in their valuation of the automotive industry. In one sense, this industry's sounds, products, and visual aesthetics seem to have positively influenced a nascent local rock scene. In another, what was sought was liberation *from* the everyday blue-collar status quo. Historicizing this issue, Waksman writes:

> While this may have been a music born out of Fordism, and out of a white male working-class sensibility, it was also founded upon a rejection

of working-class life insofar as that life was perceived to be crippling in its lack of opportunity. Thus the MC5's music, along with the music of other Detroit bands like the Stooges, may be judged as an outgrowth of that moment in history when the significance of Fordism shifted from representing the American Dream to standing for the failure of that dream. (2009, 215)

But *Testimonial*'s representation of Detroit's automotive industry does not make it clear that the American Dream – regardless of its rejection by the MC5 – has failed. Instead, a nearly propagandistic sense of pride in the Motor City's industry is divulged through in the film's opening credits, and even in the decidedly post-Fordist footage from the 2000s, factories are consistently shown dotting the horizon of Detroit's freeways. In one sense, the band's attempted subversion is sublimated to nostalgia for what appears to be the "lost glory days" of the industrial United States. In another, though, the film's assertion of this industry's dominance helps to substantiate the MC5's power to co-opt its noises as a means for composing and performing "high-energy" music capable of radicalizing Detroit's youth. So, the MC5 are positioned as attempting to resist the American Dream while simultaneously valuing and using – as an agent of spatial agency – one of the primary status symbols of that Dream.

Testimonial, Nostalgia, and the Problem of Selective Historicization

Testimonial's nostalgic framing of Detroit functions through the juxtaposition of present-day and archival footage. But reading *Testimonial* against the social and economic history of Detroit in the 1960s and 70s reveals that this nostalgia is more mythical than realistic: the film's representation of Detroit glosses over issues of spatial segregation, poverty, job loss, deindustrialization, and white suburban flight, ultimately occluding the entrenched race and class inequalities that structured the city's landscape and social geography. In terms of deindustrialization: despite the film's attention to a seemingly thriving automotive industry, a combination of decentralization and manufacturing plant closings had begun to drastically modify Detroit's built landscape during the MC5's active years. As Sugrue writes in his seminal book on Detroit, "Events in *the 1950s* reminded workers that even the factory buildings that seemed like permanent landmarks on Detroit's skyline were mortal. Bustling plants were abandoned and boarded up as companies moved production outside the city or went out of business" (2005, 143–4, emphasis mine). Though Detroit's decline and present-day association with economic blight and ruin are symbolically available in the shots of the abandoned Grande Ballroom that open and close the film, these seem to be the result of a process that had not yet started in the 1960s.

This is not to suggest that *Testimonial*'s representation of Detroit is entirely ahistorical. Rather, the film's preservation of urban social and political history is driven by the band's perspective, which is asserted through interviews and sound recordings. Consider the 1967 Detroit riots, which are introduced through an audio-visual montage. This montage includes archival news anchor voice-overs, the MC5's recording of "Motor City Is Burning," and footage of rioters, fires, cops, and the National Guard rolling down the freeway. The MC5's "Motor City Is Burning," which was recorded live at the Grande for their debut album, *Kick Out the Jams* (1969), is slower, heavier, and longer than John Lee Hooker's 1967 original. And, as Whiteley suggests, the slightly modified lyrics of the MC5's version are more explicitly pro-riot, "suggesting a supportive reference to the 1967 Detroit riots and the role of the Black Panther snipers" (2013, 22). In *Testimonial*, sound editing highlights this lyrical stance: after a brief cutaway, the riot montage continues first with someone yelling "burn, baby burn," followed quickly by the sound of an explosion. Then, cutting to footage of a burned-out block filmed from the vantage point of a moving car, "Motor City Is Burning" returns to the soundtrack on the lyric "*You best get out there in the street, check it out/Because the Motor City's burning.*" Further, as Platoff has noted, it is crucial to understand the meaning of rock songs not just through their words, but also through the delivery and musical contextualization of those words (2005, 250). In this regard, while the faster tempo and vocal/guitar call and response in Hooker's version do not suggest the soundworld of a city in crisis, the MC5's recording, with Tyner's near-shout vocal delivery in a loud and distorted instrumental context, can be easily heard as a transmission from a riotous zone. In *Testimonial*, this impression is amplified through the sonic layering of "Motor City Is Burning" with the sounds of firebombs, sirens, and urban subjects yelling on Detroit's burning streets.

Brief documentation of nationally intensifying militant and counter-cultural rebellion contextualizes these events, but at the same time, the film ignores the spatial segregation, police violence, and employment discrimination that fuelled the 1967 riots – particularly significant omissions considering the film's celebratory projection of the MC5's privileged spatial agency. When post-war industrial decentralization moved jobs out of Detroit, many White, middle-class residents were able to follow those jobs to the suburbs. As Detroit became blacker and poorer, the crises of unemployment and inadequate housing worsened for the residents who were unable to leave. Sugrue describes Detroit's social geography of the post-war years as based on violently-defended racial boundaries: "The combination of neighbourhood violence, real estate practices, covenants, and the operations of the housing market sharply circumscribed the housing opportunities available to Detroit's African American population. Persistent housing segregation stigmatized blacks, reinforced unequal race relations, and perpetuated racial divisions" (2005, 257). Yet the film eschews issue of race here, with the riots positioned as just another manifestation of increasingly radical anti-establishment sentiment – a sentiment that the band, and the film, celebrate with "Motor City Is Burning."

Gotta Keep Movin', If You Can: Spatial Agency as Sonic Agency

In a segment detailing how the band responded to conservative backlash in the wake of their increased popularity and support for the riots, the MC5's spatial agency is again confirmed: they can just pick up and drive away. This scene assembles the MC5 track "Gotta Keep Movin'" with palpably mobile footage of both present-day and archival Detroit. Following Sinclair's description of an instance of Detroit Police Department harassment, the film quickly cuts to a shot of present-day Kramer, who is standing assertively, seemingly posed, in front of Detroit's defunct Michigan Central Station. As with the Grande Ballroom in the opening credit sequence, this momentary incursion of urban geographical decline is quickly left behind, eclipsed by the past. Looking directly into the camera, Kramer proclaims: "It was getting too dangerous in Detroit for the MC5, so we had to get outta town." Then, in fast motion, the camera zooms backwards as Kramer claps, which seemingly becomes the cue for "Gotta Keep Movin'" to enter the soundtrack. As the first verse plays, archival footage shows Rob Tyner behind the wheel, initially driving through downtown Detroit, then on the freeway, with the city's skyline being left behind. This journey ends with the MC5 arriving in Ann Arbor, which is announced as the band's new home.

The upbeat blues "Gotta Keep Movin'" is mobilized as driving music here, just as it was earlier on Kramer's car radio. Significantly, despite what might be suggested by the song's title and filmic contextualization, its lyrical content focuses not on physical mobility, but rather on political resistance, which is framed as a confrontational declaration by counter-cultural youth against the elders in power: "teachers, parents, and politicians." But through its use in the film, "Gotta Keep Movin'" becomes both thematically and symbolically available as a road song. Its propulsive, riff-based groove sonically celebrates the visualized auto-mobility of the band, expressing the freedom and escape afforded by the open road and a car. Significantly, the band's spatial agency – their ability to leave Detroit – is conflated with the anti-establishment political assertions of "Gotta Keep Movin'," illustrating the film's suggestion of a relationship between embodied and musical agency. As the last lyrics of this track we hear declare: "*Can't stop me now 'cause I'm movin' too fast.*"

Here, and throughout *Testimonial*, the MC5's music is played over – or really takes over, as in voice-over – images of Detroit. While this assemblage of sound and place offers a psychogeographical analysis of the MC5's musical production, it notably does so without visually representing one of psychogeography's most typical practices: walking. Coverley, outlining some main trends in psychogeographical explorations, notes the prominence of a "spirit of political radicalism" and an "inquiry into the methods by which we can transform our relationship to the urban environment," both of which are engaged in *Testimonial* (2006, 14). But the potentially subversive act of self-conscious urban wandering is entirely absent. Instead, the film situates the act of driving – of engaging with the car as a commodity, an experience, and a sound – as a means by which the MC5 draw on the technological power of Detroit's automotive industry while also rejecting the working-class norms of that industry. By promoting an affinity between the MC5's heavy, loud music and the car, *Testimonial* ties together spatial and sonic agency, and in doing so applauds the liberating potential of the MC5's impact on Detroit. But *Testimonial* occludes the privileged nature of the band's spatial agency, their power to sonically expand into space and claim it – with cars and guitars. Ultimately, the stakes of this agency are degraded through the film's tendency towards nostalgia, resulting in a mythicization of Detroit's past that erases the racial capitalism that ruled that past.

Notes

1. Examples include *Hype!* (Doug Pray, USA, 1996), *The Filth and the Fury* (Julien Temple, UK, 2000), *Made in Sheffield* (Eve Wood, UK, 2001), *Kill Your Idols* (Scott Crary, USA, 2004), *Joy Division* (Grant Gee, UK, 2007), *Patti Smith: Dream of Life* (Steven Sebring, USA, 2008), *Pearl Jam Twenty* (Cameron Crowe, USA, 2011), *Pulp: A Film About Life, Death, and Supermarkets* (Florian Habicht, UK, 2014), and *Gimme Danger* (Jim Jarmusch, USA, 2016).
2. Following its premiere in November 2002 at the International Documentary Film Festival in Amsterdam, *Testimonial* was shown at a number of other film festivals in 2002 and 2003, and was met with critical acclaim. However, due to a contractual dispute with MC5 guitarist Wayne Kramer, director David C. Thomas and producer Laurel Leger were unable to retain the synchronization rights for the MC5's music. As a result, the film has not seen a commercial theatrical run or been released on DVD. For further details regarding the ongoing legal dispute between the filmmakers and Kramer, see Sinclair 2016, 226–32.

References

Bartkowiak, Mathew. 2007. "Motor City Burning: Rock and Rebellion in the WPP and the MC5." *Journal for the Study of Radicalism* 1(2): 55–76.
Carson, David A. 2005. *Grit, Noise, and Revolution: The Birth of Detroit Rock 'n' Roll*. Ann Arbor, MI: University of Michigan Press.
Coverley, Merlin. 2006. *Psychogeography*. Harpenden: Pocket Essentials.
Debord, Guy. 2006. "Introduction to a Critique of Urban Geography." In *Situationist*

Krims, Adam. 2007. *Music and Urban Geography*. New York: Routledge.
McLeese, Don. 2005. *Kick Out the Jams*. New York: Continuum.
Montgomery, Alesia. 2016. "Reappearance of the Public: Placemaking, Minoritization and Resistance in Detroit." *International Journal of Urban and Regional Research* 40(4): 776–99.
Plant, Sadie. 1992. *The Most Radical Gesture: The Situationist International in a Postmodern Age*. New York: Routledge.
Platoff, John. 2002. "John Lennon, 'Revolution,' and the Politics of Musical Reception." *The Journal of Musicology* 22(2): 241–67.
Ryan, Brent D. and Daniel Campo. 2012. "Autopia's End: The Decline and Fall of Detroit's Automotive Manufacturing Landscape." *Journal of Planning History* 12(2): 95–132.
Sinclair, John. 2016. "DKT/MC5: The Truest Possible Testimonial." In *Heaven Was Detroit: From Jazz to Hip-Hop and Beyond*, ed. M. L. Liebler. Detroit: Wayne State University Press: 222–32.
Sugrue, Thomas J. 2005. *The Origins of the Urban Crisis: Race and Inequality in Postwar Detroit*. Princeton, NJ: Princeton University Press.
Waksman, Steve. 2009. *This Ain't the Summer of Love: Conflict and Crossover in Heavy Metal and Punk*. Berkeley, CA: University of California Press.
Whiteley, Sheila. 2013. "'Kick Out the Jams': Creative Anarchy and Noise in 1960s Rock." In *Resonances: Noise and Contemporary Music*, eds Michael Goddard, Benjamin Halligan, and Nicola Spelman, New York: Bloomsbury: 13–23.

PART V

FUTURES

21. UNKNOWABLE DOGS

Gary Kibbins

Man: Hello my boy. What is your dog's name?
Boy: I don't know, but we call him Rover.[1]

In her soundtrack/film/experimental rockumentary *Heart of a Dog* (USA, 2015), Laurie Anderson claims to have loved her dog, but not her mother. To not love one's mother belongs to a special category of actions or states of mind which, if universal, would have serious consequences for our species' self-identity. If the love between offspring and mothers were to disappear, if none of us loved our mothers, would we still be recognizable as human? If the answer to that question is no, is Laurie Anderson, who has acknowledged not loving her mother, human? Or human, but with an asterisk? It has been a consistent and fundamental feature of the defining of the human that the difference between human and animal be carefully articulated. Crocodiles seem not to love their mothers, and for that reason, and others, we don't feel much kinship with them. But what about elephants and dogs? There is strong evidence that an adult dog, even after a long separation, can still recognize its mother by smell, although whether or not that constitutes love in any way recognizable to us is anybody's guess. We aren't very good at recognizing the subtle emotional states of animals – unless they are directed at us. We believe we know when dogs love us, and Laurie Anderson is as certain that her dog loves her as she is that she loves her dog. When people say that their dog is "almost human" or that they "think that they're people," they are referring, it

21.1 An Affront to Humanism. Laurie Anderson's *Heart of a Dog* (2015).

seems, to that obscure understanding through which they can love us, and can be loved by us in turn. What makes them people-like, then, is not of course language – the other great measuring device for separating the human from the non-human – but love. Dogs have love but no language, while humans have both. We're able to say with words that we love, or don't love, our mothers, but animals aren't.

Anderson's love for her dog Lolabelle is unconditional. She declares as much in her dream of having had the dog sewn into her stomach, so that she could experience being her biological birth mother. On giving birth to her dog, she consents to a virtual experience of the non-human, while proclaiming what human mothers characteristically do on giving birth: "I'll love you forever." And in this non-human state, she will succeed where her own birth mother is thought to have failed.

All this seems an affront to humanism, which has long proclaimed the self-aware, self-fabricating, features of being human, and has shown an oversized confidence in the process and products of human agency. There is of course a robust tradition of articulating humanism by separating the human from the animal – and then patching it back up by acknowledging our "animal nature." Blessed with reason and language (both of which are "unnatural"), humans are, in a defining sense, not-animal. But our evolutionary heritage and our biological infrastructure, being hard to ignore, are inevitably reintroduced, reluctantly by some, as an obligatory supplement, and we become the human-animal, or the rational, thinking-animal.

Here, the self-awareness so valued by humanism becomes trapped in its anthropocentric assumptions, and becomes the object of critique from multiple perspectives. The more we learn about animals and fail to articulate what constitutes an essential humanity, and the more we reflect on a developing "human condition," the more the heartfelt traditions and self-regard of humanism just seem to fade away. Much of the current, and vibrant, anti- or post-humanist critique is aimed at the compulsion to impose our self-image on our world wherever possible, through anthropomorphized projections. This is particularly observable with dogs, and it's important to see just how extraordinary Anderson's birth fantasy is in this regard. The most neutral way to see the human-animal interface is abstractly relational, that is, without any preconception of the relative status of the related parts. But we know that this is always an asymmetrical relation; humans are always on top. (Observations that dogs are like people come effortlessly, but can we say as easily that people are like dogs?) Even among those who might proclaim "equal status" among humans and animals, it's inevitably an anthropocentric equality, ordained on humanity's terms.

*

Anderson's dog-birth fantasy expunges the traditionally asymmetrical quality of the dog-human relation, leaving open the question of what kind of relation it is. The shock effect of hearing her story at the beginning of the film permeates the film's subsequent segments. In the seventh segment of the rockumentary, "How to Feel Sad Without Being Sad" – a phrase learned from her meditation teacher – Lolabelle, we are told, acquires the skill of empathy. Did Lola learn this skill from humans? Or did it naturally surface from an inherited canine moral infrastructure? Anderson suspends the context for posing this question, for this is not, as she says, about "being." At roughly the halfway point through this "song," a string accompaniment slowly emerges which sounds, according to the emotional tags we habitually attach to non-lyrical music, *sad*.

Considering Anderson's custom of using highly stylized irony in her musical and performance works, it is notable that *Heart of a Dog* is largely without noticeably incongruous music. For a sad theme, use congruously sad-sounding music. But the viewer experiencing this segment is not expected to either become sad or feel sad, but instead is invited to ponder the distinction between being and feeling. Even when emotionally invested while listening to a musical work, it is not the case that one feels one's self as intrinsically identical with that emotion. The events that give rise to the emotions experienced when listening to music, reading novels or watching films are not directly our events; we come as outsiders to the emotions that we experience in such works. Perhaps the distinction between feeling and being has an analogue with the distinction between emotions and moods. Moods, unlike emotions, are diffuse and don't have specific intentional objects, persons, or events, and so, unlike emotions, don't motivate focused actions as responses. Similarly, empathy, being a second-order, vicarious experience, is not a claim about possessing the experience, but mirroring or mentalizing it. Empathy occurs when one experiences another person's feelings, while also imagining the context and frame of reference which gave shape to those feelings. Strictly speaking, cross-species empathy shouldn't be possible. Sympathy yes, but can humans and dogs really imagine the frames of reference and contexts of the other? It is, as Anderson says, "really hard to do."

This question of whether to *feel* or *to be*, appropriate as it is to ask of the subject, can also be asked of the object. Does the musical accompaniment itself embody "sadness"? Does it import the concept of sadness from Anderson's voice/text as a kind of provisional quality? There is sadness, but where is it located? Whether or not artworks possess the qualities often attributed to them is a point of disagreement between aesthetic realists and anti-realists. The realist will claim that the artwork's qualities inhere in the artwork, while the anti-realist will say that it is an attribution. It seems a lesser commitment for a person to feel sad than to be sad, as if being sad is somehow part of the self's infrastructure while feeling sad is (only) ephemeral. But the reverse seems true of the art object. It may be just a habit of speech, but to say that a musical piece *is* sad sounds uncontroversial and would receive the approval of the aesthetic realist. Or it may be "a function of the auratic, artistic, or commodity residue still clinging to them, a function, in other words of human sensibility, imagination, pragmatic need, greed, etc." (Bennett 2015, 95). Saying that an object, art or not, can *feel* sad, on the other hand, is "a way to think about vitality that is not dependent upon a dichotomy between organic and inorganic matter." This is what Jane Bennett calls "animacy," or "registers of liveliness." (Bennett 2015, 98).

*

Heart of a Dog is an indifferent exercise in non-identity filmmaking – indifferent as it doesn't so much actively critique identity thinking as simply ignore it. This merges effectively with the various post- and anti-humanisms, as it seems now certain that any hope of articulating an essential identity of the human – at least insofar as it has been identified by the various strands of humanism – is over. The human desire to master its animal nature through reason and knowledge has turned out about as well as one would expect when one is left in charge of one's own narrative. Humans can pretty much make up anything (. . . who's watching?) provided that it is appropriately sensitive to the requirements of human self-aspiring. It's all, as we say, a construction. "Homo sapiens, then, is neither a clearly defined species, nor a substance; it is rather, a machine or device for producing the recognition of the human" says Giorgio Agamben (Agamben 2004, 26) Agamben identifies an "anthropo-

21.2 The Anthropological Machine is switched off. Laurie Anderson's *Heart of a Dog* (2015).

logical machine" as the agency which polices the border between animal and human, ensuring that our self-image remains sacred to ourselves. He suggests that we make the anthropological machine "inoperative," that we suspend its operations, through profanity and play. And accordingly, Anderson doesn't so much critique the anthropological machine, as simply carry on as if it doesn't exist. In *Heart of a Dog*, the anthropological machine is switched off, and what at first seem like familiar doggie anthropomorphizations (Lola can paint! Lola can make music!) turns out to be something else entirely. The more Lola is seen as becoming-human, the more the human of the anthropological machine recedes from view.

Anderson remembers being in a hospital as child, recovering from a broken back, where a doctor informed her that she would never walk again. Anderson comments: "And I remember thinking: This guy is crazy. I mean, is he even a doctor? Who knows?" In this expanded world of the inoperative, there are no real doctors, just as there are no real artists and no real humans, no real dogs. Similarly, Anderson relates a memory of Moses, a man who every day, regardless of the weather, could be seen at the top of telephone poles, doing repair work, opening boxes, hammering things. He was thanked warmly by passersby for his services. Moses, however, did not work for the phone company: ". . . he just lived in another world." This may be the first step in letting go of the illusions of selfhood and identity; perhaps this is the only experience of pure existence that we can grasp. There is the real, of course, readily available to experience, but no concepts that we engineer to understand and represent the real can be themselves real. You can't have both. The more we insist that our concepts of the real are themselves real, the more the *real* real recedes from view. So perhaps that was indeed a doctor, but not a real one. Just as Lola and Laurie Anderson are indeed artists and musicians, but not real ones.

*

If, beyond the operations of the anthropological machine, humans experience a divided relationship with themselves as species-specific, their relationship with animals, dogs included, is of course no less divided. Even the most earnest dog lovers are not particularly good at seeing dogs as ends-in-themselves. They are viewed primarily as ends-for-us – a core of instrumentality wrapped in affection. This is not surprising, as the respective phenomenal worlds of dogs and human are largely unintelligible, one having a nose close to the ground dominated by the sense of smell, the other having risen on hind legs dominated by the sense of sight. Humans, after all, struggle just to comprehend the experience of having a body of their own. As Anderson helps us understand, the *umwelt* of the dog is far too strange for us to understand – and it's likely as close as one gets to the animal as other. Humanity has a very, shall we say, mixed record in grasping otherness, which no doubt explains why Humanism works so hard to domesticate strangeness. It recognizes the importance of managing the mysteries of being a human animal, and to channel those alienating energies into a satisfyingly human telos whose reality may not otherwise survive scrutiny.

If, contrary to the basic tenets of Humanism, there is no Humanity, only individual humans, then the human telos is (if we think that, being human, we still must embody a telos) death. And that is indeed what happens to Lola, Anderson's mother, the sculptor Gordon Matta-Clark, many of the children in the Anderson's wing of the hospital, her husband Lou Reed, and the victims of 9/11. Almost all criss-crossing mini-narratives in the film end up there, including, as we may well surmise, that concerning the massive and life-denying state surveillance in the USA somewhat paratactically described in the rockumentary. I recently crossed the border into Tibet, where a Chinese security agent confiscated my copy of *The Tibetan Book of the Dead*, and tossed it into the bin of book-death. That is the text, originally called *Bardo Thödol*, which Anderson uses to guide Lola after her death. It is not clear how often *The Tibetan Book of the Dead* is used to assist in the after-death experience of an animal, as it was initially designed to help the recently deceased from being reborn as one. With the help of this text, all Tibetans are regularly reminded of death's inevitability.[2] Anderson helps Lola through the bewildering and frightening transformation from death to rebirth, for *The Tibetan Book of the Dead* provides an essential concept of death absent all the qualities of the living that prevent us from seeing what death is.

When entering the *bardo*, or the time/place of the experience that separates death and rebirth, the recently deceased, who may not yet fully grasp the fact that they are dead, are advised not to be attached to the life that was once theirs, and that the sometimes violent and disturbing visions that they may soon encounter are not real. What is now gone is the body, although not yet consciousness. Bodily dissimilarity is removed from the list of human-animal differences, leaving only consciousness and its human or animal experience of death, and whatever differences between the two may subsist there.

*

When we make the anthropological machine inoperative, Agamben says, we release the animal-human relation into the "zone of non-knowledge." "To render inoperative the machine that governs our conception of man will therefore mean to seek new – more effective or more authentic – articulations, but rather to no longer show the central emptiness, the hiatus that – within man – separates man and animal, and to risk ourselves in this emptiness . . ." (Agamben 2004, 92). The most compelling gesture of inoperativity in *Heart of a Dog* occurs when Anderson guides Lola through the *bardo*. ". . . the purpose of death is the release of love," Anderson says; love replaces the the anthropological machine; love complements the experience of non-knowledge, giving it shape, enabling the move beyond the aporetic condition of human-animal inertia. This approach can be translated into artistic method. In a study of the poems of Wallace Stevens, Simon Critchley sketches two distinct approaches undertaken by poets: "On the one hand, literature is an act of idealization governed by the desire to assimilate all reality to the ego and to view the former as the latter's projection . . . On the other hand, the second slope of literature does not aim to reduce reality to the imagination, but rather to let things be in their separateness from us"[3] (Critchley 2005, 86). Anderson makes no effort to assimilate the world that she encounters. Instead her heterotopic film/album asks the viewer to risk themselves in the emptiness.

Not all major material elements of *Heart of a Dog* – language, music, image, and voice – contribute to this inoperative emptiness, for Anderson plays both sides of the divide articulated by Critchley. Despite being spoken in the first person, *Heart of a Dog* is both a "language-based" and a "subject-based" work. The difference from a more consistently language-based artist like Gertrude Stein or Samuel Beckett is that she gets there having started initially from a subjectivist place, with the seemingly authoritative "I" of first-person discourse. *Heart of a Dog* starts and ends with Anderson's voice, which pulls image, music, and language into its orbit. But here the voice is a divisible thing, with two capacities. The first is that of a pure sonic instance, emanating from the body and from Anderson's distinctness, which, before it says anything at all, says no more than "I am a person; I have language; I can speak" – pure voice innocent of actual words. And secondly there are the words. The words say and mean things, but with Anderson's fragmented form, strange hesitations and characteristically odd elocutions. Anderson's speech, full of caesuras or pauses, has something of the enjambment of poetry – when a sentence or phrase in a poem carries over the end of a line. If the pauses with which she irregularly fragments the lines of her text were seen in written form, it might look like this:

> And it's almost
> A perfect moment
> Except
> That the joy is mixed with
> Quite a lot of
> Guilt

or

> To feel sad, without
> Being sad[4]

But it is not the quasi-poetic tendencies in Anderson's reading or text that make her voice – singing or non-singing – the central organizing principle in *Heart of a Dog*. She has what Roland Barthes would call the "grain of the voice" (Barthes 1977). Empty and powerful at the same time, hers is also the paradox of the Voice – it exceeds the person whose voice it is. The voice may remain immanent in the world it encounters, and it may speak directly of and to that world – of the recognizable vagaries of memory and loss, for example – but unlike many works which are based in critique or negation, signification in *Heart of a Dog* is placed in parentheses – human, animal, painting, hawks, the State, and so on. Even seemingly fundamental philosophical-aesthetic principles like "we structure the world by representing it" seem unreliable. Like Moses operating "in a different world," the imperatives of communication as such precede what is communicated. Take away everything that is said and there is still Anderson's voice; her voice is, in a sense, the Image of the spoken text. This is not the "escape from the tyranny of meaning" (Barthes 1977, 185) that Barthes valorizes in his grain of the voice, but the momentary and necessary break that the artwork makes with the world it so much wants to know and describe. The process of putting into parentheses the things said is not negation, but an immersion of the artwork in the sensations of presence and thought that the artist may not be able to advance herself. The artwork can do things and be things that people can't, and is frequently called to tasks difficult or unachievable by the artist or viewer.

*

Often the simultaneity of image and voice shows a strong referential link (we hear of hawks, and see hawks), sometimes weak or absent ones (we hear of a dying mother, and see snow landing on a windshield). Some of the images accompanying anecdotes are drawn from family super-8 films, and so might claim a kind of authenticity. Others are re-enacted. There is footage of Gordon Matta-Clarke, and there is also footage of an actor playing Gordon Matta-Clarke; the attentive viewer not already familiar with the real Gordon Matta-Clarke won't know which is which. The majority of images are "processed," that is, significantly modified in post-production. This diversity of form reminds us, as so much visual art does, that images are not concepts, and should not be counted on to do the work of concepts. Somewhat in the spirit of paradox found in René Magritte's *La Trahison des images* (1929), James Elkin writes "Pictures ... have no words, and therefore do not 'say' anything" (Elkins 1994, 255).[5] In *Heart of a Dog* we are presented primarily with the image as an image, and secondarily with the image as a stand-in for something not present. *Heart of a Dog* – odd for a work familiarly categorized as a "documentary," a "rockumentary," or even an "experimental rockumentary" – uses the image as an "artificial presence," but with the emphasis heavily weighted towards the artificiality rather than the presence.

*

What is powerful about *Heart of a Dog* is its essential strangeness. The voice, the image, the music, are simultaneously very artificial and surprisingly intimate, two seeming opposites orbiting each other – yet in it all one can easily recognize a shared world. The representation offered up by image and language seems indifferent to what is thought to be a key responsibility – providing some much-needed clarity about the world while enlightening us about ourselves. But that is the paradox of the artwork; it wishes to speak of the world but it can only do so through misrepresentation.

Maybe then it's the Image and not the Voice which holds *Heart of a Dog* together. It is a somewhat familiar idea, sometimes true, that the artist replaces a concept with an image. The concept is "non-identical" with the thing it conceptualizes; it's never enough, it will always misrepresent or mask what is "really" there. At the same time that they make things intelligible, concepts also estrange us from what they conceptualize. Images are not conceptual; what advantage does that provide?

People, things, events have a plural existence, they both are, and they want to be perceived, experienced. With this dual ontology they become a cloud of virtual self-images, a haze of potentialities which detach themselves from the originary person, thing, or event. The world becomes strange, and artificial, and it is that world which the artist seizes on and wishes to explore. Maurice Blanchot articulates the most extreme version of this approach. When we stare at something, he says, it has already "sunk into its image . . . and once it has become an image it instantly becomes ungraspable . . ." (Blanchot 1981, 80).[6] The image, then, is not something that "comes after," it is not subordinate to the thing represented, or dependent on that thing for its existence. The image attains independence by virtue of difference, and makes its own distinctive contribution to perception and understanding. "Certainly," continues Blanchot, "we can always recapture the image and make it serve the truth of the world; but then we would be reversing the relationship that characterizes it: in this case, the image becomes the follower of the object . . ." (Blanchot 1981, 80).[7] The task of these sometimes referential, highly processed images is not to become believable, but to make believability inoperative.

Jean-Luc Nancy sees the relation between the image and text (language) concerning neither one nor the other as such, but as manifested in an "oscillation" between the two. They are "heterogenous, yet stuck to one another . . . strangers to each other and because, at the same time, each discerns itself in the other: each one distinguishes a tinge, a vague outline of itself in the ground of the other, deep in its eye or throat" (Nancy 2004, 64). What image and text do not do is respectively illustrate or explain or illuminate one another. Oscillation is firstly a formal procedure, which attempts to describe a process whereby the image provisionally imbibes some of the characteristics of language, while language takes on some of the characteristics of the image, but without essentializing them. The borrowed characteristics, however, are conditional; they don't stick, and we remain uncertain what they achieve. But the primary effect is not expressed in what image and text do to each other, but what their interaction creates. The oscillation is a third thing, neither image nor language, but a relation which takes on a virtual existence.

*

There are no translations or paraphrases to be had between language and music, as both originate in incommensurate systems. As Elkins might say, music has no words and therefore doesn't say anything. All forms of commentary or analysis on musical works must resort to formal description or, no doubt more sympathetically for most, metaphorical language. Like the incommensurate systems of language and image, the incommensurate systems of language and music have the potential to oscillate. Unless of course there are lyrics. In that case we might ask if the music and language come as a package deal, jointly inscribed. If so – and continuing to use a metaphor of distance suggested by oscillation – if music and lyrics are bumped up against each other, each mirroring and fortifying the other, perhaps there is no room for oscillation, so tightly are word and music inscribed in each other. With the exception of a few passages in *Heart of a Dog* there are no lyrics, strictly speaking; the text is spoken rather than sung. Anderson does not modify her tone or cadence to accommodate the music track, creating space between voice and music, and affording each a high degree of autonomy.

The strategies devised to confront the incommensurability of juxtaposed representational systems or divergent meaning systems are boundless, but might be generalized in three ways. One approach is to be absolutist about the difference. One thinks of Rosalind Krauss, who speaks of the silence of the viewer when confronting abstract painting, or Michael Fried, who sees scandal when language penetrates the visual realm, or Stan Brakhage, who would protect the image from the corrupting influence of language. This approach has perhaps been most visible when the specificity of the medium was a dominant critical and artistic concern. Or – the most common approach – one can overcome incommensurability, and cultivate potential linkages, as when literature is designed specifically to stimulate mental imagery, or when the image is "read" as a "text," or when any non-linguistic material is thought to be "discursive" – the "linguistic desire of the image" (Groys 2011, 98). Or, one can work with the stringent challenges offered up by incommensurability, and carry on. Collage, particularly more radical collage, embraces incommensurability as a calculated opportunity. One might think of works by Leslie Thornton, where the voice/sound tracks from films are heard – Kung Fu films and sequences from Roman Polanski's *The Tenant* – while accompanied by silent images of ducks bobbing around in a pond, or water rushing backwards and forwards. The spirit of incommensurability can also be seen, for example, in Stravinsky, who wrote works for violin and piano, while judging the sound of the two instruments to be incompatible.

*

Much of the material in *Heart of a Dog* – personal stories about family and friends and a dog – feels disarmingly familiar, conventional even, and is significant enough in its effects to have the film identified and circulated as a documentary and rockumentary. But while the various incommensurabilities of image, language and music in *Heart of a Dog* are not statistically dominant, they are strategically essential, and are significant enough to compel a puzzled programmer to ask one of the editors "what the film was actually about."[7] It's a revealing question, for which there is no real answer. Dogs, mothers, love, death, our selves – in contradistinction to a culture forcefully committed to knowledge, and far too accepting of State surveillance, *Heart of a Dog* suggests that maybe we really don't know too much about these things, and maybe it's best to start a re-examination by not-knowing, or, as Agamben says, going "beyond both knowing and not knowing" (Agamben 2004, 91). This isn't about ignorance, or some kind of misplaced epistemological humility; it's concerned with recognizing that to really confront some of these questions is to confront an abyss. Incommensurabilities, non-knowledge, and strategies of non-identity are engaged in an effort to find a truly "open" artwork, one that opens onto its own world as well as the world it inhabits.

Notes

1. O'Hare, p. 122.
2. The fear of death is evidently much higher among Tibetan monks than among Hindu or Christian clerics. The reason being, as philosopher Shaun Nichols guesses, that Tibetan monks, due to cultural and religious circumstances, are given to think about death far more than their Christian or Hindu colleagues. "Shaun Nichols on Death and the Self," podcast, *Philosophy Bites*, April 14, 2015.
3. Simon Critchley, *Things Merely Are* (86).
4. While introducing virtual enjambments into the text through reading, Anderson reverses what frequently occurs when poets read their work. For example, a poem published in a recent edition of the *New Yorker* (August 5 & 12, 2019), "Almost Human" by Ocean Vuong, is also accompanied by an audio file so that the reader can hear the voice of the author reading the poem. The visual enjambments of the textual version are elided in the reading; that is, there are almost no pauses in the reading to indicate the enjambed line breaks in the poem's printed version.
5. Elkins adds "... it helps to remember that some pictures – like fallen leaves – are irrefutably, permanently, and wholly meaningless" (257).
6. Blanchot continues: "Not only is the image of an object not the meaning of that object, and of no help in comprehending it, but it tends to withdraw it from its meaning by maintaining it in the immobility of a resemblance that has nothing to resemble" (85).
7. Related to the author in a conversation.

References

Agamben, Giorgio. 2004. *The Open: Man and Animal*. Stanford, CA: Stanford University Press.
Barthes, Roland. 1977. "The Grain of the Voice." In *Image-Music-Text*, ed. Stephen Heath. New York: Noonday. 179–89.
Bennett, Jane. 2015. "Encounters with an Art-Thing." *Evental Aesthetics* 3(3): 71–87.
Blanchot, Maurice. 1981. "Two Versions of the Imaginary." In *The Gaze of Orpheus*. New York: Station Hill Press. 79–88.
Critchley, Simon. 2005 *Things Merely Are*. New York: Routledge.
Elkins, James. 1994. *Why Are Our Pictures Puzzles?* New York: Routledge.
Groys, Boris. 2011. "The Border Between Word and Image." *Theory Culture and Society* 28(2): 94–108.
Nancy, Jean-Luc. 2005. *The Ground of the Image* New York: Fordham University Press.
Nichols, Shaun. 2015. "On Death and the Self." Podcast, *Philosophy Bites*, April 14, 2015.
O'Hare, Mick, ed. 2008. *Do Polar Bears Get Lonely?* London: Profile Books.

22. "THIS IS A F**KING BUSINESS": THE CONCERT SHOW AND TOUR IN 1970S HOLLYWOOD FICTION FILMS

Julie Lobalzo Wright

INTRODUCTION

Cinematic representations of the merging of art and commerce have existed since the emergence of the rock 'n' roll genre in the 1950s. Early British and American rock 'n' roll exploitation films habitually included dishonest music people preying on young musical discoveries, such as Johnny Jackson (Laurence Harvey) in *Expresso Bongo* (Val Guest, UK, 1959) who transforms Bert Rudge into the wildly successful Bongo Herbert (Cliff Richard), before Bongo terminates his exploitative contract with Jackson. Elvis Presley's second and third films (*Loving You* (Hal Kanter, USA, 1957) and *Jailhouse Rock* (Richard Thorpe, USA, 1957)) featured his character's transition from obscurity to stardom and the promoters who helped and hindered his ascent. The performances in these exploitation films took place at county fairs, in café bars, or in theaters, and on television, mirroring the spaces where rock 'n' roll artists regularly performed in the late 1950s and early 1960s. Concerts in auditoriums and stadiums only became commonplace in the mid- to late-1960s when live music became more sought after by audiences and the music industry monetized concert tours. By the 1970s, the concert venue (arenas, outdoor stadiums), transportation to venues (buses, helicopters, private aeroplanes, limousines), and the ravenous rock audience were omnipresent in popular music and cinematic representations of the contemporary music scene.

In addition to defining rockumentaries from this period, such as *The Last*

Waltz (Martin Scorsese, USA, 1978), fiction films reflected the importance of live music and concert tours by both celebrating the live music experience and critiquing the demands of concert tours. *A Star is Born* (Frank Pierson, USA, 1976), *Stardust* (Michael Apted, UK, 1974), *The Rose* (Mark Rydell, USA, 1979) and *Slade in Flame* (Richard Loncraine, UK, 1975), in addition to *Almost Famous* (Cameron Crowe, USA, 2000), which takes place in the 1970s, all depict touring as fundamental to the success of the rock star, but also detrimental to their well-being due to the constant travel, exposure to various off-stage vices, and necessity to play show after show.

This chapter will focus on the Hollywood films *A Star is Born* and *The Rose* as fiction films that document a particular period in the expansion of the popular music business and establishing many of the clichés that have come to be associated with the contemporary rock concert tour. Furthermore, various developments in the music and film industries led to the production and exhibition of these types of films in the late 1970s.

Music Industry

Simon Frith has argued that the music industry has developed contemporaneously with popular music and while the widespread perception endures that "the music industry is a bad thing – bad for music, bad for us" (Frith 1988, 11), in reality, music has benefited from every new "threat," whether technological, economic, or cultural (Ibid., 16). While not a "threat" per se, the concert tour was a new innovation within the music industry in the 1960s and certainly went through its own growing pains. Tours generally did not last more than a dozen shows and the organization was lacking as bands often had to criss-cross the large American landscape in a short period of time.[1] In addition, the sound in larger venues, venues that became necessary due to demand, were not equipped for popular music concerts. The Beatles tours in America in 1964 and 1965 were hampered by this issue with sound, due in part to the screaming audiences, but also their reliance on small amplifiers and public announcement systems already installed at stadiums. The speciality-built amplifiers by Vox could not even compete with the wall of sound from the crowd at many of The Beatles' shows (Phillips 2013, 62). *Stardust* includes a scene of rock star MacLaine in the mid-1960s who is unable to hear himself play to a packed auditorium with a restless crowd due to the sound issues.[2] Sound issues aside, the tours were profitable and the upsurge of music festivals like the Monterey Pop Festival (1967) and Woodstock (1969) reinforced the desire by rock fans to seek out live music.

By the early 1970s, according to K. J. Donnelly, "rock's product chain" materialized with album releases coinciding with tours and, in addition, a full-length film to publicize the various products (2013, 176). The concert film and rockumentary grew in this same period, arising from, concurrently, advancements in camera and sound technology that was able to record concerts and the growth of concerts performed by popular music artists. In one decade, from 1965 to 1975, the rockumentary became an established cinematic genre through the release of *Dont Look Back* (D. A. Pennebaker, USA, 1967) and *Woodstock* (Michael Wadleigh, USA, 1970), among many other significant films, and the concert tour became a standard by-product of the rock music industry.

Almost Famous, released in 2000 (story taking place in 1973), chronicles many of these alterations that occurred in the music industry in the 1970s, by building on the experiences of writer-director Cameron Crowe, one of *Rolling Stone* magazine's most prolific writers in this decade. If the album, tour, and concert film all coalesced in the 1970s to form the commerce side of the music industry, rock journalism sought to establish the artistry of the work and elevate rock performers as "objects of serious interest and discussion" (Coates 2011, 186). *Rolling Stone* magazine, established in 1967, had become the standard in rock reporting and interviews, even expanding into politics and featuring a wide variety of writers with their own social, cultural, and political agendas, including "gonzo" journalist Hunter S. Thompson. The significance of appearing on the cover of *Rolling Stone*, with its additional story in the magazine, was confirmed in the 1973 song "The Cover of the Rolling Stone,"[3] which satirizes the music business and laments the inability of a rock band to appear on the magazine's cover (the fictional band in *Almost Famous*, Stillwater, sing this song when they are told they will be on the cover of the magazine). Crucially, within the pages of *Rolling Stone* were detailed encounters with rock stars as the journalists would generally spend days or weeks with the interviewees in their homes, at recording studios, or, more often, while the artists were touring. This is what transpires in *Almost Famous* – the character of William Miller (based on Crowe) is given an assignment to write on Stillwater and proceeds to go out on the road with the band.

Thus, by the 1970s, rock fans were privy to the rock 'n' roll lifestyles of their heroes through concert films and rockumentaries, in addition to rock magazines like *Rolling Stone*. And there was a noticeable shift in tone from the early 1960s to the early 1970s. While the 1960s rockumentaries could be described as celebrating "the 60s myth of togetherness" (Wootton 1988: 355), in the 1970s "disintegration and nostalgia" (Wiener 1975, 25) reigned in both documentaries and fiction films. The violence and murder at Altamont in 1969, the overdose deaths of Janis Joplin and Jimi Hendrix and disbandment of The Beatles in 1970, and the overdose death of Jim Morrison in 1971, in addition to the continuing political strife in America due to the Vietnam War, generated a negative mood in popular culture, and specifically popular music. As an alternative to this negativity, nostalgia was flaunted in early rock 'n' roll-inspired music, such as glam rock and pure nostalgia acts like Sha Na Na; and in films that celebrated 1950s music and culture, such as *That'll Be the Day* (Claude Whatham, UK, 1973), *American Graffiti* (George Lucas, USA, 1973) and *Grease* (Randal Kleiser, USA, 1978). Rockumentaries and concert films became, in the words of Adrian Wootton, interested in the "paraphernalia surrounding the concerts" (Wootton 1988, 355), such as the sets, fans, and promoters, but these films also exposed other "paraphernalia" like airplanes, drugs, and groupies. As Wootton notes, one of the most significant films to chronicle the rock star life is the banned Rolling Stones documentary, *Cocksucker Blues* (Robert Frank, USA, 1972)[4] because it "clearly shows all the acknowledged excesses of being 'on the road'" (1998, 356). Concert tours illustrated the "institutional dynamics of the music industry" in the 1970s through their corporate approach to offering music to audiences (Sanjeck 2013, 101). Many of the artists in this period had come of age in the 1960s and saw this industrialization of music as a "collision" with their own values, leading to an uneasy relationship between "hipsters and money-men" (Halligan 2013, 108). Consequently, by the mid part of the decade, rock 'n' roll excesses had become clichés, evident in *Variety*'s review of *Slade in Flame* – a fiction film starring the glam rock band Slade: "the saga of greed, manipulation and disenchantment is now so familiar as to be totally predictable" (Watt 1975).

There was, in 1978, a sort of death knell for the excesses of the prior decade and the corporatization of the music industry in Martin Scorsese's *The Last Waltz*, a concert film that documented the final show of The Band, interspersed with interviews with the band members. The film features many of the artists who came of age in the optimistic (or, possibly, naïve) 1960s and were positioning themselves within the new corporate music industry, such as Joni Mitchell, Jackson Browne, Neil Young, and Bob Dylan. At one point, Robbie Robertson comments that there isn't anything else he can take from the road, and that he may be superstitious. When pressed as to what he means, Robertson states that the road has "taken many of the great ones . . . It's a goddamn impossible way of life." The film acts, as Terrence Rafferty (1983, 190) argues, as an elegy to a past time when musicians were bound to a community, but now are only bound to themselves.

Hollywood Fiction Films

While the rockumentary and concert films moved away from the communal ethos of the 1960s and appeared to disown the excesses of the 1970s, Hollywood fiction films included these elements, creating films that reflected the music industry of the 1970s in varied and interesting ways. This chapter will now focus on these fiction films.

American cinema matured in this period by incorporating advancements in sound technology and embracing a more spectacle-driven type of cinema. The Hollywood studio system expired in the late-1960s, opening up opportunities for a more youth-driven cinema and for young filmmakers to produce films that responded to the contemporary era (Such as *The Graduate* (Mike Nichols, USA, 1967); *Easy Rider* (Dennis Hopper, USA, 1969); and *Mean Streets* (Martin Scorsese, USA, 1973)). While many of these films were profitable, the more personally-driven, culturally relevant cinema produced in this decade could not sustain itself in an industry motivated by large profit margins. *Jaws* (Steven Spielberg, USA, 1975) revealed the "high concept" (Wyatt 1994) blockbuster type of cinema that would dominate the Hollywood industry for the next forty plus years. *Jaws* was an innovative film, especially in relation to its marketing and promotion,[5] but also in its use of sound. As David A. Cook argues, post-*Jaws* Hollywood produced a "new 'cinema of attractions,'" "enhanced by state-of-the-art, pre-digital special effects and . . . high-quality Dolby stereophonic sound" (2000, 43). Sound was instrumental to Hollywood's ability to reproduce the concert experience, facilitating films like *A Star is Born* and *The Rose* to include multiple full-length music performances. Gianluca Sergi (2004) suggests this period of Hollywood cinema should be referred to as "the Dolby era," coming of age in 1977 when George Lucas released *Star Wars*. As Sergi argues, the Dolby era was "born out of the revolutionary era, in aural terms, that was the 1960s" (2004, 185). While Hollywood sound had transitioned to multitrack recording and the Dolby system, recorded music had also transferred from mono to stereo sound in the 1960s (until 1963 *Billboard* included separate charts for mono and stereo releases (Smith 2009, 23)). The LP format usurped singles as the largest part of the market in the 1960s, and by 1967, albums surpassed one billion dollars in sales (Smith 2009, 23). It is unsurprising that this focus on sound was matched in the cinema, especially as many of the young filmmakers in Hollywood in this period were heavily influenced by popular music, incorporating pop music into their own films (Martin Scorsese is a good example, utilizing The Rolling Stones' back catalogue in many of his films). The shift that occurred in Hollywood meant that sound people were no longer viewed as technicians and instead were regarded as creative figures (Sergi 2004, 182). Sound, quite simply, initiated, as Sergi proposes, a "new kind of relationship between audiences and film" (2004, 184).

Popular music-based films like *A Star is Born* and *The Rose* capitalized on this new relationship, as did the cultural zeitgeist film, *Saturday Night Fever* (John Badham, USA, 1976). *Fever*'s success was predicated on the disco music and dance performances throughout the film and the experience of seeing (and hearing) the film in the cinemas. As John Travolta noted, many young people didn't really like the story, but it didn't matter because they viewed the film as "like a concert" (quoted in Cook 2000, 55). It can be argued that the musical performances in *Saturday Night Fever* are no different to the integrated performances in classical Hollywood musicals; however, the experience in the cinema was altered via the industry-wide adaption of Dolby and the installation of Dolby equipment into movie theaters. Furthermore, the concert event had become a common experience in many people's lives by the late 1970s and expectations of popular music on-screen, aurally and visually, had transformed.

A Star is Born and *The Rose*

Where *A Star is Born* and *The Rose* diverge from other successful musical films in the 1970s like *Saturday Night Fever* or *Grease*[6] is that both films are concerned with the music industry, reflecting the significance of concert tours in the consumption of popular music in this period. These films, however, are not rockumentaries or concert films, meaning the performances must be accommodated into the fictional narrative of the story. The stories mirror the "paraphernalia" surrounding concerts and tours laid bare in 1960s and 1970s rockumentaries. It is notable that the most recent telling of *A Star is Born* (Bradley Cooper, USA, 2018) included numerous concert scenes and the devastating impact of rock tours on fragile and/or addicted individuals like Jackson Maine (Bradley Cooper). 1976's *A Star is Born* features a multitude of scenes that condense the rock lifestyle of late nights, studio recordings, media intrusions, television specials, and live performances. *A Star is Born* and *The Rose* can be viewed as bookends with one charting the rise of an artist (*A Star is Born*) and the other, the destruction of an artist (*The Rose*). Both films employ the new sound technology available in the cinema and exploit audience foreknowledge about the excesses of rock tours and experience of live concerts.

The films prioritize sound from the onset, with the sound of the concert audience materializing while the initial credits appear on-screen. In a similar manner to the beginning of *Gimme Shelter* (Albert Maysles, David Maysles, and Charlotte Zwerin, 1970), which features the aural announcement of The Rolling Stones at the beginning of their Madison Square Garden show while the cinema screen remains black, *A Star is Born* begins with the exasperated voice of an announcer who asks the crowd to settle down. *The Rose*, on the other hand, begins with Rose's[7] (Bette Midler) weak and trembling voice amplified through a microphone stating that she wishes to sing a lullaby from her youth. During a short pause, a fan is heard shouting "rock 'n' roll," and this exclamation surfaces multiple times in the film as a commentary on the pleasure and sorrow of the rock star lifestyle. In a later scene, Rudge (Alan Bates), Rose's manager, enthusiastically states to Houston Dyer (Frederic Forrest) that he will love being on a rock tour, but after a breakdown by Rose on the airplane, Rudge sarcastically comments, "rock 'n' roll!" *The Rose* begins at Rose's last concert and proceeds to flashback to the week prior to this final show, taking place in Rose's hometown. While *A Star is Born* follows a conventional storyline from start to finish, it too begins and ends with live performances; however, these performances are from different individuals (and in different locations), reflecting the stardom changeover from John Norman Howard (Kris Kristofferson) to Esther Hoffman (Barbra Streisand). Remarkably, the 1976 film begins in a concert auditorium, but ends in a theater auditorium similar to the setting that opens the original *A Star is Born* (George Cukor, USA, 1954) with Judy Garland's Esther Blodgett incorporating an intoxicated Norman Maine (James Mason) into her stage act.

The sound and spectacle of these live performances are enhanced by the way they were aurally and visually recorded. *A Star is Born* was recorded in a two-channel Dolby sound that was selectively exhibited in this same optical sound (Cook 2000, 55). This type of sound permitted "well-defined noises simultaneous with dialogue" (Chion 1994, 147). This aided in recreating the overlap of multiple sounds that naturally occurs at rock concerts – performed music, screaming fans, public announcements – but was unable to be recorded until the establishment and industry-wide adaptation of Dolby sound. The beginning of *The Rose* is an excellent example, with Rose's breathing, speaking voice, and the voices of fans all audible to the film viewers.

Both films also exploited camera techniques recognizable from rockumentaries, such as helicopter shots of the concert stages and audiences. *Gimme Shelter* and *Woodstock* include helicopter shots as establishing shots for the concert locations, in addition to accentuating the large audience (this is especially true in the final shot from *Woodstock*). In *A Star is Born*, after Esther and John Norman meet, he takes her to one of his shows. The scene begins with a sonic explosion of rock music matched by the helicopter shot of a rocky terrain until the landscape reveals a large concert venue in the valley with thousands of concertgoers surrounding the stage and bleacher seats towering over the space. Esther and John Norman view this from a helicopter with Esther in complete awe, joking to John Norman about his earlier comment that he wishes he were invisible. The camera continues to scan the audience before the film cuts to the helicopter landing backstage. This sequence of shots not only captures the rock concert environment in the 1970s, but also references the many rockumentaries and concert films released before this fiction film. It is important to note that the entire scene was filmed at the Sun Devil Stadium[8] in Arizona on a day when a full concert was put on to capture live performances of Kristofferson and Streisand, in addition to performances from Carlos Santana and Peter Frampton (among others) for the crowd who were there from 7am until 6pm at night (Grant 1976).

The Rose functions more like a backstage musical, with performances interspersed throughout the film, than *A Star is Born* (although *A Star is*

Born features performances within the plot, they form a trajectory, displaying, especially, Esther's rise to stardom). The narrative of *The Rose* is motivated by Rose's struggle to survive her loneliness on the road and make it to her hometown show. The film builds to the climatic final hometown performance, the one signaled aurally at the beginning of the film. The narrative climax is equaled in the film's visual and sonic spectacle. Earlier performances in *The Rose* were shot at the Wiltern Theatre in Los Angeles with a capacity audience of under 2,000. While the sound and, especially, Midler's vocal and bodily performance are boisterous, the Wiltern scenes are shot more intimately with close-ups and medium shots of Midler and the audience, in addition to long shots (in duration) of Midler singing. The final performance sequence begins with Rose's name in bright lights before a cut to a similar helicopter shot as in *A Star is Born* with the outdoor night-time crowd illuminated by the lights from the stage. This scene was shot at the Veterans Memorial Stadium in Long Beach with a capacity of over 11,000 people. The helicopter circles around the crowd while the rock concert music blares, but this scene is much longer than the one in *A Star is Born* because it follows the helicopter that Rose arrives in, cutting between the helicopter and the excited audience members. The narrative drama of Rose's arrival, coming after the film audience has witnessed an emotionally draining phone call to her parents and the injecting of heroin, is echoed in the filmmaking through the rapturous concert audience, the explosion of fireworks, and long shots of the massive audience. By the time the music stops, the sound from the audience is deafening and it continues to intrude during Rose's final performance of "Stay With Me Baby," faithfully replicating a rock concert. In contrast, Esther's final performance in *A Star is Born* is in front of a theater-sized audience who politely applaud her when she walks on stage, but remain, mainly, off-screen while the film primarily focuses on Streisand in tight close-ups as she sings "With One More Look At You"/"Watch Closely Now." The theatre audience returns, aurally, once the film ends on a freeze frame of Esther's face, which is matched with the enthusiastic applause of the theater crowd.

Conclusion

A Star is Born and *The Rose* tell two divergent stories about popular music – its artists, industry, and culture – in the late 1960s and 1970s. While *The Rose* was released in 1979, the film takes place in 1969 due to its original inspiration, Janis Joplin.[9] The films are clearly inspired visually and sonically by rockumentaries and concert films released earlier, but also the tales of excess, greed, and manipulation that had become commonplace in popular music culture. By the 1970s, rock music managers were well-known as shrewd businessmen, such as Peter Grant with Led Zeppelin, and also as exploitation merchants who swindled their clients out of large amounts of money, such as The Rolling Stones' one-time manager, Allen Klein, who endured years of litigation with the band. Managers play an important role in both films, but Rudge in *The Rose* is continuously malicious, persistently rejecting Rose's pleas to allow her to take a year off. The demand on artists to tour had become routine in the 1970s and both films illustrate how taxing life on the road can be (as Robertson rationalized in *The Last Waltz*). John Norman Howard and Rose begin their films strung out on alcohol, drugs, and the demands of the concert tour – both characters die by the end of the films. It is only Esther who is able to flourish in the music business and this can be attributed to her single-minded and demanding approach to her career (criticisms that have also been leveled against Streisand).

These films are fascinating documents from this time in popular music and Hollywood cinema when sound technology was able to reconstruct the concert experience in the cinema. Yet, these films do more than just recreate events; in the words of J. P. Telotte, they produce "a different musical experience... one fully available only in the acoustically sophisticated, Dolby-wrap-around-sound-equipped, rocking-chair world of the movie theatre" (1980, 10). The musical moments in these films are exceptional, placing the cinema audience in places the concertgoer could never infiltrate (such as the spectacular helicopter views of the large concerts). It is also important to note that these scenes were shot by experienced cinematographers – Robert Surtees (*A Star is Born*), who had won three Academy Awards in the 1950s and was known as one of the most versatile cinematographers in Hollywood; and Vilmos Zsigmond, who was one of the most influential cinematographers in New Hollywood having worked on various films, including *McCabe & Mrs. Miller* (Robert Altman, USA, 1971) and *Close Encounters of the Third Kind* (Steven Spielberg, USA, 1977). The merging of sound and vision in these films allowed them to act as pseudo-concert films with narratives that uncovered the concurrent developments in popular music, the music industry, and music journalism/media, exposing the uneasy relationship between art and commerce in 1970s popular music. As Rudge shouts to Rose early in *The Rose*, "This is a f**king business" and these films presented how popular music had been industrialized in this period, but also the enjoyable musical experiences that were to be had at concert stadiums and at the cinema.

Notes

1. A good example was The Rolling Stones' first tour of America in 1964, where they played eleven shows in fifteen days, beginning in California and ending in New York City, with stops in Texas, Colorado and Pennsylvania, among other destinations.
2. *Stardust* charts the rise of Jim MacLaine, rock 'n' roll enthusiast in *That'll Be The Day* (Claude Whatham, USA, 1973), released two years earlier, who becomes a star

as part of the Stray Cats in the mid-1960s before going solo and eventually dying of an overdose.
3. The song was written by author Shel Silverstein and first recorded by Dr Hook and the Medicine Show in 1973.
4. The film was never officially released because while the band commissioned the film, they were concerned about much of the included footage, which features drug taking and sex. There is a court ruling in place that Frank must be present anytime the film is shown.
5. See Cook (2000) for a discussion of the marketing and promotion of *Jaws*, pp. 40–4.
6. All four films – *A Star is Born*, *The Rose*, *Saturday Night Fever*, and *Grease* – were also accompanied by successful album soundtracks, diverging from Donnelly's "rock's product chain" (2013) by focusing solely on the film and album release (or vice versa).
7. Midler portrays Mary Rose Foster in the film, who is known by her stage name, "The Rose."
8. The Sun Devil Stadium was also the location of some of the concert footage from U2's *Rattle and Hum* (Phil Joanou, USA, 1988) and was the location of the concert recorded for The Rolling Stones' concert film, *Let's Spend the Night Together* (Hal Ashby, USA, 1983).
9. The script had to be changed due to her family not permitting the filmmakers to reference her life.

References

Chion, Michel. 1994. *Audio-Vision: Sound on Screen*. New York: Columbia University Press.
Coates, Norma. 2011. "Whose Tears Go By? Marianne Faithfull at the Dawn and Twilight of Rock Culture." In *She's So Fine: Reflections on Whiteness: Femininity, Adolescence and Class in 1960s Music*, ed. Laurie Stras. Farnham, UK and Burlington, VT: Ashgate, 183–202.
Cook, David A. 2000. *Lost Illusions: American Cinema in the Shadow of Watergate and Vietnam*. Berkeley and Los Angeles: University of California.
Donnelly, Kevin J. 2013. "Visualising Live Albums: Progressive Rock and the British Concert Film in the 1970s." In *The Music Documentary: Acid Rock to Electropop*, eds Robert Edgar, Kirsty Fairclough-Isaacs, and Ben Halligan. New York and London: Routledge. 171–82.
Frith, Simon. 1988. "The Industrialization of Music." In *Music for Pleasure: Essays in the Sociology of Pop*. Cambridge: Polity Press. 11–23.
Grant, Lee. 1976. "Streisand in 'Star is Born': The Way It Is." *LA Times*, 2 May.
Phillips, Ronnie J. 2013. *Rock and Roll Fantasy?: The Reality of Going from Garage Band to Superstardom*. New York: Springer.
Rafferty, Terrence. 1983. "Martin Scorsese's Still Life." *Sight and Sound* 52(3): 186–92.
Sanjek, David, and Ben Halligan. 2013. "'You Can't Always Get What You Want': Riding on The Medicine Ball Caravan." In *The Music Documentary: Acid Rock to Electropop*, eds Robert Edgar, Kirsty Fairclough-Isaacs, and Ben Halligan. New York and London: Routledge. 100–12.
Sergi, Gianluca. 2004. *The Dolby Era: Film Sound in Contemporary Hollywood*. Manchester and New York: Manchester University Press.
Smith, Chris. 2009. *101 Albums That Changed Popular Music*. Oxford and New York: Oxford University Press.

Telotte, J. P. 1980. "Scorsese's 'The Last Waltz' and the Concert Genre." *Film Criticism* 4(2): 9–20.

Watt. 1975. Review for *Flame* (aka *Slade in Flame*). *Variety*, 19 February.

Wiener, T. 1975. "The Rise and Fall of the Rock Film." *American Film: Journal of Film and Television Arts* 1(2): 25–9.

Wootton, Adrian. 1988. "Looking Back, Dropping Out, Making Sense: A History of the Rock-Concert Movie." *Monthly Film Bulletin* 55(658): 355–56.

Wyatt, Justin. 1994. *High Concept: Movies and Marketing in Hollywood*. Austin, TX: University of Texas.

23. LIVE FROM THE MULTIPLEX: THE CONCERT FILM AS EVENT CINEMA SINCE THE 2000S

Ian Robinson

In August 2003, coinciding with the launch of his *Reality* album and his first major world tour in nearly a decade, David Bowie announced a live gig to be beamed directly to cinemas via satellite across Europe from London's Riverside Studios. Celebrated as a breakthrough for simultaneous transmission of a live rock concert to audiences in cinemas, Bowie's concert brought attention to the new possibilities for "alternative content." Alternative content, or "event cinema" as it has more recently been named by industry partners, has become part of digital exhibition in cinemas, beginning in the early 2000s. The concert was "live" in forty-two cinemas across Europe, while audiences in Asia and Australia received it the next day. Cinemas in Canada, the USA, and Brazil played the concert a week later (BBC News Online 2003).

The history of live performances on screen in movie theaters of course predates the Bowie show. Only a year earlier, Bon Jovi broadcast a concert to twenty theaters across Europe, connecting fans in local cinemas to the kinetic atmosphere of the Shepherd's Bush Empire, while the American alternative metal band Korn played live to forty cinemas across the US the same year (BBC News Online 2002a; BBC News Online 2002b). There were also studio-led experiments in theatrical television in the 1940s and 1950s and the wide use of closed-circuit broadcasts of boxing matches to theaters in the 1960s, 1970s, and 1980s. However, with the rise of digital distribution and exhibition technologies, the emergence of alternative content as a distinct form of theatrical exhibition, and its recognition by the movie industry as a source of revenue growth, is still a relevantly recent development in film history.

Bowie's 2003 concert is an instructive starting point for a consideration of the cinema's incorporation of the live rock concert and the phenomenon of event cinema over the past two decades. Since the mid-2000s, event cinema screenings have grown considerably, both in number and in terms of revenues for exhibitors, distributors, and performers alike. Yet while rock concerts such as those by David Bowie, Bon Jovi, or Korn were instrumental in demonstrating the potential of integrating satellite transmission and digital cinema for reaching new audiences in cinemas, rock has been far from the most successful genre of event cinema. Event cinema's dominance by opera, ballet, and theater since the late 2000s reflects the seriality of their art forms. The stubborn singularity of the rock concert, and its ethos of authenticity, resists serialization. In comparison to the MET Live or the National Theatre Live, the codes of audience reception are less formalized for the live rock concert screening. European audiences reportedly rushed to the screen and danced in the aisles during the screenings of Bowie's 2003 concert ("Reality at Riverside"). Other reports relay the awkwardness of clapping after a song and the hyper-awareness of the screen that accompanied the close-ups of Bowie as well as the scrolling text messages from fans across the bottom of the screen (Gallagher 2003). In an attempt to interact with audiences in real time, the Bowie concert featured a live Q&A, with audiences from various cities submitting questions. The recorded concerts in Japan, Hong Kong, Canada, USA, and Brazil also featured interactive "live" Q&A sessions with Bowie, a feature that has been adopted by many concert events in order to imbue them with a sense of liveness.[1]

Since the early 2000s, rock has provided a consistent source of material for the event cinema industry, even if its output remains less significant in terms of audience or revenue numbers than other performing arts. This chapter starts with an attempt to approach the concert event screening from a media studies perspective, and to engage with its intermedial construction as both an industry and audience experience. This performative dimension to event cinema might be considered alongside Casetti's remarks about the relocation of cinema across a multitude of screens. According to Casetti, the new technologies of the film image have given rise to a situation in which the spectator "has ceased simply to consume a show and begins to intervene in the act of consumption" (Casetti 2009, 63). The live rock concert screening provides a case study of film culture which relies less on an investment in a film text than a mode of participation in a film event. At stake in the live concert film is a particular form of media environment, an intermedial space in which the live event is produced, sold, and experienced as rock concert, film, and immersive media event. Liveness is negotiated materially and rhetorically with the goal of both transporting audiences to the concert venue and inviting them to a hypermediated singalong. Where event cinema succeeds in addressing its spectators as participants in a live rock concert, it does so by playing on the mobility of the traditional values of place and authenticity that follow rock's entry into the cinema.[2] Without displacing the indexical meaning of "I was there!" that memorializes rock concerts and provides the foundation for rock ideology and fan culture, event cinema seeks to capitalize on an extension of the experience economy to the big screen.

The Intermediality of Event Cinema

Discussions of intermediality are most often reserved for analyses of high and experimental arts. In analyzing theatrical concert films as intermedial events, this chapter seeks to extend theories of intermediality to the sphere of popular culture. Intermediality provides a critical lens to examine the historical significance of the theatrical concert film: a cinematic experience of live music mediated by a digital and televisual apparatus for distribution. The live concert film therefore bears the traces of the upheavals and transformations of the global mediascape of the early twenty-first century. Its uncertain place in film, music history, or performance history is testament to its liminal status as an art form, industry and medium.

The concept of intermediality has been most fully developed in the fields of comparative literature, music, and media studies.[3] While space does not permit for an elaborate review of the literature on intermediality, it's necessary to briefly describe some approaches to the concept that pertain to event cinema and the concert film.[4] Bolter and Grusin's analysis of the dialectical interplay between the twin processes of transparent immediacy and hypermediacy in media history offers a starting point for considering the intermedial character of the concert film (Bolter and Grusin 1999). As a work of digital cinema, the event cinema screening remediates a televisual experience of watching a live event on screen. Moreover, the event screening re-articulates the relationship between the transparent immediacy of the live event and the hypermediacy of the spectacle that constitutes live and recorded music as well as cinema. Removed from the stadium or arena, themselves hypermediated environments, the concert film addresses its audience as a doubly-mediated spectacle on screen. The close-up encounter with a band, and the audience's proximity to the stage while seated comfortably in the film theater, provide an experience of immediate presence in relation to the live concert. Interactive Q&As with the band, as deployed in the Bowie concert screenings, further add to this tension of mediated presence and distance at the concert screening, as they afford the audience a level of immersive presence that is only possible because of the hypermediated environment of the cinema receiving the concert's live feed.

Further complementing and adding nuance to Bolter and Grusin's approach to digital culture and remediation, Irina Rajewski outlines particular modalities of intermediality. In emphasizing the material and discursive constructions of various media, Rajewski argues that intermedial phenomena rely upon and ultimately draw attention to the interplay between distinct media forms. Her three modes of intermedial articulation consist of medial transposition (including adaptations from one medium to another), media combination (including works of performance of installations which combine or integrate more than one medium), and intermedial references (the imitation or evocation of the qualities of one medium in another) (Rajewski 2005, 51–2; 2010, 55–6).

Rajewski's three categories provide a fruitful analytical entry point for a consideration of the experiential qualities of the live concert film as well as its material, or medial, foundations. The category of medial transposition is both applicable in a broad sense and somewhat imprecise as a descriptor of the event cinema concert. On the one hand, the screening functions as an adaptation of the original concert. The performance remains the source and original text for the screened event. On the other hand, the emphasis on the textual product, transposed from the concert hall to the cinema, seems inadequate for an account of the mediated environment of the concert screening and the experiential qualities of the concert film as a special event. Rather than existing as an intermedial adaptation, the concert film is perhaps better approached as spectacle, which utilizes the strategies of Rajewski's second and third categories, the combination of multiple media and the referencing of one medium by another. From the former perspective, the live concert screening depends upon the co-presence of multiple media. In a live satellite cast from concert hall to cinema, the spectacle is arguably multimedial as it involves and depends on the direct presence of the concert performance beamed via satellite and digital network, and the use of the cinematic apparatus for projecting and screening the performance. The degree of transparency between performance and screen, and the experiences of presence and immersion in the cinema, are indications that the live concert film is better understood as a complex intermedial combination than an adaptation. Furthermore, the transparent transmission of performance to cinema is doubled by a hypermediated environment in which spectators are addressed as both concertgoers and event cinema audiences. The experience of presence and proximity to the rock stage are complemented by the sightlines of multiplex seating and the increasingly high-definition sonic technologies offered by movie theaters. These are configurations which, in augmenting some of the sensory experiences of the live concert, inevitably betray the experience of the mediatized environment of the cinema.

Finally, Rajewski's last category, that of intermedial references, provides perhaps the most interesting mode of event cinema's articulation of intermediality. Drawing on Rajewsksi's approach, one can consider the ways that the concert screening is constructed to evoke or imitate the performance. The live concert film depends as much on a rhetorical evocation of the aura of performance as it does on a material recreation or livecast of the "original" concert.

The Live Concert and the Movie Screen

The history of event cinema is commonly told as beginning not with Bon Jovi or David Bowie, but with New York's MET Opera, which, facing declining audiences and growing financial uncertainty, began licencing its performances for live broadcast to a network of cinemas in North America and Europe in 2006 (for example, see Barker 2013). The somewhat unexpected success led to several copycats including Opera Australia, London's National Theatre, The Bolshoi Ballet, Royal Ballet, and the Stratford Festival. The odd international football and boxing match, which had been on theater screens since the early 2000s, began showing up with more frequency in cinema listings, while live popular music shows have become a staple of the event cinema industry with the likes of Elton John, Rammstein, and Take That setting attendance records for their live screened performances. And most recently, the museum industry has moved into the event cinema sector with successful screenings of guided tours. These include the British Museum's *Pompei Live* and *Vikings Live* exhibitions as well as gallery tours such as *Michaelangelo: Love and Death* on screen.

Once commonly referred to as "alternative content" in the film and media trade press, the label of "event cinema" was solidified across the industry in 2012, with the formation of the Event Cinema Association. The birth of the professional association gave a name to the industry and a mode of cinema exhibition that distinguished it from the predominant models and strategies of film distribution and exhibition. "Event cinema" therefore names not simply a form or genre or content, but a mode of cinema exhibition which redesignates the physical space of exhibition as a live and intermedial special events venue designed to fill seats in empty theaters during commonly dark Monday–Thursday periods, while also competing against the digital platforming of film content among the multitude of competing on-demand services consumed in homes.

Event cinema trades upon liveness as a primary characteristic of its "eventfulness" and this dependency upon a shared recognition of the authentic live event could not be more important to any genre of event cinema than the concert film. The live rock concert as a cultural form sits somewhat uneasily with event cinema. It depends upon an ethos of authenticity effected by a performance of apparent contingency and spontaneity with a demonstration of technique and artistry. Whether it is David Bowie, Metallica, or Coldplay, rock concerts depend on the mythology of the singular event, the ephemeral experience only recorded in memory, or perhaps in a t-shirt or record from the merchandise booth.

Not all of what passes under the banner of event cinema is temporally synchronous with a live performance. Fathom Events has estimated that roughly 60 per cent of event screenings consist of live transmissions, with almost half of its event offerings consisting of pre-recorded material. Yet as Philip Auslander has argued, liveness is a flexible concept whose definition is a product of historical discourse. He writes that "historically, the live is actually an effect of mediatization, not the other way around. It was the development of recording technologies that made it possible to perceive existing representations as 'live'" (Auslander 2010, 56). Rock authenticity, according to Auslander, is an ideological concept and discursive effect, rather than an essential characteristic of the genre (Ibid., 82). Furthermore, "in live performance, the rock audience is exposed to the music in a context that endorses it as authentic in the terms of rock ideology" (Ibid., 95). The cultural value of rock, perhaps more than any other genre of music, is tied to its claims of delivering an authentic auditory experience. Its aura depends on the fetishization of the originality and creativity of songwriting and individual technique.

These values of authenticity and the singular experience of the concert seem anathema to the concert on screen at the multiplex. However, if live rock performance is thoroughly mediatized, in the sense that it functions to establish the authenticity of recorded music, as suggested by Auslander, the tradition of the "live album" further imbues the recorded product with an effect of authenticity. Live concert albums such as The Who's *Live at Leeds* (1970), or any of Pearl Jam's "official bootleg" albums since 2000, are fundamental to rock ideology insofar as they aim to index the singularity of a performance in space and time as the originary moment of enunciation of a rock band's creative output.[5] For Auslander, "recorded live" is no less than "an oxymoron":

> ... the audience shares neither a temporal frame nor a physical location with the performers, but experiences the performance later and usually in a different place than it occurred. The liveness of the experience of listening to or watching the recording is primarily affective: live recordings allow the listener a sense of participating in a specific performance and a vicarious relationship to the audience for that performance not accessible through studio productions. (Auslander 2010, 60)

Event cinema's remediation of live performance therefore requires a reaffirmation of rock ideology, for which the significance of the authenticity of performance and the exclusive singularity of the fan experience are central constructs. However, this does not require the complete avoidance or disguise of the cinema's mediation of the concert. As Sanden argues:

> The perception of liveness depends not necessarily on the total eschewal of electronic mediation but on the persistent perception of *characteristics*

of music's live performance within the context of – and often with the help of – various levels of such mediation. Liveness represents a perceived *trace* of that which *could be live* in the face of the threat of further or complete mediation and modification. (Sanden 2013, 6)

Therefore, in its construction of liveness, event cinema must negotiate between foregrounding its own mediation – the hypermediated experience of the event – and transparently immersing audiences in the performance. According to Sanden, audiences are complicit in the construction of liveness in mediated environments, insofar as they interpret traces of the live performance.

Bearing Auslander's and Sanden's critiques in mind, we can observe the multiple modalities of the live event that form the basis of event cinema's claim to a unique status. Sanden identifies seven categories of liveness in his study of modern music, several of which apply to the screened rock concert (Sanden 2013, 11). The first, of course, is the temporally synchronous event in which production and reception occur simultaneously, as in the live transmission from the concert hall to the cinema screen. In Sanden's categorization scheme, the temporally live broadcasts of concerts would further consist of forms of liveness derived from the "fidelity" to the unmediated concert, their delivery of the "spontaneity" of the performance, and even in their demonstration of "corporeality" of the performance. Auslander refers to this mode as the live broadcast, as it is typified by live media distribution via radio, television, or Internet channels. In remediating these other broadcast media, event cinema has pushed the spectator's experience past the normal parameters of what defines cinema as a recorded medium. Bowie's live concert from Riverside Studios in London, or more recently, Kanye West's 2016 worldwide concert and fashion broadcast live from Madison Square Garden, are hardly "concert films" in this regard since they share little with common definitions or experiences of films or filmgoing.

From this perspective, such live broadcast concerts share little with a second form of liveness, defined by the pre-recorded performance – the screening of a temporally asynchronous event. This category is exemplified by the recorded live concert, as in David Gilmour's *Live at Pompeii* concert film, which played in cinemas around the world on 13 September 2017, prior to its release on multiple formats, including DVD, less than three weeks later. Here the audience's recognition of an original temporally, spatially and corporeally live event, is crucial, even as it is not experienced as such by the audience in front of the screen. Such films are dependent upon the "perceived trace of that which could be live" and their documentary ethos often aims to render the concert as an unmediated spectacle. Like the live album, such concert films offer authenticating proof of the performance as the primary musical utterance.

Thirdly, event cinema expresses a mode of liveness which derives from the eventful and public character of the screening, often by means of a special introduction, an interactive Q&A session with a filmmaker and/or leading talent, a singalong session, or even transformative theatrer décor. This is the mode of liveness that is tied to the public gathering and which derives its claim to liveness from the temporally synchronous and spatially contiguous experience of its spectators. In August 2018, Fathom Events presented its eighth annual Grateful Dead Meet-Up at the Movies with a screening of the iconic band's July 1989 concert at JFK Stadium in Philadelphia at theaters across the US. The liveness of this concert film is attached to the gathering of a community of fans rather than the co-presence of audience and performers. That the screening was scheduled on 1 August, the date which would have been the 76th birthday of the late Jerry Garcia, only added to the atmosphere for Grateful Dead fans. This form of liveness also includes concert documentaries such as Mat Whitecross's Coldplay documentary *A Head Full of Dreams* (UK, 2018). Following the band over a span of twenty years, the film was released by Amazon Prime for streaming on 16 November 2018, two days after Trafalgar Releasing's distribution of its single-day screening at 2,500 cinemas in over seventy countries.

Whether in the audience "Meet-Up," in the example of the annual Grateful Dead screening, or in the much publicized single-screening event of *Head Full of Dreams*, this third mode of liveness is the effect of events which rhetorically address and position their audiences as a group of insider-participants. Even

23.1 *8th Annual Grateful Dead Meet-Up at the Movies* poster.

23.2 Coldplay's *A Head Full of Dreams* poster.

though Coldplay's *A Head Full of Dreams* was released on Amazon Prime two days after its theatrical release, the film nonetheless earned $3.5 million at box offices, while breaking the top five in revenues for its one-day release in several countries (McNary). For many concert event films, the scarcity of screenings is utilized as a marketing tool to increase attendance, particularly tickets per screening, and to boost future sales in other media, whether it is online streaming or DVD sales, as in the case of *The Big Four: Live from Sofia, Bulgaria* (Nick Wickhan, USA, 2010), a concert film featuring metal heavyweights Metallica, Anthrax, Slayer, and Megadeth.

In each case event cinema trades upon a liveness effect of not only feeling as if one were directly and transparently present at the concert, but that the audience is present at a hypermediated and intermedial spectacle. This illusion offers audiences their own live event, independent from the original concert. Event cinema therefore negotiates these distinctions, often oscillating between them, in appealing to its spectators. The live concert film may eventually appear as a quaint or nostalgic format in the era of live streaming, where performances may be accessed in real time or at a delay from the comfort of home on multiple devices. Event cinema's demand that audiences gather in one place implies a response to the culture of streaming and the "YouTube-ification" of film and media culture.[6] Seen in this light, the live concert film – in all its modalities of liveness – can be read as an attempt by an old medium (cinema) to remediate and incorporate characteristics of an even older one (live performance), in order to resist its obsolescence in the emerging digital culture of the twenty-first century. By turning to music and performance cultures, event cinema adopts digital technologies in order to emphasize the large screen's relevance as a site of public, eventful, and live culture.

The experience sold by event cinema is framed in terms of the rhetoric of the special event, defined by contingency, unpredictability, and singularity. Robert Allen writes about film exhibition: "What makes events eventful is that they are unique convergences of multiple individual trajectories upon particular social sites. Events are necessarily unpredictable and unreproducible" (Allen 2011, 56). What is often described in industry discourse as both the challenge and promise of event cinema is the screened exhibition of single-take performances, often considered incompatible with the normative spectatorial experience and entrenched distribution structures of theatrical film exhibition. Breaking with the dominant model of film exhibition, event cinema foregrounds itself as an intermedial experience, celebrates and accentuates its liveness, and positions itself as an extra-cinematic experience. Event cinema therefore offers a new definition of moviegoing and cinematic experience, one which has been promoted by the industry with increasing enthusiasm as that industry has begun to shift its focus towards aligning cinema with the experience economy. The notion of an experience economy, as defined by Joseph Pine and James Gilmore, ushers in a new stage of capitalism organized around the production and consumption of staged events. Event cinema has been positioned rhetorically as a bellwether for the changing film exhibition industry, which it is argued requires greater flexibility in its ability to program content and attract new audiences whose primary sites for engaging with film culture are the multiple streaming services geared towards home and mobile entertainment.

Event Cinema as Networked Distribution

The founding of the Event Cinema Association shifted the rhetoric away from what was previously called "alternative content" in industry discourse to "event cinema." At stake in the new label was more than merely a shift in terminology. As Martin Barker has suggested in his discussion of what he broadly terms "livecasting," "'alternative content' has no resonant public name, only a rather roundabout 'what it isn't' industry label. I believe this relates to still unsettled questions about these events' cultural status" (Barker 2013, 10). If "alternative content" has lacked an acknowledged cultural status, the label "event cinema" reflects a desire to foreground the special and unique qualities of cinemagoing that pertain to this emerging cultural form.

The event cinema industry – producers, distributors and exhibitors of alternative content, as well as the Event Cinema Association – has tended to express the qualities of this form with an appeal to the experiential conditions of spectatorship. Since 2012, event cinema has been driven by a boosterist rhetoric on local and community-oriented spectator experience, exhibitors' capacity for self-reinvention through niche programming and audience development, and the transformative eventfulness of the live screening. To attend an event screening is sold not simply as a matter of viewership, taste or connoisseurship, but rather as a unique experience. The goal of such one-off live, intermedial screenings of an opera, a rock concert, a gallery exhibition, or increasingly a rarely-exhibited anime film, is to "eventize" the product, to construct a theatrical experience. Here, content is no longer king. As one writer for *Boxoffice* recently wrote, echoing the mantra of the experience economy, "It is no longer about what you want to see at the movies; it's about how you want to see it."[7] Such consumer-empowering rhetoric is increasingly par for the course among industry insiders, for whom a one billion dollar market has remained a consistent, if elusive goal to be reached, at first estimate by 2015, then revised to 2017 and 2019. For Michael Gubbins, an industry consultant with Sampomedia and author of the 2014 report "Audience in the Mind," "event cinema, including opera and theatre, demonstrates the case for experience economics in the film industry at large" (Gubbins 2014, 50). He continues, "Event cinema is predicated on the ability to create an illusion of authenticity – a belief that somehow the audience is sharing in at least some of the unique individual experience as those in the actual theatres and concert halls, where the live event is taking place" (Ibid., 54). The lesson of event cinema for exhibitors, according to Gubbins, is the capacity to mobilize the theater as a social space for a unique experience. His list of possible strategies for connecting with audiences all build on the liveness of event cinema. They include: additional content/Q&As; preview screenings; audience selected programming; pop-up venues; and all-night screenings as a sampling of tactics exhibitors could employ to eventize their schedules. Such eventful tactics are seen in numerous examples, from the interactive sessions of Bowie's foundational concert to the more recent release of Frank Zappa's *Roxy: The Movie* (Frank Zappa, USA) in theaters in the spring of 2015.

The intermedial qualities of event cinema – which combine performance, screening, and broadcast media – are thus central to industry rhetoric on the future of theatrical cinema. In 2013, the 50th anniversary special of the BBC's

Doctor Who was screened on free TV and live in 1,500 theaters in Europe and North America, taking in 10.2 million in box office receipts. The success didn't go unnoticed by industry executives, such as Tim Warner, who has called for a rethinking of the multiplex as an expansive TV network for programmed content.[8] In a similar vein, Randy Blotsky, CEO of Hollywood's new digital pipeline, the Digital Cinema Distribution Coalition, claims that "the DCDC Network has effectively converted traditional movie theaters into true community entertainment centers that have successfully expanded the shared content experience for consumers to all forms of content, including movies, operas, ballets . . . from anywhere in the world."[9] While this is a long way from the first MET Live simulcasts to a handful of theaters in 2006, the live, intermedial, and experiential vision of film exhibition remains highly indebted to the lessons of alternative content. The real value of event cinema for the industry increasingly lies not simply in its command of high ticket prices, impressive year-over-year growth and its ability to fill otherwise dark theaters. Rather industry rhetoric, sometimes implicitly, reveals a growing understanding of event cinema as an experimental site for the re-imagination of film exhibition and moviegoing for the experience economy.

Due to its emphasis on live transmission, the event cinema industry has built up around a cluster of competing distributors, most of which lie outside of the major networks of film distribution. In fact, it is only recently that Hollywood has taken an interest in event cinema and so far, it has not caught up with established players in the field. Most significant to event cinema distributors, and the financial success of the industry as a whole, is the formation of broad networks of distribution across space. Even more crucial to event cinema than to the feature film industry is the maximized diffusion of the screening event across space. Since most concert screenings are singular events (with occasional encores), distribution requires a return on investment from a single transmission to as many screens as possible.

As previously discussed, the rhetorical "liveness" of the concert event, whether synchronous or recorded, largely prefigures the material or technological basis of delivery of the live event. While the single screening of a David Bowie concert, transmitted live from a London studio, might remain emblematic of event cinema's rock programming, recorded concert films such as David Gilmour's *Live at Pompeii* (UK, 2017) are constructed and exhibited as special live events, offering unique fan experiences. However, the rhetorical address to the fan experience is only one source of the concert film's eventful status. The other source remains event cinema's deep-rooted commitment to technological development and innovation in cinemas and its close connection to the realm of branded entertainment and advertizing in cinemas. The question here, then, is not just how the liveness of the concert is constructed rhetorically in the cinema and presented to audiences "as if" they were attending a live concert.

Rather, since event cinema has arguably altered the medial ground of what counts as cinema, the question regards the place and significance of the concert film and event cinema in the reconfiguration of theatrical film distribution and exhibition. From this perspective, event cinema might not be seen in terms of adaptation or imitation, but as an emerging medium of live screened performance, which remediates old and new alike. Furthermore, like many media forms, event cinema has developed largely according to instrumental logic and market-driven goals.

The competing circuits of event cinema distribution which have emerged over the past decade, and which continue to expand and collapse, are the industrial and material structures which underpin the claim to liveness. Event cinema circulates according to a logic of the spatial network rather than temporal seriality. As has been discussed, the singularity of the event screening is crucial to its construction of liveness and its appeal to audiences as a unique event. Lacking the means to recuperate investment over time, the event cinema industry has developed spatial networks of exhibitors, while partnering increasingly with producers and distributors of branded content. Above all, an exhibitor's satellite capabilities and membership – or subscription – to a distributor's digital broadcast network determines its position in the event cinema industry. The industry therefore has favored distributors with some degree of vertical integration with the exhibition business. Some of the largest distributors of event cinema have longer histories as exhibition circuits. Pathé Live, the worldwide producer and distributor of The Bolshoi Ballet Live and French distributor of The Metropolitan Opera, is of course a subsidiary of the Gaumont-Pathé cinema chain, itself a division of the historic production and distribution operation. The cinema chain forms the material basis for its exclusive satellite broadcasts through the Pathé Live Cinema Network. Albeit on a smaller scale, Picturehouse Entertainment in the UK has become an industry leader in event cinema since its formation in 2010 as the distribution arm of Picturehouse Cinemas, the British indie theater chain (actually owned by Cineworld since 2012). Picturehouse reported that in its first four years, event cinema rose from 4 per cent to 15 per cent of its box office revenues.

Particularly in the USA, a second type of integrated distributor has gained early dominance in the event cinema market through control of digital networks. Content aggregators and digital service providers such as Cinedigm were early participants in the field, utilizing their vast networks of digital service provision and VPF contracts to distribute digital events such as the World Cup, presented to cinemas live in 3D in 2010. Distributors such as Fathom Events and Screenvision have succeeded in creating event cinema circuits through building on their respective connections to the screen advertizing industry, which was an early adopter of satellite broadcasting to American cinemas. Fathom has been a key player in the industry, as the distributor of the *MET: Live in HD* since 2006, and has become one of the leading event cinema distributors in the US. However, as a division of National CineMedia (NCM) until 2014, Fathom's material position with regards to content distribution was gained through access to the latter's digital advertizing network, which the company markets as the "largest digital in-theatre network in North America." As a producer and distributor of in-theater and on-screen advertizing, NCM has developed a significant digital advertizing network with three of the largest exhibitors in the US: AMC, Cinemark and Regal, in addition to some independents. In 2014, NCM restructured Fathom as a stand-alone entity, with its ownership split between the three exhibitors and a small minority stake held by NCM.

The role of digital advertizing as a primary source of the connected cinema infrastructure is something that gets very little attention in the promotional and celebratory discourse of event cinema. Along with Fathom and NCM, a recent partnership between Screenvision Media, the second largest cinema advertizing network in the USA and occasional event cinema distributor, and KAOS Connect, an event producer/distributor founded by two former Fathom executives, promises to shake up the industry again with an overt emphasis on event cinema as branded entertainment. As an article in *Film Journal International* posited rhetorically, "Are in-theatre advertising and event cinema the exhibition industry's newest power couple?"[10] According to the company's own brandings, "KAOS Connect is the next step in the evolution of the event experience, making events more accessible and engaging both on – and beyond – the Big Screen." The future event programming of KAOS Connect and Screenvision still remains uncertain but for a partnership with music festival producer LiveXLive to bring popular music festivals to local cinemas.[11] However, what is clear in both the NCM Fathom and now Screenvision/KAOS Connect partnerships is a strong integration between event cinema distribution branded entertainment.

With the Digital Cinema Distribution Coalition, a digital satellite network initiated in 2013 by the AMC, Regal, Cinemark, Universal Pictures and Warner Bros., Hollywood has firmly asserted its control over the digital delivery of films in the USA. And with their purchase of the satellite service-provided EchoStar/Deluxe the following year, the coalition now has direct ownership of their satellite carrier as well. Beginning with the concert film, event cinema, which for the past fifteen years has mostly circulated at the margins of Hollywood, is now providing a model of live distribution and exhibition for the major players.

The live concert film might be characterized as an ephemeral genre, not only for its relatively fleeting duration due to brief one-day theatrical release windows, but also due to the uncertainty surrounding its longevity as a film and music genre and mode of distribution. Since the early 2000s, the roll-out of digital technologies in cinemas and the growth of in-cinema advertizing have given event cinema a platform for experimentation. Rock concerts have held an important place within this ecosystem since 2002 due to the popularity of their performers as well as the enthusiasm of audiences for the spaces of and publics activated by live concert screenings. The live concert film will require further innovation to keep up with the economies of scale and potential profit margins offered by streaming services and platforms from Amazon, to Facebook and Google. However, event cinema also points to the resiliency of an older medium and the possibilities for transforming, or resituating, its defining mode of experience. With the live concert film, audiences are neither concertgoers nor film patrons, but are rather hailed as participants in a popular music culture, for which the performative event remains a defining feature.

Notes

1. The official press release for the David Bowie concert and a recap of the event fifteen years later are available here: http://www.bowiewonderworld.com/press/00/cinema.htm, and https://www.davidbowie.com/blog/2018/9/8/reality-at-riverside-15-years-ago-tonight
2. On rock authenticity see Auslander, *Liveness: Performance in a Mediatized Culture*, 2nd edn (London: Routledge, 2003), 73–127.
3. See for instance: Lars Elleström, ed., *Media Borders, Multimodality and Intermediality* (Basingstoke: Palgrave Macmillan 2008); Marie-Laure Ryan and Jan Noël Thon (eds), *Storyworlds Across Media: Towards a Media Conscious Narratology* (Lincoln: University of Nebraska Press, 2014); Marina Grishakova and Marie-Laure Ryan (eds), *Intermediality and Storytelling* (Berlin: De Gruyter, 2010); Sarah Bay-Cheng et al. (eds), *Mapping Intermediality in Performance* (Amsterdam: Amsterdam University Press, 2010); Werner Wolf, *Selected Essays on Intermediality, 1992-2014*. Walter Bernhart (ed.) (Leiden: Rodopi, 2017).
4. Irina Rajevski reviews many approaches to intermediality in theory in "Intermediality, Intertextuality, and Remediation: A Literary Perspective on Intermediality." *Intermédialités* 6 (Autumn 2005): 43–64.
5. A further rhetorical use of the "live album" for records recorded "live in the studio" or "live off the floor" signals the extent to which the discursive effect of liveness depends on particular configurations of technological mediation.
6. See, for instance, Carol Vernallis, *Unruly Media: YouTube, Music Video and the New Digital Cinema* (Oxford: Oxford, 2013).
7. Loria, Daniel. "Beyond the Popcorn." *Boxoffice*. New York 153(4) (Apr 2017): 40–3.
8. http://www.latimes.com/entertainment/envelope/cotown/la-fi-ct-cinemark-satellite-20140325-story.html
9. http://www.thewrap.com/dcdc-to-expand-digital-theater-network-by-4000-screens-700-locations-by-2018/
10. http://www.filmjournal.com/features/controlled-kaos-screenvision-revives-event-cinema-new-advertising-partnership
11. See http://www.filmjournal.com/news/screenvision-kaos-connect-and-livexlive-bring-music-festivals-movie-screens

References

Allen, Robert. 2011. "Reimagining the History of the Experience of Cinema in a Post-Moviegoing Age." In *Explorations in New Cinema History: Approaches and Case Studies*, eds Richard Maltby, Daniel Biltereyst, and Philippe Meers. Malden, MA: Blackwell. 41–57.
Auslander, Philip. 2010. *Liveness: Performance in a Mediatized Culture*, 2nd edn. London: Routledge.
Barker, Martin. 2013. *Live to Your Local Cinema: The Remarkable Rise of Livecasting*. Basingstoke: Palgrave.
BBC News Online. 2002a. "Bon Jovi gig seen worldwide." 19 September 2002. <http://news.bbc.co.uk/2/hi/entertainment/2268141.stm> (last accessed 29 November, 2019).
BBC News Online. 2002b. "Digital link brings concerts to cinemas." 17 June 2002, <http://news.bbc.co.uk/2/hi/entertainment/2049887.stm> (last accessed 29 November, 2019).
BBC News Online. 2003. "Bowie to play global cinema gig." 13 August 2003. <http://news.bbc.co.uk/2/hi/entertainment/3147323.stm> (last accessed 29 November, 2019).
Bolter, David J. and Richard Grusin. 1999. *Remediation: Understanding New Media*. Boston, MA: MIT Press.
Casetti, Francesco. 2009. "Filmic Experience." *Screen* 50(1): 56–66.
Crisell, Andrew. 2012. *Liveness and Recording in the Media*. Basingstoke: Palgrave Macmillan.
Elleström, Lars. ed. 2008. *Media Borders, Multimodality and Intermediality*. Basingstoke: Palgrave Macmillan.
Gallagher, William. 2003. "Bowie thrills crowd with cinema gig." BBC News Online, 10 September 2003. <http://news.bbc.co.uk/2/hi/entertainment/3091186.stm> (last accessed 29 November, 2019).
Gubbins, Michael (SampoMedia). 2014. "Audience in the Mind." Château-Renault: Cine-Regio.
McNary, David. 2018. "Film News Roundup: Coldplay Documentary 'Head Full of Dreams' Grosses $3.5 Million in One Day." *Variety*, 15 November 2018. <https://variety.com/2018/film/box-office/film-news-roundup-coldplay-documentary-head-full-of-dreams-grosses-3-5-million-in-one-day-1203030337/> (last accessed 29 November, 2019).
Pine, Joseph and James H. Gilmore. 2011. *The Experience Economy (Updated Edition)*. Boston: Harvard University Press.
Rajewski, Irina. 2005. "Intermediality, Intertextuality, and Remediation: A Literary Perspective on Intermediality." *Intermédialités* 6: 43–64.
Rajewski, Irina. 2008. "Border Talks: The Problematic Status of Media Borders in the Current Debate about Intermediality." In *Media Borders, Multimodality and Intermediality*, ed. Lars Ellestrom. London: Palgrave Macmillan. 51–68.
Sanden, Paul. 2013. *Liveness in Modern Music: Musicians, Technology and the Perception of Performance*. New York: Routledge.
Vernallis, Carol. 2013. *Unruly Media: YouTube, Music Video and the New Digital Cinema*. Oxford: Oxford University Press.

24. DOCUMENTING DEITIES: TOUCH AND K-POP FANDOM ON YOUTUBE

Eric Chalfant and Ali Na

2020 started inauspiciously with the viral spread of a video of Pope Francis slapping the hand of a seemingly overly-aggressive pilgrim. In the video, Pope Francis is walking through St. Peter's Square during a New Year's Eve celebration. Adults and children can be seen taking Francis' hand affectionately as he moves down a line of well-wishers. When Francis turns to walk away, a woman grabs him by the hand and pulls him hard towards herself. Francis' face registers first pain and then anger as he uses his free hand to swat at the woman's hand. The short clip briefly captured public attention and served as a springboard for conversations about Francis' status as a liberal icon, the Catholic Church's gender politics, and a widely-felt pessimism about the state of global affairs. The Pope hand-slap incident demonstrates that where human beings take on qualities of the sacred, the way that they touch and are touched must be carefully negotiated. Touch is powerful. For us, this example demonstrates what we outline as a wider phenomenon of digital negotiation of touch and religious adoration.

Bringing together studies in material religion, fandom, and digital culture, we explore touch and K-pop fan videos on YouTube. We argue that K-pop fans use digital media to celebrate mediated distance from idols while advocating alternative forms of virtual intimacy. First, we outline the ways in which K-pop fandoms intersect in these ideas. Then, we unpack the rhetoric of "stan" as a Western-derived virtual alternative to the Korean concept of 사생팬 (*sasaeng pan*) – a distinction that serves to reinscribe the public/private binary in a virtual space that restricts physical violation of idols' private lives. Third, we analyze comments on YouTube videos devoted to compiling idol responses to instances of inappropriate touch, noting how commenters articulate appropriate forms of touching and intimacy. Fourth, we highlight fancams (직캠/*jig kaem*) as a particular technology for re-establishing intimacy and directness in the absence of physical touching. These virtual technologies work together to create what Claudia Benthien has called "teletactility" – a kind of mediated touch that enables "intimacy without closeness" (Benthien 2002, 221). Finally, we return to the language of the sacred to argue that teletactility, in the context of YouTube fan culture around K-pop, reveals one example of Jean-Luc Nancy's reading of physical retreat as a form of sacred touch.

Documenting Deities: K-pop on the Internet

Whereas a cinematic rockumentary might be best for understanding cultural response to the British Invasion, the Internet is vital for understanding the musical dimension of *Hallyu* (the Korean Wave). Emerging in the late 90s, *Hallyu* refers to the export of Korea in Asia and beyond (Kim and Kim 2011). The digital era has amplified and shifted *Hallyu*'s reach and influence (Lee 2015). The Korean Wave is evolving through a strongly digital technological mediation of Korean substance, through which Korean media industries, platforms, and global fandoms form complex relationships (Ono and Kwon 2013, 200). The digital age is not only the means by which K-pop fans have consumed content, but also the means by which they produce the depiction of their idols. If the Beastie Boys' concert film *Awesome; I Fuckin' Shot That!* (Adam Yauch, USA, 2006) was a novel rewriting of the rockumentary in which the fan perspective was paramount, in 2020, K-pop's primary and ubiquitous documentation is through fans on YouTube and similar online platforms. As Eun-Young Jung explains, fans' uses of social media has created "a *new* dynamic phase in transnational K-pop" (Jung 2015, 74). As illustrated in the massive global popularity of Korean artist Psy's music video on YouTube, "Gangnam Style," transnational fandoms perpetuate interconnected yet divergent fan engagements, which are often embodied forms of reperformance (Na 2017) enabled by platforms like YouTube. As Kent Ono and Jungmin Kwon contend, the interactivity of digital platforms shapes the relationship between K-pop fans and their idols (Ono and Kwon 2013, 208).

This chapter is an attempt to begin to unpack the negotiation of touch in the context of K-pop (contemporary Korean popular music), particularly as it relates to interactive digital media. We are most interested in the entanglements of fan culture, religious framing, and digital interface. The chapter begins from the presumption that there is intellectual value in approaching fan culture around K-pop as a religious or at least quasi-religious phenomenon.

As fan cultures go, K-pop fan culture seems to revel in elevating its celebrities to the status of idols. Importantly, "idol" is the standardized term for musical celebrities trained through South Korean talent agencies. As Sun Jung explains, K-pop idols are carefully manufactured in order to maximize their profitability (Jung 2011).

A number of scholars have examined experiential correlations between religion and fan culture. Fandoms have replicated quasi-religious institutions by, for example, creating works that connect fictional cosmologies with their "real" social worlds, sacralizing elements of culture that correspond with elements of their particular fan culture, forming communities with regularized practices, canonical texts, and hierarchies, developing collective identities analogous to those of active religious groups (Jindra 1994), constructing sacred spaces (Porter 2009) and pilgrimage routes (Bickerdike 2015), reflexively adopting religious and "cultic" language in self-description and subject-formation (Hills 2000; Hills 2002), and elevating celebrity culture to the privileged milieu for religious notions of belonging and recognition (Rojek 2001).

This chapter builds on this work by highlighting the dimension of touch. How might the negotiation of appropriate physical handling take place in the virtual space of digital media? Beyond the symbolic deification of K-pop idols and the ritualization of fan worship, how do K-pop fans negotiate the impulse to touch and be touched by their idols, on the one hand, and the simultaneous need to protect idols from physical violation, on the other? If the sense of touch lends itself well to establishing relationships between idols and their worshippers, how can touch be engendered when the primary avenue of contact is a virtual one?

Stanning: When Your Idols are Out of Reach

Both Merriam-Webster and the Oxford English Dictionary include definitions of "stan." As a noun, a stan is "an overzealous or obsessive fan of a particular celebrity;" as a verb, to stan is to "be an overzealous or obsessive fan of a particular celebrity" (Oxford University Press 2020). The term originates in a 2000 single, "Stan" by Eminem featuring Dido, but only achieved common enough usage to work its way into the dictionaries in 2018. The lyrics take the form of four letters – three written by the obsessed "Stan" and one written by Eminem – documenting the fan's descent into self-destruction. Throughout the song, Stan becomes increasingly enraged by Eminem's failure to respond to his letters, culminating in Stan tying up his pregnant girlfriend in the trunk of his car and then drunkenly driving the car off a bridge. In 2001, rapper Nas used the term as a noun in his song "Ether," rapping, "*You a fan, a phony, a fake, a pussy, a Stan.*" And so "Stan" quickly transitioned from describing a singular fictional character to a category of fan – one with clearly pejorative connotations. While the original character "Stan" is suicidal and murderous, Nas's "Stan" is pathetic and harmless. And as "stan" has achieved more widespread use, it seems to have lost much of its more negative characteristics, serving now primarily as a portmanteau of "stalker" and "fan," with "stalker" understood most often in a playful or ironic sense.

"Stan" raises many of the themes that define contemporary fan culture. Stan exhibits typical fan behaviors in attempting to demonstrate loyalty. For example, he demonstrates expertise by referencing Eminem's underground material, dedication by tattooing Eminem's name across his chest, and empathy by pointing out resonant experiences to Eminem's. However, Stan's primary concern is to *reach* Eminem. Stan is the embodiment of a fan whose obsession remains frustrated by an inability to *be with* the object of his obsession. Thus, as one article in the *Daily Telegraph* notes, "We are all Stan . . . Eminem's stalker classic defined internet fandom" (White 2019).

The idea of unity expressed in this sentiment, however, belies the ways that stanning is bound by the tension arising from accessibility that is increasingly more virtual than actual. Stan's frustration arises not because Eminem is utterly inaccessible, but because he is *just* out of reach. Stan notes instances in which he comes face-to-face with and even talks to Eminem, but these encounters only frustrate Stan because they lack intimacy. "Stan" translates well to the context of digital fandom because it articulates frustrations that arise from fandom today, notably that the Internet spreads K-pop idols through the ubiquity and immediacy of digital media, and yet they are on the other side of the planet, out of reach.

In spite of their violent origins, "stan" and "stanning" have become loaded terms with which fans articulate their relationship to idols, particularly in K-pop fan culture outside of Korea. As perhaps is flagged in relationship to Eminem – a sometimes controversial figure of Black appropriation – this mode of distinguishing fandoms is culturally marked. Building on ideas of racial and gendered power, David C. Oh argues that YouTube often functions as a space of White primacy in postings about K-pop (Oh 2017). Identifying with stanning is not limited to White Americans, but it does present issues for cross-cultural interpretation and identification. In the popular press article "The Eternal Struggle of Being a K-Pop Stan of Color" Isha Aran covers a KCON (since 2012, an annual convention in the US and around the world in celebration of the Korean wave) panel comprised of stans of color, who largely defended K-pop against accusations of racial appropriation and problematic behaviour, citing misunderstanding of the Korean cultural context (Aran 2017).

"Stanning" connotes the dual experience of obsession and distance that comes with being a transnational K-pop fan. "Physically dispersed, but affectively connected, K-pop fans around the world have formed a dynamic community that imagines itself as transcending national boundaries" (Swan 2018,

24.1 Still image from Fancam, Blackpink world tour in LA.

549). Stanning, in turn, provides a vocabulary with which to articulate a transnational community defined by subtler distinctions, as between "hard stans" and "soft stans," "solo stans" and "*akgaes*," and "stans" and "*sasaeng* fans." It is this latter distinction that, by way of contrast, draws out the starkest characterizations of stans as it relates to questions of privacy, intimacy, and physical touch.

In Korea, *sasaeng* fans (사생팬) are something like crowdsourced paparazzi – obsessed fans who devote their lives to gaining access to their idols' private lives. The term *sasaeng* combines the words *sa* (사), meaning "private", and *saeng* (생), meaning "life." *Pan* is the transliteration of the English loan word "fan." While this phenomenon predates *Hallyu* in the digital age, social media and digital culture have amplified its reach and scope. "*Sasaeng* fans are identified by a need to seek out their idols' exact schedules in order to be as close to them as possible, as often as possible" (Williams and Ho 2016, 82–5). And so *sasaeng* fans use digital media to acquire information and coordinate with one another in order to encounter celebrities at their homes and steal (and often sell) belongings, personal information, and even bodily fluids and detritus. Much of the media narrative around *sasaeng* fans is negatively directed at girls and women aged 13–22, and repeatedly the identified problem with *sasaeng* fans is wanting to touch too much, desiring to be too close, and ultimately making themselves too proximate to their idols.

Notably, the same level of attention has not been paid to the prevalence of 삼촌팬 (*samchon pan*) in Korean fandom. This translates to "uncle fan," with *samchon* more specifically referring to one's parent's brother. These fans are often aged in respect to the title, to the point that they are old enough to be the K-pop singer's uncle. So, while the emphasis on *sasaeng* fans has been on young women who adore male Korean celebrity figures, *samchon* fans are often unacknowledged or considered harmless. For Yeran Kim, this figuration is a way of making their obsessions normalized, "with the pretentious reformulation of the male gaze into an uncle's familial support, the male consumption of girl bodies becomes relieved of the predictable blame for pedophiliac abnormality" (Kim 2011, 340).

Many K-pop fans, including transnational stans, villainize and otherize *sasaeng* fans. Take, for example, a blog post describing the differences between "hard stans" and "*sasaeng* fans": "First, I'd like to say that 'sasaeng fans' don't exist. Simply because sasaengs are not fans. Sasaengs consider themselves as fans but they invade idols' privacy! They are REAL stalkers" ([Koigokoro [h] • #IRD | Jasla :cupid:] 2018). Respect for privacy is framed here as the issue that separates fans from non-fans, and thus stans from *sasaeng* fans. Implicit in the characterization of *sasaeng* fans as "REAL stalkers," is that stans are something akin to virtual stalkers. The connotations of stalking that accompany stanning are framed as harmless to the extent that they respect idols' privacy, but what is the notion of privacy in play here? The blog post clarifies: "What do they do exactly? They push idols. They rip off their clothes. They touch them without their consent. They run after them" ([Koigokoro [h] • #IRD | Jasla :cupid:] 2018). Each of these examples appeals to a sense of physical violation. It is precisely when fans violate an idol's physical space that they cease being fans. That the idol's privacy is violated first and foremost by touch implicitly posits virtual stalking as a harmless alternative. This contrast becomes clearer when we consider how K-pop fans on digital media react to instances of physical violation that might constitute *sasaeng*.

Don't Touch Them: Reacting to Physical Violation

One of the most salient genres of YouTube video in the context of K-pop fan culture is video compilations of K-pop idols reacting to overzealous fans. K-pop fandom online does more than illustrate how fans come to know their idols. As a mode of collective fandom, Yeran Kim argues that "K-Pop reaction videos show how the emergent culture of K-Pop has been able to draw attention of a globally networked 'attention economy' in the intertwined dynamics of active/reactive, production/consumption in visual practices" (Kim 2015, 334). Kim's insights are deeply important in understanding the currencies of how fandom contributes to the fame of the idol. Where Kim's focus is on visuality, however, we turn to the question of the haptic in order to explore the materiality of seemingly immaterial worlds.

These videos compile moments when the typical boundaries between idols and fans are violated – often when fans break through security measures and physically touch idols. These moments are fraught with the danger that they represent, and more importantly because they involve a breakdown in the symbolic order that exists between idols and fans. Just as with the Pope Francis incident, moments of inappropriate contact can expose implicit assumptions about how idols and their worshippers are supposed to act, and reactions to these moments show K-pop fans rewriting implicit codes of acceptable and unacceptable touch. Exploring these reactions can help highlight the feedback loops that shape digital fan culture. As Joseph M. Reagle, Jr. argues, online commentary can serve as a mirror that helps elucidate prevalent social values: "[O]ur reaction to things (be it a comment, an answer to a question, or the liking of a photo) has come to be seen as a way in which we define ourselves. And the way that others react to those reactions (such as by retweeting them) are seen as a valuation of those selves" (Reagle 2015, 18). Comments on these compilation videos, revealing unscripted moments in which fans violate taboos around touching and approaching idols, are used to both rewrite and reinforce notions of sacrality and humanity around K-pop idols.

A video called "Reaction K-pop Idols With Rude Fans" (Knet Entertainment 2017) has, as of February 2020, over 3,000,000 views and 5,700 comments, providing a significant snapshot of how K-pop fans on YouTube negotiate questions of appropriate fan behavior. In the ten-minute compilation, fans exhibit behavior including excessively expressing their love at fan meet-ups, throwing objects at performers at concerts, climbing on stage and hugging or pulling performers, chasing idols outside of venues, and crowding idols in public places. The most popular comments frame these behaviors as violations of appropriate fan conduct, and celebrate both idols and fans who touch appropriately. One popular comment thread celebrates a fan who can be heard yelling "Don't touch them" while other fans are chasing BTS member Jungkook. The commenter writes, "the camera girl screams don't touch them that's a true army calm protective" ([Bts_Jeongguk] 2019). Other popular comments echo this sentiment: "'Don't Touch Them' That Fangirl Are So Nice " ([Arcelia Chan] 2019); "'Don't touch them' that's the real ARMY" ([Muhammad Ridwan] 2020). At the same time, commenters celebrate the idol Kwon Ji-Yong, stage name G-Dragon, for not pushing away a fan who climbed on stage and hugged him, seen at the 4:28 mark: "I respect jiyong so much/He doesnt push that fan away/He just let her hug him" ([I know i am stupid because write a hatefull comment] 2019); "GD just let her hug him he's so sweet and respectful" ([I have too many biases] 2019).

These comments create boundary markers for not only how to touch but how to engage idols. The dynamic between YouTube K-pop fans, represented by the video comments, and the "in real life" (IRL) fans depicted in the video takes on an extra dimension when we consider the banal fact of physical avail-

24.2 Screenshot from viral YouTube Fancam.

ability. It is obvious but nonetheless important to note that the rude fans have the opportunity to be discourteous because they are in the same physical space as the idols, while the commenting fans are simply unable to violate the idols' space. Given the English-language postings, we can presume they are primarily not Korean natives. Accordingly, the YouTube fans consider the factor of the physical availability of the idols in ways that draw a connection between being physically near to the idols and engaging in appropriate touching (or non-touching). For example: "While a lot of fans can't get to see concerts, these really lucky people are treating their 'idols' like trash" ([RunnyPanda] 2018).

The replies to [RunnyPanda]'s top-level response reflect varying degrees of awareness that virtual fandom affords a different kind of reverence for K-pop idols – one that IRL fans are shown to violate: "it confuses me sm when they go and get to see 'em and treat 'em bad while us international fans are wishing that they have a concert near us (Which we usually don't have enough money for anyway 😭😭)" ([Hevelyn] 2019); "Yep, I just get to see my idols across my phone screen" ([RelyneSimple] 2019); "ye some may not have the chance to see them live ever just on a phone" ([Diamond Fury Gacha] 2019). These K-pop stans who can only touch through the digital interface thus articulate their own inability to reach their idols as the more appropriate form of intimacy.

Hence, transnational fans have an incentive to valorize new forms of touch by virtue of their physical distance from Korean Idols. As Marleen de Witte summarizes, "touch is a powerful medium of religious communication" in part because "of all the senses, we take touch to be the one least prone to trickery, the most direct of all senses, providing us with unmediated access to the real" (de Witte 2011, 149). This directness makes hapticity a particularly potent form of religious experience; where the reverent caress may enhance the sacred/profane relationship between devotee and object of devotion, inappropriate touching threatens to destroy that very relationship. For YouTube K-pop stans, idols maintain their sacred status by being unavailable to physical touch. K-pop fans transform the fact that they cannot touch into a proscription to not *want* to touch. They implicitly know the lesson of *Noli me tangere*: "[Y]ou are unable to hold or retain anything, and that is precisely what you must love and know. That is what there is of a knowledge and a love. Love what escapes you. Love the one who goes. Love that he goes" (Nancy 2008, 37).

FanCams: Touching at a Distance

If religion is at its core mediation between the sacred and the profane, media technologies in turn provide the raw material for the negotiation of appropriate forms of intimacy between the two. So it is with K-pop fans and their idols. K-pop fans who cannot or will not reach their idols in the "real world" use digital media to touch at a distance. Borrowing Claudia Benthien's formulation, we can say that K-pop fans use digital media to cultivate teletactility, by which "the sensual experience of closeness and intimacy through touch is now being linked with anonymity and physical distance" (Benthien 2002, 221). One of the most popular tools that K-pop fans have at their disposal for enabling teletactility is the Fancam.

Fancams are short, usually fan-shot video clips of K-pop idols performing on stage. In a basic sense, Fancams are any video of a K-pop performance filmed from the fan's perspective. One of the most popular early Fancams was a roughly three-minute video of a performance by EXID posted to YouTube in 2014 ([pharkil] 2014). The video reached over 30,000,000 views and significantly boosted EXID's careers (Elaine 2015). By 2018, Fancams had developed into a genre of short video clip designed to be deployed in memetic fashion. Today, Fancams are used ubiquitously by K-pop fans, often embedded in reply chains on Twitter and other social media platforms as thirty-second GIFs or videos.

Fancamming has had a tangible effect on the K-pop industry. Management companies have begun tailoring performances, music videos, and even groups to appeal to the aesthetic of Fancamming – a process that dovetails with Korea's enthusiastic development of digital culture. In addition to having the amongst the highest broadband household penetration in the world, "Korean internet culture has evolved in a way that elevates the notion of 'active user' to the highest degree. Koreans' internet use may be deemed exceptionally active" from comments to uploads (Im et al. 2010).

One of the most important aspects of Fancams is that they depict idols from the perspective of a fan who is physically present at the performance. Fan presence verifies the authenticity of the experience, which itself transcends the very notion of being there. That is, being there is less desirable than the experience of touching through Fancamming. The English term "Fancam" corresponds to the Korean 직캠 (*jig kaem*), meaning "direct cam." In fact, 직캠 appears to be an abbreviation of the longer phrase 직접 찍은 카메라 (*jigjeop jjigeun kamera*), meaning "taken by a camera first-hand." The word 직접 (*jigjeop*) is commonly translated as "in person" or "first-hand," and carries the semantic connotation of haptic immediacy. Fancams provide a virtual representation of direct perception, including the ability to focus on particular idols. While official videos and press releases tend to provide overviews of K-pop groups with time devoted to each member, Fancams very often focus on one particular member of a K-pop group. Thus, Fancams appeal to fans who have an affinity for a specific idol, allowing fans the freedom to focus their (virtual) attention to a degree closer to that of an in-person fan.

A handful of scholars working at the intersection of media studies, affect studies, and religious studies have begun to unearth how media artefacts that draw attention to their own noise can generate a kind of virtual tactility that can enhance religious experience (Chalfant 2018). Anderson Blanton, for example, has highlighted how Appalachian Pentecostals have used radio static to cultivate the feeling of touching the Holy Spirit among radio listeners/feelers (Blanton 2015). Televangelists like Oral Roberts used to have viewers place their hands on their television set so that they could feel God's healing power through the television screen – an effect that relied on the fuzz that used to emanate from old television screens. Every media technology carries its own unique kind of noise, whether in the form of material interference or irrelevant content, and media artefacts contain varying degrees of noise. Something as simple as a book may have dog-eared pages, coffee stains, and typographical errors. These examples of noise are not irrelevant – they make the book feel real, and they shape how the reader understands the story.

Fancams are a component of K-pop fan culture that revels in noise. Fancams often include the noise that is filtered out of cinematic documentation – the screaming of fans that drowns out the audio of the performance, the backs of heads and bodies that obstruct the view of the idols, and the shaky camerawork and blurring that comes from less-than-ideal recording environment, equipment, and videographer. Fancams provide a form of perception that feels like a more authentic replication of live experience by virtue of offering a less polished media artefact. Fancam videos offer more of the affects that signal direct experience in the form of noise. Thus, in the absence of being able to physically approach their idols, K-pop fans use Fancams as a way to touch at a distance – to replicate the kind of tactility and physical experience that comes with inhabiting the same space as an idol as well as a community of embodied peers.

Conclusion

In the context of K-pop fan culture on YouTube and other digital media, fans who are largely unable to achieve direct physical contact with the idols that they worship (whether we use this term in a strict or loose sense) instead develop and cultivate the haptic dimensions of virtual intimacy in order to touch K-pop idols at a distance. K-pop fans develop a sense of teletactility towards their idols in part by: articulating "stanning" as a safe form of virtual stalking that celebrates intimacy while remaining keenly aware of idols' physical unavailability; using *sasaeng* fans and depictions of inappropriate physical contact as a foil against which to consecrate physical separation and privilege virtual fandom as the proper mode of intimacy, and; circulating Fancams as a mode of perception that replicates virtual hapticity through noise and reinscribes direct contact into digital technology. These practices, perhaps contrary to intuition, should not be understood as attempts merely to replace "real" intimacy with a virtual or vicarious simulation of intimacy. Rather, the kind of teletactility developed by K-pop fans may play a positive role in constructing relationships of intimacy between fans and idols. As Nancy theorizes, the interplay of touching and separation is the hallmark of a particularly intimate experience of sacrality: "Love and truth touch by pushing away: they force the retreat of those whom they reach, for their very onset reveals, in the touch itself, that they are out of reach. It is in being unattainable that they touch us, even seize us" (Nancy 2008, 37). Virtual K-pop fans, like Nancy's Mary Magdalene, become saints *par excellence* because they hold to the point "where the touch of sense is identical to its retreat" (Nancy 2008, 42–3). This is to suggest in turn that digital media, by virtue of its virtuality, is perhaps uniquely able to engender the kind of teletactility through which fan cultures like that of K-pop can articulate and cultivate profound senses of devotion and intimacy.

References

Aran, Isha. 2017. "The Eternal Struggle of Being a K-Pop Stan of Color." *SplinterNews*. <https://splinternews.com/the-eternal-struggle-of-being-a-k-pop-stan-of-color-1796431795> (last accessed 1 February, 2020).
[Arcelia Chan] 2019. Re: *Reaction K-pop Idols With Rude Fans | KNET*. [Video File]. Knet Entertainment, June 22, 2017. <https://youtu.be/e6kO0hlY4_8> (last accessed 1 February, 2020).
Bickerdike, Jennifer Otter. 2015. *The Secular Religion of Fandom: Pop Culture Pilgrim*. Newbury Park, CA: SAGE Publishing.
Blanton, Anderson. 2015. *Hittin' the Prayer Bones: Materiality of Spirit in the Pentecostal South*. Chapel Hill, NC: The University of North Carolina Press.
[Bts_Jeongguk] 2019. Re: *Reaction K-pop Idols With Rude Fans | KNET*. [Video File]. Knet Entertainment, June 22, 2017. <https://youtu.be/e6kO0hlY4_8> (last accessed 1 February, 2020).
Chalfant, Eric. 2018. "Everything is Noise: Don Delillo's *White Noise* and the Affectivity of Media, Religion, and Divination." *Journal of Religion, Media, and Digital Culture* 7(2): 158–74.
de Witte, Marleen. 2011. "Touch." *Material Religion* 7(1): 148–55.
[Diamond Fury Gacha] 2019. Re: [RunnyPanda] Re: *Reaction K-pop Idols With Rude Fans | KNET*. [Video File]. Knet Entertainment, June 22, 2017. <https://youtu.be/e6kO0hlY4_8> (last accessed 1 February, 2020).
Elaine. 2015. "EXID Goes From Down to Up with 'Up & Down'." *SeoulBeats* January 9. <http://seoulbeats.com/2015/01/exid-goes/> (last accessed 1 February, 2020).
Eminem featuring Dido. 2000. "Stan." *The Marshall Mathers LP*. Aftermath/Shady/Interscope Records.
[Hevelyn] 2019. Re: [RunnyPanda] Re: *Reaction K-pop Idols With Rude Fans | KNET*. [Video File]. Knet Entertainment, June 22, 2017. <https://youtu.be/e6kO0hlY4_8> (last accessed 1 February, 2020).
Hills, Matt (2002), *Fan Cultures*, New York, NY: Routledge.
Hills, Matthew (2000), 'Media Fandom, Neoreligiosity, and Cult(ural) Studies,' *Velvet Light Trap* 46, pp. 133–48.
[I have too many biases] 2019. Re: *Reaction K-pop Idols With Rude Fans | KNET*. [Video File]. Knet Entertainment, June 22, 2017. <https://youtu.be/e6kO0hlY4_8> (last accessed 1 February, 2020).
[I know i am stupid because write a hatefull comment] 2019. Re: *Reaction K-pop Idols With Rude Fans | KNET*. [Video File]. Knet Entertainment, June 22, 2017. <https://youtu.be/e6kO0hlY4_8> (last accessed 1 February, 2020).
Im, Yung-Ho, Eun-mee Kim, Kyungmo Kim, and Yeran Kim. 2010. "The Emerging Mediascape, Same Old Theories? A Case Study of Online News Diffusion in Korea." *New Media & Society* 13(4): 605–25.
Jindra, Michael. 1994. "Star Trek Fandom as a Religious Phenomenon." *Sociology of Religion* 55(1): 27–51.
Jung, Eun-Young. 2015. "New Wave Formations: K-Pop Idols, Social Media, and the Remaking of the Korean Wave." In *Hallyu 2.0: The Korean Wave in the Age of Social Media*, eds Sangjoon Lee and Abé Mark Nornes. Ann Arbor, MI: University of Michigan Press. 73–89.
Jung, Sun. 2011. *Korean Masculinities and Transnational Consumption: Yonsama, Rain, Oldboy, K-pop idols*. Hong Kong: Hong Kong University Press.
Kim, Do Kyun and Min-Sun Kim. 2011. *Hallyu: Influence of Korean Popular Culture in Asia and Beyond*. Seoul: Seoul National University Press.

Kim, Yeran. 2011. "Idol Republic: The Global Emergence of Girl Industries and the Commercialization of Girl Bodies." *Journal of Gender Studies* 20(4): 333–45.

Kim, Yeran. 2015. "Globalization of the Privatized Self-Image: The Reaction Video and its Attention Economy on YouTube." In *Routledge Handbook of New Media in Asia*, eds Larissa Hjorth and Olivia Khoo.New York: Routledge. 333–42.

Knet Entertainment. 2017. "Reaction K-pop Idols With Rude Fans | KNET." [Video File]. <https://youtu.be/e6kO0hlY4_8> (last accessed 1 February, 2020).

[Koigokoro [h] • #IRD | Jasla :cupid:] 2018. "Sasaeng ≠ hard stan! Important message." *Amino*. <https://aminoapps.com/c/btsarmy/page/blog/sasaeng-hard-stan-important-message/r0wq_402feuLBMB7E0WEeekPgN52vK4eqjm> (last accessed 1 February, 2020).

Lee, Sangjoon. 2015. "Introduction: A Decade of Hallyu Scholarship: Toward a New Direction in Hallyu 2.0." In *Hallyu 2.0: The Korean Wave in the Age of Social Media*, eds Sangjoon Lee and Abé Mark Nornes. *Hallyu 2.0: The Korean Wave in the Age of Social Media*. Ann Arbor, MI: University of Michigan Press. 1-28.

[Muhammad Ridwan] 2020. Re: *Reaction K-pop Idols With Rude Fans | KNET*. [Video File] Knet Entertainment, June 22, 2017. <https://youtu.be/e6kO0hlY4_8> (last accessed 1 February, 2020).

Nancy, Jean Luc. 2008. *Noli me tangere: On the Raising of the Body*. trans. Sarah Clift, Pascale-Anne Brault, and Michael Naas. New York, NY: Fordham University Press.

Na, Ali. 2017. "Gangnam Eth(n)ic: The Transnational Politics of YouTube Reperformances." *Liminalities: A Journal of Performance Studies* 13(3): 1–17.

Nas. 2001. "Ether." *Stillmatic*. Ill Will/Columbia Records.

Ono, Kent A. and Jungmin Kwon. 2013. "Re-worlding Culture: YouTube as K-pop Interlocutor." In *The Korean Wave: Korean Media Go Global*, ed. Youna Kim. New York: Routledge. 199–214.

Oxford University Press. 2020. "Stan." *Lexico.com*. (last accessed 9 February, 2020).

[pharkil] 2014. *[직캠/Fancam] 141008 EXID(하니) 위아래 @ 파주 한마음 위문공연*. [Video File] October 9. <https://youtu.be/cmKuGxb23z0> (last accessed 1 February, 2020).

Porter, Jennifer. 2009. "Implicit Religion in Popular Culture: The Religious Dimensions of Fan Communities." *Implicit Religion* 12(3): 271–80.

Reagle Jr., Joseph M. 2015. *Reading the Comments: Likers, Haters, and Manipulators at the Bottom of the Web*. Cambridge, MA: MIT Press.

[RelyneSimple] 2019. Re: [RunnyPanda] Re: *Reaction K-pop Idols With Rude Fans | KNET*. [Video File] Knet Entertainment, June 22, 2017. <https://youtu.be/e6kO0hlY4_8> (last accessed 1 February, 2020).

Rojek, Chris. 2001. *Celebrity*. London: Reaktion Books.

Rolli, Bryan. 2019. "BTS Set Largest Worldwide Event Cinema Release With Love Yourself In Seoul." *Forbes*., <https://www.forbes.com/sites/bryanrolli/2019/01/16/bts-set-largest-worldwide-event-cinema-release-with-love-yourself-in-seoul/#1ca6ba2b6fca> (last accessed 1 February, 2020).

[RunnyPanda] 2018. Re: *Reaction K-pop Idols With Rude Fans | KNET*. [Video File] Knet Entertainment, June 22, 2017. <https://youtu.be/e6kO0hlY4_8> (last accessed 1 February, 2020).

Swan, Anna Lee. 2018."ransnational Identities and Feeling in Fandom: Place and Embodiment in K-pop Fan Reaction Videos." *Communication, Culture and Critique* 11(4): 548–65.

[ThatSuaveRaptor] 2020. Re: *Indignant Pope Francis Slaps Woman's Hand to Free Himself at New Year's Eve Gathering* [Video File]. *The Guardian*, 31 December 2019. <https://www.youtube.com/watch?v=3WySwhj2SwE> (last accessed 1 February, 2020).

White, Adam. 2019. "We Are All Stan: How Eminem's Stalker Classic Defined Internet Fandom." *The Telegraph*, April 26.

Williams, J. Patrick and Samantha Xiang Xin Ho. 2016. "'Sasaengpaen' or K-pop Fan? Singapore Youths, Authentic Identities, and Asian Media Fandom." *Deviant Behavior* 37(1): 81–94.

25. RITUAL IN TRANSFIGURED TIME

Greil Marcus

Bruce Conner's film *The White Rose* documents the removal of Jay DeFeo's painting *The Rose* from her San Francisco apartment in the fall of 1965; the film was finished in 1967. The painting itself was never finished. Begun in 1957, by 1965 it had taken over DeFeo's life. Like a mutating child, it had grown to a size of more than 1.0 feet by eight feet; it held nearly 2,000 pounds of paint. First shown in 1969, at the Pasadena Art Museum, it soon disappeared, encased behind a wall in the San Francisco Art Institute for more than two decades. In 1995, six years after DeFeo's death, it was cut out, restored, and toured the country as part of the Whitney Museum of American Art's exhibition "Beat Culture and the New America: 1950–1965." Conner's film is one day in seven minutes.

There are different narratives contained and implied in the film – different ways of telling a story, framing the picture, both the painting and the him – different genres into which the film moves the painting, different genres into which the painting moves the film.

There is the story of the story: the prosaic story, about a painting that must be removed from a building because the tenants are being evicted, or even the art history story, about a painter obsessed with her work. These stories are almost missing from Conner's film. You see something more elevated, or more sensationalistic; something more religious, and something more like a movie. There is the sacramental story. There is the tale of a child abandoned by its mother or of the child taken from its unfit mother and given to someone else. There is the monster movie. And there is the murder mystery.

With a hole already cut in the wall of her apartment – the only way the painting could be taken out – the removal took seven hours, with Bekins workmen tipping the painting away from the bay window it almost completely covered, boxing the sides, wrapping it, boxing it top and bottom, lowering it by forklift to a van on the street. Those seven hours are in Conner's seven minutes – even if at one point he had to run across town for more film. With the cuts in the movie coming when you don't expect them, no matter how attuned you have become to Conner's pace or his anti-rhythms, the film seems long and slow – as if, somehow, at the end the cavalry will ride in and return the child to its mother.

"It became the only thing in her life," Conner said in 1992. "That was her reality. The room had no electricity; when the sun came up, the room was illuminated, she worked on the painting ... She wanted a canvas that would fit exactly the size of the bay [window] ... The light went away, she left the room. The room was like a temple, as the film tries to show ... but they had to leave. They were evicted, because Jay had gotten too crazy. The neighbors were complaining. There was a dry cleaners down below, and they would see the telephone from her apartment, hanging down like a fishing line, with messages written on it – and her talking at them."

Conner describes visiting DeFeo in the aftermath of the removal: "She could not finish a constructive sentence. The subjects and the active words did not function. She talked for 20 minutes, and I could not understand anything she was saying. The only direct thing she said was, 'Bruce, you're going to have to go.' But she was moving me around, asking me to go over here – I was a part of this environment. I was to hear what was happening in her consciousness; I was a part of her. Finally she said, 'I want you to come over here,' and she took a paintbrush, and she painted a white line vertically on both of the round lenses [of my glasses], and horizontally. And then she gently led me out the door and out onto the street."

In *The White Rose* countless of Conner's images are stilled, like a secret almost told, then snatched away. You can't tell how he is telling the story, or even if, as he does so, there is any movement at all, only that you have been taken from one place to another, or one image to another. The movie is not only shot as a silent, a lot of it is shot almost as a collage of still photos – and like the pictures of a crime-scene photographer, they take you into DeFeo's studio as if you're going where you don't belong.

In her groundbreaking book *Secret Exhibition: Six California Artists of the Cold War Era* (1990), Rebecca Solnit writes about Conner, DeFeo, Wally Hedrick (in 1965, DeFeo's husband), Wallace Berman, George Herms, Jess, and others as "a hermetic tribe of icon makers" – and the archaic ring of the word "icon" sets their work, and The Rose in particular, in the realm of the primitive, the primeval. In *The White Rose* you can see this in the quick images that describe an entry into DeFeo's apartment. Everything seems to have piled up in corners, as if the place is an ancient ruin, just discovered, the filmmaker part of the archeological crew, entering a place no one has inhabited for lifetimes, documenting dead plants, rotting fixtures, and encrusted paint cans that look like the 15,000-year-old oil lamp found in the cave of Lascaux.

Conner describes the construction of the ruin: "As she did the painting, she would take the paint off – this combination of black paint with white and red. The footstool that she worked on standing up – was covered with this. The entire place was the same color, and the floor was covered. She'd take off lumps of this paint, and she'd throw it on the floor."

Solnit speaks of the work of her artists as more "ritual" than art – an enactment of a truth, rather than the making of an object that carries its own authority. She focuses on the opening shots of Conner's movie, with "the Bekins moving men milling around on the sidewalk . . . looking like doctors or monks." She describes how Conner shows the painting "lit from either side like a shrine." As the movers begin to take it down "it blocks out more and more light, until the men become silhouettes and only a halo of light surrounds it, like the sun in eclipse. It descends like Christ from the cross."

Here is the sacrament, the ritual, the enactment. In those few words Solnit catches the way the movie calls up, or calls upon, both the Pagan and the Christian, or the Paganism remaining in Christian ritual – with the workers as monks worshipping a sun god, or with the dead Christmas tree that Conner shows DeFeo carrying to the hole in her wall as if to perform some Druidic ceremony that nobody consciously remembers and no one has really forgotten.

There is also a suggestion – maybe one of the stories the movie tells in spite of itself, either because it automatically reaches for certain kinds of stories, or because, watching the film, you bring certain kinds of stories to it – of the hero and the dragon, the villagers preyed upon by the monster for generations, finally triumphing over it. When the painting is standing up against the wall it looks diseased and ugly and out of control; when it's on the floor it looks smaller, as if the monster has been killed. It's wrapped up as if in a shroud, for burial.

"When I went in there to look at the painting and talk to her about filming it," Conner says, "she left me there for about an hour and a half . . . The domination of this event, the entire room, was so strong, and so calming. But the floor – because this paint didn't dry – had a skin. It would dry on the surface – but she was taking out lumps an inch thick. You walk on [the floor] – and it was like walking over flesh."

Ritual means something that has happened over and over again – something that must be enacted in order to secure peace, power, redemption, or the survival of humankind itself. In the sacramental narrative, this event, taking place thousands and thousands of years ago in a cave in San Francisco, is a version of all human history.

But I think the film as a depiction of a rite, a ritual, a funeral, is only the first thing you see. So short, but containing so much, moving so fast, with such a sense of slowness, of resistance to its own ending, the movie demands to be shown again and again and each time you see it, the movie may become less iconic and more ordinary.

Conner is an artist of superhuman patience: an artist drawn to both repetition and reduction, to repeating the tiniest movement, whether moving a pen or editing film, again and again and again, with variations no one else could track one from the other, producing a kind of movement that can't be broken down. In *The White Rose*, the cutting of the film piles split-split-split seconds on top of one another, so that in various places each movement in the film is less a cut from one thing to another than an accumulation of cuts, of part images, of nearly subliminal part images, and this completely scrambles any sense of real time. Sometimes the pileup of images creates a sense of no-time, of time suspended, and this is where the sense of religious ritual takes shape. But when the camera eye is moving into the apartment, it seems to go very fast. Here you get a sense of homicide detectives entering the apartment in double-time – something has happened, they don't know exactly what has happened, and they have to nail down the crime scene before it's too late.

And then, in Conner's film, you see the detectives. And you can begin to see other movies – especially two of Don Siegel's movies: *Invasion of the Body Snatchers*, from 1956, and *The Lineup*, from 1958.

Conner's use of Miles Davis's 1959 "Concerto de Aranjuez," from *Sketches of Spain*, is a big part of this; this is *film noir* music, American and French. The muted, drifting opening fanfare, Davis's trumpet and Gil Evans's severe arrangement, locks *The White Rose* into a whole series of crime movies, from the first modern jazz scores snaking through post-war B-pictures to Davis's own unsettling soundtrack for Louis Malle's 1958 *Elevator to the Scaffold* and on to David Amram's soundtrack for *The Manchurian Candidate* in 1962.

The music lets you see gestures of the sinister in Conner's found, accumulating images. In the slow movements of the Bekins workers, and especially in the laconic postures of the Bekins supervisors in business suits, you can begin to see the Bekins men as pods, taking away a last symbol of creativity and anarchy, of the human spirit – and you can see DeFeo, lying on the boxed painting as if it were a bed, as Dana Wynter, from *Invasion of the Body Snatchers*, the last human woman in Santa Rosa, waiting for the inevitable change: "I was apprehensive," Conner says of finding DeFeo sitting in the window hole the painting had gone through, her legs swinging in the air like those of a child, "that she was going to go out that window with it."

The Lineup seems to arrive in the middle of *The White Rose* – it's just a moment, but everything in *The White Rose* is a moment, an instant cut up into parts, and this moment is perhaps the center of the film's gravity. You see four big, imposing Bekins men in suits standing over the boxed, wrapped painting, discussing what to do, what line to follow, and you get the queer feeling you're watching policemen discussing leads in a murder investigation.

In *The Lineup* – a black-and-white picture set in San Francisco, a film that, like *The White Rose*, makes the whites and grays of small buildings, the shades that dominate the city, visually a subject in itself – there are fabulous shots of a great, half-circle window high in the police department, opening into a perfect view of downtown and the Bay Bridge. There's Dancer, a psychopathic hired killer played by Eli Wallach, and his minder, Julian, played by the cadaverous Robert Keith, who's making a book out of the last words of all the people Dancer kills. And circling around this little engine of melodrama there are the detectives: big, beefy, stolid, clueless men, played by forgotten actors, standing in boxy suits, speaking in monotones, moving slowly – in exactly the same postures of responsibility and uncertainty that possess the Bekins' bosses.

They have the corpse; they don't have a motive. They know how to collect the evidence; the body is taken away in the Bekins' hearse. Now all they have to do is solve the case.

INDEX

#MeToo movement, 93, 109
1+1/Sympathy for the Devil (UK, 1968), 69
1991: The Year Punk Broke (USA, 1992), 11
20,000 Days on Earth (UK, 2014), 14, 198, 200, 206–9, 210

A Band Called Death (USA, 2012), 116
A Chorus Line (USA, 1985), 101
A Hard Day's Night (UK/USA, 1964), 7, 71
À soir on fait peur au monde (Canada, 1969), 251, 254–5
A Star is Born (USA, 1976), 304, 307, 308–11, 312n
A Star is Born (USA, 2018), 308
A Year and a Half in the Life of Metallica (USA, 1992), 128, 129
ABBA, 9
ABBA: The Movie (Sweden, 1977), 9
ABC (American Broadcasting Company), 28, 77
Achurra, Tomás, 233
Adler, Lou, 39, 44, 47
Agamben, Giorgio, 294–5, 297, 301
Al Unísono (Chile, 2007), 232, 235
All Things Must Pass: The Rise and Fall of Tower Records (USA, 2015), 10
All Tomorrow's Parties (UK, 2009), 203
Allende, Salvadore, 226, 227
Almost Famous (USA, 2000), 304–5
Altamont Speedway Free Festival, 92
Altman, Rick, 240
Altman, Robert, 311
Álvarez, Santiago, 68
American Bandstand (USA, 1952–1989), 4, 25, 28, 29
American Graffiti (USA, 1973), 306
American Idol (USA, 2002–), 28
American Utopia (USA, 2020), 2
Amram, David, 347
Amy (UK, 2015), 9, 86, 126

anarcho-punk, 15, 263–74
Andéchaga, Osvaldo, 247
Anderson, Benedict, 252
Anderson, Laurie, 15, 291–302
Anderson, Lindsay, 8
Animal en Extinción (Chile, 2014), 232
Anka, Paul, 6–8, 10
Anti-Nazi League, 182
Anthrax, 322
Anvil!: The Story of Anvil (USA, 2008), 11
Apple Corps, 69, 71, 73
Apted, Michael, 304
Aqqiaruq, Derek, 12
Arctic Superstar (Norway, 2016), 12
Argentina, 239–48
Argentina Beat (Argentina, 2006), 248n
Ashby, Hal, 312n
Ashley, Clarence, 22
Auslander, Philip, 319
Awesome; I Fuckin' Shot That! (USA, 2006), 9, 331
Ayala, Fernando, 242
Aykroyd, Dan, 73

Bad Seeds, The, 198–203, 205–6, 209
Badham, John, 307
Baez, Joan, 8, 69, 143, 146
Baichwal, Jennifer, 64, 74
Bailet, Mildrid, 12
Baker, Michael Brendan, 6, 8, 9, 10, 13, 126, 188, 192–3, 201, 203, 252
Baker, Rob, 74
Bale, Christian, 147
Baldwin, Craig, 10
Band, The, 74, 126, 142, 144, 213, 218
Band Aid, 100
Banderas del Publo, Las (Chile, 1964), 226
Bar-Lev, Amir, 185–92, 195–7
Baraka, Amiri, 69
Barclay, Michael, 75
Barker, Martin, 323

Barlow, John Parry, 190
Barrett, Elizabeth, 215
Barthes, Roland, 158, 164, 298
Bates, Alan, 308
Battalla de Chile, La (Chile, 1974–9), 226–7, 228, 234
Bazin, André, 51
BBC, 101, 314, 324
Beach Boys, The, 11
Beastie Boys, The, 9, 331
Beatlemania, 7,11
Beatles, The, 11, 30, 64, 65, 69–73, 118, 126, 149, 163, 165, 166, 304, 305
Beatles Anthology, The (UK, 1995), 65, 70
Beatles: Get Back, The (UK/New Zealand, 2021), 64, 73
Beatles: Rock Band, The, 203
Beattie, Keith, 203, 253
Beatty, Warren, 103, 106
bebop, 5, 67
Beckett, Samuel, 297
Bed Peace (UK, 1969), 10
Beguiled, The (USA, 1971), 214
Benjamin, Walter, 164
Bennett, Jane, 294
Benthien, Claudia, 331, 338
Berlinger, Joe, 14, 126, 203, 212
Berninger, Matt, 127, 128, 134–9
Berninger, Tom, 14, 126, 127, 128, 134–9, 212
Bernstein in Israel (USA, 1957), 4
Berry, Chuck, 5
Biafra, Jello, 274
Big Four: Live from Sofia, Bulgaria, The (USA, 2010), 322
Birthday Party, The, 199, 201, 208
Björk, 266
Black Girl (France/Senegal, 1966), 170
Black Keys, The, 143
Black Lives Matter, 68
Black Panthers, 281, 284
Black Sabbath, 9
Blanchett, Cate, 150
Blanchot, Maurice, 299–300
Bland, Edward O., 13, 64, 66, 68
Bloomfield, Mike, 43, 45
bluegrass, 16
blues, 3, 4, 16, 144, 157, 167
Bon Jovi, 314, 315, 318
Bond, Billy, 242–4
Bono, 158–68
Bono and Eugene Peterson: The Psalms (USA, 2016), 159
Boorman, John, 214
Bowie, David, 314–16, 318, 320, 324, 325, 328n

Boys Next Door, The, 199, 201, 208
Brakhage, Stan, 301
Brault, François, 254
Bravo, Sergio, 226
Bread (UK, 1971), 10
Brigade Rosse (Red Brigade), 181
British Invasion, The, 331
Brittain, Donald, 199
Brooks, Peter, 138, 139
Browne, Jackson, 306
Bruzzi, Stella, 187, 188, 192
Buckland, Jonny, 125
Buena Vista Social Club (Germany/Cuba/UK/USA, 1999), 126
Buenos Aires Beat (Argentina, 2006), 248n
Buenos Aires Rock (Argentina, 1983), 15, 240, 245–7
Bujold, Geneviève, 256
Burning Down the House: The Story of CBGB (USA, 2009), 64, 78, 79
Burnstein, Cliff, 132, 133
Bush, George H. W., 107
Bush, George W., 119, 120
Byrne, David, 2

Cabaret (USA, 1972), 101
Calexico, 143
Callenbach, Ernest, 68
Cantor-Jackson, Betty, 186
Caouette, Jonathan, 203
Cash, Johnny, 159, 162, 166, 199
Cat Power, 143, 212
Cave, Nick, 14, 198–210
CBC (Canadian Broadcasting Corporation), 75
CBGB, 78, 79
Chanan, Michael, 5, 188, 192, 241
Charlebois, Robert, 254
Charlie is My Darling (UK, 1966), 86–7, 91
Chaskel, Pedro, 226
Chenault, Gene, 30, 31
Chile, 226–35
Chion, Michel, 52, 309
Chotem, Neal, 254
Christ – The Movie (UK, 1990), 214
Chronique d'un été (France, 1961), 199
cinéma vérité/cinéma direct/direct cinema, 3, 4, 6, 11, 71, 73, 102, 108, 142, 203, 240, 255
Clark, Dick, 28, 32
Clash, The, 14, 173–8, 180–4, 263, 264, 268, 272
Clayton, Adam, 161
Cleaver, Eldridge, 69
Clements, Cowboy Jack, 162
Clifton, Peter, 9, 202

INDEX

Close Encounters of the Third Kind (USA, 1977), 311
Cobain, Kurt, 11, 94
Cocksucker Blues (USA, 1972), 8, 86, 88, 90, 91, 94, 95, 306
Cohen, Jem, 203
Coldplay, 3, 125, 318
Coldplay: A Head Full of Dreams (UK, 2018), 3, 9, 125, 321–2
cold war, 67
Coleman, Ornette, 68
Color Humano, 242, 243
Columbia Records, 6, 27, 140, 204
Compton, Richard, 214
Conner, Bruce, 16, 344–7
Contours, The, 65
Control (UK/USA, 2007), 11
cool jazz, 66, 67
Cooper, Bradley, 308
Cooper, James D., 10
Corbijn, Anton, 11
Cott, Jonathan, 70, 71
country music, 3, 120, 122
COVID-19, 2, 78
Crary, Scott, 286n
Crass, 9, 15, 263–74
Crazy Horse, 126
Cream: Farewell Concert (UK, 1969), 65
Crews, Harry, 212, 218
Crosby, Stills, Nash & Young, 87
Crossfire Hurricane (USA, 2012), 10, 86, 89, 91, 94, 95
Crowe, Cameron, 286n, 304, 305
Cry of Jazz, The (USA, 1959), 13, 64, 66, 68
Cuarón, Alfonso, 209
Curbishley, Bill, 77
Curtis, Ian, 11
Cutler, Sam, 191,192

D.O.A.: A Right of Passage (UK, 1981), 201
Dalton, David, 70
Daltrey, Roger, 76–7
Damned, The, 173, 263
Dansereau, Jean, 254
David Crosby: Remember My Name (USA, 2019), 65
Davis, Jesse Ed, 12
Davis, Michael, 281
Davis, Miles, 68, 347
de Pencier, Nicholas, 64, 74
de Witte, Marleen, 338
Deadhead, 186, 187
Dead Kennedys, 274
Debord, Guy, 276–8
Decca Records, 88

Decline of Western Civilization, The (USA, 1981), 9, 201
DeCurtis, Anthony, 150
DeFeo, Jay, 344–6
Deliverance (USA, 1972), 214
Demme, Jonathan, 9
Denmark, 12
des Barres, Pamela, 90
Dessner, Aaron, 135
Dido, 322
Dixie Chicks, 14, 113–23
Dixieland, 5, 26, 67
Doggett, Peter, 69
Dolby, 307, 309
Dominik, Andrew, 209
Don't Look Back (USA, 1967), 2–4, 8, 10, 13, 24, 142, 150, 152, 203–6, 212, 305
Douglas, Andrew, 212, 213, 215–17, 219, 220
Dowd, Johnny, 212, 219
Downie, Gord, 13, 74–6
Dr Hook and the Medicine Show, 312
Drake, Bill, 2, 30, 142
Dubuque, Bill, 214
Duffield, Mike, 264, 271
Dylan, Bob, 3, 8, 10, 21, 140, 141, 142–7, 150–3, 157–60, 163, 204–9, 213, 218, 306

Eastwood, Clint, 214
Easy Rider (USA, 1969), 307
Eat the Document (USA, 1972), 142, 152
Echobrain, 129
Edwards, David Eugene, 212, 219
El Derecho de Vivir en Paz (Chile, 1999), 230–1, 232
El extraño de pelo largo (Argentina, 1970), 242
El Frío Misterio (Chile, 2010), 232
Electrodomésticos (band), 232
Elkins, James, 299, 300
Ellis, Warren, 198
Elphick, Denise, 233
Elsaesser, Thomas, 138
Elvis '68 ('Comeback Special') (USA, 1968), 65
EMI, 244
Eminem, 332–3
Emociones Clandestinas (band), 229, 232
Entwistle, John, 76
Estamos Bien (Chile, 2009), 232
event cinema, 16, 314–28
EXID, 338
EXIT, 269, 271
expanded cinema, 3
Expresso Bongo (UK, 1959), 303

351

Fade to Black (USA, 2004), 10, 65
fancamming, 12, 16, 331, 338–40
Faraldo, Claude, 255
Farmer, Denis, 254, 258
Fauteux, Monique, 254, 258
Filth and the Fury, The (UK, 2000), 10, 267, 286n
Fiori, Serge, 250, 254, 256, 258–60
Fisher, Jeff, 254, 258
Fiskales Ad Hok, 233
Flux of Pink Indians, 266
Flying Burrito Brothers, The, 87
folk, 23, 86, 213
Forestier, Louise, 254
Forrest, Frederic, 308
Forsyth, Iain, 198–200, 202, 206–8
Fortier, Robert, 15, 254–61
Fraas, Arne Philip, 2
Frampton, Peter, 309
Frank, Robert, 8, 88, 89, 93, 306
Free Cinema, 5
free jazz, 68
Fried, Michael, 301
Frith, Simon, 304
Frontwoman, La Historia de Denise de Aguaturbia (Chile, 2009), 233
Fulano, 232

G-Dragon, 336
Gagnon, Monika Kin, 65
Gallagher, Liam and Noel, 125
Game of Death (Hong Kong, 2000), 178
García, Charly, 242
Garcia, Jerry, 185, 186, 190, 191, 195, 196, 321
Gee, Grant, 286n
George Harrison: Living in the Material World (USA, 2011), 8
Gere, Richard, 151
Gieco, Leon, 242, 243, 245, 246
Gilbert, Charlene, 215
Gilmour, David, 320, 325
Gimme Danger (USA, 2016), 9, 286n
Gimme Shelter (USA, 1970), 2, 7, 10, 33, 34n, 69, 77, 86–8, 91, 95, 114, 142, 212, 240, 308, 309
Ginsberg, Allen, 88, 143, 149, 160
Godard, Jean-Luc, 69, 152
Godchaux, Donna Jean, 189, 192
Godchaux, Keith, 189, 192
Gold Diggers of 1933 (USA, 1933), 101
González, Rosario, 235
Gordon, Kim, 11
gospel, 5, 157
Gould, Ester, 108
Graduate, The (USA, 1967), 307

Grant, Peter, 310–11
Grateful Dead, The, 14, 87, 185–96, 321
Gravity (US, 2013), 209
Gray, F. Gary, 11
Grease (USA, 1978), 306, 308, 312n
Great Rock 'n' Roll Swindle, The (UK, 1980), 173
Green, David Gordon, 215
Grinderman, 198
Gringo Rojo (Chile, 2016), 232
Gritos de Fin de Siglo (Chile, 2013), 232
Grossman, Albert, 205
Guest, Val, 303
Guthrie, Woody, 4, 144, 145, 151, 152
Guzmán, Patricio, 226, 228

Habicht, Florian, 286n
Haisman, Steve, 213, 217, 219
Hallström, Lasse, 9
Hallyu (the Korean Wave), 331, 334
Hammett, Kirk, 130, 133
Handsome Family, The, 212, 220
Hansard, Glen, 143
Hardcore, La Revolución Inconclusa (Chile, 2011), 232
Haring, Keith, 107
Harmonium, 15, 250, 251, 254, 256–60
Harmonium in California (Canada, 1980), 15, 250–52, 255, 257, 260, 261
Harrison, George, 64, 70, 71, 73
Hart, Mickey, 190, 191
Harvey, Laurence, 303
Hawks, The, 142, 150
Haynes, Todd, 14, 143–46, 148, 150–2
Hazan, Jack, 174
Hazel Green and Company (USA, 1927), 26
Headon, Topper, 177, 178
Heart of a Dog (USA, 2015), 15, 291–302
heavy metal, 11, 129, 131, 230
Hendrix, Jimi, 12, 163, 192, 305
Her Smell (USA, 2018), 1, 3, 16
Herreros de Chile (Chile, 2014), 232
Herring, Christie, 215
Hetfield, James, 130–3, 137–9
Hill, Faith, 121
hip hop, 3,12
Hip-Hop Evolution (Canada/USA, 2016–), 9
History of Rock 'n' Roll, The (USA, 1995), 2, 10, 25, 30, 31, 33, 142
HIV/AIDS, 99, 107–10
Hoffman, David, 13, 21, 22
Holliday, Billie, 163
Hooker, John Lee, 284
hooks, bell, 106
Hopkins, Jerry, 30

Hopper, Dennis, 307
Horne, Lena, 69
Houston, Whitney, 86
Hudson, Garth, 144
Hunter, Meredith, 77, 87
Hurley, Erin, 251, 252
Hüsker Dü, 65
Huston, John, 214
Hype (USA, 1996), 286n

I Am Trying to Break Your Heart: A Film About Wilco (USA, 2002), 212
I'm Not There (USA/Germany, 2007), 14, 141, 143, 149, 151–3
Ice-T, 9
If You Were There (UK, 1986), 8
Ignorant, Steve, 264, 265, 272, 273
IMAX, 3
Indigenous rights, 12, 75
Instagram, 115, 118
Instrument (USA, 1999), 203
Invasion of the Body Snatchers (USA, 1956), 347
Irglová, Markéta, 143
Iris, 242

Jackson, Mahalia, 42
Jackson, Peter, 64, 73
Jagger, Bianca, 93
Jagger, Mick, 77, 87, 88, 91–5
Jailhouse Rock (USA, 1957), 303
Jam, The, 268
James, David E., 71, 203, 204
Jara, Victor, 228, 230–1
Jarmusch, Jim, 78, 88, 161, 286n
Jaws (USA, 1975), 307, 312n
Jay-Z, 9, 10, 65
jazz, 3, 5, 16, 66, 67, 68
Jazz Dance (USA, 1957), 4
Jazz on a Summer's Day (USA, 1959), 4–7, 66, 24, 30, 200
Jazz Singer, The (USA, 1927), 25
Jefferson Airplane, 71, 87, 92
Joanou, Phil, 165, 168, 170, 312n
Joe Strummer: The Future is Unwritten (Ireland/UK, 2007), 126
Johansen, David, 220
John, Elton, 318
Jones, Mick, 178, 179, 182
Jones, Sam, 212
Joplin, Janis, 192, 305, 310
Joy Division (UK, 2007), 286n
Joy Division, 11
Jubilee! Day 1977 On the River: Sex Pistols (UK, 1977), 69
Jung, Sun, 332

Kanter, Hal, 303
K-pop, 16, 330–40
Kapadia, Asif, 9
Kazan, Elia, 214
KCON (K-pop convention), 333
Kerouac, Jack, 88, 160
Keshishian, Alek, 102, 103, 106
Kids are Alright, The (UK/USA, 1979), 10, 65, 126
Kill Your Idols (USA, 2004), 286n
Kim, Yeran, 334, 335
Kimsey, John, 72
King Jr., Martin Luther, 169
King, B. B., 160, 163, 167, 168
King, Kerry, 129
Klein, Allen, 88
Kleiser, Randal, 306
Koenig, Wolf, 6
Kopple, Barbara, 14, 114–18, 121–3
Korn, 314, 315
Kowalski, Lech, 201
Kramer, Wayne, 278, 281, 282, 285
Krauss, Rosalind, 301
Kreutzmann, Bill, 196
Kristal, Hilly, 78, 79
Kristofferson, Kris, 309
Kroitor, Roman, 6
KUKL, 266
Kwon, Jungmin, 331

La Nueva Canción Chilena, 227
La Joven Guardia, 242
Ladies and Gentlemen... Mr. Leonard Cohen (Canada, 1965), 199
Lady Gaga, 86
Lambert and Stamp (USA, 2014), 10
Lambert, Kit, 10
Lang, Fritz, 101
Last Waltz, The (USA, 1978), 4, 13, 126, 203, 303–4, 306, 311
Laurel Canyon: A Place in Time (USA, 2020), 65
Leacock, Richard, 4
Ledger, Heath, 148
Led Zeppelin, 9, 310
Lee, Bruce, 178
Lee, Spike, 2
Lennon, John, 10, 64, 69–73, 163, 246
Leonard, Dennis 'The Wiz', 185–8, 190, 192, 196
Lerner, Irving, 4
Lerner, Murray, 143
Lesage, Jean, 253
Lesh, Phil, 194
Let It Be (UK, 1970), 8, 13, 64, 69–73, 126, 129

Let's Spend the Night Together (USA, 1983), 312n
Letts, Don, 267
Lévesque, René, 15, 250, 253–6, 260, 261
Lewis, Jerry Lee, 166
Lindsay-Hogg, Michael, 8, 13, 64, 69, 71, 72
Lineup, The (USA, 1958), 347, 348
Live Aid, 100
Live at Pompeii (UK, 2017), 320, 325
Livingston, Jennie, 108
Loncraine, Richard, 304
Lonely Boy (Canada, 1962), 3, 6, 7, 8, 10
Long Strange Trip: The Untold Story of The Grateful Dead (USA, 2017), 14, 185, 186, 188, 194
Long Time Running (Canada, 2017), 13, 64, 74, 77
Long, Stanley A., 10
Loog Oldham, Andrew, 87
Los Angeles Negros (Chile, 2007), 232
Los Blue Splendor (Chile, 2007), 232
Los Jaivas, La Vorágine (Chile, 2011), 231
Los Prisioneros (band), 229
Love & Mercy (USA, 2014), 11
Love, Courtney, 94
Loving You (USA, 1957), 303
Lucas, George, 306
Lundsford, Bascom Lamar, 21, 22

McCabe and Mrs. Miller (USA, 1971), 311
McCartney, Paul, 69, 70, 72, 73, 129
MacElreath, Bill, 22
McElwee, Ross, 215
McKernan, Ron 'Pigpen', 189, 190, 192
McLaren, Malcolm, 268
Macon County Line (USA, 1974), 214
Made in Sheffield (UK, 2001), 286n
Madonna, 3, 14, 86, 97–110
Magritte, René, 299
Maguire, Martie, 114, 118, 122
Mailer, Norman, 66
Maines, Natalie, 113, 114, 117, 119
Malditos: La Historia de Fiskales Ad-Hok (Chile, 2004), 233
Malle, Louis, 347
Manchurian Candidate, The (USA, 1962), 347
Marcha del Carbón, La (Chile, 1963), 226
Marcus, Greil, 13, 15, 16, 76, 77, 212, 213, 217–19
Marsh, Dave, 76
Massot, Joe, 9, 202
Matorral, 232
Matta-Clark, Gordon, 296, 299
Maxwell, Emily, 64

Maysles, Albert and David, 2, 7, 37, 88, 212, 240, 247, 308
MC5, 15, 278–86
MC5: A True Testimonial (USA, 2005), 15, 278–86
Mean Streets (USA, 1973), 307
Megadeth, 322
Mekas, Jonas, 68
melodrama, 14, 138, 139
Mencken, H. L., 213, 214
Metallica, 65, 129, 131–3, 137, 318, 322
Metallica: Some Kind of Monster (USA, 2004), 14, 126–30, 132–9, 203, 212
Metropolis (Germany, 1927), 101
Mi Nuevo Estilo de Baile (Chile, 2012), 232
Michael Jackson's This Is It (USA, 2009), 65
Midler, Bette, 308, 310, 312n
Midnight in the Garden of Good and Evil (USA, 1997), 214
Miller, Glenn, 65
Mingay, David, 174, 175
Mississippi Burning (USA, 1988), 214
Mistaken for Strangers (USA, 2013), 14, 126–8, 134–9, 212
Mitchell, Joni, 306
modal jazz, 68
Momma Don't Allow (UK, 1955), 4, 5
Montage of Heck (USA, 2015), 94
Monterey International Pop Festival, 304
Monterey Pop (USA, 1968), 2, 7, 13, 192, 241, 247
Morgen, Brett, 89, 94
Morin, Edgar, 199, 214–15
Morrison, Jim, 305
Moss, Elizabeth, 1
Moveon.org, 120
MTV, 14, 98, 99, 133, 202
Mullen Jr., Larry, 160, 161, 169
Murvin, Junior, 177
Music Makers of the Blue Ridge (USA, 1966), 13, 23

N.W.A., 11
Nancy, Jean-Luc, 300, 331, 340
Napster, 128, 133
Nas, 332
National, The, 127, 134–6, 139
National Educational Television, 21
National Film Board of Canada/Office national du film (NFB/ONF), 6, 250, 254, 255, 258, 260
National Front, 264
Neaverson, Bob, 70
Nebbia, Litto, 242
Negativland, 10
Neville Brothers, The, 162

New Orleans jazz, 67, 26
New Voices of Freedom Choir, 163
Newport Folk Festival, 140, 143, 147, 150
Newport Jazz Festival, 5, 200
Newsted, Jason, 128, 129, 133
Nichols, Bill, 267
Nichols, Mike, 307
Niebling, Laura, 4, 13
Nirvana, 94
Nixon, Richard, 73
No Depression, 213
No Direction Home (USA, 2005), 143, 146
Normandeau, Michel, 254
Northern Haze: Living the Dream (Canada, 2011), 12
Norway, 12
Now! (Cuba, 1965), 69
Nueva Canción Chilena (Chile, 1985), 227–9

O'Brien: Las Edades del Hombre (Chile, 2016), 231, 232
Oasis, 125
Oasis: Supersonic (UK, 2016), 125
Obama, Barack, 136
Oey, Alexander, 9, 15, 264, 266, 268, 269, 271, 272
Offenbach, 255
Oh, David C., 333
Olivera, Héctor, 240, 242, 245, 247
Once Were Brothers: Robbie Robertson and the Band (Canada, 2019), 65
One Direction: This Is Us (UK/USA, 2013), 29
One More Time With Feeling (UK, 2016), 209
Ono, Kent, 331
Ono, Yoko, 10
Ortega, Sergio, 227
Osbourne, Ozzy, 133
Osbournes, The (USA, 2002–2005), 133
Other Side of the Mirror: Bob Dylan at the Newport Folk Festival, The (USA, 2017), 143, 150
Ozark (USA, 2017–2018), 214

Paglia, Camille, 57
Paramount Pictures, 163
Paris is Burning (USA, 1990), 108, 110
Paris, Texas (West Germany/France, 1984), 161
Parker, Alan, 11
Parot, Carmen Luz, 230, 231, 236
Parra, Violeta, 227
Parti Québécois (PQ), 250, 253–7, 261

Pat Garrett and Billy the Kid (USA, 1973), 141, 151
Patti Smith: Dream of Life (USA, 2008), 286n
Pearl Jam, 319
Pearl Jam Twenty (USA, 2011), 286n
Peck, Cecilia, 14, 114, 115, 117, 118, 121–3
Peckinpah, Sam, 151
Pennebaker, D.A., 4, 10, 13, 37, 142, 150, 203–5, 212, 241, 247, 305
Perry, Alex Ross, 1
Perry, Katy, 86
Pescado Rabiosa, 242, 244–5
Peterson, Eugene, 159
Pew, Tracy, 208
Piedra Roja (Chile, 2011), 231
Pierson, Frank, 304
Pink Floyd, 2, 9, 126
Pink Floyd: Live at Pompeii (UK/France/Belgium/West Germany, 1972), 2, 202, 209
Pink Floyd: The Wall (UK, 1982), 11
Pinochet Boys, 229
Pintura Fresca, 242
Planet, Gonzalo, 232
Plastercaster, Cynthia, 90
PLO (Palestinian Liberation Organization), 69
Podell, Jules, 6
Pogo, El Peor de Chile (Chile, 2009), 232
Pohlad, Bill, 11
Poison Girls, 266, 271
Polanski, Roman, 301
Pollard, Jane, 198–200, 202, 206–8
pop, 3, 16, 86, 90
Pop, Iggy, 9
Pope Francis, 330
Prey, Doug, 286n
Presley, Elvis, 65, 158, 160, 166, 199, 220, 303
Preston, Billy, 71
Prima Rock (Argentina, 1982), 247
Prine, John, 162
progressive rock, 15, 251–3
Psy, 331
psychogeography, 276–8, 279, 286
Pull My Daisy (USA, 1959), 66
Pulp: A Film about Life, Death, and Supermarkets (UK, 2004), 286n
punk, 173–7, 179, 180, 183, 184, 263, 264, 267, 268, 271–2
Punk Rock Movie, The (UK, 1978), 173
Pursey, Jimmy, 182

Quadrophenia (UK, 1979), 11
Que sea rock (Argentina, 2006), 246

INDEX

Queen Elizabeth II, 69
Quilapayún, *Más Allá de la Canción* (Chile, 2015), 232

R&B, 66
Ra, Sun, 66–7
RAF (Red Army Faction), 181, 182
Ragnarock (Norway, 1973), 2
Raitt, Bonnie, 120
Rajewski, Irina, 317, 328n
Rammstein, 318
Ramones, The, 78, 158
rap, 9, 332–3
Rattle and Hum (USA, 1988), 14, 157, 158, 160, 163–5, 167, 169, 170, 312n
Red Hot Chili Peppers, 117
Reed, Lou, 9, 296
reggae, 175, 177, 178
Reiner, Rob, 201
Reisz, Karel, 4, 5
religion/religiosity, 101, 106, 141, 158, 159
Renaldo and Clara (USA, 1978), 143
Richards, Keith, 93, 163
Richardson, Tony, 4, 5
Rimbaud, Penny, 264–72
Ríos, Héctor, 231
Ripley, Arthur, 214
Road to God Knows Where, The (Germany, 1990), 14, 200, 202, 204–6, 210
Roberts, Oral, 339
Robertson, Robbie, 12, 306, 311
Robinson, Andre, 215
Robison, Emily, 114, 122
Rock Against Racism, 10, 179, 181, 182
Rock, Bob, 129, 132
Rock libre du Québec, 254
Rock Until the Sun Sets (Argentina, 1973), 2, 15, 240, 242–5, 247
Roddam, Franc, 11
Rodríguez, Silvio, 229
Rolling Stone (magazine), 30, 305
Rolling Stones, The, 8, 10, 13, 14, 30, 69, 73, 85–9, 91, 93–5, 306, 307, 311n
Rolling Thunder Revue: A Bob Dylan Story by Martin Scorsese (USA, 2019), 143
Rose, The (USA, 1979), 16, 304, 307, 308–11, 312n
Rosenbaum, Martin, 220
Rotolo, Suze, 146, 148
Rouch, Jean, 199
Roxy: The Movie (USA, 2015), 324
Rubin, Rick, 117
Rude Boy (UK, 1980), 14, 173, 174, 176, 177, 180, 183
Ruidos Molestos (Chile, 2007), 232

Rumble: Indians Who Rocked the World (Canada, 2017), 12
Rush: Time Stand Still (Canada, 2016), 65
Rust Never Sleeps (USA, 1979), 125
Rutles: All You Need is Cash, The (UK, 1978), 11
Rydell, Mark, 304

Sainte-Marie, Buffy, 12
Salvatore, Dominic, 68
Sandburg, Carl, 213, 218
Santana, Carlos, 309
Santiago del Nuevo Extremo, 229
Sargent, Joseph, 214
Saturday Night Fever (USA, 1976), 307–8, 312n
Saturday Night Live (USA, 1975–), 73
Schafer, R. Murray, 194
Schindel, Sebastián, 246
Schwenke y Nilo, 229
Schulman, Nina, 46
Schüppel, Uli M., 200, 202, 204, 205, 206
Scorsese, Martin, 94, 126, 143, 146, 203, 304, 306, 307
Searching for Sugar Man (Sweden/UK/Finland, 2012), 116
Searching for the Wrong-Eyed Jesus (USA/UK, 2003), 15, 212–21
Sebring, Steven, 286n
Seeger, Pete, 4, 143, 218
Seidl, Ulrich, 216
Sembene, Ousmane, 170
Sergi, Gianluca, 307
Sex Pistols, The, 9, 10, 66, 69, 173, 175, 183, 263, 268, 271
Sha Na Na, 306
Shaath, Zeinab, 69
Sham 69, 182
Shammout, Ismail, 69
Shankar, Ravi, 37
Sharp Objects (USA, 2018), 214
Sherman's March (USA, 1985), 215
Shine a Light (UK/USA, 2008), 94
Shut Up & Sing (USA, 2006), 14, 114–22
Siegel, Don, 214, 347
Silverstein, Shel, 312n
Simonon, Paul, 177, 178
Sinclair, John, 280, 281, 285
Sinofsky, Bruce, 14, 126, 203, 212
Sire Records, 78
skiffle, 5
Sky TV, 98, 99
Slade, 304
Slade in Flame (UK, 1975), 304, 306
Slayer, 129, 322
Slick, Grace, 92

Slickers, The, 178
SlinCraze, 12
Solar Arkestra, 66
Smith, Chad, 117
Smith, Patti, 79, 265, 272
Solnit, Rebecca, 345, 346
Something from Nothing: The Art of Rap (USA, 2012), 9
Sometimes I am Haunted by Memories of Red Dirt Clay (USA, 1999), 215
Song Remains the Same, The (UK, 1976), 9, 202
Sonic Outlaws (USA, 1995), 10
Sonic Youth, 11, 143
Southern Gothic, 15, 213–17
Spector, Phil, 72
Spheeris, Penelope, 9, 201
Spielberg, Steven, 307, 311
Spinetta, Luis Alberto, 242, 245, 247, 248n
Springsteen, Bruce, 120
Stamp, Chris, 10
Stanley, Owsley, 187
Stanley, Robert, 254
stans/stanning, 16, 330, 332–5
Staples, Mavis, 143
Stardust (UK, 1974), 304, 311n
Star Wars (USA, 1977), 307
Starr, Ringo, 70, 73
Stein, Gertrude, 297
Stein, Mandy, 64, 78
Stein, Seymour, 78
Stern, Burt, 5, 6, 7, 200
Sterne, Jonathan, 188, 195
Stooges, The, 283
Stop Making Sense (USA, 1984), 9, 101, 126, 157
Straight Outta Compton (USA, 2015), 11
Stranger Than Paradise (USA/West Germany, 1984), 161
Stranger with a Camera (USA, 1999), 215
Streisand, Barbara, 309, 311
Strike a Pose (Belgium/The Netherlands, 2016), 100, 103, 108, 110
Strong, Catherine, 13
Strummer, Joe, 177, 180, 181, 182, 265
Subirana, Libert, 254
Sui Generis, 242
Sumé, 12
Sumé: The Sound of a Revolution (Greenland/Denmark/Norway, 2014), 12
Summer of Love, 7
Surtees, Robert, 311
swing, 26, 67
Swingle, Melissa, 219
Szwed, John, 66

Tabarnac (Canada, 1975), 251, 255
Take That, 318
Talking Heads, 9, 78, 101, 126
Temple, Julien, 69, 267, 286n
Tenant, The (France, 1976), 301
That'll be the Day (UK, 1973), 306, 311n
Thatcher, Margaret, 174, 183, 271, 272
The Edge, 161, 169
There Is No Authority but Yourself (The Netherlands, 2006), 9,15, 264, 266–8, 273, 274
This is Spinal Tap (USA, 1984), 11, 114, 134, 201
Thomas, David C., 278
Thompson, Dennis, 281
Thompson, Hunter S., 305
Thorpe, Richard, 303
Thunder Road (USA, 1958), 214
Tilton, Roger, 4
To Hear Your Banjo Play (USA, 1947), 4, 5
Toque de Queda (Chile, 2014), 233, 235
Towle, Phil, 128–30, 132
Townshend, Pete, 76, 77
Tragically Hip, The, 13, 73–5
Travolta, John, 307
Trocha, Angosta, 242
True Detective (USA, 2014–), 214
Trudeau, Justin, 75
Trujillo, Robert, 128, 131, 133
Truth and Reconciliation Commission of Canada, 76
Truth or Dare (a.k.a. *In Bed with Madonna*; USA, 1991), 11, 14, 97–110
Tupac: Resurrection (USA, 2003), 65
Turner, Tina, 92
Twain, Shania, 121
Twitter, 115,118
Tyner, Rob, 278, 284, 285

U2, 10, 14, 157, 160–7, 169, 170, 312n
Ulrich, Lars, 130–3, 137–9
Underwood, Carrie, 121
Unfinished Plan, El Camino de Alain Johannes (Chile, 2016), 232
Urgent Call of Palestine, The (Palestine, 1973), 69
Uset, Aníbal, 2, 240, 242, 243, 244, 246

V8, 246
Vallée, Jean-Marc, 214
Van Dyke, Willard, 4
Van Zandt, Steve, 78
Vaucher, Gee, 264, 266, 267, 269, 271, 272
Vaudeville, 26
Vertov, Dziga, 51
Vitaphone, 3, 27, 32

INDEX

Vitaphone Varieties (USA, 1926–1932), 25–8
Vox Dei, 242

Wadleigh, Michael, 2, 37, 59, 212, 240, 305
Waking in Mississippi (USA, 1998), 215
Wall of Sound (Grateful Dead), 193, 194, 195
Warner Bros. (WB), 3, 25, 26, 27, 191, 192, 215, 327
Watts, Charlie, 77
Weir, Bob, 191
Wenders, Wim, 126, 161, 200
West, Kanye, 320
Westwood, Vivienne, 268
WE UP: Indigenous Hip Hop in the Circumpolar North (USA, 2018), 12
Wham!, 8
Whatham, Claude, 306, 311n
What's Happening! The Beatles in the U.S.A. (USA, 1964), 7, 34n, 240
White, Jim, 212, 215, 216, 218, 219
Whitecross, Mat, 3, 321
Whitehead, Peter, 87
White Panther Party, 280–1
White Lightning (USA, 1973), 214
White Riot (UK, 2019), 10
White Rose, The (USA, 1967), 16, 344–8
Winehouse, Amy, 9, 86, 126
Whitney (USA/UK, 2018), 86
Who, The, 10, 13, 65, 74, 76–8, 319

Who: The Night That Changed Rock, The (USA, 2019), 13, 64, 76, 77
Wickhan, Nick, 322
Wild Man Blues (USA, 1997), 115
Wild River (USA, 1960), 214
Williams, Hank, 206
Wilson, Brian, 11, 33
Wilson, Gretchen, 121
Wings of Desire (West Germany/France, 1987), 200, 201, 205
Winston, Brian, 241
Wise Blood (USA, 1979), 214
Wood, Eve, 286n
Woodstock, 240, 304
Woodstock (USA, 1970), 2, 7, 10, 24, 33, 114, 142, 192, 212, 240, 241, 243, 247, 305, 309
Wray, Link, 12
Wyman, Bill, 91

Yauch, Adam, 9, 331
Year of the Horse (USA, 1997), 125
Young, Neil [a.k.a. Bernard Shakey], 125, 126, 306
YouTube, 2, 11, 16, 89, 323, 330, 331, 335–8, 340

Zappa, Frank, 324
Zwaan, Reijer, 108
Ziggy Stardust and the Spiders from Mars (UK, 1979), 65
Zsigmond, Vilmos, 311
Zwerin, Charlotte, 2, 37, 212, 240, 308

EU representative:
Easy Access System Europe
Mustamäe tee 50, 10621 Tallinn, Estonia
Gpsr.requests@easproject.com